Soft
Furnishings

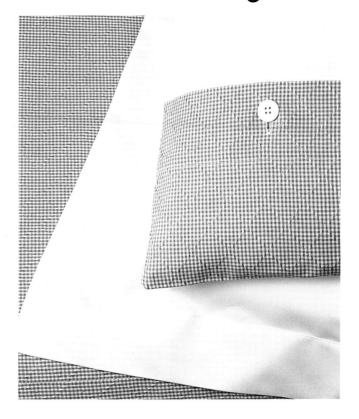

Soft Furnishings

Over 50 easy-to-make designs for beds,
chairs, tables and windows

Chris Jefferys

NEW HOLLAND

First published in 2005 by New Holland Publishers (UK) Ltd
London • Cape Town • Sydney • Auckland

Garfield House, 86–88 Edgware Road
London W2 2EA
United Kingdom
www.newhollandpublishers.com

80 McKenzie Street
Cape Town, 8001
South Africa

Level 1, Unit 4, 14 Aquatic Drive
Frenchs Forest, NSW 2086
Australia

218 Lake Road, Northcote
Auckland,
New Zealand

10 9 8 7 6 5 4 3 2 1

ISBN 1 84330 824 X

Senior Editor: Clare Sayer
Photographer: Shona Wood
Design: Frances de Rees
Illustrations: Coral Mula
Copyeditor: Patsy North
Production: Hazel Kirkman
Editorial Direction: Rosemary Wilkinson

Reproduction by Modern Age Repro, Hong Kong
Printed and bound by Times Offset (M) Sdn Bhd, Malaysia

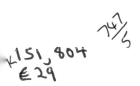

Contents

Introduction

Soft furnishings are a quick and easy way to change or update the colour scheme of a room. It could be the simplest thing – a drape around the window, a throw over a sofa and some new cushions will do the trick in next to no time. There are of course some more complex soft furnishing projects where the wide choice of fabrics available will make it possible to change to a new colour scheme at a fraction of the cost of buying ready-made items. By making your own soft furnishings, you have the reward of designing and creating your own look to suit your taste and lifestyle and the chance to work with a wonderful array of fabric colours and textures. The projects in this book vary from simple cushions and bedcovers to more sophisticated bolsters and fitted covers, so there is always an option for the beginner as well as the more experienced stitcher. For those new to making their own soft furnishings, there is a basics section that includes step-by-step colour photographs to take you through all the techniques needed to complete the projects successfully, from basic pinning to inserting zips and trimming with piping.

The projects are designed for maximum style combined with simplicity: if there is an easy way to create a look, you'll find it here. The book is divided into sections

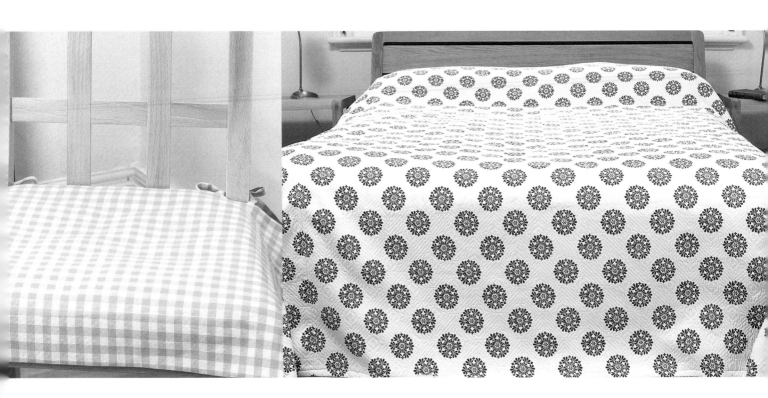

according to how the items are be used. The Chairs section contains stylish cushions, luxurious throws and gorgeous seat covers that are easy to make and elegant.

In Tables, there are tablecloths, both round and square, with a choice of lovely decorative edges, a great napkin collection and elegant table runners to add style to the smartest table settings.

The Beds section has a full selection of pillowcase and duvet designs, an amazingly simple canopy and bedhead and a straightforward but stunning patchwork quilt as well as valances and bedcovers.

The Windows chapter combines a wonderful array of window treatments with easy-to-make, almost no-sew drapes, and lined and unlined curtains that use tab tops and clip tops as well as conventional headings. I have included quick ways to line curtains and make pelmets as well as the more traditional methods. There are roller blinds and Roman blinds, including a really quick method which does away with all those battens and rings.

Whatever your level of experience, I am sure you will plenty of inspiration and essential practical advice in the projects that follow.

Materials and equipment

BASIC SEWING EQUIPMENT

Dressmaker's scissors
Bent-handled dressmaker's scissors or shears are the most comfortable to use for cutting fabric accurately as the angle of the handle allows the fabric to lie flat.

Dressmaking pins
Pins are available with metal, glass or pearlized heads. Pins with coloured heads are easier to spot and pick up, though selecting pins which are fine and sharp is the main importance. Extra-fine pins are available for lace.

Erasable marker
Air-erasable and water-erasable marker pens are easily available and are a useful addition to your sewing kit. Air-erasable marks will disappear after a fairly short time. Water-erasable marks will remain until touched with water.

Needles
Various types of needles are available and a mixed pack of multi-purpose needles is often the best option. Choose needles which are fine and sharp with eyes large enough to thread easily. Extra-fine needles are also available.

Ruler
A metal or plastic ruler is handy to measure and mark short distances and as a guide for drawing straight lines.

Small scissors or snips
Small sharp scissors or special snips are useful for snipping thread ends and can be used close to the fabric where larger scissors would be unwieldy.

Tape measure
A plastic-coated or cloth tape measure is used to measure longer distances and around curves. A retractable tape measure is a neat option.

HABERDASHERY

Bias binding

This is a strip of fabric cut on the cross grain and comes with the edges pressed over ready for use. It is available in cotton and satin and in various widths.

Blind cord

A strong, fine cord that is threaded through the blind rings and pulled or released to raise or lower the blind.

Blind rings

Small plastic or brass rings that are stitched to the wrong side of Roman and festoon blinds as part of the lowering and raising system.

Buttons

Often made from plastic or pearl, buttons fasten through buttonholes or loops to close an opening. Fabric-covered buttons can be made by covering metal or plastic moulds.

Curtain heading tape

A stiff tape available in different widths and styles that is stitched to the top of curtains and pulled up to form pleats or gathers.

Decorative trims

Tassels, rickrack, piping, and ribbons are all decorative trims that can be inserted in seams or stitched to the surface of items.

Eyelets

Chrome or brass metal rings are used to make holes in fabric to thread a pole or cord through or simply as a decorative feature.

Lining fabric

Used to line curtains when required to give extra weight and body. Lining can also be used to cover the wrong side of an item when it will not show.

Press-stud tape

A tape with poppers ready attached at intervals. Used to fasten long openings such as duvet cover openings.

Thread

Multi-purpose polyester thread for use on all types of fabric is available in a wide range of colours. Cotton and silk thread is also available for use on their respective fabrics. Invisible thread is a strong nylon thread and buttonhole twist or bold thread is a thicker, stronger thread, useful for handsewing heavier fabrics.

Velcro

A fastener that comes in two parts, with hooks on one and soft loops on the other, which stick together when closed. Available in strip form or spots and for sewing or sticking on.

Zips

These are fasteners with metal or plastic teeth that interlock together when the zip tag is pulled over them. Used widely in openings for cushion covers.

THE SEWING MACHINE

Most sewing machines are run by electricity through a foot pedal, which is attached by one cable to the machine and another to the electricity supply. Pressure on the foot pedal will start the machine going and, as more pressure is added, the speed will increase. A hand wheel at the right of the machine is also usually employed when starting and stopping a piece of machine-stitching to help control and smooth the process.

Machine-stitching is formed from two threads: the top thread and the bobbin thread. Thread is first wound from the thread reel onto the bobbin by a system usually situated on the top of the machine. The top thread is then slotted through a number of guides and down and through the needle. The wound bobbin is placed into the bobbin case, which is under the needle. During the stitching process, the top thread forms the stitch on the top of the fabric and the bobbin thread forms the stitch on the underside with the two interlinking within the fabric.

Needles for sewing machines come in a variety of different sizes. The lower the number, the finer the needle point.

Basic techniques

This section takes you through all the essential techniques needed to complete the projects in this book, from pinning and tacking to more advanced techniques such as piping. Once mastered, the basics will be used again and again to complete rewarding projects.

Pinning, tacking and handstitches

PINNING AND TACKING
Crossways pinning
Place the edges to be joined together and pin the two layers together with pins at right angles to the edge. Place the pins about 5 cm (2 in) apart; on firm fabric, you can space them further apart. Pin diagonally at corners.

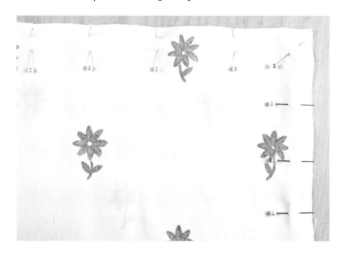

Lengthways pinning
Lengthways pins are placed along the seamline where it will be stitched. This method can be more effective in tricky areas such as fitting a curved edge to a straight edge. When tacking or stitching, remove these pins as you reach them.

Pinning hems
Hems can be pinned with crossways pins or with pins lying in the same direction as the inner fold of the hem. Crossways pins are more effective if any fullness is being eased in, such as on a curved hem. Remove the pins when tacking or stitching, in the same way as before.

Tacking
Using sewing thread or special tacking thread, begin and finish tacking with one or two backstitches. Tack by stitching in and out through the layers of fabric, making stitches 1–1.5 cm ($^3/_8$–$^5/_8$ in) long. Work the tacking over crossways pins and remove the pins afterwards. Or, on lengthways pinning, remove the pins as you reach them.

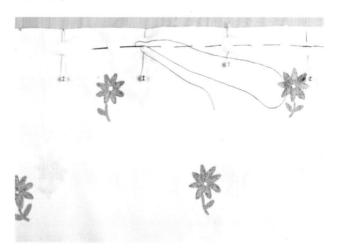

HANDSTITCHES
Backstitches
These stitches are worked one on top of the other and are used to start and finish handstitching. When tacking, the stitches can be 6 mm ($\frac{1}{4}$ in) long. In other areas it is best to make them as small as possible and position them where they are least noticeable. Insert the needle into the fabric and out again, return the needle to the beginning and work two or three more stitches on top of the first one.

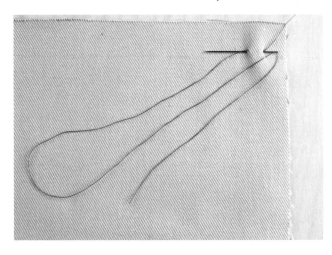

Slip hem
Used to stitch hems and the inner edge of bias binding. Begin with backstitches near the fold of the hem. Stitch across to pick up just a thread of fabric above the hem, then stitch along diagonally back through the hem again. Repeat, taking care not to pull too tight. When stitching binding, instead of picking up a fabric thread the stitch can pass through the back of the machine stitching.

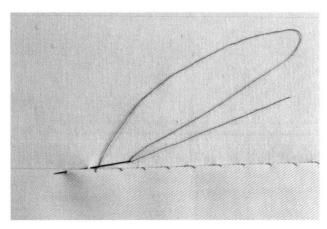

Slipstitch
This stitch is used to sew lining to curtains. Make each stitch about 1.5 cm ($\frac{5}{8}$ in) long. Slide the needle along under the main fabric then out to pick up a couple of threads at the edge of the lining. Take the needle back to the main fabric and slide it along again to make the next stitch.

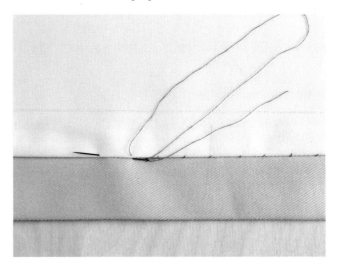

Ladder stitch
This is used to stitch two butting folded edges together. Start with backstitches, then take the needle along inside the fold of one edge for about 3–6 mm ($\frac{1}{8}$–$\frac{1}{4}$ in). Bring the needle out at the fold, take it directly across to the other fold edge and stitch along inside that fold in the same way. Repeat.

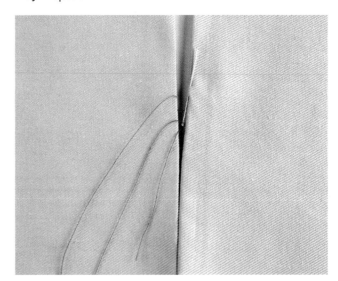

Blanket stitch

A decorative stitch, used to finish the edges of blankets and throws on fabrics that do not fray. Work from left to right. Begin with backstitches on the wrong side and bring the needle out to the right side about 12 mm–1.5 cm ($\frac{1}{2}$–$\frac{5}{8}$ in) in from the edge. Moving the needle along about 12 mm ($\frac{1}{2}$ in), take it through to the wrong side and downwards so that its point projects beyond the fabric edge. Loop the thread under the needle, then pull the needle through. Repeat. At each corner, work three stitches into the same hole as shown.

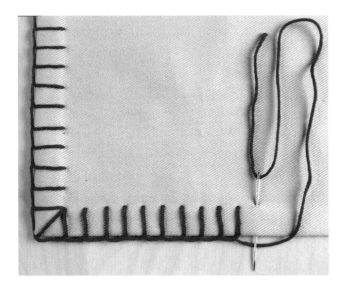

Long stitch

This is used to stitch the side hems on interlined curtains where it holds the hem to the interlining. Make a horizontal stitch across from right to left, then take the needle down diagonally for about 4 cm (1$\frac{1}{2}$ in) and repeat.

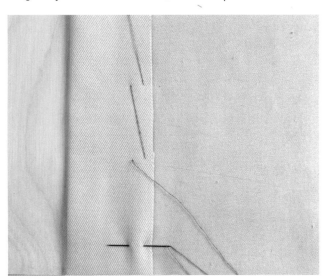

Herringbone stitch

Used to stitch hems on interlined curtains and to join butted edges of wadding and interlining. Work from left to right and begin with backstitches. Bring the needle through the hem, take it diagonally up to the right and take a stitch through above the hem from right to left. Bring the needle diagonally down to the right and take a stitch through the hem again from right to left. Repeat.

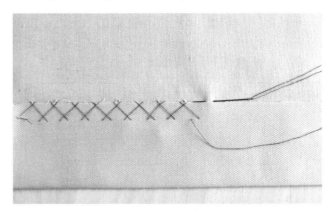

Lockstitch

Used to stitch interlining to curtain fabric on interlined curtains. Fold back the interlining at the required position. Begin with back stitches on the interlining, then move the needle along and take a stitch through the fold of the interlining. Leave a loop of thread between the previous stitch and the needle eye and take a small stitch to pick up the curtain fabric within this loop. Pull the stitch through but do not pull it tight. Space the stitches at intervals of about 10 cm (4 in).

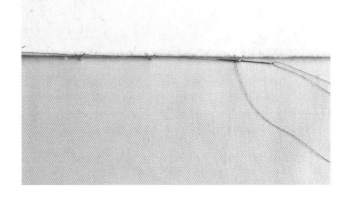

Seams and hems

Whether you tack as well as pin your fabrics together before machining is a matter of personal preference. The less experienced may wish to pin and tack before stitching, while those with more confidence may prefer just to pin and remove the pins as the stitching reaches them.

Plain seam

A plain seam is used to join two pieces of fabric together. it can be pressed open when joining widths of fabric or left with the edges together, such as around the edge of a cushion. The seam allowance is usually 1.5 cm (⅝ in) wide. If it varies, this will be stated in the instructions.

1 Place the fabric pieces together with right sides facing and raw edges level. Stitch along 1.5 cm (⅝ in) in from the edge.

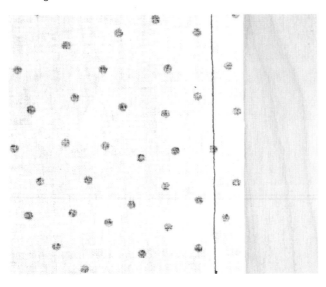

2 Open out the fabric and press the seam open, using the point of the iron. If the raw edges are exposed, zigzag stitch along each edge to neaten.

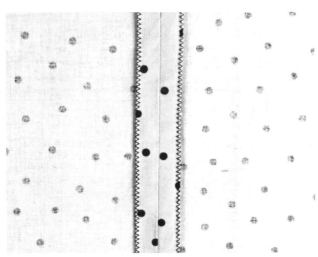

Narrow seam

This type of seam is used on sheer fabrics, as it is neater and less noticeable than a seam pressed open.
Stitch the seam as for a Plain seam, step 1. Trim both seam allowances together to about half their original width. Zigzag stitch the two raw edges together. Open out the fabric and press the seam to one side.

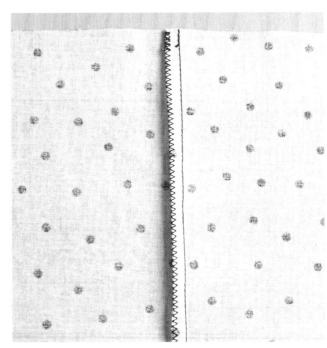

Trimming and snipping

The seam allowances are usually left intact, but if they cause too much bulk at the edge of an item, they can be trimmed to about half their original width.

Outer corners First make a diagonal cut across the corner, then cut away wedges from either side of the diagonal cut.

Inner corners On an internal corner, snip into the corner to a few threads from the stitching, but take care not to snip too close to the stitching.

Curves On a concave curve, snip into the seam allowance so that the seam allowance can expand when turned right side out. On a convex curve, cut out small wedge-shaped notches. The tighter the curve, the closer together the notches and snips should be.

Flat fell seam

A flat fell seam is used to join fabrics where a strong, easy-to-launder seam is required.

1 Place the two edges together with wrong sides facing and raw edges level. Stitch 1.5 cm (⅝ in) in from the edge. Trim one seam allowance to 6 mm (¼ in).

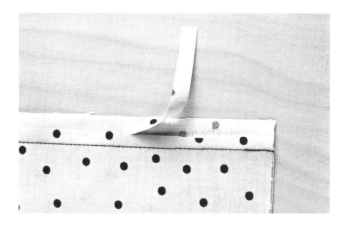

2 Open out the fabric and press the seam so the wider seam allowance lies on top of the trimmed one. Tuck the wider seam allowance under the trimmed edge and press. Stitch along close to the pressed fold by machine. The finished seam will have two rows of machine stitching on the right side.

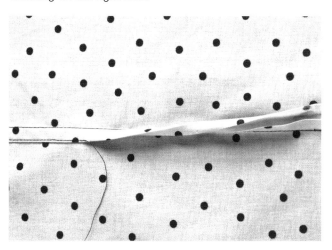

Basic hem

Press 1–1.5 cm ($^3/_8$–$^5/_8$ in) to the wrong side, then press the hem depth to the wrong side and stitch in place by hand or machine.

Double hem

This type of hem is used on sheer fabrics to conceal the inner layer of the hem.

First press the hem depth to the wrong side, then press the same amount again and stitch in place by hand or machine.

Blind hemstitched hem

Most machines have a blind hemstitch, which consists of a few straight stitches followed by a wide zigzag stitch. The straight stitches are worked along the hem edge and the zigzag stitch catches the hem to the main fabric. The stitch can be fiddly to set up accurately, but is worth the effort when stitching long lengths.

Form the hem as described above. Then, with the wrong side uppermost, fold back the hem under the main fabric with the hem edge projecting and stitch in place.

Bias binding and piping

BIAS BINDING

Bias binding can be bought or made. To make your own bias strips for both binding and covering piping cord, cut strips four times the required finished width diagonally across the fabric. For binding, then press both long edges in so that they almost meet at the centre.

Joining strips

1 Open out the binding folds and trim the two ends on the straight grain. Place the two ends together with right sides facing, the straight ends level and the foldlines intersecting 6 mm ($^{1}/_{4}$ in) in. Pin to hold. Stitch the two ends together, taking a 6 mm ($^{1}/_{4}$ in) seam.

2 Open out the binding and press the seam open. Trim off the corners of the seam level with the edge of the binding and re-press the binding folds.

Binding an edge

1 Unfold one edge of the binding and place the raw edge level with the fabric edge on the right side of the fabric. Stitch in place along the fold.

2 Fold the other edge of the binding over to the wrong side so that its edge is level with the machine stitching and stitch in place by hand.

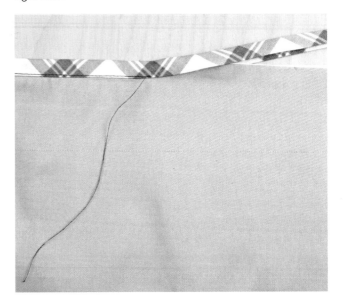

Sandwich method

Before stitching, fold and press the binding in half lengthways so that the upper half, which will be on the right side, is slightly narrower than the lower half. Sandwich the fabric into the binding and stitch in place from the right side.

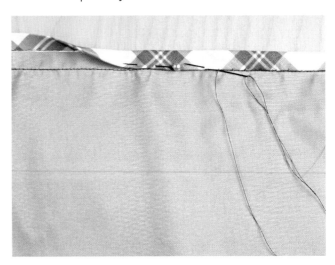

Double binding method

This is a neat method for lighter-weight fabrics and wider bindings.

1 Cut the bias strip six times the required finished width and press the binding in half lengthways. Place the raw edges level with the fabric edge on the wrong side and stitch in place the required width of the binding in from the edge.

2 Fold the other edge over to the right side so that it just covers the stitching and machine-stitch in place.

Joining ends

Join the ends with a diagonal seam before the stitching is complete, using the same method as for joining lengths of bias binding.

Alternatively, an easier method is to overlap the finishing end over the starting end, tucking the raw end under as shown, and then complete the stitching.

Using bought bias binding

Ready-made bias binding can be found in a range of colours and is also available with a satin finish as well as in plain cotton. It is also available in a variety of widths and some specialist haberdashers will have patterned bias binding (see Roller blind with scalloped border, page 144). It comes ready folded and is attached in the same way as for homemade binding strips.

PIPING

Piping can be bought ready-made with a projecting flange to insert into a seam or it can be made by covering piping cord with a strip of bias-cut fabric.

Stitching piping

1 Cut the bias strip wide enough to fit around the cord plus two seam allowances of 1.5 cm ($^5/_8$ in). Wrap the strip around the cord and, using a zipper foot, stitch along close to the cord but not right next to it.

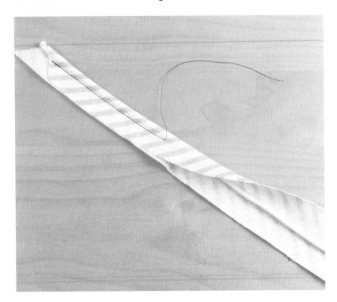

2 Place the piping onto the right side of one fabric layer and stitch in place along the line of the first stitching.

3 Sandwich the piping with the other layer of the seam. Then turn the piece over so that the previous stitching is uppermost. Stitch in place just inside the previous stitching so that the first two rows will be hidden.

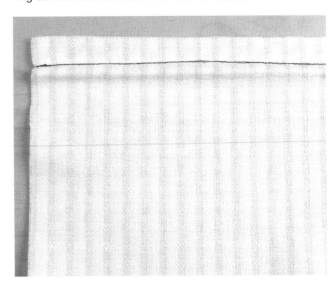

Piping around a corner

Snip the flat flange 1.5 cm ($^5/_8$ in) in from the corner so that it will open out to fit around the corner, ensuring that the raw edges are level with the next edge. If the corner is curved, make three snips around it.

Joining piping ends, method one

1 Leave about 2.5 cm (1 in) unstitched at each end of the piping. Cut the piping so that it overlaps the first end by 2 cm (³⁄₄ in). Unpick the end of the piping to reveal the cord and snip away the cord only, so that it butts up to the beginning of the cord.

2 Fold under 1 cm (³⁄₈ in) on the overlapping end of the piping and lap it over the beginning of the piping. Then complete the stitching, overlapping the beginning of the stitching line.

Joining piping ends, method two

With this method, the ends of the piping are overlapped at an angle and finished inside the seam. This method can also be used for purchased piping where it is not possible to cut away the inner piping cord. In this case, press the overlapped ends as flat as possible before stitching across them.

Leave the piping unstitched for 2.5 cm (1 in) on each side of the join and allow some excess at each end of the piping. Overlap the ends at the seamline, unpick the fabric covering and trim the cords where they overlap. Replace the covering and overlap the flat ends diagonally into the seam allowance. Then complete the stitching, overlapping the beginning of the stitching line.

Fringing and frills

FRINGING

Fringing can be purchased as a trim or made by pulling away the threads from a woven fabric. Some woven fabrics do not fringe well, so check before purchasing.

Applying fringing trim

1 Press a narrow turning, just wide enough to be covered by the braid part of the fringe, onto the right side.

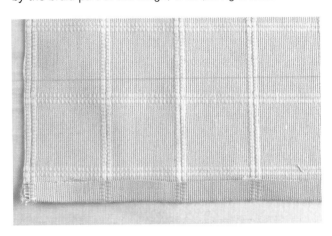

2 Lay the fringing braid along the turning to cover it. Stitch in place with a row of stitching near the fabric edge and another just above the raw edge so that it is enclosed.

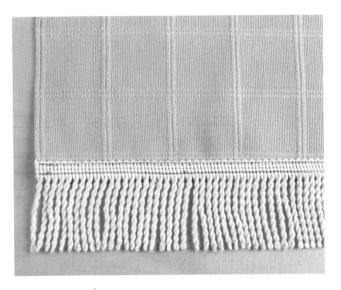

Fringing fabric

A fringe can be made by simply pulling the fabric threads away from the fabric edge. For a more durable fringe, particularly on items that will be laundered, first stitch a row of narrow zigzag stitching in a matching colour across the fabric at the top of the fringe. Then fringe the fabric back to the stitching.

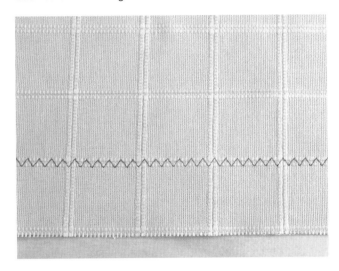

Knotting and plaiting

Both knotting and plaiting will reduce the length of a fringe considerably, so, whenever possible, test on a piece of spare fabric.

To knot, simply gather a bunch of threads together and knot them near the top of the fringe.

For a plait, gather a bunch in the same way, divide it into three sections and plait together. Finish near the base with a thread wrapped round and round and knotted firmly.

FRILLS

Frills can be made from a single layer of fabric with a hemmed edge or from fabric folded double so that no hem is needed. The frills shown here are gathered, but they could be pleated instead. A lace frill can be attached in the same way. For a gathered frill, allow 1½ times the length of the edge it will be trimming.

Single frill

1 Cut the frill to the required width plus 12 mm (½ in) for the hem and 1.5 cm (⅝ in) seam allowance. Press 6 mm (¼ in), then another 6 mm (¼ in) to the wrong side along one long edge of the frill and stitch in place. If the ends will show, hem them in the same way.

2 Adjust the machine stitch to its longest length and stitch along 1.5 cm (⅝ in) from the other edge. Stitch a second row of gathering 6 mm (¼ in) inside the first row. On long frills, stop and restart the stitching to divide the gathered edge up into about 75 cm (30 in) lengths.

3 Divide the frill and the edge to which it will be stitched into an equal number of sections and mark with pins. With right sides facing, pin the edges together at the marker pins. Pull the gathering threads on the wrong side of the frill together while sliding the fabric along to form gathers.

4 When gathered to fit, wind the thread ends around a pin in a figure-of-eight to hold. Adjust the gathers evenly and stitch in place just below the inner row of gathers.

Double frill

Cut the frill twice the required finished width plus 3 cm (1¼ in). If the ends will show, fold the frill in half with right sides together, stitch across the ends, then turn the frill right sides out. Press the frill in half lengthways with the right sides outside. Gather and attach the frill as for the single frill, steps 2, 3 and 4.

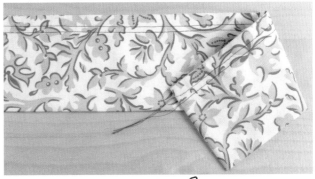

Borders and mitred borders

Block border

Used in traditional patchwork, a blocked border is stitched first to two opposite edges. The borders that are then stitched to the remaining two edges continue across the ends of the first borders. If the centre panel is rectangular, stitch the two longer edges first.

Measure the first two edges and cut borders to this length by the desired finished width plus 3 cm (1¼ in). With right sides facing, stitch the borders to the centre panel, taking 1.5 cm (⅝ in) seam allowances. Press the seams towards the borders. Measure the two remaining edges, including the ends of the first borders, and cut borders to this length and the same width. Stitch in place and press in the same way as the first borders.

Single mitred border

Decide on the desired finished width of the border and add on 3 cm (1¼ in). For the length, measure the length of the centre panel including seam allowances and add twice the width of the finished border.

1 Mark and match the centre of the borders to the centre edges to which they are being stitched. Stitch the borders to the edges, starting and finishing the stitching 1.5 cm (⅝ in) in from the edge of the centre panel. Stitch all the borders in this way.

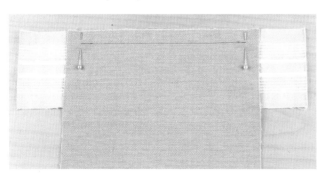

2 Fold the centre panel diagonally, so that two adjoining borders are level. Draw a diagonal line from the end of the previous stitching to the outer corner of the border. Stitch along the line. Trim away the corners 1 cm (⅜ in) outside the line and press the seam open. Stitch all corners in this way. Then press the panel seams towards the borders.

Double mitred border

To calculate the width to cut the borders, decide on the desired finished width of the border, double this and add on 3 cm (1¼ in) seam allowances. For the length, measure the length of the centre panel including seam allowances, plus twice the width of the finished border.

1 Fold the borders in half with the wrong sides outside. Overlap the ends of two borders at right angles, with the fold edges on the outer edges and the ends projecting by 1.5 cm (⅝ in), and pin.

Draw a seam line diagonally across the corner between the points where the borders intersect. Mark the seam allowance 1 cm (⅜ in) outside the seamline. Turn the border over and repeat on the other side. Trim along the outer lines.

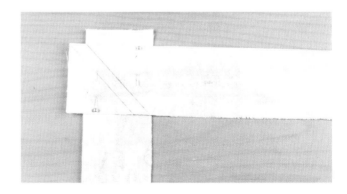

2 Unpin the borders; open them out and mark the seam-line on the unmarked half of each border. Place the appropriate two borders together with right sides facing and stitch along the marked lines, starting and finishing 1.5 cm (⅝ in) in from the side edges of the border. Trim the point and press the seam open. Stitch all four corners in this way.

3 Place the right side of one border edge to the wrong side of the centre panel. Pin together, making sure all four corners match, so that the end of the border stitching is 1.5 cm (⅝ in) from each edge at the corners. Stitch each edge separately, stopping and restarting at each corner.

4 Press the seam allowance to the wrong side along the remaining edge of the border. Then place it over to the right side of the centre panel so that it just covers the previous stitching and the seam is enclosed. Stitch in place.

Mitred hem

1 Press the appropriate double hem in place, then unfold. Fold the corner over diagonally level with the inner pressed corner. Press the fold and trim the corner away 1 cm (⅜ in) inside the fold.

2 Refold the corners with right sides facing so that the pressed lines match. Stitch along the pressed line from the corner to finish at the outer hem fold. Press the mitre seam open. Refold the hem and press again.

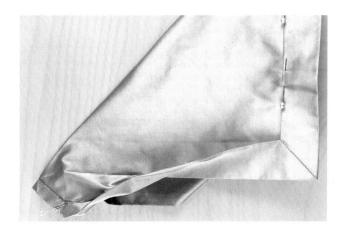

Buttons, buttonholes, ties and zips

BUTTONS
There are two main types of button: flat buttons, which have two or four holes pierced through them, and shank buttons, which have a protruding shank at the back through which they are stitched on. A shank spaces the button away from the fabric to allow fabric layers to lie flat under the button when it is fastened.

Stitching on a flat button
Using a double thread, stitch a couple of backstitches one on top of the other at the button position. Pass the needle up through one hole, then back down through the other hole and through the fabric. Work four to six stitches in this way to secure the button. On buttons with four holes, work two parallel sets of stitches or form the stitches into a cross, then fasten off the thread with more backstitches behind the fabric.

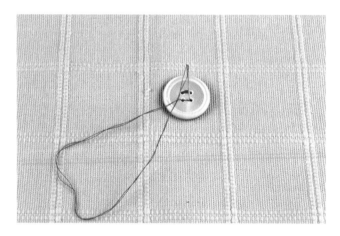

Making a shank for a flat button
1 Stitch on the button in the same way as for a button with holes, but work over a toothpick or thick needle placed on top of the button as a spacer.

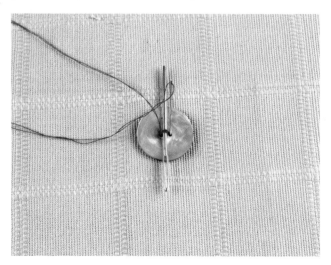

2 Before finishing off, take the thread through to between the button and the fabric. Remove the spacer and wind the thread around the stitches between the button and fabric to form a thread shank, then finish off on the reverse.

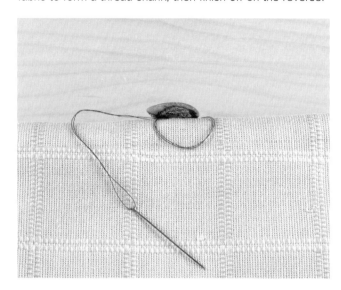

Stitching on a shank button
Using a double thread, secure the thread ends with backstitch at the button position. Stitch alternately through the shank and the fabric four to six times, then finish off with backstitches on the wrong side behind the button.

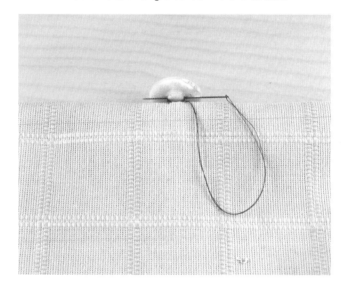

MAKING BUTTONHOLES

Buttonholes are quick and easy to work by machine. The exact method varies according to the machine model and will be explained in your manual.

Buttonholes are stitched with a close zigzag stitch, with wide stitches called bar tacks at each end and stitches half as wide along each side of the buttonhole. Cut the buttonhole along the centre after stitching, using small scissors to cut from each end towards the centre.

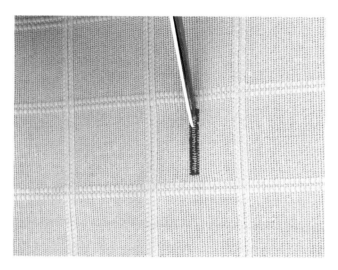

TIES

1 Press 1 cm (³⁄₈ in) to the wrong side across one short end, or both ends if they are exposed, and along both long edges.

2 Fold the tie in half lengthways and press again. Stitch down the length of the tie. On wide ties, stitch across the pressed end as well. On narrow 12 mm (¹⁄₂ in) wide ties, the end can be left unstitched.

ZIPS

1 Stitch the seam at either end of the zip position, leaving an opening the length of the zip teeth. Press the seam open and the turnings to the wrong side across the opening edges. Working with right sides uppermost, pin and tack the zip behind the opening so that one edge of the opening is just outside the zip teeth. Using a zipper foot, stitch in place near the edge.

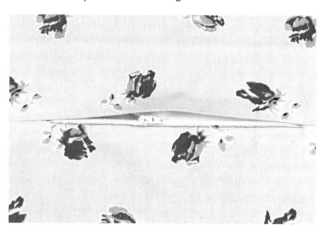

2 Arrange the other edge of the opening level with the stitching. Pin then tack this edge to the zip tape. Stitch in place across each end and along the zip tape as shown.

Pleats and tucks

PLEATS

Pleated frills and skirts make attractive trims and are a little more tailored than gathered frills and skirts. All types of pleat can be left unpressed so that the pleats are held only at the top edge, or the pleats can be pressed in place down their length for a more formal look.

Making knife pleats

Measure and mark the depth of the pleats at the top edge with pins or an erasable marker pen. Fold one marking over to meet the other. Pin then tack along the seamline at the top edge. If making rows of pleats, stitch across the top edge to hold them in place.

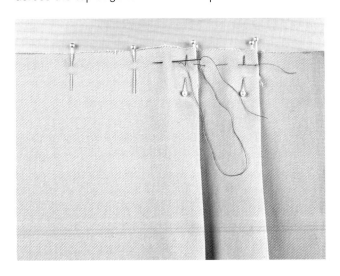

Box pleats

Box pleats are formed from two pleats facing away from each other. Measure and mark the depth of the pleats at the top edge with pins or an erasable marker pen. Fold the two inner markings outwards away from each other to meet the outer markings. Pin then tack along the seam-line at the top edge.

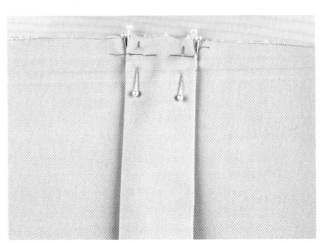

Inverted pleats

These are formed from two pleats facing towards each other so that the two folds meet at the centre of the pleat. Measure and mark the depth of the pleats at the top edge with pins or an erasable marker pen. Fold the two outer markings inwards towards each other to meet at the centre marking. Pin then tack along the seam line at the top edge.

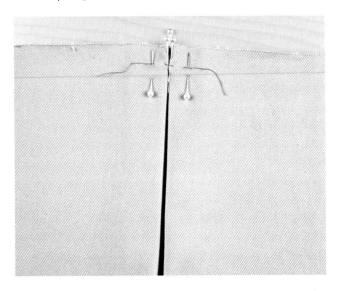

Pressed pleats

Measure and mark the pleats at intervals down the entire length of the pleat. Form the pleats and press, removing the pins as you reach them. Tack or stitch across the top edge to hold the pleats in place.

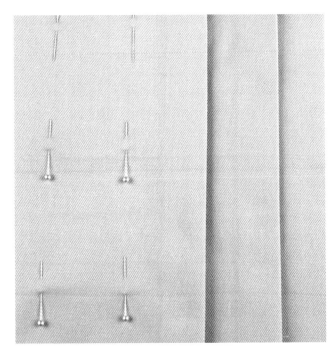

TUCKS

Tucks are stitched folds of fabric formed for a decorative effect and work particularly well with semi-sheer fabrics, as the tucks will show up well against the light. The distance of the stitching from the fold determines the type of tuck. Very fine tucks are called pin tucks. When using tucks, add twice the depth of each tuck to the fabric length.

Making pin tucks

Fold the fabric along the line of the tuck with wrong sides facing and press along the fold. With the fabric still folded, stitch along 3 mm (⅛ in) in from the fold using the machine foot as a guide. Open out the fabric and press the tuck to one side. A series of parallel pin tucks are more effective than single ones.

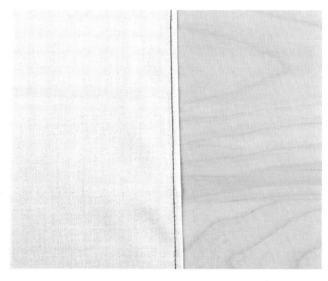

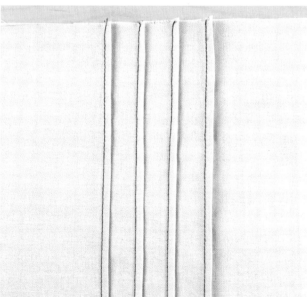

Wide tucks

Fold the fabric along the line of the tuck and press along the fold. Measure the depth of the tuck away from the fold with pins or an erasable marker pen. Tack, then stitch along the tacked line. Alternatively, stitch keeping the fabric fold against one of the guidelines on the plate beside the machine foot to keep the stitching an even distance in from the fold. Open out the fabric and press the tuck to one side.

Twin needle tucks

A machine twin needle, which stitches two parallel rows, gives a fine tucked effect on lightweight fabric such as lawn. First press a crease to form a line for the tuck. Open out the fabric and stitch along the pressed crease so that it is central between the two needles.

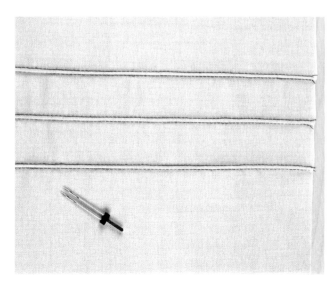

Chairs

Flap back cushion cover

This quick and easy method is ideal for square or rectangular cushions. The opening on the back of the cushion cover is formed by two overlapping edges between which the cushion pad is slipped in. Overlap the edges by 10 cm (4 in) on cushions up to 35 cm (13³/₄ in) square or by 15 cm (6 in) on larger cushions. For a rectangular cushion, place the overlap across the width of the cover rather than the length so that the opening does not gape.

DIAGRAM 2

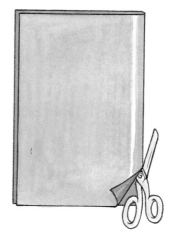

MATERIALS
Silk furnishing fabric
Sewing thread
Cushion pad

CUTTING OUT

1.5 cm (⁵/₈ in) seam allowances are included unless instructions state otherwise.

Cut out the front to the width and length of the cushion pad plus 3 cm (1¹/₄ in). Cut out the back to the same length and 14 cm (5¹/₂ in) wider than the front, or 19 cm (7¹/₂ in) wider for a larger cushion (diagram 1). Cut the back piece in half widthways (diagram 2).

1 Press a double 1 cm (³/₈ in) hem to the wrong side along the centre edges of the two back pieces. Stitch in place (diagram 3).

DIAGRAM 1

DIAGRAM 3

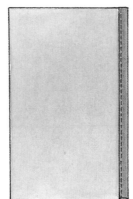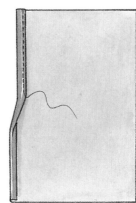

2 Place the two back pieces onto the front piece with right sides facing, arranging so that the raw edges are level all round and the hemmed edges of the back overlap. Pin together around the edge (diagram 4).

DIAGRAM 4

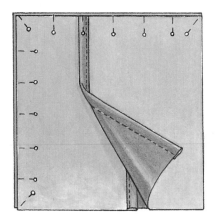

3 Stitch around the outer edge 1.5 cm ($^5/_8$ in) in from the raw edges. Trim the corners (diagram 5). Turn the cover right side out through the overlapping edges and press. Insert the cushion pad.

DIAGRAM 5

Variation

TWO-COLOUR CUSHION

For this easy decorative option, cut the cushion front from two fabrics in different colours, adding 1.5 cm ($^5/_8$ in) on the edges to be joined. Join the edges with a 1.5 cm ($^5/_8$ in) plain seam and press the seam open. Using machine straight stitch or zigzag stitch, stitch on ribbons parallel to the join. Stitch a few beads by hand along the edge of one ribbon to complete the effect. Make up in the same way as the Flap back cushion cover, page 30.

Cushion cover with zip fastening

A cushion cover fastened with a zip is a little more complicated than a flap back cover, but it has the advantage of keeping the edges of the opening pulled firmly together. You could make a feature of the zip by placing it on the front of the cover and trimming it with beads or a tassel, or use it in a purely functional way on the back of the cover. Choose a zip about 10 cm (4 in) shorter than the width of the cushion.

MATERIALS
Silk dupion or other furnishing fabric
Sewing thread
Zip fastener
Piping (optional)
Cushion pad
Tassel

CUTTING OUT

1.5 cm (⁵⁄₈ in) seam allowances are included unless instructions state otherwise.

Cut out the front to the width and height of the cushion pad plus 3 cm (1¼ in) all round. Cut the back to the same width by the height of the pad plus 6 cm (2½ in).

Cut the back piece in two the required distance down from the top edge.

33

1 Place the two cut edges of the back pieces together with right sides facing. Stitch about 6.5 cm (2½ in) in from each end, leaving a central opening the length of the zip teeth (diagram 1). Stitch the zip in place, see Zips, page 25.

DIAGRAM 1

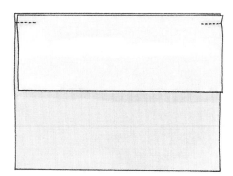

2 Make a length of piping to fit around the cushion front and, using a piping foot, stitch it in place around the edge, see Piping, page 18.

3 Open the zip. With right sides facing, place the front to the back. Stitch around the outer edge 1.5 cm (⅝ in) in from the raw edges, again using the piping foot if piping has been inserted. Trim the corners (diagram 2). Turn the cover right side out through the zip opening and press. Insert the cushion pad.

DIAGRAM 2

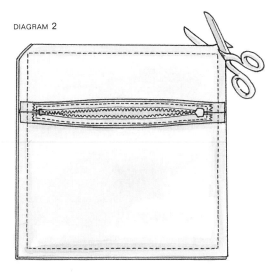

Mitred cushion cover

This cushion cover has a smart mitred border stitched around a central panel. As the border is made from separate strips, you can combine different fabrics in many imaginative ways, using subtle co-ordinating tones and textures or contrasting colours and patterns.

NOTE

The method shown here allows the cushion pad to fill the whole cushion cover. However, if you prefer, you could adapt the method so that the cushion fills the central panel only, leaving the mitred border to lie flat around it. Simply stitch the border to the central panel and complete the cushion as for the Flap back cushion cover, page 30. Then topstitch around the inner edge of the border.

MATERIALS
Furnishing fabric for border and back
Co-ordinating or contrasting fabric for central panel
Sewing thread
Cushion pad

CUTTING OUT
1.5 cm (⅝ in) seam allowances are included unless instructions state otherwise.

Cut out the central panel to the desired finished size plus 3 cm (1¼ in). Cut the borders to the desired finished width plus 3 cm (1¼ in). For each border length, measure the length or width of the central panel and add on twice the finished border width.

1 Pin and stitch the borders to the central panel (diagram 1). Mitre the corners, see Single mitred border, page 22.

2 Cut out two back pieces and make up the cushion cover in the same way as the Flap back cushion cover, page 32 (diagram 2). Insert the cushion pad.

DIAGRAM 1

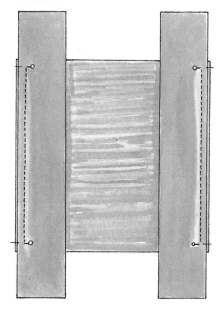

DIAGRAM 2

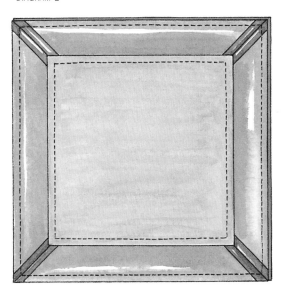

Cushion with ties

The pretty cushion is simple to make. It has a flap facing to tuck the pad behind and straight ties to hold the edges together. The facing and ties can be made from a contrast fabric or from the same fabric as the cover.

MATERIALS
Medium-weight furnishing fabric for cushion cover
Contrast fabric for facing and ties
Sewing thread
Cushion pad

CUTTING OUT

1.5 cm ($^5/_8$ in) seam allowances have been included unless instructions state otherwise.

Cut two pieces for the cover front and back the size of the cushion pad plus 3 cm (1$^1/_4$ in). Cut two facing pieces the width of the cover by 12 cm (4$^3/_4$ in) deep. Cut four ties 18 x 8 cm (7 x 3$^1/_4$ in)

1 Make the ties by folding each tie in half lengthways with right sides together and stitching across one short edge and the long edge. Trim the seams and corners, turn the ties right side out and press.

2 Place two ties to one edge of each of the front and back pieces with the ties spaced equally and the raw edges level. Place a facing piece on top of each of the front and back pieces with right sides together and stitch together along the edge so that the ends of the ties are enclosed in the seams (diagram 1).

DIAGRAM 1

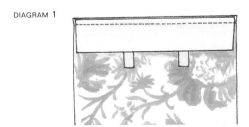

3 Open out the facings away from the cushion and press the seams open. Place the front and back together with right sides together and the facing

seams matching exactly. Stitch the front and back together around three sides, including the sides of the facing (diagram 2) .

DIAGRAM 2

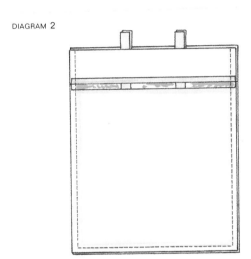

4 Trim the corners and turn the cushion cover right side out. Stitch a narrow double hem to the wrong side around the edge of the facing. Press the facing inside the cushion so that the seam is at the edge. Open the side seams out and, working from the right side, stitch down each side seam through both the cover and facing to hold the facing in place (diagram 3). Insert the cushion pad.

DIAGRAM 3

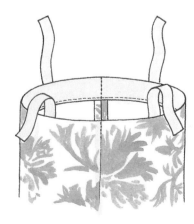

Gathered-end bolster

This long, cylindrical cushion can be made with a simple plain seam at each end, but its shape is defined more crisply if a fine piping is inserted around the seam. The circular ends are gathered and finished with a button in this version. A bolster with flat ends is given on pages 40–41. There is a zip opening in the seam at the back of the cushion.

MATERIALS
Furnishing fabric
Sewing thread
Zip about 7 cm (2³⁄₄ in) shorter than bolster pad
Piping cord
2 fabric-covered buttons
Bolster pad

CUTTING OUT
1.5 cm (⁵⁄₈ in) seam allowances are included unless instructions state otherwise.

Measure around the circumference of the bolster pad and along the pad's length. Add on 3 cm (1¹⁄₄ in) to each measurement and cut the main pieces to this size. Cut the two rectangular end pieces to the same circumference by half the diameter of the ends plus 3 cm (1¹⁄₄ in).

1 Cover the piping cord with bias strips of fabric, see Piping, page 18. Place the two lengthways edges of the main piece together with right sides facing and stitch for about 5 cm (2 in) at each end, leaving an opening at the centre the length of the zip teeth. Stitch the zip in place, taking care to keep the under-layer out of the way, see Zips, page 25. Stitch the piping around each end of the main piece.

2 Stitch the short edges of the end pieces together and press the seams open. With right sides facing and seams matching, stitch the end pieces around the ends of the main piece (diagram 1).

DIAGRAM 1

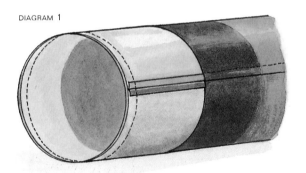

3 Open out the end pieces. Press 1.5 cm (⁵⁄₈ in) to the wrong side around the remaining edge of each end piece. Using a double thread, work running stitch around the edge and pull up the thread to gather the ends in tightly (diagram 2). Finish the thread securely and stitch on a covered button at the centre. Insert the bolster pad.

DIAGRAM 2

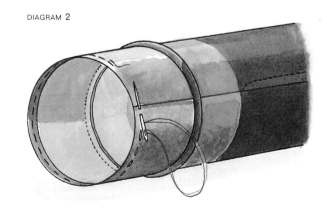

Plain-end bolster

Co-ordinating fabrics are used effectively on this smart bolster cover with plain round ends. The main section is cut in two pieces to combine the striped and patterned fabric and the ends are neatly piped in the striped fabric cut on the cross. There is a zip opening in a seam at the back.

MATERIALS
2 coordinating furnishing fabrics
Sewing thread
Zip about 7 cm (2³⁄₄ in) shorter than bolster pad
Piping cord
Bolster pad

CUTTING OUT

1.5 cm (⁵⁄₈ in) seam allowances are included unless instructions state otherwise.

Measure around the circumference of the bolster pad and along the pad's length. Divide up the length as desired between the two fabrics. Add on 3 cm (1¼ in) to each measurement and cut the main pieces to this size. Cut two circular end pieces the same size as the end of the pad plus 1.5 cm (⁵⁄₈ in) all round.

1 With right sides facing, stitch the two fabrics together to make one main piece. Place the two lengthways edges of the main piece together with right sides facing and stitch for about 5 cm (2 in) at each end, leaving an opening at the centre the length of the zip teeth (diagram 1).

DIAGRAM 1

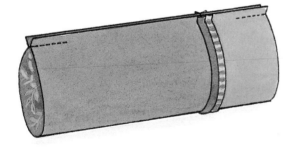

2 Stitch the zip in place, taking care to keep the under-layer out of the way, see Zips, page 25. Cover piping cord with bias strips of fabric and then stitch the piping around each end of the main piece, see Piping, page 18 (diagram 2).

DIAGRAM 2

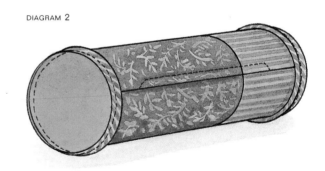

3 Divide each end of the main piece into four equal sections and mark with pins. In the same way, use pins to mark four equal sections around the edge of the circular end pieces. Leaving the zip open, place the end pieces to the main piece with right sides facing, matching the pins. Pin together at these points (diagram 3).

DIAGRAM 3

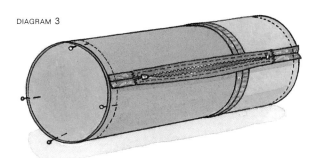

4 Working from the circle side, pin the end pieces to the main piece between the marker pins, easing the fabric in to fit. It is advisable to tack the seams firmly. Stitch the seams as in Piping, page 18 (diagram 4). Turn right side out through the zip opening and insert the bolster pad.

DIAGRAM 4

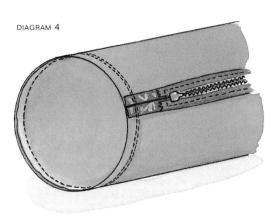

Seat pad with skirt

This style of seat pad has a flat skirt of fabric that protrudes over the chair seat around the front and side edges. It is fastened to the chair uprights with ties at the back. The seat area is padded with medium-weight wadding, but you could substitute 12 mm ($\frac{1}{2}$ in) foam for extra padding if you wish. If you are using a patterned fabric, arrange the pattern to run from the front to the back of the seat.

MATERIALS
Furnishing fabric
Sewing thread
Medium-weight wadding

CUTTING OUT

1.5 cm ($\frac{5}{8}$ in) seam allowances are included unless instructions state otherwise.

Measure the seat size, then add on 13 cm ($5\frac{1}{8}$ in) to the width and 8 cm ($3\frac{1}{4}$ in) to the depth from front to back. Cut out two pieces of fabric to these measurements. You may need to cut out a section at the back corners to accommodate the chair uprights. Cut four fabric ties 36 cm (14 in) by 5 cm (2 in).

1 Make four ties, see Ties, page 25. Place the ties onto the right side of the pad front, positioning them in pairs at each back corner so that they match the chair uprights. Arrange the ends of the ties level with the raw edge and stitch in place 1.5 cm ($\frac{5}{8}$ in) from the edge (diagram 1).

2 Place the back and front pad pieces together with right sides facing. Stitch the pieces together 1.5 cm ($\frac{5}{8}$ in) from the edges, beginning and finishing on the back edge 5 cm (2 in) in from the corners (diagram 2). Trim the corners, turn the pad right side out and press the seam at the edge.

DIAGRAM 1

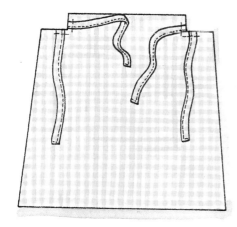

DIAGRAM 2

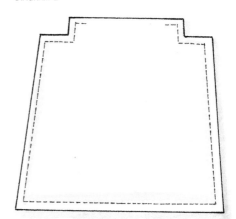

3 Beginning and finishing at the back edge, stitch around the sides and front edge of the pad, 5 cm (2 in) in from the edge, to form the skirt (diagram 3).

DIAGRAM 3

4 Cut the medium-weight wadding to the shape of the seat area of the pad. Slip the wadding in through the opening on the back edge. Tuck in the raw edges along the back edge and handstitch the opening closed (diagram 4).

DIAGRAM 4

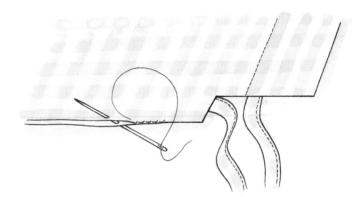

Patchwork seat pad

This version of the seat pad is made by joining fabric squares together to form a patchwork before cutting out the top. Stitch the patchwork squares along the side edges first to make three rows of three. Then stitch the rows together along their long edges. For a balanced design, number the fabrics and stitch them together in order 1 2 3 for the top row, 3 1 2 for the middle row and 2 3 1 for the base row.

MATERIALS
3 patchwork fabrics
Pattern paper
Fabric for pad back
Sewing thread
Medium-weight wadding

CUTTING OUT

1.5 cm ($^5/_8$ in) seam allowances are included unless instructions state otherwise.

Make a paper pattern to the size of your chair seat. Measure the longest distance front to back or side to side and divide this by three. Add 3 cm ($1^1/_4$ in) to this measurement and cut nine patchwork squares to that size. Cut four fabric ties 36 cm (14 in) by 5 cm (2 in).

1 Stitch the side edges of the top row of patchwork pieces together 1.5cm (⁵⁄₈ in) in from the edge. Trim the seam allowances and press them open. Stitch the middle row and base row in the same way. In the same way stitch the rows together to make one piece, matching the seams carefully (diagram 1).

2 Place the paper pattern on the fabric. Add on 1.5 cm (⁵⁄₈ in) seam allowance all around and cut out (diagram 2). Cut out the fabric for the pad back to the same size. Make four ties, see Ties, page 25, and then make up in the same way as the Seat pad with skirt, pages 42–44, but omitting the skirt stitching.

DIAGRAM 1

DIAGRAM 2

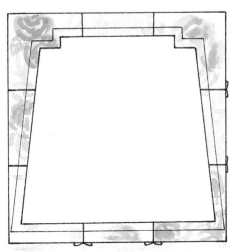

Box cushion

This piped cushion cover with a gusset can be used to re-cover an existing seat pad or fitted over a new foam pad. It has a zip opening at the back of the gusset, so that it can easily be removed for cleaning. Choose a zip length about one third of the whole gusset length.

MATERIALS
Furnishing fabric
Sewing thread
Zip, about one third of gusset length
Piping cord
Foam pad

NOTE

You can buy foam from specialist foam suppliers, who will cut it to size for you. Ask for advice on the most suitable type of foam and, if possible, choose a medium-density, flame-resistant type.

CUTTING OUT

1.5 cm ($^5/_8$ in) seam allowances are included unless instructions state otherwise.

Cut out a top and base piece to the size of the foam plus 1.5 cm ($^5/_8$ in) all round. Measure around the foam for the required finished gusset length. Cut the zipped section of the gusset the length of the zip plus 5 cm (2 in) by the foam depth plus 6 cm (2$^1/_4$ in). Then cut this section in half along its length. Cut the other section of the gusset the remainder of the length plus 3 cm (1$^1/_4$ in) by the foam depth plus 3 cm (1$^1/_4$ in).

1 With right sides facing and raw edges level, stitch two long edges of the zip gussets together for 2.5 cm (1 in) at each end, leaving an opening the length of the zip teeth at the centre. Stitch the zip into the opening, see Zips, page 25 (diagram 1).

DIAGRAM 1

2 With right sides facing and raw edges level, stitch the short edges of the long gusset to the short edges of the zip gusset. Press the seams open (diagram 2).

DIAGRAM 2

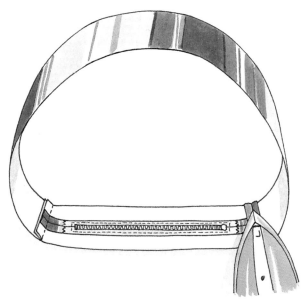

3 Stitch the piping around the edges of the top and the base pieces, see Piping, page 18.

4 Divide the edges of the top and base pieces into quarters and mark with pins (diagram 3). In the same way, mark both edges of the gusset into quarters.

DIAGRAM 3

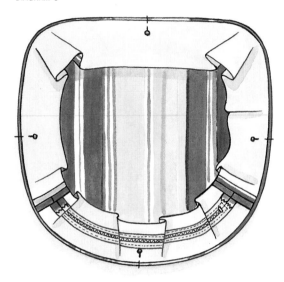

5 Open the zip. Place the top edge of the gusset to the top piece with right sides facing and raw edges level. Match the marker pins and pin together at these points, then pin between the marks.

6 For a cover with rounded corners, make several snips close together into the gusset seam allowance at each curve – the tighter the curve, the closer the snips need to be (diagram 4). On a cushion cover with square corners, make a single snip into the gusset seam allowance at each corner, so that the allowance will open out to fit around the corner (diagram 5). Tack, then stitch the gusset in place. Stitch the base to the other edge of the gusset in the same way. Turn right side out and press. Insert the foam pad.

DIAGRAM 4

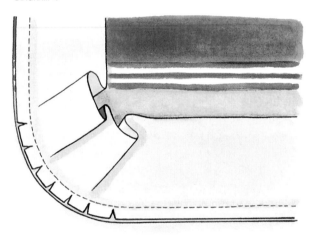

DIAGRAM 5

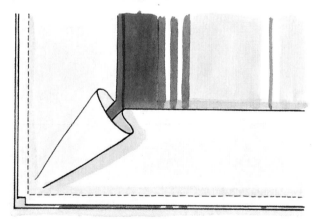

Variation

A box cushion can be made in almost any shape – just make sure that you make an accurate template of the seat area before you start.

Throw with mitred border

The double mitred border on this throw looks as good on the back as on the front. This is a very useful method of trimming reversible fabric, giving it a fine, professional-looking finish.

MATERIALS
Heavyweight main fabric, such as velvet, wool or chenille
Border fabric
Sewing thread

CUTTING OUT

1.5 cm ($^5/_8$ in) seam allowances are included unless instructions state otherwise.

Cut the main fabric to the required size. Cut the borders 17 cm ($6^1/_2$ in) wide for a finished width of 7 cm ($2^3/_4$ in) by the length of the centre panel plus twice the finished width of the border.

1 Stitch the borders following Double mitred border, page 22 which also explains how to work out different sizes and border widths.

Throw edging variations

THROW WITH BEADED TRIM

A whole range of ready-made trims is now available – sew a double hem and then stitch on the beaded trim.

THROW WITH BLANKET STITCH

Blanket stitch is a simple hand-stitched edging for a throw, see Blanket stitch, page 13. On non-fray fabrics it can be worked directly over the edge, but even here a better finish is often achieved if a single hem to the depth of the stitching is folded to the wrong side first. This gives a firm edge and also gives a good line for keeping the stitching even. On fabrics that fray such as velvet, fold a double hem before blanket stitching over it. Use a thick thread, such as wool, or a fine ribbon, as shown here.

THROW WITH FRINGED EDGE

Before you buy the fabric, check that it will fray neatly when the threads are pulled away. On closely woven fabric the threads can just be pulled away to make a fringed edge. On loosely woven fabrics and for a more durable finish, stitch a line of narrow zigzag stitch in matching thread at the top of the fringe before fraying, see Fringing fabric, page 20.

THROW WITH BINDING

Binding gives a luxurious finish to a throw, especially if a fine satin or silk is used. If you cannot find silk or satin binding, make your own from ribbon or fabric. The double binding method will give a very smart finish if a wide binding is preferred, see Double binding method, page 17.

Tailored slip cover

This smart linen slipcover will give a new lease of life to a jaded dining room chair. It is made from natural linen with fine cream piping outlining the seat and the sides of the back. There are inverted pleats at the front corners of the skirt.

MATERIALS
Medium-weight furnishing fabric
Sewing thread
Piping cord
Contrast fabric for piping

CUTTING OUT

1.5 cm (⅝ in) seam allowances are included unless instructions state otherwise.

Decide on the desired depth of the skirt. Beginning at the top of the chair seat, measure up the back of the chair back, across the top, down the front of the chair back and across the seat to the front edge, then add on the skirt depth plus 3 cm (1¼ in). Measure across the back or seat, whichever is wider, add on 5 cm (2 in) and cut the main panel to this size. Measure the skirt around the two sides and front of the chair and add on 40 cm (16 in) for pleats and 5 cm (2 in) for side hem allowances. Cut the skirt to this length by the skirt depth plus 3 cm (1¼ in).

1   Try the main piece on the chair, leaving the extra fabric allowed for the skirt depth, plus 1.5 cm (⅝ in) hem allowance, hanging down at the back. Pin down the sides of the chair back (diagram 1). Check the fit on both the back and seat and adjust if required, remembering to allow for seam allowances. Mark the top edge of the chair back, then unpin the fabric and remove from the chair.

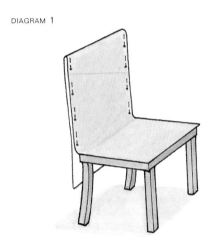

DIAGRAM 1

2   Cover the piping cord with bias-cut strips, see Piping, page 18, to make sufficient to fit around the sides and front of the chair seat and up the side seams on the chair back. Starting at the top of the chair back, stitch piping to the front of the main piece down one side edge, around the chair seat and back up the other side edge, finishing the ends into the seam allowance (diagram 2).

DIAGRAM 2

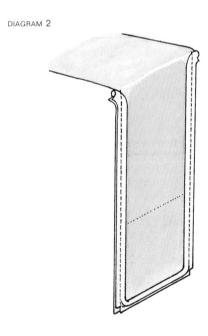

3 With right sides facing, stitch the front to the back down the side seams, leaving the skirt depth plus 1.5 cm (⅝ in) to hang free at the base of the back (diagram 3) .

DIAGRAM 3

4 With right sides facing, match the centre of the seat front on the main panel with the centre of the top edge of the skirt, then pin the skirt out to the front corners. At each corner, form a 10 cm (4 in) wide inverted pleat on the skirt, with its centre at the corner, and snip into the seam allowance at the

centre of the pleat (diagram 4). Continue pinning the skirt to the seat sides up to the back corners, leaving 2.5 cm (1 in) projecting beyond the back edges for the side hems. Tack, then stitch the skirt in place.

DIAGRAM 4

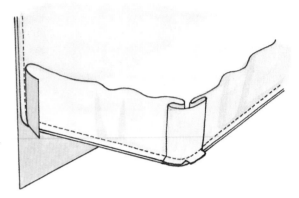

5 Zigzag stitch the lower edges of the skirt and back, and the remaining side edges of the skirt and back at the back corners. Press and stitch 1.5 cm (⅝ in) hems to the wrong side along the lower edges of the skirt and back. Press and stitch the hems to the wrong side down the remaining side edges of the skirt and back. Turn right side out and press. Add a small bar stitch at the two front corners to hold the pleats neatly in place.

Simple slip cover

Surprisingly effective, the simple slip cover is basically just a rectangle of fabric, lined edge to edge, which drapes over the chair and fastens at the sides with fabric ties. A soft interlining is sandwiched between the fabric and lining to add a little luxury.

MATERIALS
Medium-weight furnishing fabric
Lining fabric
Soft interlining
Sewing thread

CUTTING OUT

1.5 cm (⅝ in) seam allowances are included unless instructions state otherwise.

Measure the area to be covered up the back of the chair, down the front, across the seat and down the front edge and add on 3 cm (1¼ in). Measure the width required at the widest point and add on 7 cm (2¾ in). Cut out the main fabric to these measurements. Cut eight ties 4 x 30 cm (1½ x 12 in).

1 Try the main piece on the chair. Check the fit on both the back and seat and adjust if required, remembering to allow for seams. Mark the positions for the ties on both the front and back with pins. Remove the fabric from the chair.

2 Cut the lining to the same size as the main fabric and the interlining 1.5 cm ($^5/_8$ in) smaller all round. Place the interlining to the wrong side of the main fabric. Press the edge of the main fabric over the edge of the interlining. Pin and tack the ties at the marked positions with their ends level with the raw fabric edge and the ties pointing outwards (diagram 1).

DIAGRAM 1

3 Place the lining to the main fabric with wrong sides facing. Tuck the raw edges of the lining under just inside the edge of the main fabric and stitch in place, catching in the ends of the ties (diagram 2).

DIAGRAM 2

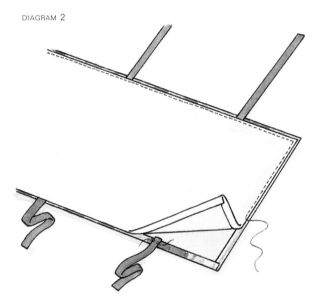

Tables

Square tablecloth

A classic square or rectangular tablecloth can protect a table top for everyday use or dress a table elegantly for a special meal. The square cloth shown here is finished with a deep hem for a classic look. The hem can be made on the wrong side of the fabric in the usual way for a plain look. If the fabric is reversible, you could make a feature of the hem by turning it onto the right side to give the effect of a mitred border. The finished hem is 4 cm (1½ in) deep, but you can make it narrower if you prefer.

MATERIALS
Cotton furnishing fabric
Sewing thread

CUTTING OUT

Cut out the cloth to the required size, adding 10 cm (4 in) to both the length and the width for the hem.

NOTE
Whenever possible, choose a fabric that is wide enough to make the tablecloth without joins. If joins are unavoidable, use a whole width of fabric for the centre of the cloth and add half widths, or whatever is required, to each side. Join the pieces with a flat fell seam, see Seams, page 14.

1 Press 1 cm (³⁄₈ in), then 4 cm (1½ in) to the chosen side of the fabric to form the hem. Form and stitch mitres at the corners, see Mitred hem, page 23 (diagram 1).

DIAGRAM 1

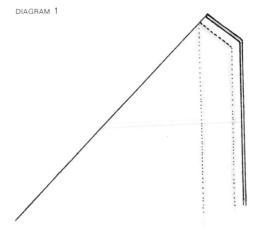

2 Refold the hem and press the corners. Pin, or tack in place if preferred, then stitch the hem along the inner fold (diagram 2).

DIAGRAM 2

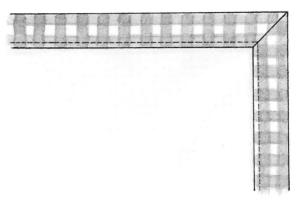

Tablecloth edging variations

TABLECLOTH WITH ORGANDIE BORDER

You will need fabric, sewing thread and organdie for the border. Cut the cloth to required size. Cut the organdie borders 11 cm (4¼ in) wide, for a finished border width of 4 cm (1½ in), by the length of the cloth plus twice the finished border width. Make and stitch the borders as in Double mitred border, page 22, trimming all the seam allowances to 5 mm (¼ in) as they are stitched.

TABLECLOTH WITH LACE EDGING

A lace edging will add a lovely touch to a plain white tablecloth. You can buy lace trims such as broderie anglaise in haberdashers but it is worth looking out for old lace tablecloths in antique markets that you can recycle.

Stitch a double 1 cm (⅜ in) hem around the tablecloth. Overlap the finished hem edge over the inner edge of the lace and stitch in place.

TABLECLOTH WITH ZIGZAG BORDER

You will need materials as for the basic square tablecloth plus contrasting cotton perlé or stranded cotton embroidery thread, an embroidery needle and matching sewing thread. Make the cloth as for the basic square tablecloth with the hem on the wrong side. Thread a long length of embroidery thread into the needle, bring it through to the front of the cloth from the wrong side and lay it along the hem, using the stitching as a guide. Using a close machine zigzag stitch, work over the embroidery thread to create a decorative border. Finish the ends of all the threads on the wrong side.

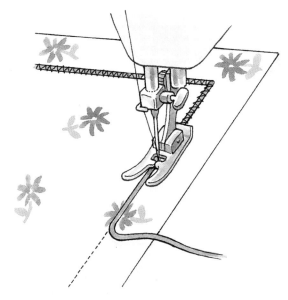

Circular tablecloth

Circular cloths are used to dress round dining tables and can be practical or luxurious depending on the fabric you choose. You can also make a feature of a small occasional table by making a circular cloth with a stylishly deep drop.

MATERIALS
Lightweight furnishing fabric
Sewing thread
Brown paper
String
Pencil

CUTTING OUT

1.5 cm (⁵⁄₈ in) seam allowances are included unless instructions state otherwise.

Tie the pencil onto the end of the string. Measure and mark half the required diameter plus 1.5 cm (⁵⁄₈ in) along the string from the pencil. Hold the marked string at one corner of the paper and, keeping the string taut, draw a quarter circle with the pencil (diagram 1).

Cut the paper along the drawn line. Fold the fabric into four, then place the straight edges of the pattern level with the folded edges of the fabric. Pin the paper in place and cut around the circular edge through all four layers of fabric.

NOTE
Because of the restriction of the fabric width, most circular tablecloths need to be joined. Use a full fabric width for a central panel and stitch more fabric to each side to make up the required width. Join the pieces before cutting out, using flat fell seams if the cloth is to be laundered frequently or plain seams if the cloth is mainly decorative, see Seams, page 14.

1 Open the fabric out. Stitch around the circle 1.5 cm (⁵⁄₈ in) in from the edge. Fold the raw edge over to the wrong side along the stitched line, pressing as you go. The stitching will naturally roll over to just inside the fold, giving a smooth curve.

2 Carefully turn under the raw edge to make a double hem. Press it as you go, easing in any fullness. Pin, tack, then stitch the hem in place (diagram 2).

DIAGRAM 2

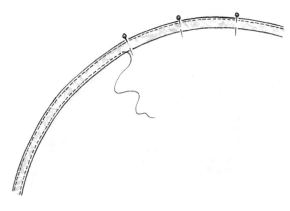

DIAGRAM 1

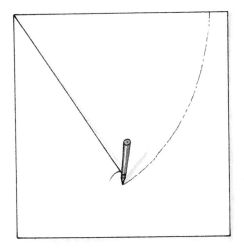

Beaded napkins

These pretty silk napkins with beaded trims are perfect for special occasions. The measurements given will make napkins with a generous finished size of 45 cm (17³⁄₄ in) square. If you prefer smaller napkins, cut the fabric 48 cm (19 in) square for a finished size of 40 cm (15³⁄₄ in)

MATERIALS
Silk fabric
Sewing thread
Small seed beads (optional)
Fine needle

CUTTING OUT

Cut out the fabric to 53 cm (21 in) square for each napkin.

1 Press 1 cm (³⁄₈ in), then 3 cm (1¹⁄₄ in) to the wrong side of the fabric to form the hem. Form and stitch mitres at the corners, see Mitred hem, page 23 (diagram 1).

DIAGRAM 1

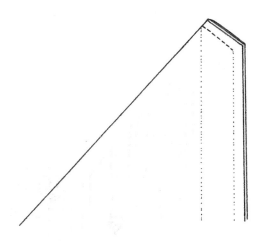

2 Stitch the hem in place. Using a fine needle, apply a row of small beads near the outer fold of the hem, spacing them about 3 cm (1¹⁄₄ in) apart. Stitch each bead with two small backstitches before slipping the needle along inside the hem to the next bead position (diagram 2). Alternatively, stitch the beads in clusters of three along the centre of the hem or in radiating lines at the corners.

DIAGRAM 2

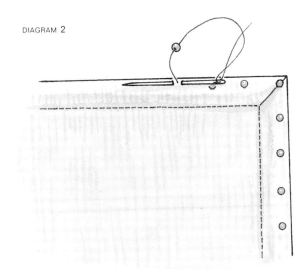

Napkin variations

CLASSIC LINEN NAPKIN

Cut out and make the napkin as in step 1 of the
Beaded napkins, page 66, but fold the hem onto the
right side of the fabric. Stitch the hem in place near
its inner edge.

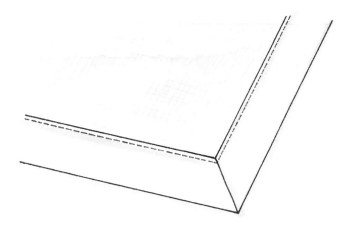

ORGANDIE BORDER NAPKIN

Cut the napkin fabric 40 cm (15¾ in) square. Cut the organdie borders 9 cm (3½ in), for a finished width of 3 cm (1¼ in), by the length of the napkin fabric plus twice the finished border. Make and stitch the borders as in Double mitred border, page 22, trimming all the seam allowances to 6 mm (¼ in) as they are stitched.

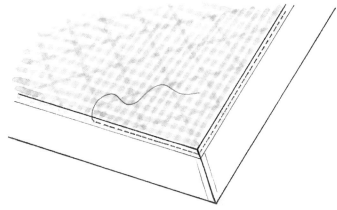

Silk table runner with tassel

This sumptuous silk table runner is lined edge to edge and is trimmed with a matching velvet ribbon. The points at each end are decorated with an elegant beaded tassel. The measurements given make a table runner with a finished size of 90 x 30 cm (35½ x 12 in).

MATERIALS
Silk fabric
Lining fabric
Pencil or marker
Ruler
Sewing thread
Velvet ribbon, 2 m (2¼ yds)
2 tassels

CUTTING OUT

1.5 cm (⅝ in) seam allowances are included unless instructions state otherwise.

Cut out a piece of fabric 93 x 33 cm (36½ x 13 in). Mark the centre of each end with a pin. Measure 23 cm (9 in) in from each end along each side edge and mark with a pin. Draw lines between the central pins and the side pins. Cut the fabric along the marked lines to make the pointed ends (diagram 1). Mark and cut both ends of the lining in the same way.

DIAGRAM 1

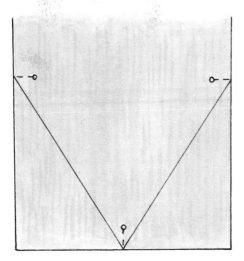

1 Place the lining and fabric right sides facing with raw edges level. Stitch together 1.5 cm (⅝ in) from the raw edges, leaving a 15 cm (6 in) opening on one long edge (diagram 2).

DIAGRAM 2

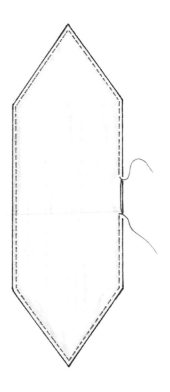

2 Trim the corners and turn the runner right side out. Press the seam allowance to the inside along the opening and slip stitch the opening edges together. Pin and tack the velvet ribbon around the outer edge. Stitch the ribbon in place along both long edges. Stitch a tassel to the point at each end (diagram 3).

DIAGRAM 3

Table runner with organza border

The elegant oblong table runner has a fine linen centre panel surrounded by a wide mitred border made from gold organza. The finished runner is 41 cm (16 in) wide.

MATERIALS
Linen fabric for centre panel
Organza border fabric
Sewing thread

CUTTING OUT

1.5 cm ($^5/_8$ in) seam allowances are included unless instructions state otherwise.

Cut out two centre panels 28 cm (11 in) wide by the required length minus 13 cm ($5^1/_8$ in). For the border, cut four strips 19 cm ($7^1/_2$ in) wide by the required length, see Double mitred border, page 22.

1 Stitch the strips together to form a double mitred border. Trim the mitre seams to 5 mm (¼ in) and press them open. Press the border with raw edges level and right sides outside. With right sides facing, stitch both raw edges of the border together to the outer edge of the front centre panel. Press the seam towards the centre panel (diagram 1).

DIAGRAM 1

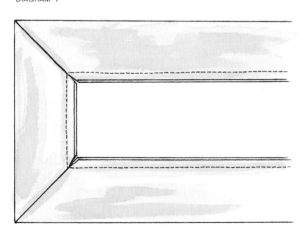

2 Press the seam allowance to the wrong side around the back centre panel. Place this panel to the wrong side of the runner and stitch in place by hand along the line of the previous stitching (diagram 2).

DIAGRAM 2

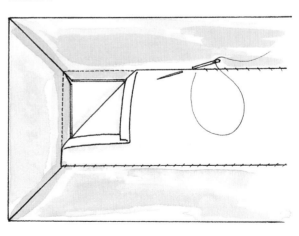

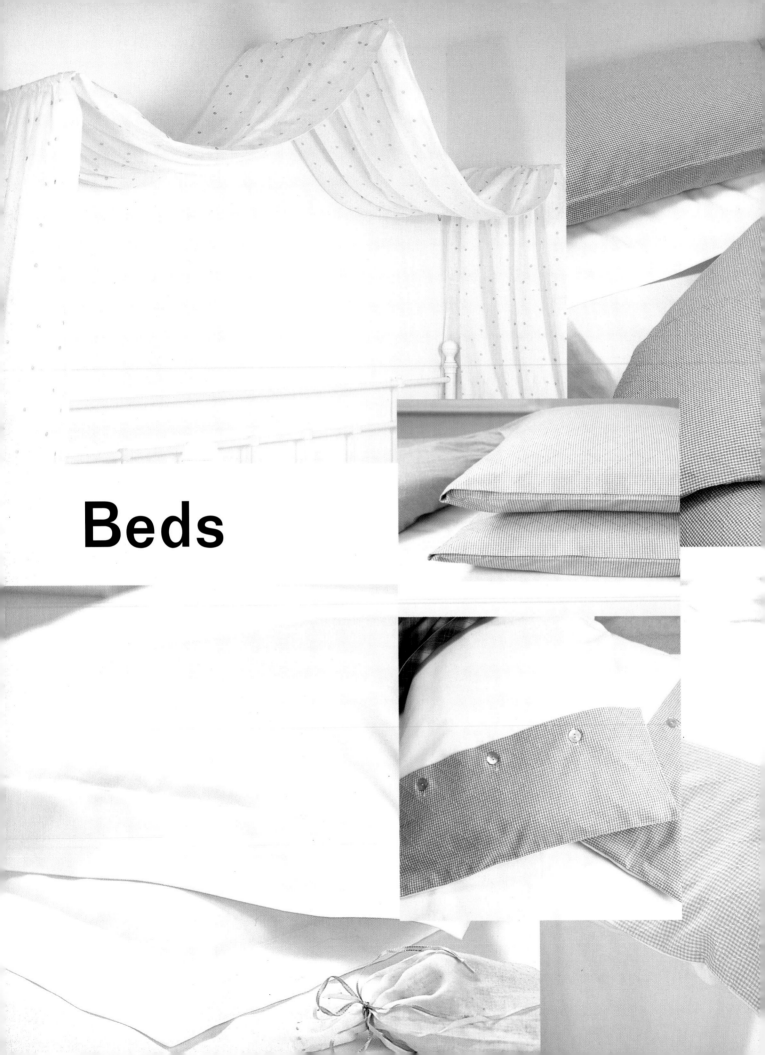

Beds

Buttoned pillowcase

The stylish buttoned pillowcases have deep hems on the two front panels which overlap and button together. The end panels are made in contrasting fabric to co-ordinate with the buttoned duvet cover on page 85.

MATERIALS
Cotton or polycotton sheeting
Sewing thread
3 buttons, 2 cm ($^3/_4$ in) in diameter

NOTE
A standard British pillowcase measures
75 x 50 cm (29$^1/_2$ x 19$^3/_4$ in)

DIAGRAM 2

CUTTING OUT

1.5 cm ($^5/_8$ in) seam allowances are included unless instructions state otherwise.

For the pillowcase back, measure the length and width of the pillow and add on 3 cm (1$^1/_4$ in) to each measurement. Cut out a piece of fabric to this size. Cut the front end panel to the same width and 35 cm (13$^3/_4$ in) deep. Cut the main front panel the same width as the back and 2.5 cm (1 in) longer.

1 Press and stitch a double 7.5 cm (3 in) hem to the wrong side along one long edge of the front end panel and along one short edge of the main front panel (diagram 1).

DIAGRAM 1

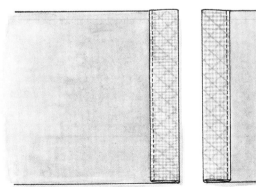

2 Mark three buttonhole positions centrally on the hem of the front end panel, placing one buttonhole at the centre of the hem and one on either side, midway between the central one and the edge. Stitch the buttonholes at right angles to the edge (diagram 2).

3 Place the front end panel to one end of the pillowcase back with right sides facing and raw edges level. Place the main front panel to the other end of the back in the same way, so that the hems overlap. Stitch the front panels to the back around all four edges (diagram 3).

DIAGRAM 3

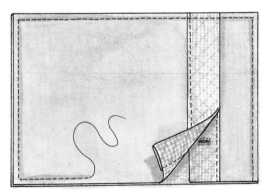

4 Trim the seam to 1 cm ($^3/_8$ in) and zigzag stitch the edges together to prevent fraying. Turn the pillowcase right side out and press the seam at the edge.

5 Stitch buttons to the main front panel hem to correspond with the buttonholes, placing the buttons to sit at the outer end of the buttonholes.

Housewife pillowcase

This simple, plain pillowcase is finished with a deep hem on the opening end and has a flap inside to hold the pillow in place.

MATERIALS
Cotton or polycotton fabric
Sewing thread

CUTTING OUT

1.5 cm ($^5/_8$ in) seam allowances are included unless instructions state otherwise.

Measure the length of the pillow, double this and add on 25 cm (10 in). Measure the width and add on 3 cm ($1^1/_4$ in). Cut out a piece of fabric to this size.

1 Press and stitch a double 1.5 cm ($^5/_8$ in) hem across one short end. At the other short end press 1 cm ($^3/_8$ in), then 5 cm (2 in) to the wrong side to make a deep hem and stitch in place.

2 With right sides facing, fold the end with the deep hem over so that it is 16 cm ($6^1/_4$ in) in from the edge with the narrow hem. Fold the projecting fabric back over the deep hem edge to form the flap (diagram 1).

DIAGRAM 1

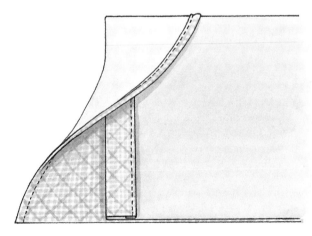

3 Stitch along both side edges, taking 1.5 cm ($^5/_8$ in) seam allowances. Trim the seams to 1 cm ($^3/_8$ in) and zigzag stitch the edges together to prevent fraying. Turn the pillowcase right side out and press.

Oxford pillowcase

This smart tailored pillowcase has a generously wide 7 cm (2³⁄₄ in) border around the edge of the filled area. The inner edge of the border is trimmed with a row a decorative zigzag stitching worked over an embroidery thread.

MATERIALS
Cotton or polycotton fabric
Sewing thread
Stranded embroidery cotton or coton perlé embroidery thread

CUTTING OUT
1.5 cm (⁵⁄₈ in) seam allowances are included unless instructions state otherwise.

Measure the length of the pillow, double this and add on 50 cm (19³⁄₄ in). Measure the width of the pillow and add on 17 cm (6³⁄₄ in). Cut out a piece of fabric to this size.

1 Press and stitch a double 1.5 cm (⁵⁄₈ in) hem to the wrong side along each short edge.

2 With right sides together, fold one short edge over so that it is 33 cm (13 in) in from the other short edge. Fold the projecting short edge back over so that it overlaps the other short edge by 16 cm (6¹⁄₄ in)

(diagram 1). Stitch along both side edges, allowing for seams. Trim the seams to 1 cm (³⁄₈ in).

DIAGRAM 1

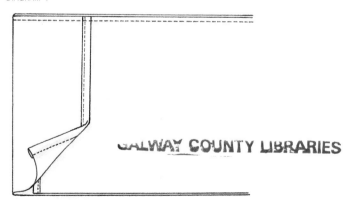

3 Turn the pillowcase right side out and press the seams at the edges. Tack the overlapping flap to hold it in place. To create the border, stitch around the pillowcase 7 cm (2³⁄₄ in) in from the outer edges. For a more decorative finish, stitch around the pillowcase again using a machine zigzag stitch worked over a length of coton perlé embroidery thread or all six strands of stranded embroidery cotton. Remove the tacking from the flap.

Basic duvet cover

This plain and simple duvet cover is easy to make and has an opening in the hem across the base edge of the cover.

MATERIALS
Cotton or polycotton sheeting
Sewing thread
Press-stud tape

NOTE
Standard duvet sizes are as follows: 135 x 200 cm (53 x 78½ in) for a single and 200 x 200 cm (78½ x 78½ in) for a double. Many furnishing fabrics are wide enough for a single duvet cover, though they may not wash well and often require a lot of ironing. Only custom-made sheeting is wide enough for a double duvet cover and has the advantage of an easy-care finish.

CUTTING OUT

1.5 cm (⅝ in) seam allowances are included unless instructions state otherwise.

Measure the length and width of the duvet, add 11 cm (4¼ in) to the length and 3 cm (1¼ in) to the width and cut out two pieces of fabric to this size.

1   Press and stitch a double 3 cm (1¼ in) hem to the wrong side along the lower edges of both pieces.

2   Place the two hemmed edges together with right sides facing. Stitch the hemmed edges together just inside the inner fold of the hem for 30 cm (12 in) from each side, leaving an opening at the centre (diagram 1).

3   Cut the press-stud tape 5 cm (2 in) longer than the opening, avoiding having a press stud near the ends. Separate the two halves of the tape. Position one half on one hem so that it projects beyond the opening for 2.5 cm (1 in) at each end (diagram 2). Using a zipper foot, stitch the tape in place along both its long edges.

4   Fasten the second half of the tape to the first, then pin it to the opposite hem – this ensures that the two halves match exactly. Unfasten the tape and stitch the second half in place in the same way as the first (diagram 2).

DIAGRAM 1

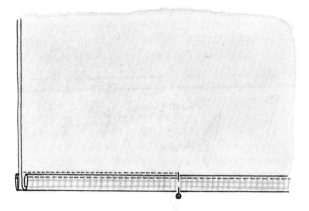

DIAGRAM 2

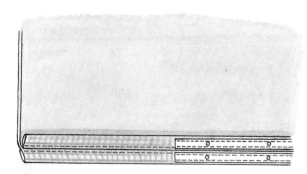

5 Fasten the tape. Stitch across the hems 2.5 cm (1 in) in from each end of the tape so the ends are enclosed.

6 With right sides facing and raw edges level, stitch the pieces together around the remaining three edges, taking a 1.5 cm ($^5/_8$ in) seam allowance. Trim the seams to 1 cm ($^3/_8$ in) and zigzag stitch the raw edges together (diagram 3). Turn the duvet cover right side out and press the seams at the edges.

DIAGRAM 3

Duvet cover with flange

This version of the duvet cover has a generous 7 cm (2¾ in) wide flange and will co-ordinate with the Oxford pillowcase, page 79. The duvet fills the inner pocket, which is sized to cover the duvet, leaving the flange flat at the edges.

MATERIALS
Cotton or polycotton sheeting
Sewing thread
Press-stud tape
Stranded embroidery cotton or coton perlé
embroidery thread

CUTTING OUT
1.5 cm ($^5/_8$ in) seam allowances are included unless instructions state otherwise.

Measure the length of the duvet, double this and add on 29 cm (11½ in). Measure the width of the duvet and add on 17 cm (6¾ in). Cut out a piece of fabric to this size.

DIAGRAM 1

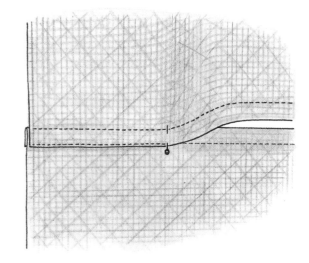

1 Press and stitch a double 3 cm (1¼ in) hem to the wrong side along the two shorter edges.

2 With right sides uppermost, lap one hemmed edge over the other. Stitch the hems together along the edge of the uppermost hem for 30 cm (12 in) from each side, leaving an opening at the centre (diagram 1).

3 Turn the cover through to the wrong side. Cut the press-stud tape 5 cm (2 in) longer than the opening, avoiding having a press stud near the ends. Separate the two halves of the tape. Position one half on one hem so that it projects beyond the opening for 2.5 cm (1 in) at each end. Using a zipper foot, stitch the tape in place along both its long edges.

4 Fasten the second half of the tape to the first and pin it to the opposite hemmed edge – this ensures that the two halves match exactly. Unfasten the tape and stitch the second half in place in the same way as the first (diagram 2).

DIAGRAM 2

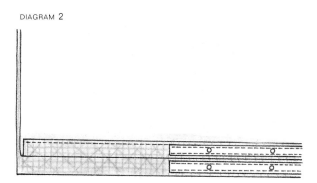

5 Fasten the tape and, working from the right side, stitch across the hems 2.5 cm (1 in) in from each end of the tape so the ends are enclosed (diagram 3).

DIAGRAM 3

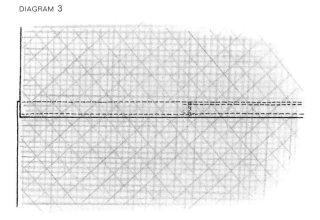

6 With right sides facing, arrange the fabric so the opening is at least 8.5 cm (3³⁄₈ in) from the lower fold edge and the raw edges are level at each side. Stitch together along both raw edges, taking 1.5 cm (⁵⁄₈ in) seam allowances (diagram 4).

DIAGRAM 4

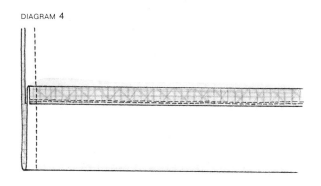

7 Trim the seams to 1 cm (³⁄₈ in). Turn the cover right side out and press the seams at the edges. To form the flange, stitch around the side and lower edges 7 cm (2³⁄₄ in) in from the outer edge (diagram 5). To give a decorative finish, stitch around the flange again using a machine zigzag stitch worked over a length of coton perlé embroidery thread or all six strands of stranded embroidery cotton (see page 63).

DIAGRAM 5

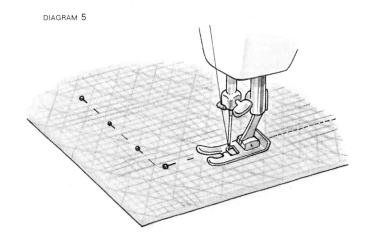

Duvet cover with border

Add a designer edge to the basic duvet cover with a crisp single mitred border stitched around a centre panel. The duvet fills the cover out to the edge of the border. Vary the look with different fabrics or combine co-ordinating checks and stripes for a country-style cover, taking care to match the pattern at the mitred corners.

MATERIALS
Cotton or polycotton sheeting
Sewing thread
Press-stud tape

CUTTING OUT

1.5 cm ($^5/_8$ in) seam allowances are included unless instructions state otherwise.

For the back of the cover, measure the length and width of the duvet, add 18 cm (7 in) to the length and 3 cm ($1^1/_4$ in) to the width and cut out one piece of fabric to this size. For the front of the cover, subtract 37 cm ($14^1/_2$ in) from the measurements of the duvet and cut out the centre panel to this size. For the border cut strips 23 cm (9 in) wide by the required length, see Single mitred border, page 22.

1 Cut a 26 cm ($10^1/_4$ in) wide strip from the lower edge of the back piece. Press and stitch a double 3 cm ($1^1/_4$ in) hem across both the cut edges. Overlap the hems and make the opening in the same way as the opening on the Duvet cover with flange, steps 2–5.

2 Stitch a mitred border around the front panel, see Single mitred border, page 22. With right sides facing, stitch the duvet front to the back around the outer edges. Trim the seam allowances to 1 cm ($^3/_8$ in) and zigzag stitch the raw edges together.

Buttoned duvet cover

The smart buttoned duvet cover has a wide contrast band across its top edge which buttons onto the main front panel to form the opening. The cover is designed to co-ordinate with the buttoned pillowcase on page 76.

MATERIALS
Cotton or polycotton sheeting
Sewing thread
Buttons, 2 cm (³/₄ in) in diameter

CUTTING OUT

1.5 cm (⁵/₈ in) seam allowances are included unless instructions state otherwise.

For the back of the duvet cover, measure the length and width of the duvet and add on 3 cm (1¹/₄ in) to each measurement. Cut out a piece of fabric to this size. Cut the top front panel to the same width by 46 cm (18 in) deep. Cut the lower front panel the same width by the length of the back minus 8.5 cm (3³/₈ in).

1 Press and stitch a double 7.5 cm (3 in) hem to the wrong side across the lower edge of the top front panel. Repeat across the top edge of the lower front panel.

2 Stitch a row of 2.5 cm (1 in) long vertical buttonholes centrally along the top panel hem, spacing them about 30 cm (12 in) apart.

3 Place the top panel to the top edge of the back piece with right sides facing and raw edges level. Place the lower front panel to the lower edge of the back in the same way, so that its hem overlaps the hem on the top panel.

4 Stitch together around all four edges, 1.5 cm (⁵/₈ in) in from the raw edges. Trim the seam to 1 cm (³/₈ in) and zigzag stitch the raw edges together to prevent fraying.

5 Turn the cover right side out and press the seam at the edge. Stitch the buttons onto the hem of the lower front panel to match the buttonhole positions, placing the buttons to sit at the lower edge of the buttonholes.

Throwover bedcover

This, the simplest of all bedcovers, is just a rectangle of fabric hemmed around the edges. When measuring up, remember to make an allowance for the cover to fit up and over the pillows.

MATERIALS
Heavyweight furnishing fabric, such as cotton matelassé
Sewing thread

CUTTING OUT

Measure the width of the bed and add on two drops to the floor plus 8 cm (3¼ in) for the hem. Measure the length of the bed and add on one drop to the floor plus 8 cm (3¼ in) for hems, remembering to add an allowance to fit over the pillows. If the fabric needs to be joined, add on 4 cm (1½ in) for each seam. Cut out the fabric to these measurements (diagram 1).

DIAGRAM 1

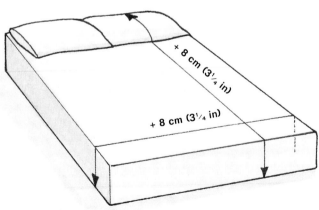

1 If the fabric is not wide enough to cut the whole required width of the bedcover as one piece, use the full width of the fabric to make a central panel and add the extra fabric required to either side. Stitch the panels together with 2 cm (¾ in) seams, neaten the raw edges together and press the seams away from the central panel (diagram 2).

DIAGRAM 2

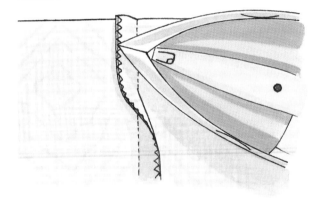

2 Press 1 cm (⅜ in), then 3 cm (1¼ in) hems to the wrong side along the side edges. Stitch the hems in place. Then press and stitch double hems along the top and bottom edges in the same way (diagram 3).

DIAGRAM 3

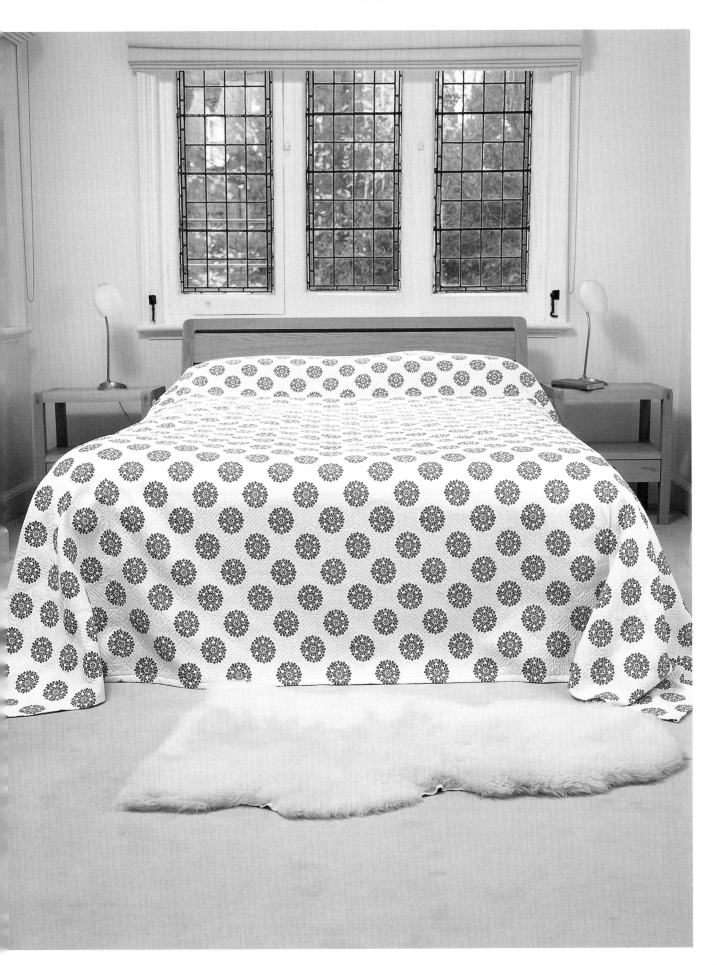

Throwover bedcover with curved corners

This is almost identical to the throwover bedcover on page 86, except that the corners are curved for a slightly more finished look.

MATERIALS
Heavyweight furnishing fabric, such as cotton matelassé
Sewing thread
Marker pen and string
Cotton fabric for binding

CUTTING OUT
Measure and cut out the fabric as for the Throwover bedcover, page 86, omitting the 8 cm (3¼ in) allowed for hems. If required, join fabric pieces as for the Throwover bedcover, step 1.

1 Mark the curved corners as follows. Measure along the fabric edges 30 cm (12 in) from either side of the first base corner and mark with pins. Place another pin equidistant from these two pins, so that the three pins and the base corner form a square. Tie the marker pen onto the string and mark the string 30 cm (12 in) away from the pen. Position the marked end of the string on the inner corner of the square. Holding the string taut, draw a curved line between the two outer pins with the pen. Trim the base corner along the curved line (diagram 1). Repeat for the second base corner.

DIAGRAM 1

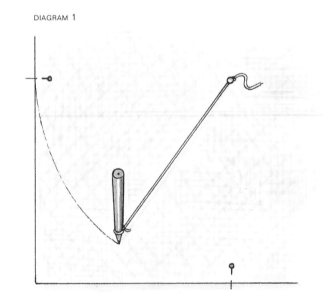

2 Cut and join bias strips to fit around the two sides, curved corners and lower edge, see Bias binding, page 16. Cut and join another strip to fit across the top edge plus 2 cm ($^3/_4$ in). Make into binding and bind the side and lower edges, see Binding an edge, page 16, easing the binding to fit around the curves (diagram 2).

3 With right sides facing, stitch the binding to the top edge, allowing 1 cm ($^3/_8$ in) to project at each end. Fold the projecting ends onto the wrong side of the binding. Turn the binding over to the wrong side and handstitch the second edge in place.

DIAGRAM 2

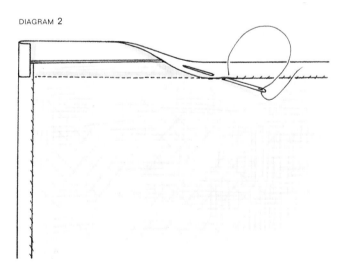

Fitted bedcover

This smart fitted cover has a straight skirt with inverted pleats. Neat piping
inserted in the seam gives the edge of the main panel a crisp outline.

MATERIALS
Medium-weight furnishing fabric
Sewing thread
Piping cord

CUTTING OUT

1.5 cm ($^5/_8$ in) seam allowances are included unless instructions state otherwise.

Cut out the main panel to the required finished width plus 3 cm (1$^1/_4$ in) by the required finished length, remembering to add an allowance to fit over the pillows, plus 5.5 cm (2$^1/_8$ in). Allow extra for any joins. Cut the skirt to the required finished depth plus 5.5 cm (2$^1/_8$ in). For the skirt length, double the required finished length of the main panel, plus its width, plus 20 cm (8 in) for each pleat and 8 cm (3$^1/_4$ in) for hems. Plan the pleats so one is positioned at each corner. Allow extra for joins.

1 If required, join the fabric to make up the width of the main panel, using the full width of fabric for a central panel and adding narrower widths at either side. Drawing around a saucer, mark curves at the two lower corners to match the mattress shape and trim the fabric.

2 On the skirt allow 4 cm (1$^1/_2$ in) for the side hem, then measure the distance to the first pleat, i.e. 30 cm (12 in) for the bedcover shown here, and mark with a pin. Measure along another 10 cm (4 in) and mark with a pin, then a further 10 cm (4 in) and mark with a pin. Bring the two outer pins over to meet at the central pin to form an inverted pleat, see Inverted

pleats, page 26. Pin and tack the pleat in place across the top edge. Measure the required distance to the next pleat, i.e. 25 cm (10 in), then mark and form the pleat in the same way.

3 Continue joining fabric where required at the back fold of the pleats until all pleats are tacked. The distance, including hem allowance, between the last pleat and the edge of the skirt should be the same as at the beginning (34 cm/13$^1/_2$ in). Stitch around the top edge to hold the pleats in place (diagram 1).

DIAGRAM 1

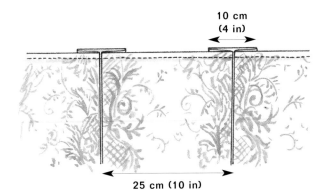

4 Cover the piping cord, see Piping, page 18. Beginning and finishing 4 cm (1$^1/_2$ in) in from the top edge, stitch the piping around the sides and lower edge of the main panel, snipping into the edge of the piping to fit around the curved corners.

5 Place the top edge of the skirt onto the piped edge of the main panel with right sides facing and raw edges level. Match and pin the ends of the skirt to the top corners of the panel and the corner pleats to the centre of the curved corners. Then pin the edges together between these points and tack (diagram 2). Stitch in place with the main panel uppermost.

DIAGRAM 2

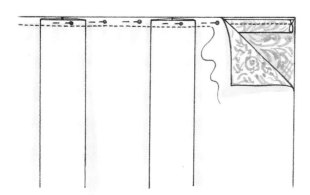

6 Press 1cm (³⁄₈ in), then 3 cm (1¼ in) to the wrong side to form a hem around the lower edge of the skirt and stitch in place. Press and stitch a hem across the ends of the skirt and top of the main panel in the same way. Form the pleats along the length of the skirt and press in place.

Patchwork quilt

A patchwork quilt is an eye-catching feature in a bedroom and this version, with its big, bold squares, does not take long to make. Three squares across by five down make a quilt with a finished size of 100 x 150 cm (39 x 59 in). Each square has a finished size of 25 cm (10 in) and the border is 12.5 cm (5 in) wide.

MATERIALS
Selection of cotton fabrics for patchwork
Sewing thread
110 g (4 oz) wadding
Cotton backing fabric

CUTTING OUT

1.5 cm ($^5/_8$ in) seam allowances have been included unless instructions state otherwise.

Cut out as many 28 cm (11 in) patchwork squares as required. Cut the strips for the mitred border 15.5 cm (6 in) wide by the length and width of the finished patchwork plus 25 cm (10 in). Cut the wadding and backing fabric to the size of the finished patchwork with mitred border attached.

1 Arrange the patchwork pieces as required. With right sides facing and raw edges level, pin and stitch a horizontal row of squares together along their side edges. Stitch the remaining squares into horizontal rows in the same way and press the seams open (diagram 1).

DIAGRAM 1

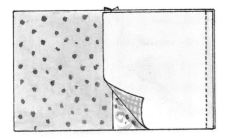

2 With right sides facing, place the top of one row to the base of the row above it, pinning the seams together before stitching so that they match exactly. Stitch all the rows together in this way and press the seams open (diagram 2).

DIAGRAM 2

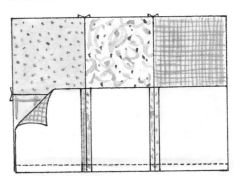

3 Pin on the borders, matching the centre of the border to the centre of the patchwork edge and working outwards towards the corners. Stitch the borders in place and mitre the corners, see Single mitred border, page 22. Press the border seams open (diagram 3).

DIAGRAM 3

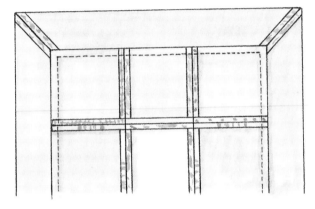

4 Place the wadding to the wrong side of the quilt and trim to fit. If the wadding needs to be joined, butt the edges together and stitch with large, loose herringbone stitch, see Herringbone stitch, page 13. Pin and tack around the edge. With right sides facing, pin and tack the backing fabric to the right side of the quilt. Stitch together around the outer edges (diagram 4), leaving a 20 cm (8 in) gap to turn through. Trim the excess wadding from the seam allowance. Trim the corners, turn the quilt right side out and arrange the seam neatly at the edge. Tuck in the seam allowances along the opening and stitch it closed by hand.

DIAGRAM 4

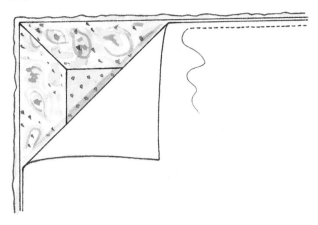

5 Arrange the three layers of the patchwork quilt evenly, smoothing the fabric flat on both sides. Pin through the layers along the outer patchwork seam, then along the lines of the patchwork squares. Tack, then machine stitch along the horizontal and vertical seams (diagram 5).

DIAGRAM 5

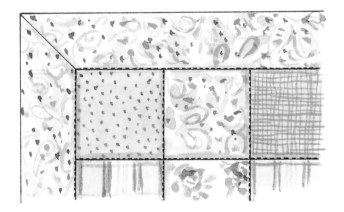

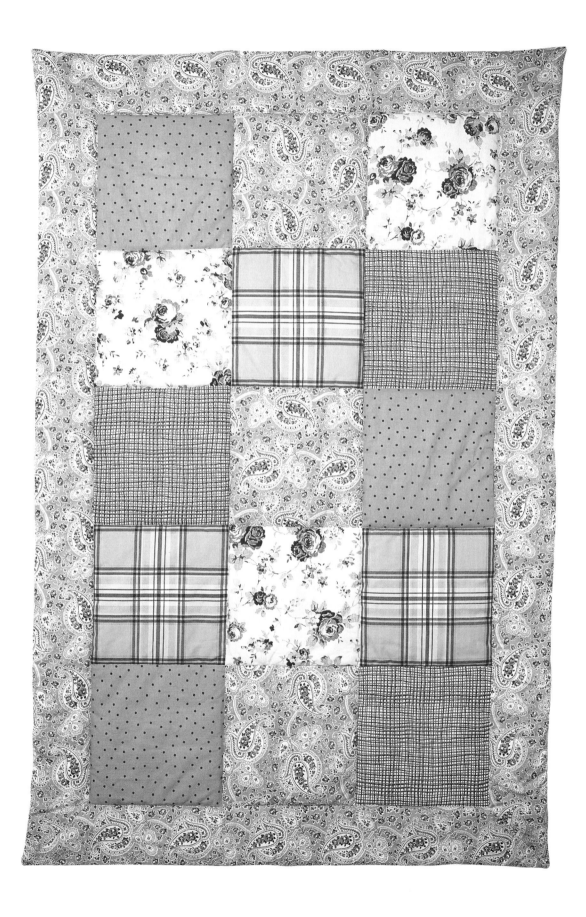

Gathered valance

A valance fits over the base of the bed underneath the mattress with a skirt that hangs to the floor to hide the bed base. Fabric with a ready-made scalloped edge gives a pretty finish to the lower edge. If you use a plain fabric for the skirt, finish the edge with a hem.

MATERIALS
**Cotton or polycotton sheeting fabric
Inexpensive fabric or old sheet (optional)
Sewing thread**

CUTTING OUT

1.5 cm ($^5/_8$ in) seam allowances are included unless instructions state otherwise.

For the bed panel, measure the length of the mattress and add on 3.5 cm ($1^3/_8$ in), then measure the width and add on 3 cm ($1^1/_4$ in). For a bed panel with a border, see Note below, cut out the central section from inexpensive fabric and cut 10 cm (4 in) wide borders from the skirt fabric to fit around its side and base edges to make up the required size. For the skirt depth, measure from the top of the bed base to the floor and add on 6.5 cm ($2^1/_4$ in) for a hemmed lower edge, or 1.5 cm ($^5/_8$ in) if using fabric with a ready-made scalloped edge. For the skirt length, add the bed width to twice its length and double that measurement.

NOTE

For economy, you can cut the central area of the bed panel, which will not be seen, from an old sheet or inexpensive fabric, adding a narrow border of the skirt fabric around the edge where it might show. If you prefer to use sheeting, you can cut the whole bed panel as one piece.

1 If required, make up the size of the bed panel by joining the borders to the edges of the central section with narrow seams, see Seams and hems, page 14. Drawing around a saucer, mark curves at the two lower corners of the bed panel and trim to shape (diagram 1).

DIAGRAM 1

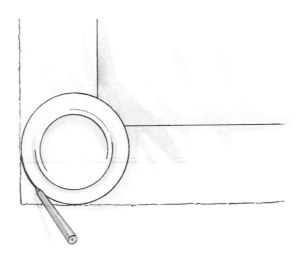

2 Cut as many fabric widths as required to make up the skirt length. Join the skirt pieces with narrow seams. If required, press a double 2.5 cm (1 in) hem to the wrong side around the lower edge of the skirt and stitch in place.

3 Measure the side and base edges of the bed panel and divide into six equal lengths. Mark with pins. Divide the top edge of the skirt into six equal lengths and mark with pins in the same way. Gather the top edge of the skirt, stopping and restarting at the pins (diagram 2). Stitch the skirt to the bed panel, matching the marked points, see Frills, page 21.

DIAGRAM 2

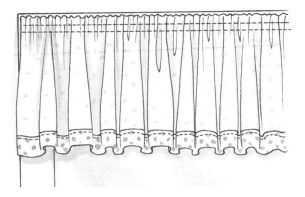

4 Press a double 1 cm (³⁄₈ in) hem to the wrong side along the side edges of the skirt and across the top edge of the bed panel (diagram 3).

DIAGRAM 3

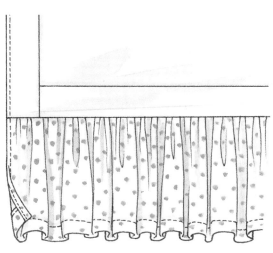

Fitted valance

The fitted valance is plain along the side and base edges with inverted pleats at the corners for a smart tailored look. This valance is made with square corners to emphasise the sharp lines.

MATERIALS
Cotton or polycotton sheeting
Sewing thread

CUTTING OUT

1.5 cm (⁵⁄₈ in) seam allowances are included unless instructions state otherwise.

For the bed panel, measure the length of the mattress and add on 3.5 cm (1³⁄₈ in), then measure the width and add on 3 cm (1¹⁄₄ in). For the skirt depth, measure from the top of the bed base to the floor and add on 6.5 cm (2¹⁄₂ in). For the skirt length, add the bed width to twice its length and add on 84 cm (33 in).

If you wish to make the central section of the bed panel from inexpensive fabric, cut out the fabric and add borders as for the Gathered valance, page 96.

1 If required, make up the size of the bed panel by joining the borders to the edges of the central section with narrow seams, see Seams and hems, page 14.

2 Cut as many fabric widths as required to make up the skirt length. Join the skirt pieces with narrow seams. Press a double 2.5 cm (1 in) hem to the wrong side around the lower edge of the skirt and stitch in place.

3 Measure the length of the side edge of the bed panel minus 1.5 cm (⁵⁄₈ in) along the top edge of the skirt. Mark with a pin. Measure along a further 20 cm (8 in) and then another 20 cm (8 in) and mark with pins. Bring the outer pins over to meet at the central pin to form an inverted pleat. Tack the pleat in place along the top edge (diagram 1). Measuring from the other end of the skirt, make another pleat in the same way, see Pleats, page 26.

4 With right sides facing and raw edges level, pin the skirt around the side and base edges of the bed panel, checking that the pleats align with the lower corners. Snip the fabric at the centre of the pleats so that it fits around the corners. Tack and stitch in place.

5 Press a double 1 cm (³⁄₈ in) hem to the wrong side along the side edges of the skirt and across the top edge of the bed panel. Stitch in place.

DIAGRAM 1

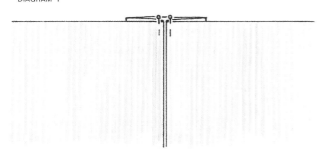

Bedhead

The pretty padded cover simply folds over the bedhead and ties at the sides. The narrow stripes have a clean country look and add charm and co-ordination to a fresh colour scheme. By replacing the lining with a contrasting fabric, you can make the bedhead reversible too.

MATERIALS
Cotton furnishing fabric
Sewing thread
100 g (4 oz) wadding
Lining fabric

CUTTING OUT

1.5 cm ($^5/_8$ in) seam allowances are included unless instructions state otherwise.

Measure the width of the bedhead and add 7 cm ($2^3/_4$ in) Measure the required depth, double this and add on the thickness of the bedhead plus 3 cm ($1^1/_4$ in). Cut out the main fabric, wadding and lining fabric to the established measurements. Cut out four ties 43 x 4 cm (17 x $1^1/_2$ in).

1 Make the ties, see Ties, page 25. Fold the main fabric in half with right sides outside. Mark the positions for the ties at the side edges of both fabric layers, placing the top pair 15 cm (6 in) down from the fold and the lower pair 17 cm ($6^3/_4$ in) up from the lower edge. Adjust the position for the ties if desired. Unfold the fabric and tack the ties to the marked positions on the right side of the fabric with their raw ends level with the raw edges of the fabric (diagram 1).

DIAGRAM 1

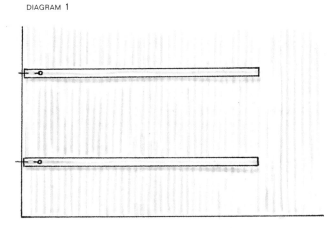

2 Place the wadding to the wrong side of the fabric and tack around the edge. With right sides facing, pin and stitch the lining to the fabric around all edges, leaving a 30 cm (12 in) opening at the centre of the back lower edge (diagram 2).

DIAGRAM 2

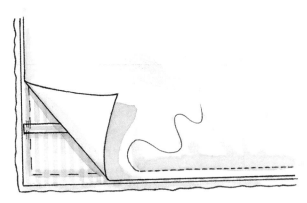

3 Trim the wadding from the seam allowances. Turn the bedhead right side out through the opening. Lightly press the seam at the edge. Press in the raw edges along the opening and slipstitch the opening closed.

Canopy

A pretty draped canopy will add bags of style to a simple day bed. The fabric is held in place by means of stitched-on casings that are slipped over wooden rods attached to the wall with brackets.

MATERIALS
Lightweight furnishing fabric
Sewing thread
3 wooden rods
3 brackets

NOTE
Choose a fairly lightweight fabric that drapes well and allow plenty of fullness. The width of the lightweight linen illustrated is about $2\frac{1}{2}$ times the length of the rods; if you use a thicker fabric, you could reduce the fullness. Using the full width of fabric avoids the need for hems at the front and back edges.

1 Cut the wooden rods to the required length; the rods illustrated are 54 cm ($21\frac{1}{4}$ in) long for 140 cm (55 in) wide fabric. Paint the rods white if you wish. Fix the rods to the top of the brackets and fix the brackets to the wall at the required positions. The centre rod shown here is 2 m (78 in) up from the floor and the side rods are 30 cm (12 in) lower.

2 Drape the fabric over the rods to establish the required length and mark the positions for the casings on the fabric at each rod. Cut the fabric to the required length and stitch a close zigzag stitch across each end to neaten.

3 Cut three casing strips wide enough to accommodate the rod and bracket plus 2 cm ($\frac{3}{4}$ in). Press 1 cm ($\frac{3}{8}$ in) to the wrong side along the long edges of each casing. Place the casings to the wrong side of the fabric across its width at the positions marked for the rods. Stitch in place along both long edges and the front edge.

4 Press the canopy, then, starting at the back edge, thread each casing onto its appropriate rod and bracket. Arrange the fullness evenly.

Windows

Unlined tab top curtains

The top edge of these simple unlined curtains is finished with fabric tabs so that you can hang them from a curtain pole.

MATERIALS
Lightweight curtain fabric
Sewing thread

CUTTING OUT

1.5 cm ($^5/_8$ in) seam allowances are included unless the instructions state otherwise.

Decide how full you want the curtains to be. Unless a window is extremely narrow, you will need to join widths of fabric to get the required curtain width. Work out the required curtain width and add on 10 cm (4 in). Measure the required length and add on 17.5 cm (7 in). Cut the tabs twice the required width plus 3 cm (1$^1/_4$ in) by 22 cm (8$^3/_4$ in) long. Cut an 8 cm (3$^1/_4$ in) deep facing to the required curtain width plus 3 cm (1$^1/_4$ in).

NOTE

The width and length of the tabs can be adjusted to suit the fabric and the size of the pole. A heavy fabric hung from a thick pole will require larger tabs than a fine fabric hung from a thin pole. Tabs that are cut 10 cm (4 in) wide will have a finished width of 3.5 cm (1$^3/_8$ in) and are suitable for lightweight or medium-weight fabrics.

1 Join any fabric widths if required with plain seams pressed open. Press 2.5 cm (1 in) double hems to the wrong side along the side edges of the curtain and stitch in place.

2 Fold the tabs in half lengthways with right sides facing and stitch the two raw edges together. Trim the seam and press it open. Turn the tabs right side out and press the seam to one edge (diagram 1).

DIAGRAM 1

3 Fold each tab in half widthways and pin it, pointing downwards, to the right side of the curtain with its raw edges level with the top edge of the curtain. Place a tab at each side edge and arrange the others evenly in between, about 12–15 cm (4³⁄₄–6 in) apart. Pin and tack the tabs in place (diagram 2).

DIAGRAM 2

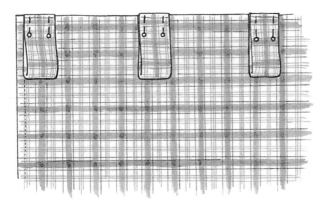

4 With right sides facing and top raw edges level, place the facing across the curtain on top of the tabs, allowing it to project for 1.5 cm (⁵⁄₈ in) at each end. Stitch in place across the top edge (diagram 3).

DIAGRAM 3

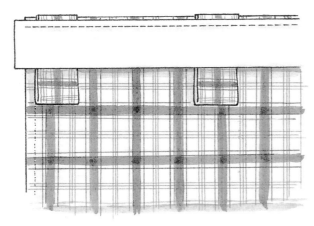

5 Press the facing over to the wrong side. If your chosen fabric is translucent, trim the fabric seam allowances to 1 cm (³⁄₈ in). Press the seam allowances to the wrong side of the fabric along both sides and across the lower edge of the facing. Stitch the facing to the curtain along the pressed edges. Topstitch across the top edge of the facing (diagram 4).

DIAGRAM 4

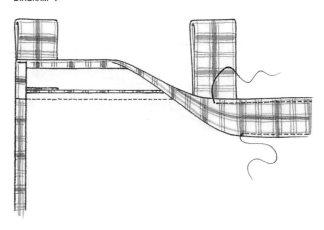

6 Press an 8 cm (3¹⁄₄ in) deep double hem to the wrong side across the lower edge of the curtain and stitch in place.

Variation

This curtain, using very sheer, embroidered fabric, is particularly effective and looks lovely when the light shines through the fabric.

Unlined curtain with fold-over top

On this pretty curtain, a section of the fabric at the top is simply folded over and attached to clip-on hooks to hang from curtain rings. Stitched tucks, which show up well against the light, are worked across the curtain on the fold-over section and above the base hem. Choose a reversible fabric, as the back of the fabric forms the front of the fold-over.

MATERIALS
Reversible sheer curtain fabric
Sewing thread
Curtain clips

1 If side hems are required, press 1 cm ($^3/_8$ in) double hems to the wrong side along the two side edges of the curtain and stitch in place.

2 At the top edge, press the depth of the fold-over section plus 14 cm ($5^1/_2$ in) for the tucks and hem over onto the right side. At the lower edge of the fold-over, press a double 4 cm ($1^1/_2$ in) hem to the wrong side and stitch in place. On the right side of the fold-over, fold and press a crease 4.5 cm ($1^3/_4$ in) up from the top of the hem. Stitch 1.5 cm ($^5/_8$ in) in from the crease to form a tuck, see Tucks, page 27 (diagram 1).

CUTTING OUT
1.5 cm ($^5/_8$ in) seam allowances are included unless instructions state otherwise.

Decide how full you want the curtain to be and measure the required width. Add on 4 cm ($1^1/_2$ in) if side hems are required; alternatively, use the fabric selvedges as the side edges. Measure the required length and add on the depth of the fold-over plus 20 cm (8 in) for hems and 15 cm (6 in) for tucks.

3 Press the tuck downwards. Press a second crease 4.5 cm ($1^3/_4$ in) above the previous tuck stitching and stitch a second tuck 1.5 cm ($^5/_8$ in) in from the crease.

4 On the main part of the curtain, fold a double 6 cm ($2^1/_4$ in) hem to the wrong side across the lower edge and stitch. Make three tucks above the hem in the same way as the previous tucks (diagram 2). Clip on curtain clips at regular intervals along the top of the curtain.

DIAGRAM 1

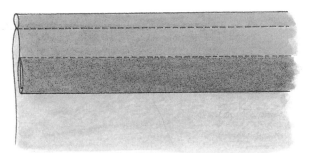

DIAGRAM 2

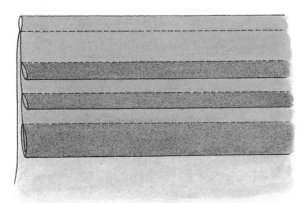

Unlined curtain panel

A patchwork of fine lawn panels creates a vibrant mosaic effect on this translucent curtain. It has a simple fold-over casing at the top, so that it can be threaded onto a tension rod or wooden dowelling. A separate casing at the lower edge holds a length of dowelling to add weight to the curtain.

MATERIALS
Lawn fabrics
Sewing thread
Ribbons for trimming
Wooden dowelling

CUTTING OUT

Cut out as many fabric panels of varying sizes as required, allowing 1 cm ($\frac{3}{8}$ in) for seams for joining the pieces, 2 cm ($\frac{3}{4}$ in) for the side hems, and 3.5 cm ($1\frac{3}{8}$ in) for the top casing. For the lower casing, cut a strip 12 cm ($4\frac{3}{4}$ in) deep by the required width of the curtain panel.

1 Lay out the lawn panels in vertical rows – each panel within a row should have the same width. Join the lawn panels widthways with 1 cm ($\frac{3}{8}$ in) seams to make vertical panels. If you wish, stitch ribbon trims along selected seams. Then join the panels lengthways with 1 cm ($\frac{3}{8}$ in) seams to make the whole curtain panel, adding ribbon trims if required.

DIAGRAM 1

2 To make a window patch, take a smaller rectangle of lawn, press the raw edges under and stitch the piece onto a lawn panel. Trim away the fabric behind the patch. Neaten the raw edges at the back with machine zigzag stitch (diagram 1).

3 Stitch double 1 cm ($\frac{3}{8}$ in) hems to the wrong side along the side edges of the curtain and lower casing. Press 1 cm ($\frac{3}{8}$ in), then 2.5 cm (1 in) to the wrong side across the top edge and stitch to make a casing. Fold the lower casing in half with the right sides outside. Stitch the casing to the lower edge with right sides facing and raw edges level, then press the casing downwards (diagram 2).

DIAGRAM 2

Tube-lined curtains

Tube-lined curtains are the easiest type of lined curtain to make. The lining is cut narrower than the fabric and the side edges of the lining and curtain are simply seamed together. The narrower lining pulls the fabric over to the wrong side to give the effect of a hem. However, these hems will have to be realigned and re-pressed each time the curtain is laundered.

CALCULATING FABRIC AMOUNTS FOR CURTAINS

For the curtain width, multiply the width of the curtain track or pole by the amount of fullness required by the heading tape – this is usually 2–2$\frac{1}{2}$ times the track or pole length. Add on allowances for side hems and joins as given for each project. Then, if necessary, round up the amount to the next full width or half width. For the length, add on allowances for the top hem and lower hem as given for each project. Multiply the length required by the number of widths to give the fabric amount. If the fabric has a pattern that needs to be matched, you will need to allow for it on each fabric width or half width.

MATERIALS
Curtain fabric
Sewing thread
Lining fabric
Heading tape

CUTTING OUT

1.5 cm ($\frac{5}{8}$ in) seam allowances are included unless instructions state otherwise.

Calculate the fabric amounts (see left). For the width, allow 4 cm (1$\frac{1}{2}$ in) for each side hem and 3 cm (1$\frac{1}{4}$ in) for each join. For the length, add on 4 cm (1$\frac{1}{2}$ in) for the top hem and 15 cm (6 in) for the lower hem. If the curtains are long, you may wish to make a deeper hem.

Cut the lining 4 cm (1$\frac{1}{2}$ in) shorter than the curtain fabric at the top edge and 10 cm (4 in) narrower than the width.

1 Join any fabric and lining widths if required with plain seams pressed open. Place the lining to the fabric with right sides facing and the top of the lining 4 cm (1$\frac{1}{2}$ in) below the top of the curtain fabric. Arrange the side edges level and stitch the lining to the fabric 1.5 cm ($\frac{5}{8}$ in) in from the raw edges, finishing the stitching above the hem level (diagram 1).

DIAGRAM 1

2 Turn the curtain right side out. The narrower lining will pull the side edges of the curtain over to the wrong side for 2.5 cm (1 in). Arrange the hems evenly on both side edges and press in place (diagram 2).

DIAGRAM **2**

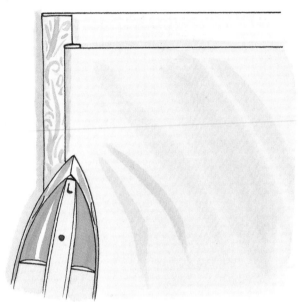

3 Press 4 cm (1 ½ in) over to the wrong side at the top edge of the curtain. Cut a length of heading tape 5 cm (2 in) longer than the curtain width and, with wrong sides facing, place it 3 mm (⅛ in) below the top edge of the curtain. Turn under the ends of the heading tape for 2.5 cm (1 in) at each side edge, level with the edge of the curtain (diagram 3).

DIAGRAM **3**

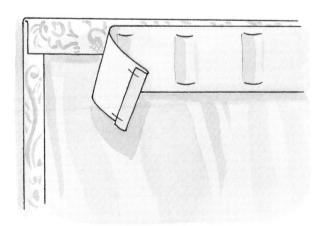

4 Stitch the heading tape in place up the side edge, across one long edge of the tape and down the opposite side edge. Stitch the other edge of the tape in the same way, so that the ends are stitched twice to ensure the cords are caught firmly in the stitching (diagram 4).

DIAGRAM **4**

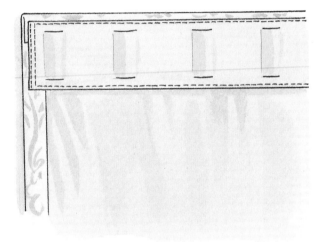

5 Trim the lower edge of the lining 2 cm (¾ in) shorter than the lower edge of the curtains. Press a 7.5 cm (3 in) double hem to the wrong side on the curtain and stitch in place (diagram 5).

DIAGRAM **5**

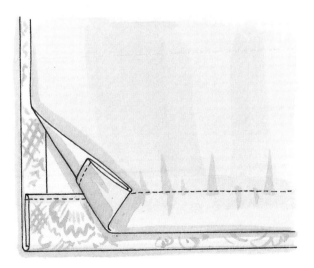

6 Make the lining hem in the same way so that it faces
   the curtain hem. Finish stitching the lining to the side
   hems by hand (diagram 6). Gather the curtains along
   the top edge, see Cord tidies and curtain weights,
   page 120.

DIAGRAM 6

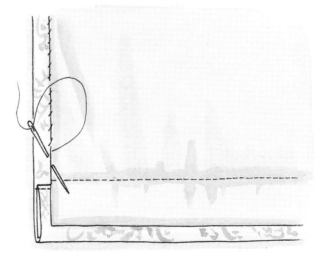

Loose-lined curtains

Loose-lined curtains are hemmed along the side edges of the fabric before the lining is attached. The lining is then stitched to the hems by hand, but left loose across the width of the curtain. You can stitch the hems at the sides and across the lower edge of the curtain by hand or machine. Stitching by hand gives a finer finish, whereas machine stitching is quicker and more durable. For large curtains, it is well worthwhile mastering the machined blind hemstitch, see page 15.

MATERIALS
Curtain fabric
Sewing thread
Lining fabric
Heading tape

CUTTING OUT

1.5 cm ($^5/_8$ in) seam allowances are included unless instructions state otherwise.

Calculate the fabric amount as for the Tube-lined curtains, page 114. For the width, allow 6 cm ($2^1/_4$ in) for each side hem and 3 cm ($1^1/_4$ in) for each join. For the length, add on 4 cm ($1^1/_2$ in) for the top hem and 15–40 cm (6–16 in) for the lower hem. Cut the lining 4 cm ($1^1/_2$ in) shorter than the curtain fabric at the top edge and 12 cm ($4^3/_4$ in) narrower than the width.

1 Join fabric and lining widths if required with plain seams pressed open. Press a 3 cm ($1^1/_4$ in) wide double hem to the wrong side along the side edges of the curtain. Stitch in place by hand or machine.

2 Press 2 cm ($^3/_4$ in) to the wrong side along the side edges of the lining. Place the lining to the wrong side of the curtains so that the lining edges overlap the side hems by 1 cm ($^3/_8$ in) and the top of the lining is 4 cm ($1^1/_2$ in) down from the top of the curtain.

3 Handstitch the lining to the side hems, finishing the stitching above the top of the lower hem. Trim the lining 3 cm ($1^1/_4$ in) shorter than the fabric at the lower edge (diagram 1).

DIAGRAM 1

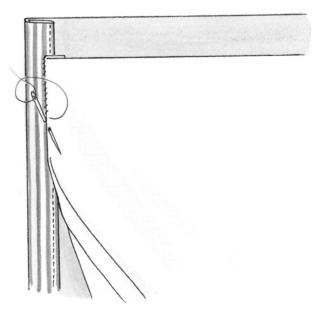

4 Press 4 cm (1½ in) to the wrong side across the top edge and stitch on the heading tape in the same way as for the Tube-lined curtains, steps 3 and 4, page 116.

5 Press a double hem of the required depth to the wrong side. Unfold the hem and the unstitched part of the side hem. At one side edge, press the corner in at an angle on a line that begins at the side edge on the top fold and intersects the inner edge of the side hem at the lower fold (diagram 2).

DIAGRAM 2

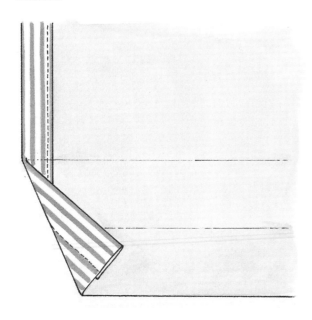

6 Refold the hem so that it forms a neat mitre at the corner. Mitre the other corner in the same way. Handstitch the mitres in place and stitch the hem in place by hand or machine (diagram 3).

DIAGRAM 3

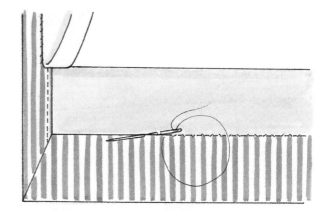

CORD TIDIES AND CURTAIN WEIGHTS

To gather curtains, pull all cords simultaneously at the centre of the heading tape and gradually push the gathers or pleats away to each side. Once the curtain is fully gathered or pleated, the cords can be wrapped neatly around a cord tidy.

Curtain weights add weight to the hems of large curtains to improve their hang. They come in two forms: round coin-like weights and long string-like weights. The coins are retained in small fabric pouches, which are stitched inside the hem at each corner and at the base of any joins. The string-like weights sit in the base of the hem and are attached with light stitching at the corners and joins.

7 Make a double hem on the lining the same depth as the one on the curtain and machine stitch it in place. Finish stitching the side edges of the lining to the curtain side hems by hand (diagram 4). Gather the curtains along the top edge, see below.

DIAGRAM **4**

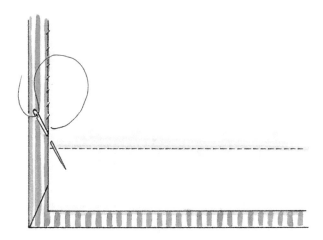

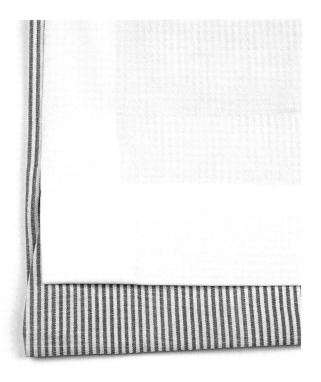

Interlined curtain

Interlining is a layer of specially made soft fabric that is sandwiched between the curtain fabric and the lining. It adds weight to lightweight fabric and gives a sumptuous finish to the curtains. Interlined curtains also help reduce draughts and keep out the cold.

MATERIALS
Curtain fabric
Sewing thread
Interlining
Lining fabric
Heading tape

CUTTING OUT

1.5 cm ($^5/_8$ in) seam allowances are included unless instructions state otherwise.

Calculate the fabric amount as for the Tube-lined curtains, page 114. For the width, allow 6 cm (2$^1/_2$ in) for each side hem and 3 cm (1$^1/_4$ in) for each join. For the length, add on 4 cm (1$^1/_2$ in) for the top hem and 12 cm (4$^3/_4$ in) for the lower hem. Cut the lining fabric and interlining to the same size.

NOTE

The interlining is held in place against the curtain fabric with lines of lockstitch, see page 13, worked from the top to the base of the curtain. Curtains made from one fabric width should be lockstitched a third of the width in from each side. Wider curtains, made from more than one fabric width, should be lockstitched at each seam and twice between each seam, as well as between the outer seams and the side edges of the curtain. A thick interlining may need to be trimmed along the fold of the lower hem to reduce bulk.

1 Join fabric and lining widths if required with plain seams pressed open. If required, join interlining widths by butting the edges together and stitching across the join with herringbone stitch, see page 13.

2 Place the curtain fabric right side down on a worktop and smooth it out flat. Place the interlining on top with edges and seams lined up.

3 Fold back the interlining to the furthest seam or position of lockstitch line. Lockstitch the interlining to the fabric from 5 cm (2 in) below the top edge to the lower edge, picking up just a thread of curtain fabric so that the stitching does not show. Space the stitches wide apart and do not pull them tight (diagram 1).

DIAGRAM **1**

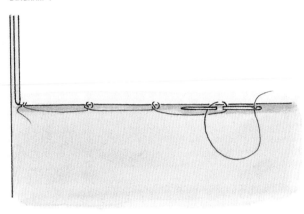

4 When the first line of lockstitch is complete, smooth the interlining back across the fabric to the position for the next lockstitch line and lockstitch in the same way. Repeat until all lines of lockstitch are complete.

5 Fold both interlining and fabric together over to the wrong side for 6 cm (2$\frac{1}{2}$ in) along both side edges. At the lower edge, fold a 12 cm (4$\frac{3}{4}$ in) hem to the wrong side. Mark the inner edge of each hem at the corner where they intersect (diagram 2).

DIAGRAM **2**

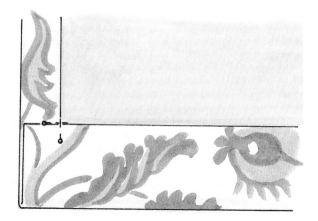

6 Open out the hems and refold the corner diagonally to the wrong side between the marked points. If you are using heavy interlining, trim it along the pressed line (diagram 3).

DIAGRAM **3**

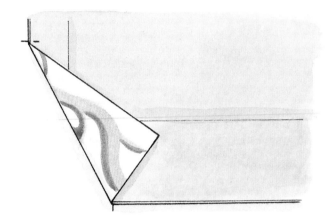

7 Refold the hems to form a mitred corner. Stitch along the side edges with long stitch, see page 13, spacing the stitches about 4 cm (1$\frac{1}{2}$ in) apart and taking the stitches through both layers of interlining but not the main fabric.

8 Slipstitch the edges of the corner mitres together. Stitch the lower hem with 2 cm ($\frac{3}{4}$ in) long herringbone stitches (diagram 4).

DIAGRAM **4**

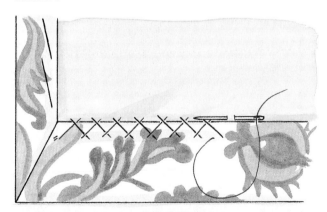

9 Place the lining centrally on top of the interlining with raw edges matching along the top edge. Lockstitch it in place in the same way as the interlining, finishing the stitching above the hem and 5 cm (2 in) down from the top edge. Trim the side edges of the lining level with the edges of the curtain. Tuck under the raw edges along the sides of the lining so that 3 cm (1 1/4 in) of curtain side hem shows. Pin and slip hem the lining in place along the side edges to just above the lower hem, see page 12.

DIAGRAM 5

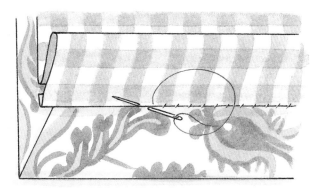

10 Trim the lining to 6 cm (2 1/2 in) longer than the curtain. Press 1.5 cm (5/8 in) to the wrong side along the lower edge of the lining. Pin in place so the raw edge of the lining is level with the raw edge of the hem and slip hem the lining to the hem along the pressed edge (diagram 5).

DIAGRAM 6

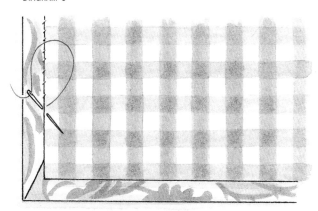

11 Allow the excess lining to fall downwards, forming a pleat. Finish stitching the lining to the side hems down to the bottom of the lining (diagram 6).

12 At the top edge of the curtain, fold back the lining and trim the interlining 4 cm (1 1/2 in) below the top edge (diagram 7). Fold both the lining and fabric over to the wrong side for 4 cm (1 1/2 in) along the top edge. Stitch on the heading tape in the same way as for the Tube-lined curtains, steps 3 and 4, page 116. Gather the curtains along the top edge, see Cord tidies and curtain weights, page 120.

DIAGRAM 7

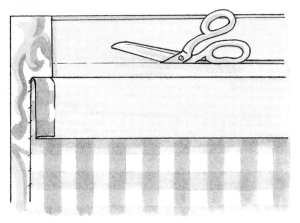

Shaped tieback

This formal style of tieback has an elegant curved shape and is made by covering stiff interfacing, pelmet interfacing or buckram with fabric that matches or contrasts with the curtain. The tiebacks can be left untrimmed or finished with cord or piping around the outer edge. They are fixed to a hook on the wall by two small rings.

TIEBACKS

First work out the required length and width of the curved tieback – the pattern illustrated is for a tieback about 28 cm (11 in) long and 12 cm (5 in) wide at the fold. Draw the pattern for half the shape of the tieback on a large piece of folded paper. Cut out the shape through both layers of paper, then open out the pattern to its full length. Try the pattern on the curtain to check the length and fit, and adjust the size and smoothness of the curve as required.

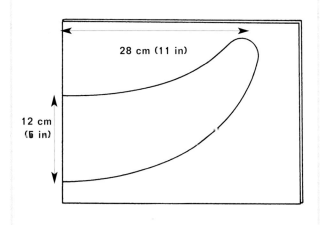

28 cm (11 in)

12 cm
(5 in)

CUTTING OUT

1.5 cm (⅝ in) seam allowances are included unless instructions state otherwise.

Cut out the front fabric 1.5 cm (⅝ in) larger than the pattern all round. Cut out the lining fabric and interlining 6 mm (¼ in) larger than the pattern all round. Cut the heavyweight iron-on interfacing or buckram to the pattern size.

MATERIALS
Curtain fabric
Sewing thread
Heavyweight iron-on interfacing or buckram
Interlining
Lining fabric
Cord (optional)
4 small rings (two for each tieback)
2 wall hooks

1 Centre the heavyweight iron-on interfacing, fusible side up, on the interlining and pin in place. Snip the projecting fabric at curves and snip out notches around the ends.

2 Fold the projecting edges of the interlining over onto the iron-on interfacing and press to fuse them in place. Take care to press on the interlining only and remove pins as you reach them (diagram 1).

DIAGRAM 1

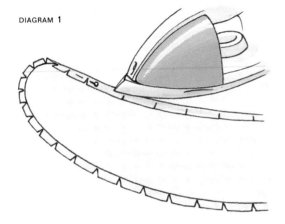

3 Pin the interlined piece, fusible side up, on the wrong side of the fabric. Snip and notch the fabric edges and fuse them in place in the same way as the interlining (diagram 2).

DIAGRAM 2

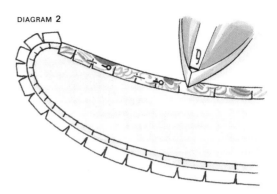

4 Snip and notch 6 mm (¹/₄ in) into the edge of the lining. Press 6 mm (¹/₄ in) to the wrong side all round the lining. Pin the lining to the wrong side of the tieback and handstitch in place around the edges (diagram 3).

DIAGRAM 3

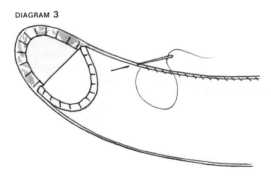

5 If you require a cord trim, handstitch the cord around the edge of the tieback, finishing the ends inside the lining in an inconspicuous place. Stitch small rings to the wrong side of the tieback at each end to fasten onto a hook on the wall.

Straight tieback

This simple straight tieback looks very effective on curtains that are partially drawn back and pulled up into a swag. It can be fastened with eyelets or rings to a hook beside the window.

MATERIALS
Curtain fabric
Sewing thread
Heavyweight iron-on interfacing
Large eyelets

CUTTING OUT

1.5 cm (⁵/₈ in) seam allowances are included unless instructions state otherwise.

Cut the tieback 10 cm (4 in) wide by the required length plus 3 cm (⁵/₈ in) all round. Cut the interfacing to same length but half the width.

1 Apply the iron-on interfacing lengthways to the wrong side of half the fabric. Fold the tieback in half lengthways with right sides facing. Stitch across each short edge and along the long edge, leaving a 10 cm (4 in) opening partway along the long edge (diagram 1).

DIAGRAM 1

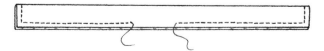

2 Trim the seams and corners and turn the tieback right side out. Press the seam at the edge and press the seam allowance inside along the opening. Slipstitch the opening closed.

3 Following the manufacturer's instructions, attach an eyelet centrally at each end of the tieback to fasten onto a hook on the wall (diagram 2).

DIAGRAM 2

Eyelet café curtain

This simple café curtain is made from a basic rectangle of fabric trimmed with a fabric flap along the top edge. It is threaded onto a narrow pole through large metal eyelets.

MATERIALS
Lightweight curtain fabric
Sewing thread
Large eyelets

CUTTING OUT

1.5 cm ($^5/_8$ in) seam allowances are included unless instructions state otherwise.

Measure the required finished size, then add on 20 cm (8 in) to the width for fullness and hems, and 9.5 cm ($3^3/_4$ in) to the length. Cut out the main piece to this size. Cut the flap the same width by a third of the curtain length plus 3.5 cm ($1^3/_8$ in).

1 Press 1 cm ($^3/_8$ in) double hems to the wrong side along both side edges of the main piece and stitch in place. Press a double 4 cm ($1^1/_2$ in) hem across the lower edge and stitch in place.

NOTE
When attaching the eyelets, work on a solid surface – concrete or paving is best.

2 Press 1 cm ($^3/_8$ in) double hems to the wrong side along the sides and lower edge of the flap and stitch in place. Place the right side of the flap to the wrong side of curtain with the top edges level and stitch together across the top edge (diagram 1). Turn the flap over to the right side and press.

DIAGRAM 1

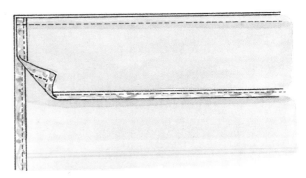

3 Mark the eyelet positions 2 cm ($^3/_4$ in) down from the top and 2 cm ($^3/_4$ in) in from the side edges. Space the others evenly about 13 cm (5 in) apart. Attach the eyelets through the double fabric layer, following the manufacturer's instructions (diagram 2).

DIAGRAM 2

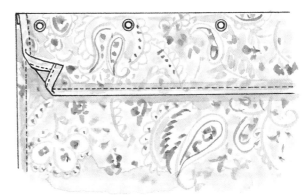

Self-frill café curtain

This curtain has a casing along the top so that it can be gathered onto a pole or wire. The narrow fold of fabric above the casing forms a pretty self frill.

MATERIALS
Lightweight curtain fabric
Sewing thread
Curtain pole or tension rod

CUTTING OUT

1.5 cm (⁵⁄₈ in) seam allowances are included unless instructions state otherwise.

Measure the width across the pole and the required length from the pole to the sill. Cut the curtain twice the pole width by the required length plus 18 cm (7 in).

1 Press a 1 cm (³⁄₈ in) double hem to the wrong side along both side edges of the curtain and stitch in place.

2 Press 1 cm (³⁄₈ in), then 6 cm (2¹⁄₄ in) to the wrong side across the top edge. Stitch along the pressed edge and again 3 cm (1¹⁄₄ in) above it to form a casing (diagram 1).

DIAGRAM **1**

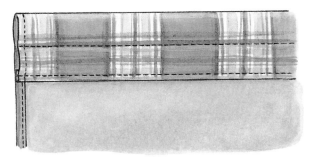

3 At the lower edge, press a double 4 cm (1¹⁄₂ in) hem to the wrong side and stitch in place.

Café curtain with ties

Fabric ties are used to attach this stylish curtain to a pole. The fabric is finished with a scalloped edge or an alternative hem could be made.

MATERIALS
**Lightweight curtain fabric with optional scalloped edge
Sewing thread
Tension rod or curtain pole**

CUTTING OUT

1.5 cm ($^5/_8$ in) seam allowances are included unless instructions state otherwise.

Measure the required finished size, then add 14 cm ($5^1/_2$ in) to the width for fullness and hems. Add 9.5 cm ($3^3/_4$ in) to the length, or just 1.5 cm ($^5/_8$ in) if the lower edge is ready finished. Cut out the main piece to this size. Cut a facing 2 cm ($^3/_4$ in) wider than the finished size by 6.5 cm ($2^5/_8$ in) deep. Cut ties 50 cm ($19^3/_4$ in) by 4 cm ($1^1/_2$ in).

1 Press 1 cm ($^3/_8$ in) wide double hems to the wrong side along both side edges of the main piece and stitch in place.

2 Press 1 cm ($^3/_8$ in) to the wrong side around all edges of the ties. Press the ties in half lengthways and stitch along the long edges.

3 Fold the ties in half. With the fold 6 mm ($^1/_4$ in) down from the top edge and the ends pointing downwards, pin the ties to the right side of the main piece about 15 cm (6 in) apart. Tack the ties in place.

4 Place the facing across the top edge of the main piece with right sides together and raw edges level, allowing it to project 1 cm ($^3/_8$ in) at each end. Stitch in place across the top edge and trim the seam to 1 cm ($^3/_8$ in) (diagram 1) .

DIAGRAM 1

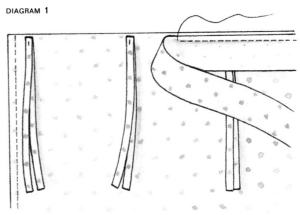

5 Press 1 cm ($^3/_8$ in) to the wrong side around the other edges of the facing. Fold the facing over to the wrong side and press the seam at the edge. Stitch around the side and lower edges of the facing. If required, press a 4 cm ($1^1/_2$ in) double hem to the wrong side across the lower edge of the curtain and stitch in place.

Voile swag

A simple length of fine linen, voile or muslin will drape beautifully over a pole to make an amazingly simple but effective window treatment. A single drape looped behind the pole at each end will frame a window perfectly. Alternatively, you can experiment with more elaborate options. First fix the pole, then drape the fabric over to establish the length required.

MATERIALS
Fine curtain fabric
Sewing thread
Sticky fixers (optional)

1 Stitch across the fabric ends with a close zigzag stitch.

2 Arrange the drape over the pole. If it slips out of place, use sticky fixers to secure the fabric to the pole at the back where they will not be visible.

Swag variations

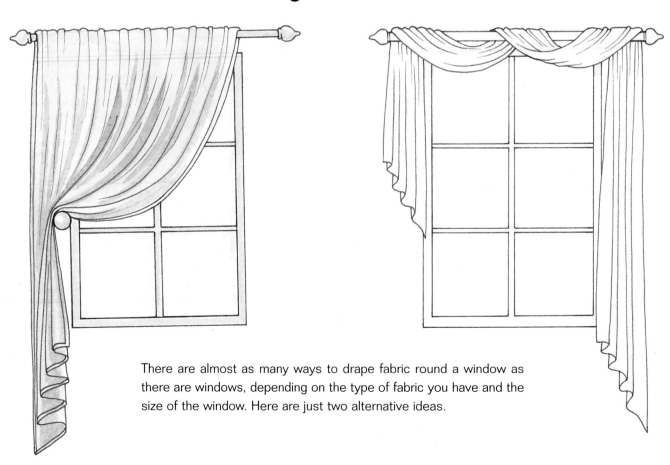

There are almost as many ways to drape fabric round a window as there are windows, depending on the type of fabric you have and the size of the window. Here are just two alternative ideas.

Pelmet with fold-over casing

This neat pelmet provides a pretty country-style treatment for a small window in a recess. It is also useful to soften the effect of a bare kitchen window, where curtains might intrude onto the work surface. The top edge is finished with a simple fold-over casing through which a tension rod is inserted to support the pelmet within the recess.

MATERIALS
Curtain fabric
Sewing thread
Lining fabric
Tension rod

CUTTING OUT

1.5 cm ($^5/_8$ in) seam allowances are included unless instructions state otherwise.

Measure the length of the rod and cut the fabric width to twice this measurement plus 3 cm ($1^1/_4$ in) for side seams. Decide on the depth of the pelmet and add 7 cm ($2^3/_4$ in) for hems. Cut the lining to the same width as the main fabric, but 8 cm ($3^1/_4$ in) shorter.

1 Place the lining fabric and main fabric together with right sides facing and lower edges level. Stitch together across the lower edge (diagram 1).

DIAGRAM **1**

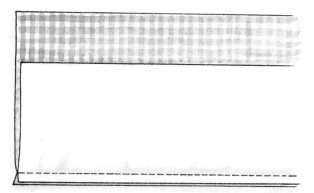

2 Open out and press the seam allowances towards the lining. Refold with right sides facing so that the seam is 5 mm ($^1/_4$ in) above the fold on the lining side. Stitch together along the side edges (diagram 2).

DIAGRAM **2**

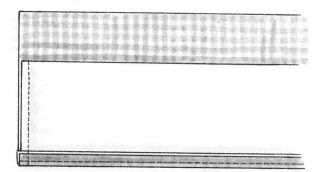

3 Turn right side out. Press 1 cm ($^3/_8$ in) to the wrong side along the top edge of the fabric. Then press 4 cm (1$^1/_2$ in) to the wrong side along the top edge, so that it overlaps the top edge of the lining to form a casing.

4 Stitch the casing in place along its lower edge and again just inside the top fold edge (diagram 3).

DIAGRAM 3

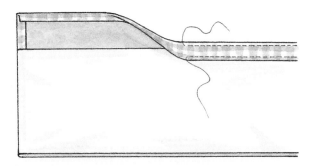

Pencil pleat pelmet

This more formal style of pelmet is finished with heading tape at the top and is drawn up into pleats or gathers. A special type of curtain track is available with an extra rail from which you can hang the pelmet. Alternatively, you can fix the pelmet with Velcro to a narrow pelmet shelf with rounded front corners. This is secured to the wall above the window.

MATERIALS
Curtain fabric
Sewing thread
Lining fabric
Heading tape
Curtain hooks or Stick-and-stitch Velcro

CUTTING OUT

1.5 cm ($^5/_8$ in) seam allowances are included unless instructions state otherwise.

Calculate the number of fabric widths required for the pelmet in the same way as for Tube-lined curtains, page 114. Decide on the depth of the pelmet and add 6.5 cm (2$^1/_2$ in) for hems. Cut the lining pieces to the same width as the main fabric, but 6 cm (2$^1/_4$ in) shorter.

1 Place the lining and fabric together with right sides facing and lower edges level. Stitch together across the lower edge.

2 Open out and press the seam allowances towards the lining. Refold with right sides facing so that the seam is 1 cm ($^3/_8$ in) above the fold on the lining side. Stitch together along the side edges (diagram 1).

DIAGRAM 1

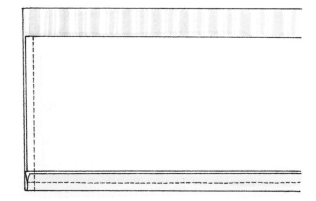

3 Turn right side out. Press 4 cm (1½ in) over to the wrong side along the top edge. Stitch on the heading tape in the same way as for Tube-lined curtains, steps 3 and 4, page 116 (diagram 2). Pull up the heading tape to the required width and arrange the fullness evenly.

4 If you are hanging the pelmet from a track, insert curtain hooks. If you are using a pelmet shelf, cut the Velcro to fit around the edge of the shelf. Stick the adhesive side of the Velcro to the edge of the shelf. Place the "stitch" part to the wrong side of the heading tape and handstitch in place to the back folds of the pleats or gathers.

DIAGRAM 2

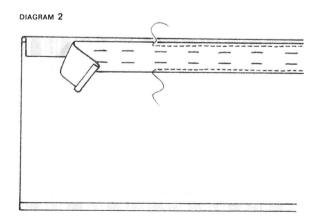

Door curtain

A lightweight door curtain is a useful accessory for a door with a glass panel, as it provides privacy while still letting the light in. A door curtain also gives a stylish look to a cupboard with a glass panel door. The curtain is held taut at top and bottom by lengths of plastic-covered tension wire secured with metal screw eyes hooked onto small screw hooks on the door.

MATERIALS
Lightweight fabric
Sewing thread
Tension wire
Screw hooks and eyes

CUTTING OUT

1.5 cm ($^5/_8$ in) seam allowances are included unless instructions state otherwise.
Measure the required width and double it for fullness.
Measure the length and add on 6 cm (2$^1/_4$ in) for hems.
Cut out the fabric to these measurements.

1 Press 1 cm ($^3/_8$ in) wide double hems along both side edges. Stitch in place (diagram 1).

DIAGRAM **1**

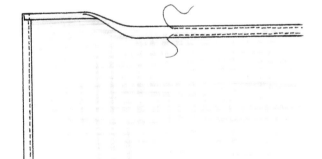

2 At the top and lower edges, press 1 cm ($^3/_8$ in), then 2 cm ($^3/_4$ in) to the wrong side to make casings. Stitch in place along both edges of the casing (diagram 2). Insert lengths of tension wire into the casings.

DIAGRAM **2**

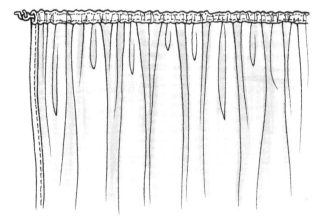

Basic roller blind

A roller blind is one of the simplest window treatments. It consists of a piece of stiffened fabric that hangs from a roller at the top and wraps neatly around it when the blind is raised. A roller blind can be hung alone or used as a sunshade in conjunction with curtains. Roller blinds are ideal for the kitchen and bathroom, where curtains might drag on a work surface or become splashed.

MATERIALS
Medium-weight fabric
Stiffening solution or spray
Roller blind kit

CUTTING OUT

Cut the fabric to about 2 in (5 cm) wider than required by 12 in (30 cm) longer to allow for the lower hem and to wrap around the roller. Ensure that the edges are straight and check that the side edges are at right angles to the top edge by using a protractor or carpenter's try square. If you do not have these tools, refer to diagram 1 – if A to B measures three units, A to C equals four units and B to C equals five units, the angle will be a right angle. Any fabric pulled or printed off grain will not roll evenly and should be avoided.

NOTE

There are two main types of roller blind: those operated by a tension roller and those with a side winder mechanism. The latter are the more widely available and usually come as a kit containing the roller, fixing brackets, winding mechanism and batten for the lower edge.

Before you make up the blind, spray or soak the fabric to stiffen it and prevent the side edges from fraying. There are various products on the market for these purposes. The soaking method is generally thought to be the more successful of the two. The fabric should not come right to the end of the roller. Leave a gap of 2 cm (³⁄₄ in) between the fabric and the side walls on a blind to be hung in a recess.

DIAGRAM 1

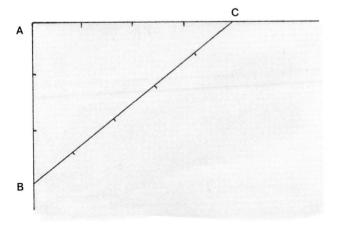

1 Stiffen the fabric with a stiffening solution or spray, following the manufacturer's instructions. When the fabric is stiffened, trim the side edges so that the blind is the required width. Press 1 cm (³⁄₈ in), then 3.5 cm (1³⁄₈ in) to the wrong side across the lower edge and stitch in place to make a channel for the batten.

2 Secure the fabric to the roller (which is usually supplied with a length of double-sided adhesive tape stuck to it for this purpose). Insert the batten into the channel and screw on the blind pull. Fix the blind in position inside or outside the window recess, as required.

Roller blind variations

ROLLER BLIND WITH EYELET TRIM

Prepare the fabric and make up the blind as for the Basic roller blind, page 142. Determine the positions for the eyelets, placing them about 12 cm (4¾ in) up from the lower edge and spaced about 15 cm (6 in) apart. Insert the eyelets, following the manufacturer's instructions.

ROLLER BLIND WITH SCALLOPED BORDER

Stiffen the fabric and trim to the required width. Draw out the shape of the scallops on a paper pattern, adjusting their size to fit across the desired width. The scallops shown are 7 cm (2¾ in) deep and 38 cm (15 in) wide. Cut a 5 cm (2 in) wide bias strip and bind the scalloped edge, see Bias binding, page 16. With right sides facing, fold the blind 7 cm (2¾ in) above the top of the binding and stitch 3.5 cm (1⅜ in) in from the fold. Press the stitched pleat down to make a channel for the batten. Make up the blind as for the Basic roller blind, step 2, page 142.

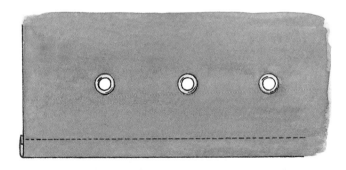

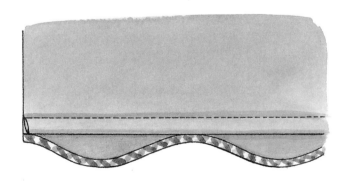

ROLLER BLIND WITH SHAPED EDGE AND DOWEL ROD

Stiffen the fabric and trim to the required width. Press 18 cm (7 in) to the wrong side across the lower edge. If the fabric is still tending to fray, apply iron-on buckram to the pressed-back turning. Stitch 5 mm (¼ in) down from the cut edge of the pressed-back turning, then again 3.5 cm (1³⁄₈ in) below that to make a channel for the batten. Draw a paper pattern, adjusting the size and number of cutouts to fit across the width of the blind. The cutouts shown are 18 cm (7 in) wide, 6.5 cm (2½ in) deep and 5 cm (2 in) apart. Mark and cut out the cutouts. Stitch across 2 cm (¾ in) up from the folds to make channels to thread a dowel rod through. Make up the blind as for the Basic roller blind, step 2, page 142.

ROLLER BLIND WITH LACE TRIM

Stiffen the fabric and trim to the required width. Press 1 cm (³⁄₈ in), then 4 cm (1½ in) to the wrong side across the lower edge and stitch in place. Lap the top edge of the lace under the lower edge of the hem and stitch in place. Make up the blind as for the Basic roller blind, step 2, page 142.

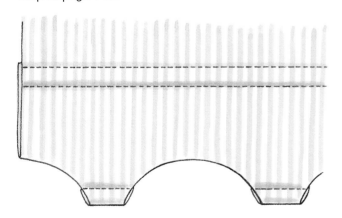

Roman blind

A Roman blind lies flat when it is lowered, but concertinas into elegant pleats across its width when raised. The pleats are created by thin lengths of dowel inserted into casings at the back of the blind and pulled up by a system of rings and cords.

MATERIALS

Closely woven furnishing fabric
Sewing thread
Wooden batten, 30 mm (1¼ in) square
Screw eyes
Stick-and-stitch Velcro
Blind rings
Lengths of dowel, 6 mm (¼ in) in diameter
Lath, 30 x 6 mm (1¼ x ¼ in)
Cleat (to hold cords in place)
Blind cord and acorn

CUTTING OUT

1.5 cm (⅝ in) seam allowances are included unless instructions state otherwise.

Before cutting out, decide how many casing rods you will need. Allow about 25 x 33 cm (10–13 in) between the rods and half this distance between the top of the lower hem and the first casing.

For the width of the blind, measure across the front of the batten and add on 10 cm (4 in). For the length, measure from the top of the batten to the window sill, add on 3 cm (1¼ in) for each dowel casing and 7 cm (2¾ in) for turnings.

PREPARATION

The blind is attached with Velcro to a wooden batten fixed to the wall above the window. Prepare the batten as follows. Fix a screw eye 10 cm (4 in), or 15 cm (6 in) for a wider blind, from each end of the wooden batten, placing it midway between the front and back edges. This will be the underside. Fix another screw eye, again placing it centrally, 1.5 cm (⅝ in) from the end where the cord will be used to pull the blind up. If the window is wide, add another supporting screw eye at the centre of the batten. Stick the adhesive half of the Velcro across the front of the batten. Fix the batten above the window, using a spirit level to ensure it is straight. Fix the cleat to the wall.

1 Press 1 cm (⅜ in), then 4 cm (1½ in) deep hems to the wrong side along both side edges. Stitch the hems in place close to the inner fold (diagram 1).

2 Press a 1 cm (⅜ in), then 5 cm (2 in) hem to the wrong side across the lower edge. Stitch the hem in place close to the inner fold. Leave the side edges of the hem open (diagram 1).

3 Mark the casing positions on the wrong side of the fabric with two parallel lines spaced 3 cm (1¼ in) apart (diagram 1).

DIAGRAM 1

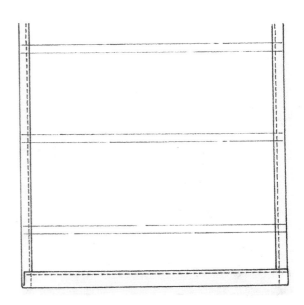

4 With right sides together, fold the fabric along the centre between the lines so that the lines match. Stitch along the lines to form 1.5 cm (⁵⁄₈ in) deep casings. Stitch all the casings in this way.

5 Using a double thread, stitch a ring to the fold of each casing 10 cm (4 in) in from each side edge on a narrow blind, and 15 cm (6 in) in from each side edge on a wider blind (diagram 2).

DIAGRAM 2

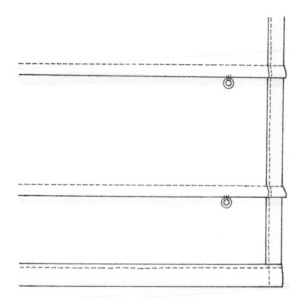

6 Press 1 cm (³⁄₈ in) to the wrong side across the top edge of the blind. Pin the "stitch" half of the Velcro across the top edge to cover the turning and stitch in place around all four edges (diagram 3).

DIAGRAM 3

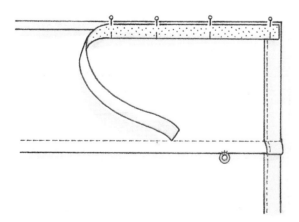

7 Insert a length of dowel into each casing and hand-stitch the ends of the casings closed. Insert the lath into the hem at the lower edge of the blind and hand-stitch the ends closed.

8 Tie a cord to the lowest ring on the opposite side to the cleat and thread up through the rings to the top. Then allow enough cord to go across the top of the blind and down the cleat side to reach the cleat (diagram 4) .

9 In the same way, thread a separate cord up through the rings near the opposite edge, allowing enough cord to go across and down to the cleat. This will be shorter than the first cord (diagram 4).

10 Attach the Velcro on the blind to the Velcro on the wall batten. Thread the cords through the screw eyes as shown (diagram 4). Pull the cords to raise the blind and fasten around the cleat. Trim the cords if required, thread on the acorn and knot the ends below it.

DIAGRAM 4

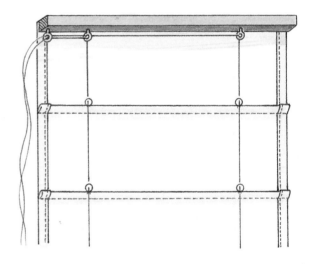

NOTE

As well as plain fabrics, vertical stripes or small prints work well for a Roman blind. Avoid horizontal stripes and any large prints as the horizontal casings will cut across the design.

Roman blind variations

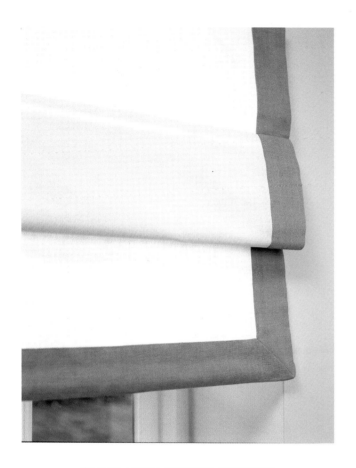

BLIND WITH MITRED BORDER

A neat mitred border gives a crisp edge to a Roman blind for a smart, contemporary look. The border is most effective if it is visible when the blind is pulled up. To achieve this, allow the same distance between the finished lower edge and the first casing as between the other casings.

When cutting out, allow a seam allowance only at the side edges of the blind. Stitch the outer edge of the border to the wrong side of the blind down the side edges. Stitch the lower border to the right side across the lower edge so the stitching is level with the top of the hem allowance. Snip into the side seam allowance at the top of hem and join the border corners, see Mitred borders, page 22. Make the hem, keeping the border out of the way, then topstitch the inner edge of the border in place. The casings are then stitched across the border.

BLIND WITH PINTUCKED LOWER EDGE

A panel of tucks adds discreet but stylish detail to a plain blind. Use bold contrasting topstitching on the right side of the tucks to highlight the detail. To ensure the tucks are visible when the blind is pulled up, allow the same distance between the finished lower edge and the first casing as between the other casings.

When working out the length of the blind, add twice the finished depth of the tucks multiplied by the number of tucks.

Make the hems at the sides and lower edge of the blind, then stitch the tucks so that the fold of each tuck is just above the stitching of the previous tuck, see Tucks, page 27.

Quick Roman blind

This quick version of the Roman blind pulls up into concertina pleats in a similar way to the traditional Roman blind, but does not use the same system of dowels and rings. Instead, just one length of dowel is used in the lowest casing and fine cords are stitched through the casings on the wrong side to pull the blind up. If you wish to make the blind firmer, you could insert stiff wires into the casings. Work out the positions and spacing of the casings in the same way as for the Roman blind, page 146.

MATERIALS

Closely woven furnishing fabric
Sewing thread
Wooden batten, 30 mm (1¼ in) square
Screw eyes
Stick-and-stitch Velcro
Dowel, 6 mm (¼ in) in diameter
Cleat (to hold cords in place)
Fine cord and acorn

CUTTING OUT

1.5 cm (⅝ in) seam allowances are included unless instructions state otherwise.

Measure the required width and add on 6 cm (2¼ in). For the length, measure from the top of the batten to the window sill and add on 2 cm (¾ in) for each casing plus 4 cm (1½ in) for turnings.

2 Measure and mark parallel lines across the blind the required distance apart for the casings (diagram 1).

3 With right sides together, fold the blind along the marked lines and stitch across 1 cm (⅜ in) away from each fold. Slip the dowel into the lowest casing and handstitch across each end of the casing (diagram 2).

DIAGRAM 2

1 Press 1 cm (⅜ in), then 2 cm (¾ in) hems to the wrong side along both side edges. Stitch the hems in place close to the inner fold. Make a hem across the lower edge in the same way (diagram 1).

DIAGRAM 1

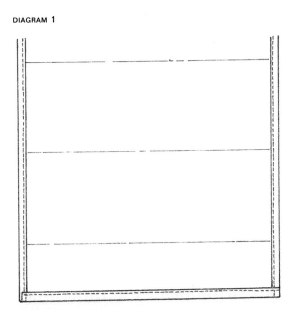

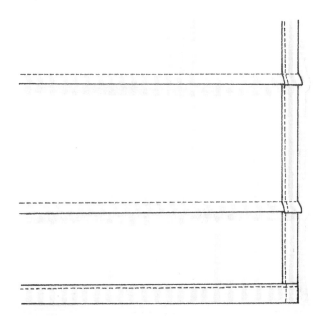

4 Press 1 cm (³⁄₈ in) over to the wrong side across the top edge. Place the "stitch" half of the Velcro across to cover the raw edge. Pin and stitch the Velcro in place around all four edges (diagram 3).

DIAGRAM **3**

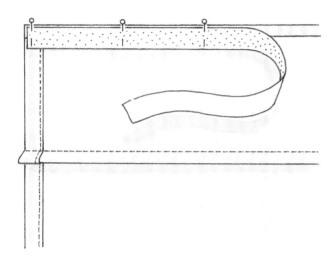

5 Allow enough cord to go up the blind, across the top of the blind and down the cleat side to reach the cleat. Make a large knot at the end of the cord and thread the cord into a needle. Stitch the cord through the centre of the lower casing, 10 cm (4 in) in from the side edge (diagram 4).

6 Then stitch through each of the casings above it in the same way. Stitch a separate cord through the casings on the opposite edge in the same way (diagram 4).

DIAGRAM **4**

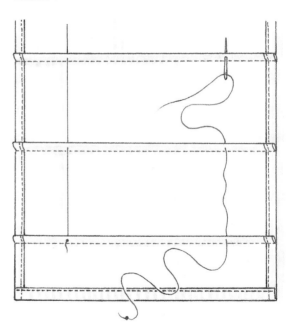

7 Hang the blind in the same way as the Roman blind, step 10, page 148.

London blind

This type of blind has a soft, ruched appearance and looks best on windows where the blind is left lowered for most of the time so that the gently gathered fabric is displayed to advantage. To retain the ruched effect even when the blind is pulled down, allow extra length when cutting out the fabric. Choose a fairly densely woven furnishing fabric for a London blind – plains and small prints work well.

MATERIALS
Closely woven furnishing fabric
Sewing thread
Wooden batten, 30 mm (1¼ in) square
Screw eyes
Stick-and-stitch Velcro
Dowel or lath, 1 cm (³⁄₈ in) in diameter
Blind cord, blind rings and acorn
Cleat (to hold cords in place)
2 tassels (optional)

PREPARATION
Prepare the batten for hanging in the same way as for the Roman blind, page 146, but aligning the screw eyes with the rings.

CUTTING OUT
1.5 cm (⁵⁄₈ in) seam allowances are included unless instructions state otherwise.

For the width of the blind, measure across the front of the batten and add on 40 cm (16 in) for the pleats and side hems. For the length, measure from the top of the batten to the window sill and add on 6 cm (2¼ in).

1 Press 1 cm (³⁄₈ in), then 4 cm (1½ in) hems to the wrong side around the side and lower edges of the blind. Mitre the corners as in Mitred hem, page 23. Stitch the hems in place (diagram 1).

2 On the wrong side of the top edge, measure and mark 20 cm (8 in) and 35 cm (13¾ in) in from one side edge. Measure and mark the same distances in from the other side edge (diagram 1).

DIAGRAM 1

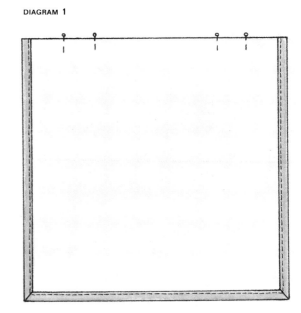

3 Fold the fabric vertically with right sides facing to match the first two marks. Stitch for 5 cm (2 in) down from the top edge to form an inverted pleat. Stitch a second inverted pleat at the other side of the fabric in the same way (diagram 2).

4 Open out each pleat and arrange centrally behind the stitching, then press in place just at the top, see Pleats, page 26 (diagram 2).

DIAGRAM **2**

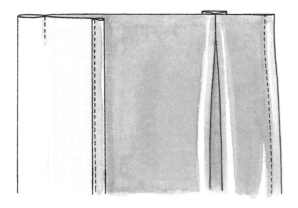

5 Press 1 cm (³⁄₈ in) to the wrong side across the top edge of the blind. Pin the "stitch" part of the Velcro across the top edge to cover the turning and stitch in place around all four edges (diagram 3).

DIAGRAM **3**

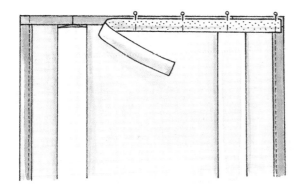

6 On the wrong side, lightly mark a line 20 cm (8 in) in from each side edge in line with the centre of the pleats. Start 10 cm (4 in) above the lower edge and stitch on rings spaced at 20 cm (8 in) intervals, ending at least 10 cm (4 in) below the base of the pleat stitching (diagram 4).

DIAGRAM **4**

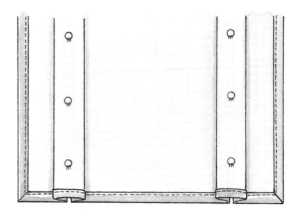

7 Cut the dowel or lath to match the length between the centre of the pleats at the top. Cut a fabric strip 7 cm (2³⁄₄ in) wide to the same length plus 3 cm (1¼ in). Fold the fabric strip in half lengthways with right sides together and raw edges level. Stitch across one short end and the long edge 1 cm (³⁄₈ in) in from raw edges to make a casing (diagram 5).

DIAGRAM **5**

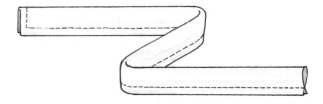

8 Turn the strip right side out and press. Insert the dowel or lath into the casing. Tuck the raw ends of the fabric to the inside and slipstitch them together neatly.

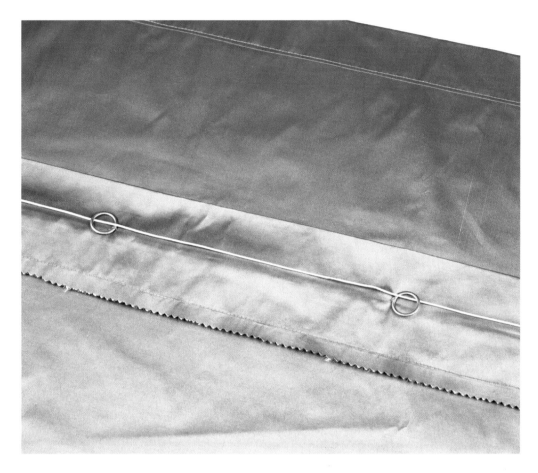

9 Place the casing to the wrong side of the blind just below the lower rings and handstitch each end of the casing to the blind (diagram 6).

10 Stitch tassels to the lower edge of the blind hem in line with the rings at the centre of the pleats. Thread the cord and hang the blind in the same way as for the Roman blind, steps 8–10, page 148.

DIAGRAM 6

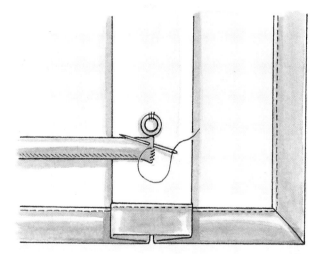

NOTE

If you need to join the fabric to make up the width required, place the seams at the back folds of the pleats.

Fabric glossary

Batiste
Fine, sheer, plain woven fabric, usually cotton, used for lightweight curtains.

Broderie anglaise
A decorative embroidered cotton fabric with punched embroidered holes available as both a fabric and edging trim. Available in white and pastel colours and used as a trim on towels, pillowcases and tablecloths.

Calico
A cheap, plain cotton fabric available in various weights and usually in an unbleached cream colour. It creases easily and may shrink when washed. Used for inner cushion and pillow covers and trial items.

Cambric
A fine, firm, closely woven plain-weave cotton fabric. Used for inner covers on cushions, pillows and duvets.

Chambray
A fine, woven, cotton fabric with white weft threads and a single colour for the warp threads (often blue). The effect is of a fine denim. Used for cushions, curtains and tablecloths.

Chenille
A soft fabric with a thick, velvety pile. Originally made from wool or cotton, it can now also be synthetic. Used for throws, bedcovers and curtains.

Chintz
Medium-weight woven cotton fabric, often printed with a bold floral design, with shiny glazed finish. Used for cushions, curtains, tablecloths and chair covers.

Corduroy
A hard wearing pile fabric with distinctive lengthways cords of pile, available in different weights, from lightweight needlecord to heavyweight elephant cord. Used for cushions.

Crushed velvet
A velvet pile fabric, processed to flatten the pile so the tufts lay in different directions to give an interesting texture. Used for cushions, curtains and bedcovers.

Damask
A firmly woven, self-patterned fabric made on a jacquard loom usually from cotton or a combination of fibres. Traditionally used for tablecloths and napkins.

Denim
Very hardwearing twill-weave, cotton fabric traditionally with white weft threads and blue warp threads, which give a mottled, faded look. Used for cushions, curtains and chair seat covers.

Domette
A very soft, open-weave fabric with a napped surface. Made from cotton or synthetic fibres, domette is used as an interlining between the fabric and the lining in curtains, to add warmth and very light padding.

Drill
A hardwearing, twill-weave, cotton fabric usually plain dyed. Made in various weights. Used for cushions and chair covers.

Flannel
A soft, plain or twill-weave fabric with a flat napped surface usually made from wool. Used for throws, bedcovers and cushions.

Georgette
A fine fabric with a crêpe texture which drapes well and is used for sheer curtains and bed drapes.

Gingham
Lightweight, cotton fabric with white and a single coloured yarn woven to form a characteristic check pattern. Available in checks of varying size. Used for lightweight curtains and tablecloths.

Hopsack
A coarse-weave, medium-weight fabric made using two yarns in each direction. Can be made from wool, cotton or synthetic fibres. Used for throws and bedcovers.

Lawn
A lightweight, plain weave, soft cotton fabric used for sheer curtains and bed drapes.

Linen
A very strong fabric with a high lustre, made from fibres from the flax plant. Linen fabrics are available in all weights from fine lawn to heavy furnishing fabrics. Most linens crease easily. Used for all types of soft furnishing from window drapes to chair covers.

Lining
A secondary fabric used to back curtains or other fabric items, to improve drape and cut out light, or provide a neat backing. A firmly woven cotton sateen is the most usual and it comes in cream, beige, white and a range of colours.

Matelassé
A thick double cloth with a quilted effect; it is woven from a double set of warp and weft threads which interlink at intervals producing the quilted effect. Used for cushions, throws and bedcovers.

Organdie
A very sheer, cotton fabric with a crisp finish which washing may remove. It

creases very easily. Used for edgings and speciality cushion covers.

Organza

A very sheer, fine fabric similar to organdie but made from silk, viscose or polyester fibres. It creases very easily. Used for edgings and speciality cushion covers.

Piqué

A crisp, light- to medium-weight cotton fabric, often plain white, with a textured surface of fine ribs or a small geometric pattern. Used for tablecloths, napkins, cushions and curtains.

Polycotton

A fabric, usually plain weave, made from a mix of polyester and cotton fibres. This combines the comfort and absorbency of cotton with the crease-resistance and strength of polyester. Used for sheets, duvet covers and pillowcases.

Polyester

A versatile synthetic fibre, polyester can be spun to imitate the natural fibres – cotton, wool, silk and linen. It is strong and crease-resistant and is often mixed with natural fibres to add these qualities.

Poplin

A medium-weight, hardwearing, plain weave fabric with a slight surface sheen. It is usually made from cotton, or a mixture of polyester and cotton fibres. Used for sheeting, pillowcases and duvet covers.

Sateen

A strong, plain cotton fabric woven to give a shiny smooth surface on the right side and a matt finish on the wrong side. It is mainly used for lining curtains.

Sheeting

An extra wide fabric, usually a polyester/cotton mixture, produced especially wide enough to make sheets and duvet covers.

Silk

Soft but strong, silk fibres are obtained from the cocoons of silk worms. Silk fibres absorb dyes easily to produce a good range of deep colours and can be woven into various fabrics. Used for cushion covers, table runners and curtains

Silk dupion

A medium-weight fabric with a fine but uneven slub weave caused by the natural thickening of the silk fibres in some areas. Used for cushion covers, table runners and curtains.

Toile de jouy

A traditional cotton print in a single colour on a beige or off-white background. The prints typically show romantic rustic scenes of figures and foliage. Used for curtains, cushions, tablecloths and chair covers.

Twill

A type of weave which forms diagonal lines on the right side of the fabric. There are various types of twill weaves and any fibres can be woven this way.

Velvet

A woven fabric with a surface pile. Originally made from silk, now it is often made from cotton or polyester. Used for cushions, curtains and throws.

Voile

A fine, lightweight, slightly open-weave fabric made from cotton, polyester or a mixture of the two. Used for sheer curtains and bed drapes.

Wool

Made from sheep's fleece, woollen fabrics are hard wearing, hairy and warm, and easy to mould. Wool, like silk, can be made into many different fabrics and weights varying from very fine to heavyweight. Most often used for blankets, throws, bedcovers or cushion covers.

Suppliers and useful addresses

UK

Baer & Ingram
Dragon Works
Leigh on Mendip
Radstock
BA3 5QZ
Tel: 01373 813800
Email: sales@baer-ingram.co.uk
www.baer-ingram.co.uk
Wide range of cotton fabrics available mail order.

Fabrick.com
Tel: 01620 842841
Fax: 01620 842608
Email: info@fabrick.com
www.fabrick.com
Online supplier of fabrics by British and European designers. Also supplies trimmings and interior accessories.

Fabric World
287 High Street
Sutton
Surrey
SM1 1LL
Tel: 020 8643 5127
Fax: 020 8770 0021
Email: info@fabricworldlondon.co.uk
www.fabricworldlondon.co.uk
Fabric stockists, also available mail order by email.

G P & J Baker
Chelsea Harbour Design Centre
North Dome G18/19
London SW10 0XE
Tel: 020 7351 7760
Fax: 020 7351 7752
www.gpjbaker.co.uk
Suppliers of top quality curtain and soft furnishing fabrics.

John Lewis
Oxford Street
London
W1A 1EX
Tel: 020 7629 7711
www.johnlewis.com
Stocks a range of furnishing fabrics and accessories. Visit the website for details of branches nationwide.

Lewis & Wood
5 The Green
Uley
Gloucestershire
GL11 5SN
Tel: 01453 860080
Fax: 01453 680054
www.lewisandwood.co.uk
Suppliers of fine furnishing fabrics and wallpapers.

MacCulloch & Wallis Limited
25–26 Dering Street
London
W1R 0BH
Tel: 020 7629 0311
Fax: 020 7491 2481
Email: macculloch@psilink.co.uk
www.macculloch-wallis.co.uk
Stockists of a range of fabrics, sewing equipment and haberdashery supplies.

Malabar
31-33 The South Bank Business Centre
Ponton Road
London
SW8 5BL
Tel: 020 7501 4200
Fax: 020 7501 4210
Email: info@malabar.co.uk
www.malabar.co.uk
Designer and stockist of fabrics available through selected stockists.

Marvic Textiles Ltd
Chelsea Harbour Design Centre
Chelsea Harbour
London
SW10 0XE
Tel: 020 7352 3119
Large range of fabrics available for soft turnishing and upholstery.

Online Fabrics
388-394 Foleshill Road
Coventry
CV6 5AN
Tel: 024 7668 7776
Fax: 024 7668 1656
Email: info@online-fabrics.co.uk
www.online-fabrics.co.uk
Large online supplier of fabric.

AUSTRALIA

Lincraft
31–33 Alfred Street (Head Office)
Blackburn
Victoria 3130
Tel: 1800 640 107
www.lincraft.com.au
Major fabric, sewing and craft retailer. Branches nationwide and online supplier.

Spotlight
Head Office
100 Market Street
South Melbourne
Victoria 3205
Tel: 1300 305 405
www.spotlight.com.au
Fabric and craft superstores, branches nationwide. Visit the website or phone for mail order delivery.

SOUTH AFRICA

Cape Town
Lifestyle Fabrics, Curtain and Linen
11 Picton Road
Parow 7500
Tel/fax: 021 930 5170
Good range of fabric and soft furnishing materials.

Durban
Classic Textiles
126 Archary Rd
Clairwood
Durban
4052
Tel: 031 465 9016
Fax: 031 465 9003
Email: info@classictextiles.co.za
www.classictextiles.co.za
A comprehensive range of fabrics, haberdashery and curtaining equipment.

Gauteng
Fabric & Decor
Shop 22, Town Square
Weltevreden Park
Roodepoort
1709
Tel: 011 675 2135
Fax: 011 675 1246
Range of fabrics suitable for soft furnishing.

NEW ZEALAND

Spotlight Stores
Whangarei (09) 430 7220
Wairau Park (09) 444 0220
Henderson (09) 836 0888
Panmure (09) 527 0915
Manukau City (09) 263 6760
Hamilton (07) 839 1793
Rotorua (07) 343 6901
New Plymouth (06) 757 3575
Gisborne (06) 863 0037
Hastings (06) 878 5223
Palmerston North (06) 357 6833
Porirua (04) 238 4055
Wellington (04) 472 5600
Christchurch (03) 377 6121
Dunedin (03) 477 1478
www.spotlight.net.nz
Large selection of fabrics and haberdashery items.

Fabric & Curtain Barn
Mt Wellington (09) 573 1919
Henderson (09) 838 6481
New Lynn (09) 826 3075
Wairau Road (09) 441 2206
Fabrics and accessories for soft furnishings and curtain making.

Index

Acknowledgements

The author and publishers would like to thank the following people for their contributions to this book:

Gwen Diamond, Vicky French and Melanie Williams for their expert stitching.

Martin Short for sourcing such wonderful fabrics.

Elizabeth Johnson and Sophie Silocchi for letting us photograph in their homes.

Baer & Ingram, GP&J Baker, Lewis & Wood, Malabar and Marvic for generously donating fabric to make up the projects. For full details, see page 158.

The
Dream Traders

The
Dream Traders

E.V. THOMPSON

ROBERT HALE · LONDON

© E.V. Thompson 2010
First published in Great Britain 1981
This edition published 2010

ISBN 978-0-7090-8885-1

Robert Hale Ltd
Clerkenwell House
Clerkenwell Green
London EC1R 0HT

www.halebooks.com

2 4 6 8 10 9 7 5 3 1

Printed in Great Britain by the MPG Books Group,
Bodmin and Kings Lynn

For Celia
who has listened to my
Hong Kong reminiscences
with great patience
for so many years

PROLOGUE

CHINA in the 1830s was a country of four hundred million people and had successfully fought off progress and reality for many hundreds of years. In achieving this remarkable feat, the Emperors of 'The Heavenly Kingdom', as they called their land, gained absolute dominion over their people and regarded themselves as personally chosen by the Gods. They, and they alone, were the supreme rulers of the world. Others, whether they be kings, emperors or sultans, were mere mortals and addressed China's ruler on their knees.

The ordinary people of the countries beyond China's borders were 'barbarians' — a term used even when talking directly to them. If they were of European descent, the barbarians were also known as the Fan Qui — 'Foreign Devils', their presence impatiently tolerated.

Such an attitude was destined to bring China into collision with the remainder of the world in the nineteenth century.

While the Chinese stagnated, secure in the knowledge that they were the chosen people, a brash and arrogant nation, Great Britain, was busily building the greatest empire the world had ever known. With Great Britain frustrated in trade by China's backwardness, and scornful of her intricate network of tradition and corruption, a clash between the two nations was inevitable.

When it finally came it showed up the weaknesses and self-deception of China — but it did far more. It proved that Great Britain, cradle of nineteenth-century morality, was willing to go to war to fight in support of pride, avarice — and opium.

PART ONE

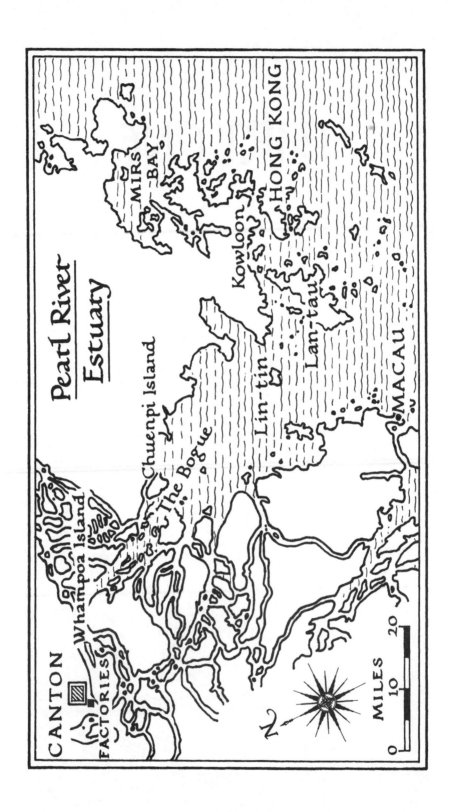

Pearl River Estuary

CANTON
FACTORIES
Whampoa Island
Chuenpi Island
The Bogue
MIRS BAY
Kowloon
HONG KONG
Lin-tin
Lan-tau
MACAU

MILES
0   10   20

One

AN UNEXPECTED gust of wind blew from the direction of the mauve haze that hid the shore. With a crack like a musket-volley, the idle sails of *The Two Brothers* bellied out and the merchantman leaned towards the distant grey skyline. On deck, Luke Trewarne gripped the guard-rail that enclosed the passengers' exercise-area as the scrubbed wooden planking tilted beneath his feet. Looking up at the raised poopdeck, Luke saw the grin on the coxswain's face as the seaman spun the wheel. The laden ship heeled over even farther, chopping through the short green waves with an uncomfortable bouncing motion.

'That's right, laddie. You cling tight to that guard-rail. Dan Gemmell has high hopes of you retrieving his trading losses for him. If I lose you now, he'll be blaming me for his failures.'

Laughing sarcastically, Captain Obadiah Innes heaved himself awkwardly through the hatchway leading from the cabins. Luke turned to make an appropriate retort, but it was lost in his surprise at seeing the captain of *The Two Brothers* wearing full ceremonial naval dress.

Gaining the deck, the heavily built captain stood straddle-legged against the movement of the ship as he fastened the gold buttons of his dark-blue longcoat. From beneath his arm he took a battered cocked hat trimmed with faded gold braid. Cramming it upon his head, he glared fiercely at Luke, who was staring with undisguised curiosity.

'I wore this hat at Trafalgar, Mr Trewarne. That would be some years before you were born, but I don't doubt that you've heard of the victory we won there? When Nelson showed the French fleet what sea fighting was all about? It's seen a deal of sea-time since then, in the service of the King – ay, and of lesser men.'

From braided cocked hat to brass-buckled shoes, Captain Innes was every inch an officer of Her Britannic Majesty's Navy, but *The Two Brothers* was a lumbering merchantman, bound for Whampoa, the island just down-river from Canton, the only port in the whole of China open to foreign traders. Luke was the sole passenger and he could think of no reason why the captain should be wearing his finery. But he said nothing. Captain Innes had an explosive and uncertain temper, and Luke had no wish to bring his ire down upon himself and the unfortunate crew of *The Two Brothers*.

Captain Innes himself supplied the answer to Luke's unspoken question. When the ship returned to an even keel he shook a fringe of white lace free from the cuff of his coat and pointed ahead of the merchantman. 'You see that brown water, laddie?'

Leaning over the side of the merchantman, Luke could see a dark-brown stain on the water. It extended shorewards for as far as he could see.

'That's mud, washed down from a thousand miles of rice fields on both sides of the Pearl River beyond Canton. There are fields enough in that one valley to cover the face of all England – and that's but a fraction of China. At the moment the Chinese are doing no more than drain off a little water so they can see to pull up the weeds. Come harvesting time there'll be muddy water stretching a hundred miles from shore. There's not a navigator – not even a Portuguese – who can't find his way to port at harvesting time. Right now it tells me we're likely to meet up with the Chinese Navy before long. *That's* why I'm wearing the Queen's uniform. I hope the Chinese will be sufficiently impressed to keep their distance.'

Luke looked at Captain Innes sharply. 'And if they're not . . . ?'

Captain Obadiah Innes thrust his chin forward belligerently. 'Then they'll negotiate with the *The Two Brothers*' cannon. I've five hundred chests of Ezra McCulloch's opium in the hold, laddie – and that's how many he'll expect me to deliver. No thieving Chinese Customs man's getting his hands on them before then.'

Luke expressed surprise. 'But you'll need to open the hatches at Macau. East India Company regulations state that all ships going up-river to Canton must call at Macau first and declare their cargoes. It's Imperial Chinese law. . . .'

Macau was the settlement on the western bank of the wide Pearl River estuary, occupied by the Portuguese for three hundred years. It was a tenuous occupancy, tolerated rather than approved of by the Chinese authorities. Aware of the fragile nature of their tenancy, the Portuguese eagerly sought ways to make themselves indispensable to their unpredictable landlords. Monitoring the shipping proceeding to and from the

4

port of Canton was one such duty the Portuguese had taken upon themselves.

'We no longer jump to the tune of the East India Company, Mr Trewarne. As for "Imperial China", I'm employed by Ezra McCulloch, and you by Dan Gemmell. You'll do well to remember that. You'll need to wait for some other day to get the smell of Macau. I'm heading straight up-river to Whampoa, same as always.'

Swinging away, Captain Obadiah Innes stomped stiff-legged to the ladder leading to the raised poopdeck, leaving Luke to ponder on his words.

Luke stayed on deck as the merchantman drew closer to the hill-lined coast of China. Before long the ship sailed slowly into a wide muddy-watered estuary with clusters of high-peaked islands on either hand. Some miles to westward the sun was reflected on the glass windows and white-painted houses of Macau. Luke would have felt happier had Captain Innes been taking *The Two Brothers* there before proceeding up-river, but he would sample the pleasures of the Portuguese colony soon enough. The Chinese, with a typical lack of logic, had decreed that the foreign 'barbarians' should remain in their Cantonese trading enclosure only during the trading months of winter. The decree was loosely adhered to only because it suited many of the European traders and their staff to go down-river to Macau for the hot stormy summer. During this season the Chinese gods of sea and air sent their great winds, the 'typhoons', scouring the seas off the Chinese coast. Ships in their path would vanish with occupants and cargo, claimed as a sacrifice by the violent gods of the elements.

Captain Innes kept his ship close to the centre of the estuary and his eyes turned away from Macau. In common with all other British sea captains in this part of the world, he was scornful of the Portuguese and the duties they had assumed on behalf of the Chinese Emperor.

There were many vessels here in the Pearl River. Mostly they were small wooden fishing sampans, manned by grey-clad Chinese fishermen wearing wide conical straw hats. Here and there a high-sterned junk with butterfly-wing sails glided silently across the surface of the brown water.

Gradually, rice-terraced hills on either side of the river began to close in about the merchantman, and long islands of mud festooned with thick bamboo undergrowth reached out

5

from the shore. As *The Two Brothers* glided past one such tangled peninsula, a look-out, posted in the ship's bow, called out urgently, 'Two junks bearing down on us . . . fine on the starboard bow.'

Luke leaned far out over the guard-rail and saw two large junks change direction in ragged unison, trying to catch the wind and head off the merchantman. From their squat main-masts fluttered long golden pennants, displaying the dragon emblem of Imperial China.

The Two Brothers was about to be intercepted by junks of China's navy.

'Mr Trewarne! Either get yourself below, or come up here where I can keep my eye on you.'

Resplendent in his naval officer's uniform, Captain Innes stood at the poopdeck rail. Over Luke's head he called to a group of seamen, brought on deck by the look-out's cry, 'One of you hoist the Union Jack, then get below. Prime the guns, but don't run them out until you get the order from me.'

As Luke climbed the ladder to the poopdeck, Captain Innes added, in a voice that was intended to carry no farther than the coxswain at the wheel, 'I hope to God they've kept their powder dry; our lives may well depend on those guns in the next few minutes. Those junks mean business. Polite words and shiny buttons won't satisfy them today.'

'Is there going to be a battle?' The thought both thrilled and appalled Luke.

'There might be. If you've no stomach for cannon-fire, you'd best lock yourself in your cabin and pray that we win. If we don't it'll be too late for prayer.'

'The thought of battle doesn't trouble me,' declared Luke honestly. He had witnessed more than one bloody skirmish in India's hill country. 'I'm more concerned about the consequences. We're not at war. Fighting the Chinese Navy won't help trade in these waters.'

'Neither will losing Ezra McCulloch's best ship,' retorted Obadiah Innes. 'Now, out of my way. . . . Hard a-port! . . . Spin that wheel, mister!'

Captain Innes roared his orders to the coxswain as the leading Chinese junk bore rapidly down upon them.

The coxswain heaved on the wheel, and another seaman sprang to his assistance. Slowly the big merchantman heeled over, her bow coming round until it pointed at the first of the

6

two junks. The stretch of sluggish brown water between the two craft narrowed so rapidly that Luke drew in a sharp breath. A collison seemed inevitable.

At the last possible moment, the nerve of the junk's commander broke. The awkward-looking craft changed direction, scraping along half the length of *The Two Brothers* and tearing away a section of her own sternboard.

Leaning over the side of the poop, Luke looked down upon the junk's untidy deck. Three Chinese seamen strained at a heavy wooden tiller, while others scattered in confusion. In the junk's blunt bow two brass cannon pointed harmlessly ahead at empty brown water.

Moments later the Imperial Chinese junk fell away, wallowing in the wake of *The Two Brothers*.

But Captain Innes had shaken off only half the intercepting force. The commander of the second Chinese man-of-war had been far enough away to see what was happening and he correctly anticipated *The Two Brothers*' new course. Taking advantage of the strong breeze in his favour, the commander sent his vessel surging through the water towards the merchantman. When still a dozen lengths away, two plumes of smoke spat simultaneously from the brass cannons mounted in the bows of the Chinese man-of-war. Before the flat 'crack!' of the shots reached Luke's ears, two cannonballs struck *The Two Brothers*.

The first ball passed through the rigging, severing no more than a rope or two before splashing harmlessly into the water a few hundred yards beyond the ship.

The second shot was more effective. It ploughed through the planking at the edge of the poopdeck; then, its momentum almost spent, struck down a seaman standing no more than an arm's length from Luke.

Luke leaped forward and prevented the reeling seaman from falling over the side of the ship — but he could do no more for him. With the right side of his chest shattered by a bronze cannonball no larger than an orange, the sailor panted his life-blood away. Taking off his coat, Luke placed it beneath the dying seaman's head.

Around them, Captain Innes's crew had been galvanized into swift retaliatory action. There were four gun-ports on either side of *The Two Brothers*. As they crashed open, the heavy guns were run out with practised speed. Both *The Two*

Brothers and the Chinese junk had changed course and were now sailing broadside on to each other. The merchantman's four starboard guns opened fire at point-blank range. For a moment billowing black smoke hid the junk from Luke's view. When the smoke blew away, the deck was a tangled mess of splintered wood and bamboo rigging, and two holes gaped in the side of the junk's hull.

The Two Brothers heeled over under full sail and executed a wide turn, in order to bring her other guns to bear on the crippled junk now spinning slowly and helplessly in the river current. The range increased rapidly, but the aim of the British gunners remained true. Four twelve-pound cannonballs ripped into the Imperial Chinese junk, reducing it to a wallowing shambles. The screams of its injured and dying crew echoed across the water as it dropped behind.

Twice more Captain Innes sailed past the battered and badly listing junk and fired a broadside into her. Not until her crew began leaping into the river did Innes break off the engagement. During all this time the other junk made no attempt to engage *The Two Brothers*, her commander sailing his vessel away from the brief but bloody battle as fast as wind and tide would allow.

A shadow fell across Luke as he kneeled beside the dying seaman. He looked up to see Captain Innes standing beside him. The expression on the face of the captain of *The Two Brothers* could have been anger – or elation.

'I'll have him taken below and see what can be done for him.'

Luke stood up and shook his head. 'Moving him will only cause him more pain. He'll be dead in a few minutes in either place. Better to leave him where he is.'

Lifting a hand to shield his eyes from the sun, Luke looked back to where the crippled junk was settling deeper into the muddy waters of the Pearl River. 'Is this the way the Chinese usually greet traders?'

'No.' Captain Innes eased the hat from his head and wiped perspiration from his forehead with a sleeve. 'Shots have been fired before, but it's never been more than a game. They fire their guns, we show them ours are bigger and better, and they go away. Honour is satisfied on both sides. Today was different. They meant business – and men have died. The Chinese can't save face by pretending this hasn't happened. They'll want

8

someone's blood for this day's work. It'll be mine for certain if I try to go up-river this voyage. I'm afraid it will be a while before you see Canton on this ship, laddie.'

'Where will you go — Macau?'

Obadiah Innes's laugh was short and without humour. 'I might as well give myself up to the Chinese. The Portuguese Governor there does as the Chinese tell him. No, laddie. We'll head for the finest anchorage in the China Seas. Ezra McCulloch has built himself a house there — though he'll not thank either of us for spreading word of it to anyone.'

Turning to the coxswain, Captain Innes called, 'I'm going below to speak to the gunners. Take us to Hong Kong, mister.'

The wounded seaman in *The Two Brothers* died within an hour of the engagement. After a perfunctory funeral service read by Captain Innes, his body was committed to the murky waters of the Pearl River estuary.

As the crew went back to their various tasks, Luke leaned over the stern of the merchantman and gazed at the hills of China. He wondered what the future held for him here. He was only twenty-two years of age, yet it seemed a lifetime since he had left his native Cornwall and sought a career and a fortune in India.

The only son of a tenant farmer, Luke had been only ten years old when his father died. Within a year, the widowed Mrs Trewarne married again, in order to retain possession of their small rented farm. She chose her new husband well. A widower, he brought to the farm three hard-working sons, all bigger and older than Luke — and each eager to prove his superiority. In the three years that followed the marriage, Luke's mother added three daughters to the family. Caught between step-brothers and half-sisters, Luke soon realized there was no longer a place for him in the house where he had been born.

Fortunately for Luke, others saw his growing unhappiness. One was the landlord, who owned the farm together with most of the land in this particular corner of Cornwall. He encouraged Luke to spend much of his time at the big house, sharing the lessons given to the landowner's own children. Luke learned well and profited by his diligence. He made a favourable impression on a visitor who came to the house in the summer of 1828, when Luke was thirteen years of age. The visitor was the landowner's brother. He was also a director of the great East India Company. At the end of that same year, Luke was on his way to India, a privileged employee of the company that ruled two hundred million people in the rich but fragmented subcontinent of India.

For nine years Luke served the Company well, and his service took him from the cool hills of northern India to the hot humid plains of Bengal. In the latter he saw for the first time the East India Company's fields of white opium poppies, extending for as far as the eye could see in every direction. The Company's expatriates saw nothing sinister in the cultivation of the poppy on such a vast scale. In the sweltering Calcutta heat they were fond of saying how much the sight reminded them of the almost forgotten snows of home.

It was while he was stationed in Calcutta that Luke first met Dan Gemmell. A quiet man, Gemmell had many years earlier established a trading company in Canton, with an ambition to rival one day the trading empire of Jardine Matheson. That was before the rigours of Far Eastern trading ruined his health, and cholera carried off his wife and infant son. Now Dan Gemmell traded because he knew nothing else and because all the family he had were buried side by side in the shadow of the church of St Antonio in Macau.

Gemmell made several visits to the East India Company offices. He took a liking to the young clerk with the soft Cornish accent and made a shrewd assessment of his work. Confident in all he did, Luke was thoroughly conversant with all the aspects of Far Eastern trading – but he had not yet been caught up in the web of corruption that ensnared so many men involved in the sale and production of opium.

Dan Gemmell was one of the very few merchants trading in Canton who refused to deal in the drug. It was an easy way to make a large profit, and the merchants were encouraged and supported in the trade by the East India Company. The Company carefully organized and controlled opium growing in India, maintaining a high standard. Patna opium from the plains of Bengal was particularly prized by the opium merchants of China. Stronger and purer than its rivals, it could be mixed with cheaper grades and sold for an enormous profit to desperate addicts who could not survive without the nerve-dulling drug.

It mattered little to either seller or purchaser that the import of opium into China was illegal, banned by an edict issued by the Celestial Emperor himself. Mandarins and government officials at all levels were content to allow the trade to continue – for a price. Chinese officialdom was riddled with corruption. The only uncertain factor facing a ship's captain bringing opium into China was the *amount* of bribery that would be squeezed from him. The rumblings of the Emperor's displeasure at the continuing trade had been growing louder in recent months, but these were largely ignored by the Europeans sailing up the Pearl River to Whampoa island. They had heard such mutterings many times before. Besides, the Imperial capital was more than a thousand miles distant. Coming from so far away, the edicts of the mysterious Emperor had an air of unreality about them.

This situation was explained in detail to Luke when Dan Gemmell offered to make him his senior trading clerk in Canton. The merchant promised Luke he would be given a free hand to run the merchandizing side of Gemmell Company – with ten per cent of all profits. By dint of hard work, and given reasonable luck, Luke might one day leave China a moderately wealthy man – or stay to become a trader himself.

Luke seized the opportunity eagerly. It was at such times that he wished he had a close family with whom to share his good fortune. He still wrote letters to his mother; but it had become a duty – no more. The letters from Cornwall had stopped after his second year away. Luke Trewarne had only himself now. His home was wherever he made it – and he was as much at home in the Far East as he would be anywhere else.

Six months after accepting Dan Gemmell's offer and giving up his post with the East India Company, Luke was still in India. He hoped he had not made a serious mistake. Dan Gemmell had returned to Canton, promising to send for Luke at the earliest opportunity. Since then Luke had heard nothing. But he had not wasted his time. Characteristically, Luke had set about learning the language of the land where he would soon be working, employing one of the East India Company's Chinese clerks as tutor.

Learning languages came easily to Luke. He had already mastered a number of Indian dialects, and he became totally absorbed in his self-imposed task. Cantonese Chinese was like no other language he had ever known. The slightest change in the sound of a single syllable could alter the meaning of a complete sentence. The construction of the sentences themselves was at first utterly bewildering to his European mind.

Nevertheless, by the time Captain Obadiah Innes arrived in Calcutta with instructions for Luke to take passage to China in *The Two Brothers*, and news that Dan Gemmell had been seriously ill, Luke had gained a sound grasp of the Chinese language. He was eager to put it to the test in China.

Now, in the year 1838, when only a few miles from Canton and a promising future, Luke wondered whether all his studying had been in vain. The battle between *The Two Brothers* and the junks of the Imperial Chinese Navy might well have signalled the end of all British trade with China.

Two

THE ANCHORAGE at Hong Kong island was a crescent-shaped bay, protected from winds coming off the China Sea by a series of ragged-peaked hills. To the north the mainland reached out gnarled granite fingers towards the island, holding back the deep-sea waves and providing a natural harbour sheltered from all but the fiercest of summer storms.

Luke conceded that Captain Innes was right; this was a very fine anchorage indeed. Others evidently agreed with his view: there were three British merchantmen anchored offshore. Two flew a blue flag on which was a white St Andrew's cross – the company flag of Jardine Matheson. The other ship was little more than a hulk, used by Ezra McCulloch as a temporary opium-receiving ship.

Captain Innes took *The Two Brothers* close inshore, anchoring midway between the beach and the opium-receiving ship. Nearby was a Chinese fishing village with a large community of sampan dwellers. A faint breeze blew spasmodically from the shore, bringing with it such a strong smell of fish and insanitary human habitation that Luke wrinkled his nose in disgust.

Captain Innes saw Luke's pained expression and smiled. He was in high humour in spite of their recent experience on the Pearl River. 'You're sampling one of the true joys of China, Mr Trewarne – the stench of its people. You'd better not let them see you pull such a face. They call this place "The Fragrant Harbour"! That should give you some idea of what to expect – but no doubt it got its name before the sampans arrived here.'

He nodded towards the floating 'village', where the sampans huddled together in close-packed disorder. 'Hoklo fishermen – water-gipsies from farther up the coast. They moved here in the hope that we'll give them protection from pirates.'

'Pirates?' Luke looked at Captain Innes to see if he was serious.

'That's what I said, mister. Our fight today would have been a different story had the other ships been Chinese pirates.

They don't give up so easily — and they leave no survivors to complain of their doings. Pirates are the scourge of the China coast hereabouts. They kill more people than do the typhoons. . . .'

Captain Innes broke off his conversation as the ship's long-boat dropped heavily into the water and one of the seamen shouted to him that they were ready to go ashore.

Calling out that he was coming, Captain Innes said, 'I'll see you later, laddie. No doubt Ezra McCulloch will know what's been happening to upset the Chinese since I was last here.'

Luke would have liked to go ashore with Captain Innes, but he had already asked and been refused. Obadiah Innes told Luke that Ezra McCulloch did not welcome uninvited visitors to his Hong Kong home. Luke watched as the longboat reached shore and was run up on to a small beach. Leaping ashore, the burly captain strode up the hill with a rolling seaman's gait, heading for a clump of trees. Beyond them Luke could see a large, almost completed granite-stone house. It was a curious fact that the Chinese, who so fiercely resisted foreign influence on the mainland, should allow the traders to do much as they wished on Hong Kong, Lin-tin and the many other islands scattered about the Pearl River estuary.

Luke stayed on deck until the sun sank below the high peaks to the west of the bay, sending long irregular shadows far across the anchorage. Then he went below to his cabin, which was situated just above the waterline. It was late summer, and the weather was stiflingly hot. There was a small porthole in the cabin, secured with ringhead bolts. Unscrewing them with some difficulty, Luke swung the small window open on protesting brass hinges. A welcome breeze entered the cabin, but it was hardly strong enough to set the yellow flame in the oil-lamp flickering.

Soon a meal was brought down to the cabin, but Luke had hardly begun to eat when a thin high-pitched voice from behind him called, in Chinese, 'Food! You give me food?'

Startled, Luke sprang to his feet. When he turned he saw a face peering at him through the open porthole. It belonged to a young girl of no more than nine years of age. Thin-faced and dark-eyed, her hair straggled untidily across her face, and she had a smudge of dirt across the bridge of her nose.

'Food! Give me food.'

'Do boat-children have no manners? Is that the way you are

taught to ask for something?' Luke snapped back at the child in Chinese.

Her mouth dropped open in surprise and the head bobbed back from the open porthole.

Luke heard her awed voice say, 'It is a barbarian . . . yet he speaks with a Chinese tongue!'

There was an amused laugh, and a pleasant female voice commented, 'Then my little sister Tik-wei will need to show respect to this clever Fan Qui.'

Luke winced. 'Fan Qui' meant, quite literally, 'Foreign Devil'. He had been told that this name, together with the word 'barbarian', was used by the Chinese to describe Europeans, even in direct conversation with them, but it was the first time he had heard it used to describe himself.

The next moment the child was peering warily in at the porthole again. For a few uncertain moments the dark eyes stared at him. Then the young girl smiled shyly, revealing a wide gap between two front teeth. 'Tik-wei is hungry. Give me some food . . . please.'

Luke gave the child an answering grin. She made a very appealing beggar. Taking up the ship-baked loaf of bread that had come with his meal, he passed it through the porthole. 'This should be enough to fill such a small belly.'

Two small hands came into sight and eagerly snatched the bread. Before she could take it, Luke called, 'Wait, Tik-wei.'

On a table in the cabin was a hairbrush. On the voyage from India it had fallen to the floor in a storm and Luke had trodden on it and broken the handle. He took the brush and handed it out to the girl.

'Here, if you want to become a successful beggar you'll need to tidy your hair – and wash your face while you're about it.'

He had to shout the last remark as Tik-wei's boat was bumped away from the side of *The Two Brothers* by other sampans, their occupants eagerly putting forward their own pleas for food. Soon grubby hands were held up to him and a dozen voices alternately pleaded for food and cursed their neighbours as more and more boat-people crowded in upon *The Two Brothers*.

Angrily, Luke slammed the port shut in disgust. Drawing the curtain, he sat down to finish his interrupted meal.

Luke was lying on his bunk reading when someone clattered down the ladder to the cabin flat. There was a knock at the door, and it opened far enough for a seaman to put his head inside the cabin. 'Cap'n Innes's compliments, Mr Trewarne. He's sent a boat to take you ashore.'

'At this time of night?' The breeze had strengthened, and *The Two Brothers* danced to its tune, snatching at the anchor chain. It was no night to take a trip in the darkness in a small boat. 'Won't whatever he wants keep until morning?'

'I wouldn't know,' replied the seaman cheerfully. 'I only know what the coxswain of the boat told me.'

Luke swung himself from his bunk, the movement sending rivulets of perspiration coursing down his limbs. It was hot and airless in the cabin. Now he had moved he felt the need to get up on deck quickly or he would collapse into a chair and begin panting like a hound.

Surprisingly, it was little cooler on deck. The wind, though by now quite fierce, was as hot as a dragon's breath. As Luke clambered down a ladder to the waiting longboat, the boat-swain of *The Two Brothers* called, 'You'll be better off ashore, Mr Trewarne. We're in for a big storm — a typhoon, I shouldn't wonder. Tell Cap'n Innes the barometer reading's already dropped off the scale. . . .'

The wind threw the remainder of his words back in his teeth as the longboat's crew strained at their oars and pulled away from the ship.

The boat bounced heavily across the choppy water on its way to the shore. Fortunately, it did not have far to travel. In a few minutes there was a scraping of gravel beneath the keel. The boat was run up on to a small beach and dragged clear of the water by a number of Chinese carrying flickering lanterns.

The seamen from *The Two Brothers* remained on the beach as Luke followed the Chinese along a narrow path that led up the hillside to the clump of trees where he had earlier seen McCulloch's house.

Soon, Luke saw lights shining into the night from unshuttered windows. The house was much larger than it had appeared from the ship. Ezra McCulloch had combined a comfortable dwelling-house with a warehouse, the whole building being constructed in the style of a fortified English manor-house.

A large belligerent man, Ezra McCulloch lolled in a chair in a downstairs room. He did no more than raise a hand in a drunken gesture when Luke was shown in. He and the captain of *The Two Brothers* had been drinking heavily, but Captain Innes acknowledged the boatswain's message soberly enough.

'Ay, I'm on my way back to the ship now,' he growled. 'Think yourself lucky that you're to be Mr McCulloch's guest tonight, laddie. There's a typhoon on its way. *The Two Brothers* will be an uncomfortable berth for a landlubber.'

Climbing heavily to his feet, the sea captain nodded to his host. 'I'll see you again when the storm has blown itself out, Ezra. In the meantime, think on what I suggested about the new markets farther along the coast. That's where the future lies for traders on the China station, believe me.'

Running a crumpled handkerchief around the neckband of his shirt, Obadiah Innes plunged out into the stormy night, a lantern-bearing Chinese servant scurrying to get ahead of him.

'So you're Dan Gemmell's new head clerk,' the merchant growled at Luke when Captain Innes had gone. 'You've brought a load of trouble along with you, by all accounts.'

Not sure whether McCulloch was serious, Luke retorted that he could hardly be blamed for an attack on two Chinese men-of-war by Ezra McCulloch's own ship.

Ezra McCulloch impatiently waved him into silence. 'I don't give a damn who's responsible. It's happened, and that's all there is about it.' The merchant slurred his words badly, but drinking had not dulled his thinking. 'Every trader in the Far East has known for years that one day it would come to this. The pity is that it had to happen when there isn't a British man-o'-war within a thousand miles.'

'Perhaps that's just as well,' said Luke thoughtfully. 'Given time, an incident involving a merchantman can be glossed over. A fight between warships could have far more serious consequences.'

'Speak in plain English, man. You mean it might lead to a war? So? It will take a war to make the Chinese realize they're not the only people on God's earth. But the fight is nothing. It's what caused it. The Chinese tried to stop *The Two Brothers* from going up-river because the Tsotang at Canton – he's the magistrate – has banned all European ships from going up-river to Whampoa. He says it's because we've been carrying opium there. The truth is that he's out to squeeze more money from us. God blast the Chinese! We've done our damnedest to trade normally with them, and had insult and humilation heaped upon us for our pains. The country is in a mess. Full of corrupt officials. Run on superstition and fear. But what can you expect? The Emperor claims he's a god and locks himself away from his own people. He spends his time painting flowers and writing poems that no one understands, living in a palace full of eunuchs who smell like tom cats. War? By God, if that's what it's going to take to drag them into the nineteenth century, then I say we should give it to them!'

Ezra McCulloch struggled to his feet and headed for a cabinet in a corner of the room. He refilled his glass from a bottle of brandy and, as an afterthought, poured one for Luke.

'You'll find out all about the bloody Chinese when you get up-river to Canton – though God only knows when that'll be. The Chinese can't even trade in a straightforward fashion. The Tsotang appoints one of his own merchants – a "Hong" – to be responsible for each of us "barbarians". Everything we buy and sell must go through him. That means we must accept his high prices. There's no one to be trusted in this God-forsaken country. Every trader is being bled white. . . .'

Looking around the room in which they were sitting, Luke listened to McCulloch's words with a great deal of scepticism. The room was furnished in a manner that would have been the envy of many a rich man in Europe. The walls were hung with a wide variety of valuable animal skins. Among them Luke recognized tiger, mountain leopard and sable. The floor was hidden by a huge colourful Persian rug, and antique vases and statuettes adorned tables and bureau tops about the room. Not all of Ezra McCulloch's profits were going into the pockets of the Chinese Hong.

The merchant saw Luke's glance and correctly read his thoughts. 'I've worked hard to get what I have. No damned Chinese is going to squeeze more out of me by sending warships after my merchantmen. To the victor go the spoils – and I'm making damn sure that Ezra McCulloch is always a winner.' He waved the brandy-glass at Luke. 'You'd do well to persuade Dan Gemmell to adopt the same attitude. Forget high and mighty principles. Dan's a fool to himself. Without opium he'll remain a poor man and be trusted by no one, European or Chinese.'

Ezra McCulloch took a swig of his brandy and frowned over the rim of the glass at Luke. 'This latest business is a damned nuisance – but no more than that, I promise you. If I can't use *The Two Brothers* for trading up to Canton, I'll transfer her general cargo to other boats and have them take it up-river – when trading's resumed. This ban will be hurting Dan Gemmell harder than me and the other traders. We have opium. I'll put the opium from *The Two Brothers* on the receiving ship and wait for customers to come to me. Either that or send Obadiah along the coast to sell it. That's what Jardine Matheson are doing. They have half a dozen fast clippers working to the north of here. But creeping around the coast of China, selling to smugglers, is not my idea of trading. Damn the Emperor again! Three thousand miles of coastline and he restricts trade to one tiny port. . . .'

Ezra McCulloch emptied a quarter of his drink down his throat. 'The trouble is that the Provincial Governor in Canton is due for promotion to the Imperial Court. Through the Tsotang he's trying to squeeze as much as he can from the Fan Qui before he goes. Last month he made all the ships arriving at Macau unload their cargoes and carry them up-river by open boat. By the time the goods arrived, what little hadn't been stolen had been ruined by rain and indifferent handling. The traders who complained had all their mer-chandise impounded for their pains! Dan Gemmell was one of them.'

Ezra McCulloch laughed and choked on his brandy. Wiping his chin with the back of his hand, he said, 'Damn fools! They'll learn. Sail direct to Whampoa, as I do. Ignore Macau and you cut out fifty per cent of your palm-greasing.'

'Even if it means sinking Chinese men-of-war?'

'Even that.' Ezra McCulloch's eyes narrowed. Leaning for-ward, he glared aggressively at Luke. 'Does that bother you? If it does, then Dan Gemmell's picked the wrong man to run his business for him. He needs a strong man – to do the things he himself has no stomach for.'

Luke shrugged his shoulders. Ezra McCulloch had a reputa-tion as a swashbuckling ruthless trader who allowed no one to stand in his way. He boasted that he would make his trading company the largest in the Far East – and no one doubted him to his face. Luke knew it would be foolish to antagonize McCulloch unnecessarily when he was in such an aggressive and drunken mood. Once Luke reached Canton he would have little to do with Ezra McCulloch. Better by far to humour him now. 'Of course sinking Chinese men-of-war bothers me. It affects profits. Which costs less, paying off the Chinese officials at Macau – or paying to have cargo taken up to Canton under guard?'

Ezra McCulloch continued to stare, but some of the belligerence had left him. Luke was speaking a language he understood: the language of profit and loss. 'I don't know,' he grumbled. 'You're the one being paid to make Dan Gemmell's trading profitable. You work it out; but, whatever you do, don't kowtow to these damned yellow savages. . . .'

'Do my people make you so angry yet again, Hau-ye?'

The words were English, but they were spoken in the singsong style of the Chinese and they referred to McCulloch as 'Lord'. Unnoticed, a Chinese girl had silently entered the room. She had been there for some minutes watching Luke, but he had not been aware of her until she spoke. Dressed in colourful silks, she was tiny and dainty. Even with her hair piled high on her head in the style of the Manchu girls of the north, she stood no more than five feet tall. Luke thought she was one of the most exquisite girls he had ever seen. He scrambled respectfully to his feet as she advanced across the room.

But the girl looked only at Ezra McCulloch. When she reached his side, she dropped down on her knees and took his hand in hers. 'It is not good you should upset yourself so, Hau-ye.'

'How can I help it? I'm living in a land where they think time has stood still for five hundred years.' Ezra McCulloch gestured impatiently for Luke to sit down.

Luke's open admiration had not been missed by the Scots trader. Reaching out, he cupped the girl's face in his hand, forcing her head back. 'I've told you before about coming into the room when I'm discussing business.' Without releasing his grip, Ezra McCulloch turned her head until Luke could see the pain on her face. 'This is Lo Asan. Before I came along she was being groomed for a useless life in the harem of the poncing Emperor. Now she's mine, paid for with damn near half a cargo of prime Patna opium. Don't go getting any ideas while you're here.'

Releasing his cruel grip on her face, Ezra McCulloch pushed her from him. 'She's an investment for the future. Lo Asan

20

has a large family, each of whom holds a high office in the Government. One day they will open the door to China for the McCulloch Trading Company, while Jardine Matheson are still searching for deserted creeks in which to land their opium and Dan Gemmell is counting farthings to see if he's made a profit.'

Ezra McCulloch sank back in his chair and leered at Luke. 'In the meantime, the waiting isn't unpleasant.'

Luke made no reply. Suddenly, there was a loud crash from somewhere outside and the doors and windows began to rattle alarmingly. It sounded as though the wild night wind was trying to smash its way into the house.

'Damn! That new window must have gone. I knew they should have shuttered up for this wind.' Struggling to his feet, Ezra McCulloch waved Luke back to his seat. 'Stay here. I'm not having you spy on everything I have stored away. Ask Lo Asan some questions about Canton. She lived there for a few years. I'll only be gone a few minutes.'

Ezra McCulloch hurried from the room, leaving Luke alone with Lo Asan. For a while there was an uncomfortable silence between them, then:

'You speak. . . .'

'I believe. . . .'

They both spoke at once, but the laugh that followed as a result took away the awkwardness that lay between them.

'You speak very good English,' said Luke. 'Isn't that unusual for a girl . . . in China?'

'Perhaps. But I live this house more than a year now. I have little else to do.' Lo Asan spoke a winsomely attractive, clipped form of English. Suddenly she switched from English to Chinese. 'But I can use the language of my people with you. I am told you speak it well. I know, too, that you teach good manners to our children – and instruct them how to beg.'

For a moment Luke looked at her blankly, then he remembered the face at the porthole of *The Two Brothers* and he smiled. 'News is a speedy traveller here.'

'Nothing that a foreigner does in China remains a secret for very long. You will do well to remember this.'

Before Luke could ask her to explain her apparent warning, there was considerable activity outside the window as a group of Chinese servants struggled to place heavy wooden shutters into position. Eventually they were successful, and Ezra McCulloch came back to the room, his hair dishevelled by the wind.

Picking up his drink, the merchant looked suspiciously from Luke to Lo Asan, and back again. 'It was as I thought. The wind had blown out a window. I don't usually entertain visitors here, but you'll be more comfortable than sitting out a typhoon aboard *The Two Brothers*. The last I heard, Dan Gemmell was in the mission hospital in Canton. As you can't get there I'll have you taken to Macau the moment the typhoon has blown itself out.'

'No, there's nothing for me in Macau. If Dan Gemmell is ill in Canton, he'll have need of me. There must be some way to get up-river.'

Ezra McCulloch looked at Luke speculatively. 'If you worked for me, I'd smuggle you up-river with some fishermen, but I know no one likely to take such a chance for Dan Gemmell.'

'He has made friends with Soo Tik-wei,' said Lo Asan quickly. 'Her father can be trusted.'

Ezra McCulloch snorted. Still looking at Luke, he said, 'I've yet to meet the Chinese I'd trust farther than I could see him — especially one who puts opium before all else. But if you're determined to get to Canton he's probably your only chance.'

'I'll ask Kuei to travel with them. She will not allow anything to go wrong.'

Only now did McCulloch shift his glance to Lo Asan. 'Ah, yes! Your water-gipsy friend. I was forgetting she's Soo Fang's daughter.' He shrugged his shoulders. 'All right, go ahead and make the arrangements. It will keep you amused.'

To Luke, Ezra McCulloch said, 'If you're caught, Trewarne, I'll deny any knowledge of the whole business. Having *The Two Brothers* run into trouble is all the bad luck I need this year.'

He suddenly chuckled. He would give a great deal to see Dan Gemmell's face if he learned that his new chief clerk's passage up-river had been paid for with opium — for that was the payment Soo Fang would demand. But McCulloch said nothing to Luke. It was a revelation he would save for another day.

Ezra McCulloch suddenly lost his humour and frowned at Luke. 'In return you'll keep a still tongue about anything you've seen here, Trewarne. If any rumours start, I'll know where to look.'

Luke knew exactly what the trader was talking about. Ezra McCulloch was a married man with a wife and daughter only forty miles away, across the Pearl River, in Macau.

Three

FOR two days and nights the typhoon waged a fierce lone battle around the island of Hong Kong. During lulls in the senseless onslaught, the rain eased and visibility momentarily improved. On these brief occasions Luke could see *The Two Brothers* bucking and pitching in the small bay. Tugging frantically at the anchors holding her at head and stern, the ship reminded Luke of a wild boar he had once seen in the Indian hill country. Chased by hunters until it was cornered, exhausted but still angry, the boar had been secured by one rope after another until it was safe for the hunters to approach and stab it to death with their spears.

Unlike the unfortunate boar, *The Two Brothers* won her battle. On the third day of his stay in the McCulloch house, Luke awoke to a morning so calm there might never have been a storm at all. The sky above the distant mainland hills was a clear and spectacular blue, and outside the hillside house there was not sufficient breeze remaining to disturb a single leaf on the trees and bushes.

Ezra McCulloch took the opportunity to cross the bay to Kowloon, no more than a mile distant. He took Obadiah Innes with him, to discuss business with an opium dealer. Before leaving, McCulloch told Luke to be ready to leave Hong Kong that night. Lo Asan had arranged for him to board the Soo family's fishing sampan after dark, when inquisitive eyes would not see him.

Luke spent the day in the company of Lo Asan. With Ezra McCulloch away it was not necessary for her to guard her every word and action, and she chattered incessantly, speaking sometimes in English, at other times in Chinese. Lo Asan talked about nothing in particular, but it did not take Luke long to realize that in the course of their conversations she was learning a great deal about him. At the same time she told him nothing of herself. When he laughingly taxed her with this, she candidly admitted it was true.

'You will be going to Canton with my very good friend, Kuei. She is specially nice girl. You will be on the sampan with her three days. All that time you all in great danger. You were on *The Two Brothers* when it had fight with ships of the Emperor. Many were killed. That is bad. If you are captured and recognized, it will mean death for you. Such an end is not dishonourable for a man, perhaps. For Kuei and little Tik-wei capture would be far worse. Men of Emperor's navy are no better than the pirates they are supposed to fight. They do not honour women. Kuei's father only takes you because I ask him. I must be sure you are not a man to do foolish things and put everyone in danger.'

'Well . . . ? Are you satisfied now?'

Lo Asan placed a hand gently on Luke's arm and smiled up at him. 'You very quiet man. Quiet men not easy to know. But is better to travel into danger with quiet man than one who makes much noise. I think Kuei will learn more of you than I. You must trust her, Luke. She and her father are of the Hoklo people. McCulloch Hau-ye calls them "water-gipsies". It is true; but no one knows the river better.'

Luke boarded Soo Fang's sampan late that night from a small beach half a mile from the house. Dressed in Chinese fishermen's garb, he was guided to the spot by Lo Asan. Before leaving the house, he had been given last-minute instructions by McCulloch. The trader then handed him a bulging pouch. It contained opium for Soo Fang. Only then did Luke learn the price of his passage to Canton. He could not raise any objections at this stage. Opium was the price demanded by Soo Fang; McCulloch had agreed to pay. Luke was warned to give the fisherman only a limited amount each day — 'to keep him going'. The bulk of the opium would be handed over when the journey had been successfully accomplished.

Just before the boat was pushed away in the darkness, Lo Asan leaned inside and, to Luke's great surprise, kissed him gently on the cheek. 'Take good care of Kuei,' she whispered. 'I am very fond of her. You will be, too, when you know her better.' Seconds later the boat slipped out into the waters of the natural harbour.

Luke was glad Ezra McCulloch had not come to see him off. Had he witnessed Lo Asan's innocent farewell gesture, Luke felt certain he would have made her suffer as a result.

Unseen in the stern of the sampan, Kuei worked the single oar from side to side in the water, using it both to steer and to propel the small vessel away from the shore. When they reached deeper, less sheltered waters Soo Fang and his daughter hoisted a small sail, both of them stepping carefully around Luke in the darkness as they carried out their work. Minutes later, the boat was gliding silently over the water, heading for the Pearl River estuary.

Soo Fang and his two daughters sat hunched up in the stern of the sampan, no more than vague shapes to Luke. He occupied the small arched canopy in the centre of the boat which would serve as sleeping-quarters and was the vessel's only shelter against the hot sun of the day. When he judged they were well clear of the shore Luke called, 'Is there anything I can do to help. . . ?'

'Yes. Until it is light enough for ears to hear only what eyes can see, you will make no noise.'

As little Tik-wei giggled at her sister's sharp words, Soo Fang remonstrated with his elder daughter for the way in which she had spoken to their passenger. Luke himself did not know whether he ought to be angry or amused. Certainly, he had heard no woman speak to a man in such a manner since he had been in the Far East.

Towards dawn, lulled by the soft lapping of water against the hull of the sampan, Luke dozed off. He woke suddenly and sat up, momentarily confused by his surroundings. Not far away, Tik-wei was curled up on a small mat, sleeping. Nearer to him, crouching on his haunches, Soo Fang was looking anxiously at Luke, his fingers nervously fighting each other as he clasped his hands together in his lap.

'You have opium for me?' he pleaded abjectly.

Luke nodded and picked up the bag he had been using as a pillow. The opium was wrapped in an oiled cloth. Breaking off a sticky piece the size of a small walnut, he handed it to Soo Fang. The fisherman snatched it without thanks. Taking it in cupped hands, he carried it carefully to the bow of the boat where a small lamp burned. Beside it lay an opium pipe. The pipe was made from a thick tube of bamboo, into the side of which a smaller tube had been inserted to form the pipe bowl. Luke watched in fascination as Soo Fang moulded a small piece of opium with trembling hands. Rolling it into a tiny ball, he heated the opium carefully over the flame of the lamp before inserting it into the pipe bowl. Now he lay down on his side in the bottom of the boat and, holding the pipe bowl over

26

the flame, inhaled deeply. His mouth completely covered the opening of the bamboo tube, and Soo Fang removed it only to allow the smoke to trickle slowly from nose and mouth.

It was the first time Luke had seen opium being smoked. He watched in fascination as the soporific drug took effect and Soo Fang's strained expression softened into a half-smile.

'Are you so happy to see a man smoke your opium you do not wish to lose one moment of his misery?'

Startled, Luke looked up to see Kuei standing over him holding out a bowl of rice and vegetables.

It had been dark when Luke boarded the sampan, and he was seeing her for the first time. She was tall for a Chinese girl. Tall and slim. Her long black hair, plaited in a single thick queue, hung down her back as far as her waist. The stark simple style accentuated her high-cheekboned face and the smoothness of her neck. She was a striking girl rather than a beautiful one, but she carried herself with a haughtiness he had not expected to find in a fisherman's daughter.

Taking the bowl of food from her, Luke said easily, 'Your father looks contented enough to me. I wish I could cast aside my cares as easily.'

'You carry only dreams for *other* men in your bag? You have only to reach inside to share his "contentment". But no, you will not do that. It is not the Fan Qui way. Only Chinese dreams can bring you riches. Watch my father very carefully when next he comes to you for opium to put in his "pipe of dreams". See his hands tremble as he tries to control the hunger for opium. Keep him waiting and the man will become a child —a child who whines that worms crawl in his stomach and rats gnaw at his shoulders. See this—as I have many, many times—*then* tell me my father is contented.'

Kuei looked at Luke angrily. 'He has known no happiness since opium became his master. Before that he was a simple fisherman. His dreams were of a fine day and a good catch of fish. He had pride in himself and his family. *That* was contentment. It will never come to him again. All he has now is a hunger that can never be satisfied. Hunger for the opium you barbarians bring to our country.'

Kuei spat the last words at Luke with so much venom that he was genuinely alarmed. This was the girl who was supposed to be *helping* him! A girl who held his life in her hands!

'With so much hatred for Europeans in your heart, why are you taking me to Canton?'

Her outburst over, much of the fire died away inside Kuei. She turned from Luke and crouched over the small cooking-lamp on which she had been warming the rice and vegetables. As she bent down, her short grey coolie-jacket rode high up her back, exposing a wide band of smooth skin and the beginning of the swelling of her small breasts.

'I help you because it is Lo Asan's wish.'

'Lo Asan is herself living with a man who trades in opium. He paid for her with opium.'

'The father of Lo Asan is the same as Soo Fang. He dreams . . . or he dies. Lo Asan is very ashamed that she was paid for by the misery of so many of our people. But she is a good daughter. She had to obey her father. Even so, Lo Asan believes she will one day make McCulloch love her so much he will sell no more opium to our people. That will bring much good to our country and make her very happy.'

Kuei spoke the words without conviction. They were Lo Asan's, not her own. She did not believe that the ambitious McCulloch would ever cease his trade in opium.

Luke was equally sceptical. Opium was the one certain saleable commodity in a very uncertain and difficult trading situation. Lo Asan might be an exceptionally intelligent and attractive girl – but Ezra McCulloch was a determined and ruthless trader.

Luke would have liked to talk some more with Kuei, but she went back to the stern oar, leaving Luke to think about the hatred she so obviously bore for all European traders. Moodily, he looked out across the waters of the estuary to the shore, where terraced cultivation clung tenaciously to the steep-sloped hillsides, utilizing every square foot of soil. Below the hills, the occupants of peasant farms and walled villages were beginning their long day, the muffled complaints of their wide-horned oxen carrying across the water.

On her sleeping-mat Tik-wei stirred and woke, stretching lazily and rubbing sleep from her eyes. She smiled shyly at Luke. Self-consciously she ran the brush he had given her through her hair and then scrambled past him to collect her breakfast-dish from the small heating-lamp. When she returned, she sat cross-legged opposite Luke and began eating, using only two thin wooden sticks as eating-utensils. She shovelled food into her mouth at an incredible rate as Luke struggled to master the simple utensils. Eventually, after some amused tuition from Tik-wei, he managed to balance a little food on the 'chopsticks' long enough to bring it to his mouth.

Before he had finished the long-drawn-out meal, Kuei called out, 'A junk is coming down-river. I am not sure, but I think it is flying an Imperial banner. Tik-wei, hide the pipe and the lamp – quickly! Then wake Father. Hurry now.'

Tik-wei scrambled to the bow of the boat and began shaking Soo Fang. He did not move. The little girl's shaking became more urgent, but still Soo Fang lay on the wooden deck of the fishing vessel, oblivious to everything about him. Luke rose to go to Tik-wei's assistance, but Kuei's cry stopped him.

'Are you a fool? Stay where you are. You must not show yourself. The junk is turning this way.'

Luke was alarmed. He was dressed as a Chinese fisherman, but his disguise would not stand up to more than a cursory glance. If the junk came too close, he would be quickly recognized for what he was – a Fan Qui.

Kuei was aware of it, too. 'Lie down on the sleeping-mat,' she called to Luke. 'Tik-wei, wrap it around him. Be quick about it. We have only a few minutes.'

Luke did as Kuei told him, lying down on the coarse rush mat beneath the low curved canopy. Moments later Tik-wei tucked the mat about his body, hiding him from head to toe.

It was hot beneath the matting, and within seconds Luke was soaked with perspiration. Running from his forehead, it collected on his eyelids. When he foolishly blinked, the salt moisture irritated his eyes almost beyond endurance. Gritting his teeth, Luke resisted the urge to raise his hand and rub his eyes clear. Next, he had an overwhelming urge to sneeze, but then he felt the solid bump of another vessel coming alongside the sampan. Luke forgot all his trifling problems, his perspiration turning to ice.

Then he heard a man's voice, calling to Kuei, asking her business.

'We go to Canton from Lan-tau.' Kuei named the large island to the west of Hong Kong.

'Wake your father. Let him speak for you.'

'My father is ill,' said Kuei, adopting the exaggerated humility expected of a girl addressing an officer of the Imperial Navy. 'He has the sickness that eats the skin and fires the body.'

'Aiyee!' Luke heard the chorus of consternation from listening crew members on board the junk. Kuei had described the symptoms of smallpox, a fatal disease for which there was no known treatment.

'I see no marks on the skin of your father.' There was uncertainty in the voice of the Chinese officer. 'He lies like a man who has been smoking opium.'

'That is how our brother was, at first,' Kuei replied tremulously, apparently on the verge of tears. 'He had the fever and we could not wake him. Now he lies dead, wrapped in a mat, here in the boat. Please, come into the boat and examine his body.'

Luke drew in his breath sharply. Kuei was taking a desperate risk in her bid to convince the Chinese naval officer.

'Are you mad, girl? the officer retorted. 'Would you have me bring the burning fever on board one of Admiral Kuan's ships? Where do you go with your brother and father?'

'To Canton, so they may lie at rest beside their ancestors.'

'You are a dutiful daughter. Tsotang Teng will not thank me for allowing you to carry fever into his province, but I am here to defend the land of the King of Heaven against his enemies, not to protect a magistrate from foolish Hoklos. Go in peace.'

'Thank you. May you bring great honour to the King of Heaven.'

As water began to slap against the bow of the fishing sampan once again, Luke relaxed. Before long he again became aware of the discomfort and the heat. Then the matting was pulled away from his face by Tik-wei, and Kuei called, 'You can uncover yourself now – but stay where you are. The junk is not far away, and there may be more of them on the river.'

Luke extricated himself from the sleeping-mat and wiped the perspiration from his face and body, grateful for the faintest of breezes that blew through the open-ended shelter.

He looked back to where Kuei was helping the sampan on its way with powerful sweeps of the stern oar. 'You did very well back there. Thank you.'

'You owe me nothing. I lied for the sake of my father.'

She had begun to show her earlier arrogance, and in a bid to put their relationship on a more light-hearted footing Luke asked, 'Weren't you even the *slightest* bit concerned for *my* safety, Kuei?'

He was smiling, but Kuei stopped working the oar and threw

him a contemptuous glance. She pointed to an island that rose high out of the water a mile away across the estuary. 'You see that place? That is Lin-tin island. Before our navy junks came to the Pearl River there were sometimes twelve, sometimes twenty barbarian opium ships there. How much misery do you think they caused? How many families did they break up for the sake of a few dollars? This morning you told me I have hatred in my heart for your people. Now you tell me – why do the Fan Qui hate *us* so much that you destroy us in this way? What have we done to you? Should you be surprised that I hate all Fan Qui?'

Kuei's frank reply both angered and hurt Luke. He was honest enough to admit to himself that he wanted her to feel some concern for him. She was a most unusual girl with a remarkable depth of feeling. It hurt his pride to know that she felt nothing but contempt for him. Not that he could really blame her. Opium had all but destroyed her way of life – and Luke had a guilty conscience about the opium trade. He had worked in the East India Company's auction rooms during the yearly opium sales, when opium was sold on the open market – on condition that it would only be traded in China. Thirty-five thousand chests had been sold the previous year. One thousand seven hundred and fifty tons of raw opium. To the Company it represented a profit of five hundred per cent on their investment. To smokers like Soo Fang . . . ? This was a facet of the trade that rarely came up in conversation in India. Luke had once tried to broach the subject, but one of the more senior Company employees had ended the discussion with the knowledgeable statement that opium smoking was no more harmful than drinking alcohol.

Now, sitting in a sampan on the Pearl River, with an opium addict unconscious in the bottom of the boat, Luke wondered whether the Europeans in India really believed their own lies. It was more probable that they sought to hide the distress that opium so blatantly brought to many families in China. Luke tried to comfort himself with the thought that opium was also used as a medicine to bring relief to many sufferers. Its medicinal value must surely outweigh its misuse by a few weak men. Opium financed a great part of the East India Company's Indian administration. Such a large-scale operation had to be sanctioned by the British Government. It would never allow the continuance of a trade that brought such misery to so many ignorant people. . . .

Luke's self-justifying argument lost all its force when he looked again at the still form of Soo Fang lying in the bottom of the sampan.

Soo Fang did not regain consciousness until the early afternoon. Then he sat huddled in the bow of the boat until Kuei steered away from the middle of the estuary, heading for one of the many islets of thick bamboo breaking up the river current away from the main channel.

'Soon we will be in a narrow part of the river,' explained Kuei curtly, in answer to Luke's question. 'There are forts on both banks and many inquisitive eyes. From here it will be better for us to move only at night. We will rest for a few hours first.'

As the sampan nosed into the tangled bamboo, Luke helped Kuei and Tik-wei to pull it forward until the bow nuzzled against a low ridge of mud and was effectively hidden from the view of anyone on the river or the shore.

They slept until the sun went down and a full plump moon rose over the distant hills to the east. It cast a warm romantic light through the grass-like leaves of the tall bamboos – but there was little romance on board the sampan. Soo Fang moved as a man living a bad dream. Kuei made it quite clear that she held Luke to blame for his condition. Her attitude made Luke angry but, rather than risk a scene with her, he left the sampan and went ashore on the hard mud of the islet.

Pushing his way through the tangled bamboo, Luke reached a small clearing on slightly higher ground. From here he could just make out the sails of a number of sampans, painted silver by the light of the moon, well out in the centre of the river. They were part of a small fishing fleet, heading down-river towards the mouth of the estuary. Inland, dim yellow lights flickered here and there in the small scattered houses of the Chinese peasant farmers. Farther up-river Luke saw a cluster of brighter lights. He guessed it must be the first of the Bogue forts, surrounded by the huts of the camp followers. Ezra McCulloch had told him of a great deal of activity hereabouts in recent weeks. The garrisons of the larger of the river forts had been reinforced by Tartar soldiers, newly arrived from the northern borders of China. Unlike the British Army, the Tartars did not travel alone. They had no settled home to which they could return at the end of a campaign. For them, home was wherever they happened to be. Where they went, there, too, went their wives and children – together with all their animals and belongings. Consequently, far from being isolated fortresses guarding the river approaches to Canton, the river forts now resembled the castles of medieval England, surrounded and half-hidden by the hastily erected shanties of their followers.

Luke stayed looking out over the moonlight-bathed countryside for about an hour. By then he was beginning to be bothered by the attentions of a host of angry mosquitoes. They appeared to resent his presence as much as did Kuei.

He was about to make his way back to the sampan when he heard someone crashing noisily through the bamboo towards him. Luke's imagination ran riot and he tensed, waiting for what was to come. Then the figure of Soo Fang stumbled into the small clearing.

'For God's sake, man! What do you think you're doing crashing around like that? On a night like this sound carries for miles. They must have heard you right across the river!' In his relief and anger, Luke had spoken in English. Realizing his error, he said more quietly in Chinese, 'Is something wrong? Are the others all right?'

Soo Fang looked at Luke stupidly for a few moments, then he said, 'I must have more opium. I am a very sick man.'

Luke looked at the fisherman in disgust. 'You made all that noise just to come and ask me for more opium? Come along, you'd better return to the boat with me.'

'Wait. . . .'

Luke shook off Soo Fang's hand and pushed his way through the bamboo towards the sampan. After only the slightest hesitation, Soo Fang hurried after him.

Kuei was in a state of near-panic. She had not seen her father leave the sampan and did not know he was the cause of the noise on the island. Soo Fang brushed aside her chiding and again urged Luke to give him more opium.

'Please!' He took Luke's hand and clung to it in desperation. 'I have a sick pain in my belly. I *must* have opium.'

'You can have opium in the morning. We'll be getting under way soon, travelling up-river towards Canton. You'll need to look and act like a fisherman if we're to arouse no suspicion. You'll be no use to anyone lying in the bottom of the boat.

Tomorrow doesn't matter. You'll be able to sleep for as long as you wish.'

'How can I fish when my belly is on fire? Please, I beg you. Give me opium . . . or I die.'

Kuei came to stand by her father, and in the bright light of the moon there was no mistaking her expression of contempt when she looked at Luke. He was being blamed for Soo Fang's abject condition. But it was to her father she spoke.

'Have you so lost your pride that you beg from a Fan Qui? Do you forget you are Hoklo – one of the boat-people? Will you behave as a beggar from the alleyways of the city? Come, Father. We must take this barbarian to Canton because I have made a promise to Lo Asan. But we will not return to Hong Kong. We will go away. Back to the home of your fathers, in Fu-kien. There we will cure you of the need for opium and forget we ever saw the Fan Qui. One day the Emperor will drive every one of them far from our lands. Then we will be as we once were. . . .'

Soo Fang was not listening. He had seen the angry look Luke had given to Kuei and, in his desperation, had misinterpreted it.

'I *plead* with you for opium. I am only a poor fisherman, but all I have is yours to take if you will only end my misery. My boat. . . .' Soo Fang licked his lips and looked quickly down at the wooden planking beneath his feet. 'My daughter. . . .'

Kuei's mouth dropped open and she looked at her father in horror. When she spoke her voice came out as a whisper of disbelief. 'You offer me to a Fan Qui? You would give me to him for his opium? No, Father. Please. . . .'

'Didn't you tell me that a daughter must obey her father?' Luke said, quietly mocking her. He had been on the receiving end of her sharp tongue since the voyage up-river had begun. Her present discomfort was something new. 'Is Lo Asan so much more of a daughter to *her* father?'

Soo Fang clung eagerly to Luke's hand. 'You want Kuei? You will give me opium?'

Luke shifted his gaze to the wretched fisherman. He would be no use to them tonight in this condition. Far better for all of them if he lay quietly in the bottom of the sampan, drugged into silence.

'Yes, Soo Fang. I'll give you opium. Here. . . .'

Opening the bag he carried, Luke dropped the whole ball

34

of opium at Soo Fang's feet. He stepped back as the fisherman dropped to his knees, grovelling in the shadows for the drug that meant more to him than his own family.

'You give my father only what is his – and for this you would take his daughter? Truly, you are a trader, barbarian. McCulloch will need to beware of you. One day you will take all that is his in the same way.'

'Perhaps I shall also take McCulloch's ways and teach you to be a little more respectful.' Luke remembered the trader's cruel grip on Lo Asan's face when she had first come into the room where he and Luke were talking. But Luke spoke only to taunt Kuei. Her father's desperate offer to him had pierced the shield of toughness she had built around herself. Luke had seen her vulnerability and taken advantage of it. He was relieved to learn she was as feminine as any other girl, but he had no intention of hurting her any more. He had never taken Soo Fang's offer seriously for a single moment.

Luke had reckoned without Kuei's own peculiar pride. In truth, he had learned the language of the Chinese well, but he knew little of the complicated code of honour by which they lived. He had suggested that Kuei was less honourable than Lo Asan. The suggestion had not been made seriously, but it *had* been made. It was necessary for Kuei to prove herself as worthy a daughter as Lo Asan.

Soo Fang had disgraced his family before this barbarian. She would not add to his dishonour, but she would obey on her own terms.

'You need teach me nothing. My father gave me to you, so I must be yours – but only for tonight. Four catties of opium will not buy me for life. . . .'A catty was about twenty-eight ounces. A ball of opium weighed seven pounds. 'Neither will I allow my sister to see my shame. We will go on the island. Come.'

Kuei turned from him and stepped over the side of the sampan on to the mud islet. Here she paused and ordered Tik-wei to look after their father, being careful to ensure he made no sound. Wide-eyed and bewildered by what was happening, Tik-wei could only nod her head.

As Kuei pushed her way through the bamboos, Luke's first instinct was to call her back, to tell her he would not take advantage of her addict father's outrageous offer. But a new and overpowering emotion had begun to stir deep inside him.

Kuei was an attractive girl and she excited him. Did it matter what he did tonight? Once they reached Canton he would probably never see her again. Besides, had she wanted to, it would have been easy for her to laugh off her father's offer to him. . . .

Luke stepped from the sampan and followed the soft-footed girl through the bamboos.

In the clearing where Soo Fang had found Luke earlier, Kuei stopped and turned to face him.

'You want me here?'

Luke's perspiration owed nothing to the heat of the night. He nodded, glad his face was shadowed from the light of the ascending moon. He still did not believe that Kuei would really go through with this. Then he sucked in his breath as she raised her arms and drew the cotton jacket over her head. Kuei wore nothing beneath it, and her small breasts heaved with the emotion that was in her. Next she reached down and wriggled out of her trousers to stand before him as naked as a new-born child.

The sight of her body in the soft moonlight sent the blood pounding in Luke's ears, and he was aware of his masculinity as he had never been before. Not daring to speak, he took a half-step towards her. Reaching out, he touched her shoulders. Slowly he traced the roundness of her body down as far as her waist, and she quivered beneath his hands.

Her chin rose, and she looked up into his face. 'You will need to tell me what to do. . . . I have not done this before.'

Luke's hands dropped away from her body as shame replaced all other emotions. His mouth opened and closed stupidly as he sought the words he wanted to say. They would not come. Turning abruptly from her, he stumbled blindly back to the sampan.

Behind him, Kuei trembled violently for a full minute before she sought her clothes and began to put them on again. She had won another battle with the Fan Qui, and she smiled. But it was not a smile of victory. The barbarian's hands had aroused feelings in her for which she would always know nothing but shame.

four

WITH a lantern attached to the stern, the sampan made steady progress up-river towards Canton. Soo Fang slept heavily inside the shelter while Luke hung over the side of the vessel with Tik-wei, making a pretence of fishing. Behind them Kuei toiled at the oar, pushing the boat against the sluggish tide. Along the great river, for as far as could be seen, fishing-lights winked at their dull reflection in the muddy river. Fish, attracted to the lights as moths to a flame, were swiftly netted and shaken out into the bottoms of the boats.

Kuei was propelling their boat much faster than any of the other sampans, so they did not catch a great many fish. Nevertheless, they did net a number of small ones, much to Tik-wei's delight.

More than once, the sampan was hailed by another fisherman. On such occasions, Kuei shouted a reply that satisfied the other fisherman and, as often as not, left him chuckling at the sauciness of the Hoklo girl. All the same, Kuei kept them as far from the other boats as was possible. In the moonlight Luke was no more than a shadowy figure, just another fisherman busy with his work.

Fortunately, they met up with no more Imperial Navy vessels — but once they were overtaken by an unlit craft that was long and slim, with an impressive bank of oars on either side. At its passing, Kuei whispered urgently for Tik-wei to extinguish the fishing-lamp and she hurriedly veered away from the silent vessel.

In answer to Luke's question, she said cryptically, 'Pirates.'

Fortunately for all of them, the pirates were after bigger game than the tiny Hoklo fishing boat. That night one of the riverside villages was raided and razed to the ground. It was no more than half a mile from a small fort manned by the part-time soldiers of the green-banner regiment of China, but the militia officers could not persuade a single 'soldier' to go to the aid of the villagers in the darkness.

Shortly before dawn, Kuei once again steered the sampan into the shelter of a bamboo-covered island for the day. This time it was a horseshoe-shaped island with a clear pool of water at the centre, hidden from outside view by the drooping bamboo.

Soo Fang was conscious again, but he sat in the bow of the boat, behaving as might a man with a colossal hangover. Staring unseeingly ahead of him, he seemed unaware of his surroundings.

Luke doubted whether he would sleep. He was still confused and upset by the events of the previous night. Kuei had said nothing to him since then, although she behaved perfectly normally in all other respects. In spite of his misgivings, Luke lay down on the coarse mat and within minutes had fallen into a deep and exhausted sleep.

He opened his eyes with a start, woken by an unusual sound. He lay still for a few moments, listening. The sun was shining in through the open end of the shelter, having already coursed three-quarters of the sky. The heat and humidity were almost unbearable. Once again Luke heard the sound that had wakened him. It was the splashing of water, this time accompanied by a half-stifled giggle.

Crawling from the cramped shelter, Luke stepped over the prostrate form of Soo Fang, shielded from the sun by the partially raised sail. Rising to his feet, Luke immediately saw the reason for the girls' merriment. Tik-wei and Kuei were swimming in the pool at the heart of the bamboo island. Both girls were naked and enjoying themselves as though they were in a safe, and private, garden.

As Tik-wei paddled about in a vain attempt to catch her more agile sister, Kuei turned on to her back, long black hair streaming out in the water about her, and urged Tik-wei on to greater efforts.

Kuei saw Luke watching from the sampan. For a fleeting moment the smile left her face; then she splashed a final handful of water at her sister and swam strongly to the sampan, hoisting herself on board with one quick agile movement. Making no attempt to hide her nakedness from Luke, she stood with her head tilted over the side of the sampan and wrung water from her long hair.

When Luke turned away in embarrassment, Kuei's low voice called mockingly to him, 'Is my body so ugly that it is only in the darkness you dare to look upon it – barbarian?'

Luke turned to look at her again. This time he stared at her long and hard, enjoying the sight of her body glistening with a million pearls of water that enhanced all yet hid nothing. He had the satisfaction of seeing her cheeks redden, but his own stomach muscles had contracted violently. He could only stammer, 'No, Kuei. Only my thoughts are ugly.'

Bending down, Kuei picked up the heap of drab grey clothing and moved away to the shelter. Last night the young barbarian had thought to humiliate her; now he deeply regretted it. Of that she was certain. Not only had she saved 'face', but she was also now well ahead of him on points scored. As she dressed and plaited her hair into a thick black queue, Kuei watched Luke through the loosely woven matting of the sleeping-shelter. Tik-wei swam to the edge of the sampan and reached up a hand for him to help her aboard. He lifted her easily, then recoiled in mock dismay as Tik-wei shook her head, flicking water over him. Kuei smiled. She had given the barbarian a hard time on the way up-river, blaming him for all the trans-gressions of the Fan Qui – of Ezra McCulloch in particular. In truth, McCulloch was the only other barbarian she had ever met. She did not like him. He was cruel to Lo Asan and made her unhappy, although Lo Asan would never admit it to anyone. Lo Asan was a Manchu girl, one of the ruling class to which the Emperor himself belonged. She was much too good for the big Fan Qui. Indeed, she was too good for anyone in this part of China. No, Kuei did not like McCulloch. But this one . . .? Kuei smiled again. She thought she could learn to like this bar-barian, 'Luke', very much. Now the event was behind her, she was ready to admit that the way he had looked at her body had excited her beyond words. And when he touched her . . . ! His hand had burned like fire, yet he had not taken her. She was glad. It was not yet time.

Kuei's father stirred and groaned, and her good humour faded quickly. Soo Fang tried to climb to his feet. Falling, he crawled to the side of the sampan and hanging his head down to within inches of the water, he retched noisily.

'Tik-wei! Fetch some food . . . and tea.'

When the retching died away, Kuei struggled to drag her father back into the boat. Luke went to her assistance and was shocked by the frailty of the fisherman. His bones were as light and as brittle as a pigeon's. Lifting Soo Fang bodily, Luke placed him inside the shelter and watched as both girls brought food and drink. While Tik-wei held the head of her emaciated father in her hands, Kuei tried to coax him to take food and drink.

Eventually, Kuei's efforts proved successful. Soo Fang ate his first food since the voyage up-river began, but for the remainder of that day he sat in the shade of the sleeping-shelter, staring vacantly before him. Even when Tik-wei sat down beside him and leaned affectionately against his shoulder, Soo Fang made no sign that he knew she was there. Stupefied by too much opium, his senses needed constant prodding before they reacted.

Luke wanted to ask Kuei when and where her father had begun smoking opium, but she seemed to be in a happier frame of mind today, and he did not wish to upset her yet again.

When the sun sank into a blanket of many colours in the western sky, Kuei eased the sampan out of the bamboos, and Soo Fang had recovered sufficiently to be able to raise the sail with Luke's help. They needed to catch some fish quickly before they resumed their journey. The river narrowed soon, and it was likely that other sampans would pass close enough for their occupants to see what was being carried. In any other circumstances, the next few hours would have been extremely pleasant, as they fished the river, helped on their way by a breeze from the sea which was cooler than of late.

Luke was fishing with a line when he hooked into an angry young shark. In the excitement of getting it on board, Kuei left her oar and came forward to help. Still fighting hard, the shark was finally dragged into the boat and lay threshing about on the wooden boards surrounded by a variety of less energetic fish. In the hostile environment the slit gills of the shark twitched open and the tiny black eyes glittered malevolently at anyone who approached too close. When Tik-wei prodded it with her foot the horseshoe slash of a mouth opened to reveal rows of wicked backward-sloping teeth. Luke thought of the two girls swimming in these waters not more than a couple of hours before and he broke out in a cold sweat. This shark undoubtedly had larger brothers not very far away.

However, there were worse dangers than sharks in these troubled waters. They entered 'The Bogue' just before midnight. Here the Pearl estuary narrowed dramatically. Until now it had been fifteen to twenty miles wide. Now it was suddenly pinched in with less than two miles separating the banks. They had entered the Pearl River proper.

Dotted about them were the lanterns of other fishing boats, with the concentration of lights from the forts on either side.

It was Tik-wei who first saw the large ship that came silently up-river behind them, its sails gleaming ghostly white in the moonlight. In an instant Kuei had swung in the lamp and extinguished it quickly. Around them on the river others were hastily doing the same.

'What is it?' Luke asked, only to be quickly silenced by Kuei.

'Hush! It is one of your Fan Qui ships. They are trying to pass the Bogue forts in the darkness. If they see us here, they will run us down so we will not warn the soldiers.'

Luke could see the vessel more clearly now as it passed them at a distance of no more than a couple of hundred yards. It was certainly a European vessel and it was taking a desperate gamble by sailing up here at night. Ezra McCulloch had charts of the estuary in his house on Hong Kong island, and Luke had spent some time studying them. The river hereabouts was scattered with rocks and small islands, and navigation was a hazardous business even in daytime. To attempt the passage in darkness was madness, even if the captain intended doing no more than clear the Bogue forts and anchor in the safer water beyond.

As the ship surged by, Luke saw the dark shadows of open ports along the whole of her length. They were gun-ports — and far too many for a merchantman. This was a man-of-war, a frigate of at least thirty-two guns.

Kuei was guiding the sampan towards a patch of dark water, shadowed by sandstone hills on one of the islands to the left of the Bogue entrance, when there came a loud hail from a boat somewhere ahead of them. The shout was taken up by someone in a second boat — and then a third, and a fourth, until eventually there was an answering cry from the nearest fort. The Chinese had a chain of boats guarding the entrance to the Bogue. Had the unknown man-of-war not appeared on the scene, Soo Fang's family and Luke would have fallen into the hands of the Imperial Chinese forces.

The sound of excited shouting and the banging of gongs echoed across the narrow waters of the Bogue, and more lights sprang into life as the Tartar soldiers tumbled from their beds and prepared for action.

'We'd better turn about, Kuei. There's going to be a battle,' Luke called softly to the girl.

'Then everyone will be far too busy to bother with us,' replied Kuei firmly. 'There is a good wind. We will be beyond the forts before they begin fighting.'

Kuei was wrong. The words were hardly out before the first shot was fired from one of the forts. Determined not to be the last to open fire, the crews of each cannon opened fire hurriedly, not bothering to take aim. This, coupled with the haphazard charging of the ancient weapons, made it dangerous for a craft to be anywhere on the river between the two main forts. Cannonballs were falling on the surface of the Bogue as though sprinkled from a giant pepper-pot.

Suddenly the unidentified warship returned the fire. It was an awesome lesson in gunnery. The first broadside threw five hundred pounds of lead shot singing over the sampan. It crashed into the fort on the left bank of the Bogue, and a similar salvo was fired at the fort on Chuenpi island on the other side of the narrow neck of water. No sooner had the first salvo struck home than the reloaded cannons thundered out for a second time.

The roar and flash of the cannons, and the splash of the Tartars' shot terrified Tik-wei. Luke caught her as she tried to rush past him in a blind panic. Soo Fang crouched in the bottom of the sampan trembling with terror, his hands clapped firmly over his ears. Only Kuei seemed unmoved by the bedlam about them. As he held the sobbing Tik-wei tightly, Luke marvelled at Kuei's calm courage. She held the sampan on course, ignoring the din of battle until they rounded a long high spit of land. With Tik-wei tucked beneath one arm, Luke leaped to adjust the sail which was flapping uselessly, robbed of wind by the high hills.

On the shore, Luke could see dark figures running back and forth between the sea and the fort, caught in the light from the fires that raged in the fort and the surrounding hovels.

Moments later the battle was behind them, hidden by the spit of land. Kuei's skill and calm courage had brought them to safety. But when Luke tried to express his honest admiration Kuei cut him short.

'It was the only way. Now you must take the oar. Keep the sampan between the islands ahead. I must attend to my father.'

Luke made his way to the stern of the little craft and took the oar from Kuei's hand. As she moved to pass him, Kuei slipped and Luke's arm went out to prevent her from falling. For a few moments he held her close to him. Then her pale face was turned to his and she twisted from his grasp.

As Luke steered the sampan between the islands, he could hear Kuei talking soothingly to her father. She spoke to him as though he were a small child. Later, with Tik-wei's help, she got him beneath the shelter and on to the matting bed. Then, protesting indignantly, Tik-wei was tucked up, too. Not until then did Kuei return to the stern of the sampan. Taking the oar from Luke's hands without comment, she pulled it hard towards her, bringing the sampan around in a tight turn. 'Now we leave the main channel. When day comes there will be too many boats here.'

Luke nodded. McCulloch's chart had shown the river between here and Canton to be a maze of islands, some large, others no more than large rocks. There were a hundred different routes they might take. Any one of them would be safer than the established route. Luke stayed in the stern of the sampan, separated from Kuei by only the oar, for most of the night. He tried to draw her into conversation, but she did not want to talk and quickly silenced him, pretending she was concentrating on sighting particular landmarks in the pale moonlight.

Luke desperately wanted to speak to her, but not until the moon had sunk below the ridge of the hills to the west of them and the sky to the east gave the first intimation of dawn did Luke take his courage in his hands and say what was on his mind. A few more minutes and Kuei would be able to see his face, then he would never say the words he had been rehearsing silently for half the night.

'Kuei . . . I . . . I'm sorry about what happened back there on the island.'

He faltered, waiting for Kuei to say something to make it easier. She remained silent.

'I wouldn't have done anything to you. Not there . . . like that.'

'Then why did you let me take off all my clothes?'

Her soft reply threw Luke into confusion.

'I don't know. . . . I didn't think you'd really do it.' He shrugged his shoulders miserably.

'Perhaps you wanted me to be ashamed, eh? Because I make you so angry?'

'No. . . . Yes! I suppose that was part of the reason,' Luke admitted. 'I'm sorry, Kuei. If we get to Canton, it will be entirely due to you. I know that. I owe you a great deal.'

Now it was Kuei's turn to shrug her shoulders. 'Why should you feel sorry? You are a barbarian. Should I expect you to behave like a Chinese?'

As soon as the words were out, Kuei regretted saying them. Luke had made a sincere apology to her. He had tried to heal the breach between them and did not deserve such a snub. It was her own father who had offered her to him. Luke would have been fully entitled to take her, on the bamboo island. Looking at Luke in the feeble light, Kuei wondered how he would have felt towards her now, had he done so. She burned hot at the thought and hoped the light was not sufficient for Luke to see the blood that had rushed to her cheeks.

Five

THE European community in Canton lived on three sides of a square beside the Pearl River, the fourth side being the river itself, three hundred yards wide at this point. Separated from the great walled city by a large sprawling suburb of shanties, the foreign traders were forbidden to enter either city or suburb. An Imperial edict had restricted them to their riverside 'factories' for more than a century.

The 'factories' were no more than large Chinese houses. The word 'factory' had originated in the days when the first factors were allowed to bring their goods to mainland China two hundred years before. The square in front of the factories was the sole exercise-area provided for the barbarian traders, and every evening when they set off to enjoy a stroll before dinner they had to contend with hordes of onlookers. Many were visitors to Canton, brought to the square by friends and relatives to look at the Fan Qui, who could not be seen in any other part of the vast Chinese empire. Many of the Chinese were not content merely to look. They wanted to touch the barbarians, feeling their clothes and even the texture of their pale skin.

This was just one of the many tribulations with which European traders were taxed. Not allowed to set foot beyond their factory bounds, they were forbidden the company of women — whether it be their wives, or the painted strumpets who giggled at them from behind the partially drawn curtains of the floating brothels moored offshore.

Many other petty restrictions were added from time to time, at the whim of local officials and mandarins. All were calculated to increase the amount of 'squeeze' extorted from the long-suffering traders. If it were not for the fact that the ships bringing in the trade goods came only as far as the island of Whampoa, more than ten miles down-river, more than one trader would have stormed on to his ship in the heat of a midsummer pique and sailed away from China for ever.

The most recent dispute between the merchants and the Chinese was more serious than usual. At its root lay the firm line adopted by the present Emperor on the question of opium smuggling. Although trade in the drug had always been illegal, judicious bribery ensured that it continued to flourish. But in the last few months the officials themselves had become worried. Drug traffickers were being arrested on the Emperor's orders and publicly executed. Those who condoned their offences were stripped of office and banished to the primitive outposts of the Chinese empire. The time had arrived for the Emperor's laws to be enforced. Unfortunately, the European traders refused to believe the Chinese authorities were any more serious than before. They were convinced this was merely one more ploy to extort more money. They carried on as usual. As a result, a number of opium cargoes were seized, tempers became frayed and Canton's Tsotang placed a total embargo on traffic between Canton and Macau.

This was how things stood when Luke reached the Canton factories. He arrived a short while before midnight, but few traders slept.

The Chinese had guard-boats patrolling the river in front of the factories, but the look-outs carried out their monotonous task with a marked lack of enthusiasm. The sampan was able to slip unnoticed between them and the factories. As the small boat bumped against the bank, Luke leaped ashore, clutching a small bag that contained little more than a European shirt, trousers and a razor. A few moments before, Luke had slipped a number of silver dollars into Tik-wei's hands. He knew better than to try to persuade Kuei to take them. Now he turned, calling a soft 'goodbye' to the two girls and their father who had brought him safely to Canton. But Kuei and Soo Fang were heaving together on the large stern oar, driving the sampan through the water to the safety of a shadowy tangle of boats. Blocking two-thirds of the wide river, they made up a vast floating village off Canton. Here were thousands of Hoklo boat-people and their kinsmen, the Tankas. Kuei and her family would be safe here. The Chinese could send an army after them and learn nothing. The water-people were fiercely loyal to their own.

Luke had been made familiar with the European enclave at Canton by Ezra McCulloch. After a quick look about him, he sprinted towards the building that housed the mission hospital.

One of the militia sentries in an offshore boat actually saw him run from the river, but before he could make up his mind what he ought to do Luke had disappeared into the shadows.

After giving the matter some troubled thought, the sentry decided it would be better if he forgot he had seen anything. To report it now would bring punishment upon his own head for not reacting sooner.

The main door of the hospital was not locked. Pushing it open, Luke found himself in a long corridor, lit only by a single low-burning lamp. However, there was a light showing through a half-open door at the far end of the corridor, and Luke hurried in that direction.

He had almost reached the door when he heard a sound behind him and a commanding voice called upon him to stop. Luke did as he was told. Turning, he could just make out a tall European standing in the corridor, wielding a stout wooden staff.

When the man spoke, it was in Chinese. 'If you are in need of help and come in peace, you are welcome. If not, I suggest you go straight back out of that door. There is little here for you to steal. Certainly nothing to make a cracked head worth while.'

Luke was still dressed in his fisherman's garb and he had been mistaken for a Chinese. Suddenly, he realized for the first time that his hazardous journey up-river was over. He had reached safety. He grinned in sheer relief.

'I come in peace,' he replied in English. 'But, with the river guarded so jealously, I thought it best to dress this way.'

'You've come up-river? But that isn't possible! Movement between Macau and Canton has been stopped for two whole weeks!' The man's voice carried an American accent. Reaching the lamp down from a shelf, he turned it up and looked more closely at Luke. 'Who are you? I haven't seen you here before.'

'My name is Trewarne – Luke Trewarne. I'm employed by Dan Gemmell – that's why I'm here.'

'Dan Gemmell . . . ? Of course! He's been worrying about you ever since the river was blockaded. He was afraid you'd fall into Chinese hands. . . . But are you telling me you've come straight from India and made your way up-river on your own?'

The American shook his head in disbelief. 'If you have, you'll be able to tell us what's happening. . . . But what am I thinking about? Keeping you here answering foolish questions. . . .' He held out his hand. 'I'm Abel Snow . . . the Reverend Abel Snow. This is my hospital. Come along to my office.'

'I'd rather see Dan Gemmell, if he's not asleep.'

'Poor Dan sleeps very little. His lungs are giving him considerable pain. There's little I can do but pray for him. His only hope of a cure is to leave China and live in a cold dry country. But perhaps your arrival will boost his spirits for a while. He's been worried about his trading company – and with just cause, I might add. Come, I'll take you to him. Then I'll hurry off and tell James Killian that you're here. Killian is the Superintendent of Trade. He's appointed by your government, but he's got into the habit of speaking for everyone. A few uncharitable merchants might tell you that he's responsible for the mess things are in right now, but he's done as well as the pressures from all sides would allow. At the moment he's at an emergency meeting with the traders. The Chinese authorities have withdrawn all labour from the factories. It could be the prelude to an attack. Canton has a new Tartar general. He arrived with his troops a few weeks ago, and no one yet knows what manner of man he is.'

While they were talking, the Reverend Abel Snow had been leading Luke along the corridor. Once through the door where Luke had seen a light, they were in the medical section of the hospital. It was a mixture of small open wards and individual rooms. The patients, too, were of a variety of races. Luke was surprised to see Europeans, Indians and Chinese occupying beds in the various wards through which he was led.

Dan Gemmell occupied a small room on his own and, when he recognized Luke, he struggled to sit up and shake his hand.

Luke was made to give a brief account of his voyage up-river before Abel Snow hurried away, leaving Luke and his sick employer to talk about Gemmell Company.

'I'm worried, Luke,' admitted Dan Gemmell. 'Not just about this temporary stoppage of traffic on the river – that affects everyone. No, it's this damned illness of mine. It's dragged on for so long that I feel I've lost my grip on the business. It's going downhill fast . . . and I know it better than anyone.'

'Well, now you can concentrate on getting better and leave me to worry about the business, Dan. Is anyone looking after your factory at the moment?'

'Your guess would probably be as good as mine! I thought there was, but just lately I'm not too sure. Before I came into hospital I took on a German, Hans Moller. I know little about him; he arrived in Macau when I was last there and seemed to have a fair knowledge of trading. Beyond that I know nothing. Where he came from . . . why. . . . I was just too sick to care. But since I came in here I've been hearing disquieting rumours about him, although no one will tell me anything specific. You sort it out for me, Luke. Do whatever you think is necessary. From this moment *you* are Gemmell Company. You've got a free hand to do whatever has to be done. If you like, I'll put that in writing.'

'That won't be necessary, Dan. Your word is good enough for me. If it wasn't, I wouldn't have come all this way to work for you.'

Dan Gemmell leaned back against his pillows and gave Luke a tired smile. 'Do you know, I feel better already, damn me if I don't. Seeing you has done more for me than all of Abel Snow's medicines – or his prayers.' The trader closed his eyes and said nothing for so long that Luke thought he slept but, when Luke rose to his feet to leave, Dan Gemmell said, 'Don't go just yet, Luke. I've got something to say to you.'

He opened his eyes again. 'You put Gemmell Company back on its feet, boy, and when I get out of here I'll make you a full partner. Give you a half-share in the Company. How will that suit you?'

It was an incredibly generous offer, but Luke realized that it was being made by a very sick man. He would not hold Dan Gemmell to his promise when he recovered.

The two men were still talking quietly when Abel Snow hurried into the room. Beaming at Luke, he said, 'I gave the news of your arrival to James Killian, and he immediately announced it at his meeting. You'd have thought he'd told them that the British fleet had arrived at Whampoa. Killian wants to meet you, right away.'

From his sickbed, Dan Gemmell smiled ruefully. 'Go over there and let them pat you on the back, Luke. It's the first time I can recall anyone from Gemmell Company doing anything to meet with their approval. They disapprove of my stand on opium trading almost as much as I dislike theirs.'

'That's a subject on which you and I will *always* agree, Dan.' The missionary spoke passionately. 'Carrying and selling opium is immoral. I've fought long and hard against the trade, as you well know, but I'm a realist. I recognize defeat when I meet with it – even though my belief in God's goodness won't always allow me to accept it. Mind you, there are faults on both sides. The refusal of the Emperor to allow China to take its place in the nineteenth century is one. . . . But there I go again, talking when I should be doing. Come, Luke, or I'll have you here all night talking about opium. It's time for Dan to pretend to take my medicine and get some rest, while I take you to meet your fellow-traders.'

James Killian had called his meeting in what had formerly been the banqueting-room of the East India Company's factory. It was fitted out in a manner befitting one of the wealthiest organizations in the world. Such luxury was in sharp contrast to the teeming squalor of Canton's suburbs viewed from the factory windows.

But it was too dark for Luke to see from the windows when Abel Snow escorted him into the room. The unexpected air of opulence, heightened by a huge chandelier of Italian crystal hanging from the centre of the ceiling, took him by surprise — as did the tumultuous reception he was given by the assembled traders.

When the applause was at its height, James Killian crossed the room and grasped Luke by the hand. 'Mr Trewarne, you've put new heart into us. God knows, sneaking up the river like a thief in the night, disguised as a Chinese, is a poor victory for an Englishman, but it's the first we've scored for a very long time. There has been no news from the outside world for longer than two weeks. What's happening out there? Do you bring despatches from Macau?'

Luke shook his head. 'I haven't been to Macau.' He told a hushed meeting of the attempted trip up-river by McCulloch's ship, *The Two Brothers*. His words were given a mixed reception. Most of the merchants were highly indignant that the Chinese Navy should fire upon a British merchantman, but more than one voice was raised in condemnation of Captain Obadiah Innes for not calling first at Macau.

'Gentlemen! Gentlemen! Let us not quarrel among ourselves. It will help no one but the Chinese. Soon I hope to see a ship of Her Britannic Majesty's Navy force a passage up-river and break this ridiculous stalemate. Captain Fish and *Midas* are due at Macau this month. I left word for him to proceed here immediately. I don't think the Chinese will dare to fire upon a warship flying the flag of our country.'

'If a warship hasn't yet arrived, then I'm afraid it wasn't successful in forcing the Bogue,' said Luke. He told the Super-

50

intendent of Trade of the night engagement between the un-known frigate and the Bogue forts.

James Killian was stunned by the news. 'If the Chinese have managed to sink *Midas*, they might well feel they are ready to launch an assault on the factories. Gentlemen, we must take immediate steps to secure our properties. Barricade yourselves in your factories and fight with whatever weapons you have to hand. If possible, we should also fly the flags of our individual nations from each building, so that the Chinese fully understand that an attack on a factory constitutes an attack on the country itself.'

Luke was bewildered by the strange negative logic of James Killian. Instead of withdrawing inside the factories, the Super-intendent of Trade should be out and about, seeking negotia-tions with the Chinese authorities. During the noisy applause given to James Killian's words, Luke whispered his views to Abel Snow.

The American missionary smiled sadly. 'It isn't quite that simple, Luke. The argument between you British and the Chinese has been going on for years. The Chinese believe they are the greatest nation on earth and expect others to pay them homage. You British *know* you are the greatest – and will pay homage to no one! So you end up with China refusing to acknowledge the existence of Britain, and Britain scorning China. You can't have a dialogue between two nations that don't exist for each other.'

Luke was astonished. 'But that's ridiculous. . . .'

Abel Snow shrugged. '*I* can see that, and so can you . . . but you won't convince the *Honourable* James Killian. He's a younger son of the Earl of Fulbrook, one of your country's oldest families, and an honest and fair man by normal standards. But he's too proud, too rigid for the post of Superintendent of Trade in Canton. The Chinese bend with the wind and expect others to do the same. The two sides can never agree for long.'

'But what will happen about the blockade, and trade?'

Abel Snow smiled. 'I only *serve* God, Luke. I'm not in His confidence. . . . But I think Mr Killian wants to talk to you.'

Luke looked up to see the Superintendent of Trade beckon-ing to him. He suggested that Luke should leave, in order to barricade the factory of Gemmell Company against the ex-pected attack.

'I look forward to speaking to you again when I have restored normality to the situation,' Killian said pompously. '*Midas* may have failed to force the Bogue, but other warships will be on the way. We still have some difficult days ahead, but with enterprising young men like yourself among us we will win through. The Chinese cannot afford to lose all their profit from trade for long.'

With these words of comfort, James Killian waved Luke an airy goodnight and dismissed him from his mind as he turned away to dispense comfort and advice to the other traders.

On the way to Gemmell Company's factory with Abel Snow, Luke expressed the misgivings he felt. 'If the other traders won't accept that *opium* lies at the root of all the trouble with China, how can we hope to reach a solution?'

'Oh, I don't doubt a solution *will* be found . . . eventually,' said the missionary surprisingly. 'As I said earlier, the Chinese bend with the wind. They'll come up with a way to resume trade – and at the same time make it look as though they've won the day.' He stopped and pointed to a building set in one of the corners of the square. 'There you are – Gemmell Company's factory. I'll leave you now and return to my hospital. Our Chinese helpers were ordered out with all the others, but we can't just close down and stop trading. Before we go, I'd like to give you a word of warning about Hans Moller. I know nothing about the work he's done for Dan, but he's a strange ungodly man with a number of very dubious friends. Take care when you get inside the factory, Luke.'

With this mysterious warning, Abel Snow raised a hand in farewell. Striding away across the window-lit square, his long-legged gait quickly carried him out of sight. Luke watched him go reluctantly. He had made a friend – and he believed he would need one in this beleaguered little trading outpost.

Luke turned his attention to Gemmell Company's factory. It was a small two-storey building, constructed of stone in a strange confusion of European and Chinese styles. There were no lights at the windows, and when Luke tried the door he found it was locked. Dan Gemmell had given him a bunch of keys, and the largest of them fitted the front door. Swinging the door open, Luke stepped inside the house which was to be both home and office for him here in Canton.

It was dark inside the factory, and Luke was unable to locate either a lamp or a candle in the hallway. Closing the door behind him, he groped his way slowly and carefully along a narrow passageway – and then he saw a faint glimmer of light showing beneath a doorway. There was something else here, too, a distinctive aroma that Luke had smelled on more than one occasion during the past few days. The bitter-sweet smell of opium smoke.

Cautiously pushing open the door, Luke stepped into a small room with closed windows and drawn curtains. Opium smoke was so thick in here that it brought tears to Luke's eyes. Flinging the door open wide, Luke strode to the window. He drew the curtains, but had a moment's difficulty with the window-catch. Then that, too, was opened wide, and Luke took deep gulps of warm, but fresh, night air.

When he was able to breathe easily once more, Luke turned back to the small room and surveyed the untidy scene revealed by the dim light of a dying lamp. The room was almost emptied of furniture, but Chinese sleeping-mats were scattered about the floor. On the mats lay three naked men. One was a paunchy middle-aged European. The others were young Chinese. All were in a deep opium-induced sleep.

None too gently, Luke set about rousing Han Moller, but he soon realized it was quite impossible. The German's dreams had taken his senses far from the unhappy factories of Canton. The body they had left behind functioned at a level so low it was only just sufficient to maintain life. Moller's pulse was barely perceptible, his breathing shallow and weak.

Luke had more success with one of Moller's Chinese companions. He stirred at Luke's touch and attempted to push him away. Luke's answer was to lift the man by the shoulders and shake him so violently that his head bounced from side to side in an alarming manner. The young Chinese began to complain irritably until, breaking from Luke's grasp, he struggled to get to his feet.

When Luke was certain the man could hear him he said, 'Get dressed and get out of here – and take your friend with you.'

The Chinese looked up at Luke for a full minute, his face devoid of all expression. Then, slowly and carefully, he reached for an untidy heap of clothing and began to dress, whilst Luke tried to rouse his companion.

It was twenty minutes before the two young Chinese were able to leave the house, one supporting the other. From the doorway of Dan Gemmell's factory, Luke watched them weaving drunkenly across the square, heading for the shadow of a dark alleyway. Slamming the door shut, Luke locked it and returned to the room where Hans Moller lay. There would be no rousing him tonight. Moller's moment of reckoning would come with the new day.

Luke found a lamp in one of the rooms and was able to make a cursory inspection of the premises. There were rooms fitted out for sleeping upstairs, but Luke decided to spend the remainder of the night on a chair in the office. From somewhere not very far away there was the continuous din of heavy gongs being beaten, occasionally accompanied by the staccato detonation of firecrackers. The sounds were part of the Chinese war of nerves against the Europeans. Neither they nor the thought of a Chinese assault on the factories kept Luke awake.

Before he drifted off into a deep dreamless sleep, Luke went over the extraordinary events of the last few days. A week ago he had been looking forward to a secure future running the affairs of an established trading company in Canton, anticipating the opportunities open to him to grow rich with Gemmell Company. Now, only a few days later, he was sharing Dan Gemmell's neglected factory with an unconscious opium addict, had been involved in a sea battle with the Imperial Chinese Navy, and faced a trading future that could only be described as bleak. He had also made a remarkable voyage up the Pearl River with a girl like no other he had ever known. Luke's last waking thought was of Kuei. He was determined to see her again – but when, where, and under what circumstances?

Luke awoke to the sound of doors being slammed and a loud voice raised in anger. Standing up stiffly, Luke limped to the door and swung it open on protesting hinges.

'Is that you, Ching? What are you doing in my office? I have told you before –' The guttural, heavily accented voice broke off as Hans Moller saw Luke standing in the office doorway.

'Who are you? What are you doing here, eh? This is Gemmell's factory . . . private property.'

Hans Moller had the symptoms of a man suffering from a colossal hangover. Grey-faced and hunch-shouldered, he wore only a grubby towel about his flabby waist. Moller was an opium addict, but its grip was not yet so strong that he had lost his taste for food and drink.

Luke viewed the older man with undisguised distaste.

'That's right, Moller, it's a factory – though by the look of things there's been no work done here since Dan Gemmell went into hospital.'

'Ah! You are the bright young man from India who is to make Gemmell Company successful overnight.' Moller snorted derisively. 'This is not India. You do not have an army to call on if the natives do not do as they are told. Here, in China, an Englishman is not God's great blessing to the world. He is the same as a Prussian, a Dutchman – or any other European. He is a barbarian – a foreign devil! The lowest form of life on the sacred soil of the Emperor's "Heavenly Kingdom". Lower than the meanest coolie. God!' – Moller pronounced it 'Gott' – 'I want to get away from here, to forget I ever heard of Canton . . . of China.'

'You were doing a good job of forgetting when I arrived in the night and kicked your friends out. When Dan Gemmell learns what's been going on in his factory I've no doubt he'll help you on your way. . . .'

'You sent them from here in the night? Ching and Ah Shun? Oh my God! Do you know what you have done? You have killed them as surely as though you had stuck a knife in them yourself. Tsotang Teng is looking for them. I have been hiding them here.'

Moller's melodramatic outburst startled Luke momentarily, but he had not spent three uncomfortable days and nights on the river to hear about the troubles of Hans Moller's friends.

'I've come here to take over Gemmell Company. Harbouring Chinese criminals has nothing to do with trading. If you are going to remain under this roof, we'd better get a few things understood – but first I need to eat. Show me the way to the kitchen, I'll cook some breakfast while you tell me something of the trading situation as it stands at the moment.'

'Go to hell!' Moller shouted angrily. 'You are the clever one – find out for yourself. I will get dressed and move out now. I am finished with Gemmell and his company. I will stay at the Dutch factory until I can take a ship out of here. If you had any sense, you would do the same – but you will not. You are British. Damn you and Gemmell's company. You deserve one another.'

Hans Moller made his way angrily along the corridor, and Luke grinned at the back of the departing German. It was difficult to take a man seriously when he was dressed only in a towel – and Luke was relieved he was not going to have to share the factory with him.

Luke found the kitchen and was searching through cupboards occupied only by hungry cockroaches when Abel Snow arrived, letting himself in through the open door of the factory.

'Good morning, Luke. I saw Moller hurrying across the square a few minutes ago, clutching all his worldly possessions. I thought you might care to share my breakfast. It's only salt pork and Chinese beans, but until the blockade is lifted I doubt if you'll do better anywhere else.'

Luke accepted the invitation gratefully. He felt the need to talk to someone this morning – someone who could make sense of the confusion existing at the Canton factories.

Luke talked with Abel Snow until mid-morning. After accepting an invitation to dine with him that evening, he made his way back to the factory. As he was about to go inside, the look-out posted by Killian on the roof of the tallest factory shouted an excited warning.

'They're coming! The whole damn Chinese Army is coming this way.' With these words of alarm, the look-out, a diminutive Irishman, shinned down a waiting ladder and ran to the factory occupied by the Superintendent of Trade.

Luke went inside Dan Gemmell's factory and checked that all doors and windows were secured. It was more to give himself something to do than anything else. The factory was indefensible. Indeed, the whole of the factory area could be taken within an hour. The traders might barricade themselves in, but they had no more than half a dozen weapons between them all.

As it happened, the Irish look-out was guilty of considerable exaggeration. The 'army' consisted of a hundred soldiers of the Tartar blue-banner regiment, although, as they marched out of the gate of the walled city of Canton, they might have *appeared* to be an army. Armed with a miscellany of swords, spears and aged matchlock muskets, the Tartars carried round metal shields which caught the sun's rays and hurled them back at the many excited onlookers. The soldiers appeared ragged and ill-disciplined, yet with an army of these men the Tartar general Shengan had won more than fifty impressive victories. He had fought the Emperor's enemies in the high snow mountains of Tibet and on the arid plains of Mongolia, putting down rebellions in every province in the country. He and his men had earned for themselves a reputation as fearless and ruthless fighters. Shengan's successes had also brought him a ruby button to wear in his hat, a symbol of the Emperor's esteem for all to see. With the button went the rank of a mandarin of the first grade – the highest in the land – and the right to embroider the insignia of a unicorn on the blue banners of Shengan's regiment. The Emperor knew the wisdom of keeping a strong and loyal Tartar army. These were the troops who had brought the Manchu dynasty into being. Without their support the throne would topple.

The Tartars marched from Canton, across the bridge isolating the factories from the suburbs, and into the square. Behind them came a long procession in which were many senior dignitaries of the city with their retainers. There was the Tsotang, the mayor, and officers of the militia, all borne in sedan chairs high on the shoulders of uniformed servants. At the rear of the long procession were a number of police runners. They carried two bamboo cages, suspended from long sagging poles. Each cage was hardly large enough to hold a medium-sized dog, but huddled inside was an unhappy Chinese, crouched in the foetal position, heavy chains securing wrists and ankles. Following the official procession came a mob of noisy spectators, beating gongs and shouting the praises of the mandarins.

When the last of the Chinese had entered the square, the Tartar soldiers began beating back the spectators, clearing a large space in the centre. Inside the factories, the residents braced themselves for the onslaught they were convinced was now about to begin.

But the Chinese had more subtle plans for 'persuading' the small trading community to fall in with their wishes. They were determined to prevent opium from entering their vast country – but not at the expense of legitimate trade. Today the Canton authorities would leave the Fan Qui in no doubt about the risks involved in trading in opium.

When sufficient space had been cleared, a shelter of bamboo and matting was hastily erected in the square. Beneath its shade the Chinese dignitaries took their seats in anticipation of the forthcoming spectacle. About twenty yards from them, two wooden crosses, each six feet high, were carefully hammered into the ground side by side. When officers of the army and police had checked the steadfastness of the crosses and bowed their approval towards the seated officials, the occupants of the two cages were dumped unceremoniously on the ground. With much rough manhandling, they were dragged to the upright crosses and secured with ropes, arms outstretched and bricks beneath their feet to raise them to a more convenient height.

From Gemmell Company's factory, Luke was watching the proceedings from the office window and he paled when he saw the faces of the two prisoners. They were the men he had ejected from the factory during the night. He remembered with growing misgivings Hans Moller's hysterical outburst about their fate at the hands of the Chinese authorities. He had no doubt that the two men were to be executed, but he was unprepared for the method used, and the total lack of formality with which the sentence was carried out.

A silk cord was looped about each man's neck and passed through a hole in the wooden upright, immediately above the crosspiece. A stick was passed through the loop. Then, with no ceremony, and no signal that Luke could perceive, the bricks were kicked from beneath the unfortunate victims' feet. At the same time, the sticks were twisted until the cords dug deep into the throats of the two men. One died without uttering a sound, but Luke could hear the painful choking of his companion as his tongue protruded from his mouth and he fought a losing battle for breath against the slowly tightening cord.

Luke was witnessing the traditional Chinese method of execution, but it was all over so quickly that he hardly had time to take in the full horror of the act. When he looked at the seated officials, it was apparent that no more than half were aware that the sentence had been carried out. The others talked and joked as though they were attending a rare social gathering.

The crowd, too, was slow to appreciate that the judicial sentence had been implemented. When realization came, a howl of disappointment rose on the warm morning air. Before it blotted out all other sounds, Luke imagined he heard a cry of despair from a single throat. It appeared to come from the direction of the Dutch factory.

With the crowd giving voice to such noisy disappointment at the speedy end to their promised entertainment, it seemed likely they would vent their frustration upon the factories of the traders – but General Shengan had anticipated such a possibility. His soldiers began to clear the square, brutally beating the onlookers before them as the city dignitaries were whisked back to homes and offices. Behind them, the two dead criminals stared open-mouthed at the hushed factories.

Soon only the dead men and a handful of soldiers remained – together with their general.

General Shengan was mounted on a shaggy pony born and bred on the vast plateau of Mongolia. A pony like its owner, tough and durable. Surrounded by a small bodyguard, Shengan advanced across the square – heading for the Gemmell factory.

Luke drew back from the window, his heart beating madly. He knew instinctively they were coming for him. In a moment of panic, he tried to remember the geography of the factory, seeking a way of escape. The moment quickly passed. There *was* no escape. In front of the factory were the soldiers. Behind, the great city of Canton. The Tartar soldiers began hammering imperiously at the door of the factory, and Luke walked slowly to open it to them before they smashed it down.

When the door swung open he found himself looking into the flat and expressionless faces of men without pity. Fighting men who had never sought or given quarter. One of them, apparently an officer, spoke to Luke in Manchu, the language of the Tartars. Luke shook his head, indicating he did not understand what was being said. He was immediately pounced upon, dragged down the steps in front of the factory and flung to the ground in front of General Shengan.

The General grunted a single Manchu word and the soldiers backed away, leaving Luke to climb to his feet and brush himself off, doing his best to maintain a composure he did not feel. Standing beside General Shengan's stirrup was a small Chinese whom Luke quickly learned was an interpreter.

'You . . . this factory belong you?'

The interpreter enunciated the English words as though he were speaking Chinese, and Luke had to concentrate on them in order to understand what was being said.

'I'm in charge. The owner is ill – sick.' Luke realized that the interpreter had even more difficulty understanding him and he passed on far more information to General Shengan than Luke had given to him. In a bid to improve matters, Luke said, 'Does the General speak Cantonese? If he does, we could talk direct. . . .'

Immediately, the interpreter rounded on Luke angrily, spitting words at him. 'General Shengan not speak to Fan Qui.

You speak me. I speak General. How long you work this place?'

Answering truthfully would lead to even more difficult questions. 'I left the East India Company to work for Mr Gemmell almost a year ago,' Luke declared ambiguously. He spoke in Cantonese and could see by Shengan's surprised expression that the Tartar general understood.

'Speak English to me!' The interpreter was so angry, Luke thought he was about to strike him. This was the greatest moment in the interpreter's hitherto uneventful life – an opportunity to use the English he had picked up whilst working on the quay at Whampoa, to interpret for China's greatest general. He did not intend to allow this English barbarian to spoil the great moment.

'You . . . how much opium you have your factory?'

The question took Luke by surprise. 'None. Gemmell Company does not trade in opium.' Again Luke spoke in Cantonese.

'You lie!' The interpreter extended a quivering arm in the direction of the two crucified Chinese. 'They smoke opium your place. Where they get it, eh?'

The Chinese interpreter had gone too far in his bid to impress his hero. The questions were his own and not the General's. Shengan did not understand the English spoken, but he realized the interpreter was pursuing his own line of questioning. General Shengan was a man of action. Kicking his heels into the pony's flanks, he drove the animal forward, sending the interpreter sprawling amidst the grinning Tartar troops. To Luke he said, in perfect Cantonese, 'What is your name?'

'Luke Trewarne.'

General Shengan was tall and solidly built, with wide powerful shoulders and an air of proud authority that would have singled him out in any crowd. But it was his eyes that immediately captured the attention of those who met him for the first time. Black and deep, they were capable of striking terror into the hearts of his enemies. A lone man who had never known a close friend, he was adored by the fierce Tartar warriors he commanded. Because of this, he was probably the most powerful man in the kingdom. Only unquestionable loyalty kept him clear of those whose duty it was to eliminate all subjects whose personal popularity might one day threaten the Emperor.

'Luke Trewarne. . . .' The sound of the name pleased General Shengan and he repeated it twice. 'Luke Trewarne, last night you put two men from your factory. Why?'

'They had no right to be there.' Luke looked towards the two bodies and remembered hearing the dying man choke to death. 'Had I known what would happen, I might have let them stay.'

'Why?' The Tartar general expressed genuine surprise. 'They were nothing to you. You had never seen them before. You will never see them again. Alive they were a nuisance. Dead . . . ? They can provide an end to your troubles. . . .'

The angry voice of James Killian broke in upon the General's words. Accompanied by two traders, the Superintendent of Trade had left his factory when he saw Luke brought before Shengan. He was protesting loudly as the Tartars prevented him from coming closer, beating him back with spear-handles and shields.

'Who is that?' General Shengan demanded.

'James Killian, the Superintendent of Trade.'

'Ah! The man who is deaf to the words of the Emperor, and so is now Superintendent-without-trade.'

In Manchu, General Shengan called for James Killian to be allowed to come to him. To Luke he said, 'You will stay and interpret his words for me.' It was not a request, but a command.

Allowed to pass by the Tartars, the furious James Killian confronted Shengan. 'This exhibition is a disgrace . . . an insult to the flag of Great Britain.' He pointed to the Union Jack, hanging limply from the flagstaff behind the two executed men.

Luke translated swiftly, and General Shengan gave a nod of acknowledgement. 'A flag is no more than a piece of cloth, made by man. It cannot see, or speak, or hear. Should I have ordered the flag to be taken down before having two criminals strangled?'

'He is deliberately misunderstanding my meaning,' spluttered Killian, when Luke passed on the General's reply. 'Executing criminals in this square is a deliberate provocation. Technically this is British territory. *That* is why the flag of Great Britain flies here.'

When Luke translated, General Shengan jerked cruelly on the rein of his restless pony. His dark eyes glittering dangerously, he said, 'A piece of cloth flying on a pole does not take a single speck of dust away from China. *All* this belongs to the Emperor.' He waved a hand to encompass factories and squares. 'I gave the order for these two men to be strangled in this place because their deaths have been brought about by you.

They were executed for selling Fan Qui opium to their own countrymen. In future, all Chinese caught selling opium will be executed here and their bodies will remain until you have no space to exercise between them – regardless of what flag is flying.'

James Killian listened in tight-lipped silence. When Luke had ended he said, 'Tell the General he leaves me no alternative but to order the British flag lowered. This means there will be no more trade between our countries. The flag will not be raised again until I receive an assurance that the Chinese will treat the flag and the subjects of Great Britain with the respect accorded to them by more civilized countries. Tell General Shengan the traders wish to leave. Will he please arrange for the embargo on river traffic to be lifted so that we may proceed down-river to Macau?'

'Such a weighty burden of pride can cause a man to stumble and fall on his face before the whole world,' said General Shengan when Luke passed on Killian's decision. 'The Superintendent-without-trade speaks empty words. Can he take something he does not have? Tell him to throw off his anger and take counsel with wiser men before he makes decisions that will hurt you and your country more than China. Now, hear my words. I am pleased with you, Luke Trewarne. You do not allow criminals to hide in your factory, and I believe you when you tell me you do not trade in opium. I have made my thoughts known to the Governor of this province and he agrees that such a responsible attitude deserves reward. The river between Canton and Macau is open once more. Tell the Superintendent-without-trade he can take his flag to Macau when he wishes – or he can stay and become a Superintendent who has trade once more.'

When Luke translated General Shengan's news the faces of the two traders who accompanied Killian broke into smiles of delighted relief. Not so Killian himself. He went pale as he realized that General Shengan and his own anger had led him into a neat trap. He could either carry out his threat and withdraw from Canton with those traders who would follow him, or he would have to abandon his stand. If he took the latter course, he would lose face with Shengan and all those to whom the story was repeated. Such a course was unthinkable for Her Britannic Majesty's Superintendent of Trade. Tight-faced, the Honourable James Killian said, 'Nothing has changed. Unless there is an apology from the Provincial Governor himself, then the British traders – and possibly many others – will leave Canton before nightfall.'

General Shengan shrugged his shoulders nonchalantly when Luke passed on Killian's ultimatum. 'He will be back. But you. What will you do? Go, or stay?'

'Stay,' declared Luke without hesitation. He had not come all this way only to leave almost immediately to satisfy another man's pride. Besides, Dan Gemmell was not well enough to leave. He would have to remain behind in the mission hospital.

'Good.' Working at his reins, General Shengan sawed cruelly at the mouth of his restless pony. 'Then it will not be necessary for me to enquire into the manner of your arrival at Canton. Instead I will compliment you on your resourcefulness.'

Something that might have been a smile crossed the Chinese general's face. Jerking at the rein of his pony, the hero of China rode away, surrounded by a handful of ragged Tartar soldiers.

Six

JAMES KILLIAN left Canton the day after his angry confrontation with General Shengan. Such was the strength of British influence that he was accompanied by most of the traders, British and foreign, who normally operated from Canton. Only the Dutch, the Americans and Luke remained.

Reasons for the strength of Killian's support were not hard to find. The Honourable James Killian was an arrogant man who put his own pride before the interests of the merchants, but as Superintendent of Trade he represented the greatest trading nation in the world – and Great Britain possessed a navy jealous of its reputation for protecting the business interests of her subjects, and their friends. Over the years British men-of-war had prevented the Chinese authorities and greedy mandarins from pushing the long-suffering traders too far on many occasions. Without such protection, their cargoes – opium in particular – would have proved an irresistible target for every pirate and corrupt official on the Chinese coast.

The Dutch, characteristically, refused to follow Killian's lead because they were still smarting at recent action by Britain which had forced them to relinquish their hold on Belgium, and they had never forgiven Britain for ousting the Dutch East India Company from almost all its Far Eastern trading strongholds.

The Americans, ever anxious to assert their independence from all things British, were not prepared to abandon their trade for James Killian. Indeed, the present situation offered them a wonderful opportunity to increase their own share of the Chinese market.

Only Luke had misgivings about staying. He told James Killian that Gemmell Company could not afford a further break in trading if it were to survive. It was true, but he did not enjoy the thought that he might be letting down his countrymen. Nevertheless, he argued his case stubbornly when a thin-lipped Superintendent of Trade accused him of condoning a serious insult to the British flag.

'I don't see it that way. The root of all the trouble is opium.

Gemmell Company doesn't trade in opium. That means this isn't our fight.'

'It's likely to be everybody's fight before long,' retorted James Killian angrily. 'China's behaviour is leading her into a war with Britain. If that happens while you are in Canton, it will be no use crying for protection. Your last opportunity to leave may be now.'

'I'll take my chances here,' said Luke defiantly.

His bravado ebbed away slightly when he watched all the grim-visaged traders embarking from the main factory quay that evening, but he had made his decision and he soon found many other things to think about.

When he began going through the haphazardly kept account-books belonging to Gemmell Company, Luke found them depressing reading. Dan Gemmell had a small brigantine, *Black Swan*, somewhere on the seas between Ceylon and Canton, hopefully loaded with goods that would produce a small profit. This was the only glimmer of hope Luke could find. There was nothing stored away in the Gemmell warehouse – known locally as a 'godown' – on Whampoa island, or in those belonging to the Hongs. It was a gloomy picture but, if *Black Swan* arrived in Canton soon, Luke could take advantage of the present situation to sell high, whilst buying local goods at rock-bottom prices.

Luke did his best to keep the gloomy state of affairs from Dan Gemmell, but one night, when he was walking from the hospital accompanied by Abel Snow, he confessed to the missionary that the future was depressing. 'I can understand why the other traders deal in opium,' he added bitterly. 'Even a single cargo would put Gemmell Company comfortably on its feet again.'

Abel Snow stopped walking abruptly and turned to face Luke. 'I'd rather see Gemmell Company go out of business, Luke. A good man can face up to financial ruin and fight his way back again. The thousands – no, *millions* – of Chinese addicted to opium have only one way out – death! And they'll suffer the pangs of hell long before they leave this life. All because a few greedy and unscrupulous men want to get rich quick. You doubt my words? All right, you don't have to believe me. I'll *show* you. Come with me. . . .'

Taking Luke's arm, the missionary doctor guided him into

an alleyway that divided two of the largest factories. It was muddy here, and on either side were flimsy and ill-lit shanties.

'This is Hog Lane,' Abel Snow whispered. 'Talk only Chinese here. The sound of a European voice is inviting a knife between your ribs.'

Luke nodded. The stench between the enclosed walls was so bad that he wondered aloud whether the animals that had given the lane its name were still in residence.

'There are things here to disgrace any animal,' declared Abel Snow grimly. He went to the dimly lit entrance of a large 'building', constructed entirely of bamboo and heavy matting. Holding aside the entrance curtain, he called, 'Take a look in here. This is how the ordinary man *enjoys* the pleasure of opium.'

Luke put his head inside the opening and recoiled in disgust. It smelled worse than a gamekeeper's backyard. Steeling himself against the offensive smell, he looked inside again, more cautiously this time. It was indescribably squalid. A number of foul mats were strewn about on the mud floor, some occupied by unconscious men with cold opium pipes lying beside them. Others breathed in opium fumes, eyes closed as the smoke transported them from agony to oblivion. Here and there sat men who had awakened from their dreams, but were not yet at one with their surroundings. Glassy-eyed, they scratched languidly at a flea-bite, or picked an overactive louse from their emaciated bodies. Luke recoiled in horror from the sordid scene, but Abel Snow had not finished with him yet. He forced him to look inside three more opium shanties, each worse than the first.

'These are the better-class establishments,' said Abel Snow. 'One or two cater for women – and the sailors from the ships at Whampoa. Farther along the lane are hovels where even I dare not show my face.'

'How did you learn of this place?' askel Luke, shocked by what he had just seen.

'I'm called here frequently,' replied Abel Snow. 'Whenever a man abuses his body once too often. If he were to die here, the wrath of the magistrate would come down upon the owners of these places. They call me in to carry away the unfortunate addicts. I do my best for them, but I've never saved one yet. It plays havoc with my patient-recovery statistics, but it assures some poor soul of more comfort in death than he's ever known in life. Do you still think that one cargo of opium will make no difference to anyone?'

'Have you brought Dan Gemmell here?'

'I have — and many of his colleagues, too; but all men don't have the conscience of Dan Gemmell.'

Luke had witnessesd scenes of degradation in Hog Lane that would remain with him all his life, but before he could say more to Abel Snow a Chinese darted from the shadows between two of the opium shanties.

'There is a very sick man along here. I think he must soon die.'

'Has he been smoking your opium?'

'My opium is good. The best Patna from the Company. No, this man comes with friends. They must have brought bad opium with them. You will come?'

'I'll come.'

Abel Snow and Luke followed the Chinese to an opium den that was as filthy and fetid as any they had yet seen. Stepping carelessly over the men sprawled on the floor, the Chinese led them to where two men crouched beside a body on one of the mats. The unconscious man was lying on his side, and Abel Snow swiftly turned him on to his back. The limp body rolled over easily, and as the pale light from a nearby opium lamp fell across the man's face Luke expelled his breath in a gasp of dismay.

Dropping to his knees beside the prostrate Chinese, Luke asked, 'Is he alive?'

'Only just. You know him?'

'Yes. His name is Soo Fang. He's the fisherman who brought me up-river from Hong Kong. He and his two daughters. He was smoking opium for most of the voyage. . . .' Luke left the explanation there. Soo Fang had been smoking opium given to him for making the voyage to Canton. If anyone was to blame for his present condition, it was Luke himself.

'Then his condition will come as no surprise to anyone. Help me with him, Luke. Quickly now. I don't want to be carrying a dead man if the Chinese militia stop us on the way back to the mission.'

Carrying Soo Fang presented no problem. As Luke had observed on an earlier occasion, there was little weight to the fisherman. Luke picked Soo Fang up in his arms and followed the American missionary from the hut.

Soo Fang was still alive when they reached the mission hospital, and Abel Snow worked hard to bring him back to consciousness. Salts were burned beneath the fisherman's nose and foul-smelling medicines poured down his throat. While this was going on, Luke told Abel Snow of Kuei and Tik-wei. A convalescing Chinese patient was roused from his bed and sent to the floating village to find Kuei urgently.

'With any luck at all, this one will survive,' Abel Snow explained to Luke. 'If he does, then the moment he realizes we are trying to effect a cure he'll go berserk and scream for his freedom. Unless I have authorization from his family to keep him here, the Tsotang will take great delight in arresting me for abducting Soo Fang.'

Kuei arrived at the hospital within the hour. Breathless from hurrying and full of concern for her father, she was bemused by the unfamiliar surroundings. As Abel Snow explained patiently why he had sent for her, Kuei listened in wide-eyed consternation, a very different girl from the one who had been in full command of herself and the others during the hazardous voyage up-river.

When Abel Snow ended his explanation, Kuei hesitated, reluctant to put her father's life in the hands of this Fan Qui.

'It's the only way to save his life,' Luke said gently. He still felt guilty about Soo Fang and, watching Kuei trying to cope with such an important decision in these strange surroundings, his heart went out to her. He wanted Soo Fang to recover – for *her* sake.

'You truly believe this?' Kuei's eyes searched his face for any sign of deception. She saw only his concern for her.

'Yes.'

'All right. My father must stay here.'

'Good girl!' Abel Snow squeezed her shoulder. 'He'll recover. I promise you that. But when he wants opium again, and we refuse to give it to him, he's going to suffer more pain than he's ever known before. He'll hate everyone – you more than anyone else. Go back to your boat, away from here, and I'll send someone to keep you informed of his progress.'

Suddenly, Abel Snow wanted this girl away from the factories. He had intercepted the look Luke had given Kuei. The missionary had seen such looks before – but never here, in Canton. It contained all the qualities that Abel Snow had spent a lifetime teaching to his fellow-men. Compassion, tenderness – and love.

68

But when such emotions were shown by a European man towards a Chinese girl they could have tragic consequences.

'I will stay here with my father.' Kuei cut across Abel Snow's thoughts. 'It will be better if I am here when he wakes.'

'Women are forbidden in the factories – and I believe you have a younger sister.'

'Tik-wei is with friends, and I am not in the factories. I am in your hospital. Besides, there are very few Fan Qui left. General Shengan has chased them all away.'

Abel Snow made no attempt to correct Kuei's version of the departure from Canton of the traders. His concern was for the Fan Qui who was in the room at the moment; but he thought it inadvisable to pursue the matter now.

'Very well, but you must remain in the hospital.'

Kuei nodded. Had the Fan Qui missionary forced her to go, she would have taken Soo Fang with her. That would have been regrettable. She had heard only good things about the mission hospital, but she would not trust the tall Fan Qui with her father unless she remained with him. The Fan Qui missionary would one day preach of a deity who loved his enemies – and the next day would cut out offending devils from a man's body with a knife. Kuei, in common with most Chinese, could no more understand the idea of a single God than she could comprehend the aims of Western surgery.

Luke returned to the empty factory that night convinced that Dan Gemmell and Abel Snow were right. The opium trade had to be stamped out; but he believed that the Chinese were incapable of doing it by themselves. They needed the willing help of Great Britain, and a start would have to be made in the fields of India, not in the cities of China.

The following day, Luke continued his work in Gemmell Company's office, redoubling his efforts to find a glimmer of hope in the situation of the trading company. He succeeded in depressing himself even more than before. Far from reaping the rich rewards he had anticipated, Luke had been given a percentage of – nothing. The only relief in the gloom was that the Company was owed money by its Chinese Hong.

The Chinese Government's insistence that all merchandise, imports and exports, pass through the hands of a Hong meant that the Chinese merchant controlled the purse strings – and the Hongs were notoriously slow to settle their debts. Gemmell Company's affairs were in the hands of Lien Ling, the oldest and most influential of the Hongs. He was also the craftiest. Recovering the money might prove difficult.

Late that evening, Luke was poring over the accounts, trying to determine the exact amount owing to the Company, when there came a soft knocking at the main door of the factory. Frowning at the unexpected interruption, Luke strode to the door and flung it open irritably.

Standing outside in the darkness was Kuei.

Luke's immediate thought was that something must have happened to Soo Fang, but Kuei was far too cheerful. She walked past Luke into the factory as though she came calling every day.

'Hello. I have come to visit you.'

Luke took a hasty look out into the square before closing the door and hurrying after Kuei. Her unexpected visit had thrown him completely off balance. 'Kuei . . . women aren't allowed in the factories. You could land yourself in serious trouble. . . .'

She had reached the open door of the office now, and turned to face him. With the light behind her he was unable to read her expression.

'Nobody saw me come. There is very little light outside, and I was very careful. But no matter. If you want me to go. . . .'

'Of course I don't want you to leave.' Luke gathered his scattered wits together. 'Here, sit down. I . . . have some tea.' Luke had quickly adapted to the Indian and Chinese habit of always having a pot of cold tea available. He poured some quickly, the delicate cup rattling noisily against the saucer in his clumsy eagerness to please her.

Kuei smiled as she took the tea from him and perched herself precariously on the edge of a chair, doing her best not to allow herself to be overawed by her surroundings.

'How is your father?'

Luke asked the question just as Kuei had decided that to drink the tea she should bring cup and saucer to her mouth without parting them. She lowered them and realized her error as Luke lifted only his cup. The Fan Qui had many strange habits. She would need to watch carefully if she wished to learn their ways.

'My father is suffering much pain in his belly. He begs to be given opium, but your barbarian doctor gives him only medicine to make him sleep. It will be a long time before he is better . . . but I must thank you. If you had not found him last night, he would be dead. I know that. Thank you . . . Hau-ye – or should I call you "Master"?'

The unfamiliar use of the words by Kuei jarred on Luke. He remembered her natural arrogance during the time she was bringing him to safety on the Pearl River.

'I am not your master; neither am I lord of anything. My name is Luke.'

'Luke.' Kuei had difficulty with the name, pronouncing it 'Ruke'. She seemed pleased with the sound, but she was also puzzled. 'McCulloch makes all Chinese call him "Master", or "Hau-ye", because he is Lord of Hong Kong.'

'I'm not Ezra McCulloch.' Luke frowned. 'But I'm as much to blame as he is for your father's condition. I let him pay for my passage up-river with opium.'

'Oh, no,' replied Kuei quickly. 'It would have made no difference how you paid him. He would have exchanged anything else he was given for opium – or bought it with money. No, this time it is my fault. I quarrelled with him and said he must give up opium. I threw all he had in the river.' Kuei shrugged. 'That was stupid of me. He came ashore and found some bad opium.'

For a moment, Luke thought she might cry. Instead, she stood up and put her cup on the desk in front of her. 'Please, I would like you to show me this house.'

'Certainly.' Luke put aside his concern about Kuei's presence in Gemmell Company's factory. Delighted with her unexpected friendliness, he first showed her the offices and then took her upstairs to the living-quarters.

Kuei was particularly interested in Luke's room, but appalled at his lack of possessions. He had been able to bring to Canton only what he could cram into a small bag. The remainder of his clothes and belongings had been off-loaded from *The Two Brothers* at Hong Kong. 'I'll get them soon,' he explained. 'When traffic is normal again on the river. I might even come to Hong Kong myself to pick them up.'

He smiled at Kuei. 'I'll come and visit you there.'

Kuei did not answer his smile. She was tracing a finger in the dust on top of a bedside table, looking down at the pattern with a serious expression.

'I have spoken much to the barbarian doctor. He told me that you work for a man who will not bring opium to China '

Luke made no reply. Kuei had more to say.

'Now Gemmell Company is sick. . . .' Luke carefully avoided a smile. 'You are the master. Will you bring in opium?'

'After seeing what it had done to your father and the other poor creatures in Hog Lane? No, Kuei. I stand with Dr Snow. Gemmell Company will never import opium while I am with them. The day Dan Gemmell changes his policy, I leave.'

Luke was not making his statement in a bid to please Kuei — although at this moment he desperately wanted to impress her. After his visit to Hog Lane, Luke had vowed never to have anything to do with the opium trade. Rather, he intended doing everything within his limited power to bring it to a rapid end.

Kuei was pleased with his reply. 'That is what the barbarian doctor told me. He said you are a good man — not the same as other Fan Qui.' She smiled at him. 'I gave you a bad time on the river . . . Luke.'

Her use of his name delighted Luke, and he smiled at her. 'Yes, Kuei. You gave me a bad time.'

'I am sorry. I was very worried about my father. We can be friends now, perhaps?'

'Friends . . . ?'

Kuei looked apprehensive as Luke moved towards her and took her by the shoulders. She remembered the last occasion on which Luke had held her like this.

Luke remembered, too, and he trembled at the memory of her soft body in the moonlight. 'I'll try, Kuei.'

She smiled up at him, and suddenly Luke's self-control snapped. Cupping her face in his hands, he brought his mouth down hard upon hers. For a moment she struggled, breathing fear against his face. Then the fear became something else, and her hands came up to touch his cheek, her fingertips moving over his features as might those of a blind person.

Luke released her reluctantly, and her eyes stayed closed for a long time. When she opened them her dark eyes looked at him in awe. 'Lo Asan told me that the Fan Qui touch lips . . . but I never knew it would feel like that.'

Luke kissed her again, and this time their bodies shared the embrace. When Luke realized how hard he was holding her to him he released her for fear he was hurting her, but Kuei moaned and pressed herself even harder to him.

Luke's hands moved up inside her loose grey jacket, and she moved to allow him to hold the roundness of her more easily.

'Wait, Luke . . . please wait!'

Gasping for breath, Kuei stayed the progress of his other hand and she stepped away from him. He watched her jacket and trousers fall to the floor, as they had once before. But now there was no bargain struck with her father to come between them.

Seven

ABEL SNOW disapproved strongly of the new relationship between Luke and Kuei. The missionary told Luke so, in no uncertain terms, after Luke and Kuei had spent their third night together in the tiny bedroom in Gemmell Company's factory.

'I'm not concerned about the rules laid down by the Chinese, Luke – though you flout them at your peril. I'm talking about Christian laws. The need to set an example to people who have not yet discovered God.'

'What I'm doing is hurting nobody,' retorted Luke. 'Save your sermons on good and evil for those who trade in opium.'

Luke was unduly sharp with Abel Snow because the missionary's knowledge of the state of affairs had taken him by surprise. He had thought it a close secret and was concerned that it might affect the happiness he had so unexpectedly found with Kuei.

'You are hurting yourself and Kuei,' persisted Abel Snow quietly. 'I'm not blind, Luke. I know that most of the traders keep a Chinese mistress in Macau. But their relationships mean little, either to them or to the girls involved. I think I know you well enough to realize that this is different. You are not a young man to have a casual affair – any more than Kuei would agree to be passed on to another man should you leave or tire of her. I saw the way you looked at her when you were first together in my hospital. I prayed then that there would never be anything more than a look between you. Taking Kuei for your mistress can only lead to unhappiness – perhaps even disaster. Please look at things logically, Luke. What can come of this? You are an up-and-coming trader, with the chance to show others that it isn't necessary to carry opium in order to make a profit. . . .'

Luke snorted derisively, but Abel Snow continued patiently. 'All right, things *don't* look so good for Gemmell Company right now, but remember the Company has been running itself for months. Now you are here things will change. I *know* they will. Before long you'll be an influential man in this part of the world. Kuei is a Hoklo – a gipsy of the water. Her people are wild and free. Try to keep hold of her and she'll break your heart, for sure. Not only that; along the way, you'll make her an outcast from her own people. Be fair to both of you, Luke. End this affair right here and now.'

After angrily telling Abel Snow to 'stick to medicine and mind your own damned business', Luke left the hospital without paying his daily call upon Dan Gemmell. No doubt the medical missionary was convinced he was giving Luke sound advice, but Luke had fallen deeply in love with Kuei. Right now, she was more important to him than anything else in life.

Luke waited for Kuei to say something to him, certain that Abel Snow would have spoken to her along similar lines during her daily visit to her father, but the American missionary had said all he had to say on the subject to Luke. What happened now would be a matter for Luke's conscience – providing there was no outside interference from the Canton magistrate.

Kuei had arranged a special meal for Luke that night. Appalled by what she found in the far-from-well-stocked larder of the factory, she had bought a variety of foods in the floating village and prepared them herself in the factory kitchen.

There were a number of fish dishes, prawns served piping hot in a clear soup, fried rice, bamboo shoots and water chestnuts, all washed down with a heady rice wine bought especially for the occasion in Canton's walled city. Using chopsticks was still a problem for Luke and he dropped more than he was able to carry to his mouth. Whenever he tried to complain Kuei skilfully popped a choice titbit into his mouth, effectively silencing him and reducing herself to fits of happy giggling.

Later, Luke lay on the bed with Kuei in his arms. It was unbearably hot, and they were both naked. They had made love, and now Kuei dozed. Luke stroked her arm, delighting in the smooth skin beneath his touch.

Sounds carried far on the still air. From the walled city there came the night-time hubbub of a city occupied by a million people. Closer to the factories there were more distinct noises. The desperate squealing of a family pig, objecting vociferously to having its throat cut by the hand that had provided food for nine idle months; the crackle of firecrackers, chasing evil spirits from a house where a family prepared for bed; the clip-clop of wooden-soled sandals on the hard ground of the lane behind the factories. From the river there was the occasional call of one fisherman to another; a baby crying in the floating village where Tik-wei slept; and the incessant throaty grunting of romantic bullfrogs.

Through the open window, Luke could see far across the river the lights of a Buddhist monastery, isolated high on a hillside.

The sounds and sights promoted a remarkable feeling of well-being in Luke. There was a timelessness in China that soaked into a man. A feeling that nothing would ever change. Then he remembered what Abel Snow had said to him. Involuntarily, Luke tightened his arms about Kuei.

He had thought she was asleep, but now she nuzzled his ear and said, 'I feel your body close to mine, my Luke – but where are your thoughts?'

'They are here, too, Kuei. I am thinking about the future. *Our* future.'

Kuei hugged him. 'Why? You are going to be very rich and have me to live with you always. You will buy so many nice things for your mistress, Kuei, that every Hoklo girl will want a Fan Qui. I shall be very happy.'

'Will you, Kuei? If it were possible for us to be together always, would you be happy away from your own people?'

Kuei was silent for such a long time that Luke thought he had offended her in some way, but then she spoke, her voice low and husky.

'You think I am happy with the Hoklo, Luke? You think that is the life I want? No, the Hoklo are not my people. They are all I have, but they are still not my people. They have never let me forget that.'

'I don't understand. Soo Fang . . . ?'

'Soo Fang is a good man, but I am the daughter of his heart and not of his loins. He found me floating in the King Ling River, in Fu-kien, when I was a baby. I wore very nice clothes – not the clothes of the water-people. Soo Fang thought there had been an accident. He made enquiries for my family, but no one knew anything. That was a bad year in Fu-kien. There had been no rain, and the rivers were so low that there was no water for the crops. Many people had died, and girl-babies were being put into the river so that mothers' milk could keep the boy-children alive. Soo Fang kept me. The Hoklo – those you say

76

are my people – they told Soo Fang that keeping me was fool-ishness. After all, what is another girl-baby? But Soo Fang has always had a good heart. He kept me and looked after me as though I were his own.'

Kuei had raised herself on one elbow and was plucking at the bedsheet as she talked. 'My mother – Soo Fang's wife – she, too, was very kind. No daughter ever had a better mother. She died when Tik-wei was born.'

Luke saw the tears glistening on Kuei's eyelashes. 'For many years after my mother died things were hard for us. The fish did not come close inshore, the rains failed again and again. Then someone said it was my fault. That I had been put in the river as an offering to the Sea Gods, and Soo Fang had offended them by taking me from the water. No one would talk to us. They even spoke of killing me and throwing my body back into the sea. When things became too bad Soo Fang left Fu-kien and brought Tik-wei and myself to Hong Kong. We told the Hoklo here nothing of our troubles, but for a long time – until Lo Asan came to Hong Kong – I made no friends. Even so, we had a good life here, until Soo Fang began smoking "the pipe of dreams". You ask me if I will be happy away from "my" people. I tell you, I do not know who my people are.'

Kuei put a hand flat on Luke's bare chest and laid her head against it. 'But I am very happy now, my Luke. Happier than I have ever been. I know it will not last – it cannot last. When Soo Fang is better I will have to take him back to Hong Kong and you will need to stay here. But until it is time I will pretend. . . .'

Luke protested that she, Tik-wei and Soo Fang could live at Canton, but she silenced him by placing a finger on his lips. 'Hush! One day all the other Fan Qui will return to Canton. What would you do then . . . ? Dress me as a man and tell them I am your cook-boy? No, my Luke. The Hoklo at Fu-kien might be right. If I belong to the Sea Gods, they will be angry because you make me happy. Then you, too, would suffer. It will be enough to be together for a little while. We must not hope for more.'

Luke told Kuei she was talking a lot of superstitious non-sense, but she effectively silenced him again, this time by kiss-ing him and insisting that he made love to her. Meeting the demands of Kuei's body drove all thoughts of talking from Lukes's mind. Afterwards he fell into a deep sleep. When he woke, the sun was sending its rays in through the window, and Kuei had gone.

That was the day *Black Swan* arrived at Whampoa. Its captain immediately came up-river to the offices of Gemmell Company to report his arrival. To Luke's surprise, Gideon Pyke was not many years older than himself.

A fellow-countryman of Abel Snow, Pyke was a tough 'Yankee' from the island of Nantucket, off the coast of Massachusetts. Born of a fisherman father, he was deep-sea fishing off the Newfoundland Banks at an age when most children were being taught to recite the Lord's Prayer.

Gideon Pyke never did get around to learning that particular prayer – but he quickly mastered the art of handling a boat. A mate on a whaling ship for two years, he afterwards worked for a year as the mate of a slaver on the West African coast run. Conscience eventually scored a victory over the high rewards to be earned from slaving, and Gideon spent two adventurous years commanding a gun-runner for the Mexican government of General Antonio Lopez de Santa-Anna. Then, in March 1836, Santa-Anna stormed a fort on the Alamo and wrote the names of its defenders into America's history. Sickened by the slaughter of his own countrymen, Santa-Anna's gun-running captain moved on.

Six months later he arrived in Macau. He was immediately taken on by Dan Gemmell and put in command of *Black Swan*. Gemmell never had reason to regret his decision. Gideon Pyke was a tough, godless, swashbuckling giant of a man. He was also honest, hard-working and unswervingly loyal to his employer.

Gideon Pyke came into Gemmell Company's office like a breath of fresh salt air, and after mutual introductions had been made he asked for Dan Gemmell. When Luke told him the merchant was in the mission hospital Pyke grunted and sat down on the edge of the desk where Luke had the accounts spread out before him.

'Dan should have given up and gone home years ago.'

Taking a tobacco-pouch and a wooden pipe from a pocket, he began filling the huge carved bowl with tobacco. 'The word in Macau is that you broke the Chinese blockade all by yourself.'

'I made the trip in a sampan – mostly at night. But I just kept

78

my head down. The Chinese fishing family who brought me took all the risks.'

Gideon Pyke nodded, his teeth clenched about the pipe stem as he put a light to the tobacco. It was dry and crackled like a corn-stubble fire, sending out clouds of blue aromatic smoke.

'You figuring on staying with Dan Gemmell for long?'

Waving smoke from the air before him, Luke replied, 'That depends on how much cargo you're carrying. I was hoping to stay here until I'd made a fortune but, unless Gemmell Company increases its trade, one lifetime won't be long enough.'

Taking the pipe from his mouth and holding it up before him, Gideon Pyke leaked smoke as he spoke. 'This is an old Sioux Indian peace-pipe. I brought it here, hoping it might just do a bit of good. I ain't yet found one damn Chinaman ready to take a single puff at it. I reckon life's just plain cussed like that. Never does do what you think it ought.' Slapping a few sheets of stained and creased paper down on the desk before Luke, he said, 'Here's a list of what I've brought you – and I'm owed fifteen hundred dollars by the Company. I heard of some ginseng, off-loaded in a godown in Manila. I bought the lot, using my own money.'

Luke nodded his approval. Gideon Pyke had added almost a thousand miles to his homeward voyage, but had picked up a cargo of a root herb highly valued by the Chinese. The American was more than a good captain. He possessed a shrewd trading brain – as his next remark quickly confirmed.

'I've also brought some cargo up-river from Macau for Lancelot Fox. He's one of the traders sulking at Macau with Killian. I trebled the usual freight rate – and might have got more had I been prepared to hold out a while longer.'

Luke put down *Black Swan*'s cargo manifests and stared hard at the other man. 'How many fully laden ships are held up at Macau?'

Gideon Pyke shrugged. 'I didn't count. Certainly upwards of a dozen. Why?'

'If you brought a full load up-river for whoever would pay the highest freight rate, how much would we make?'

A great cloud of smoke escaped from Gideon Pyke's mouth as he followed Luke's thinking. 'About five times as much as we'll make from our own cargo.'

'Then that's what we'll do. What's more, there are warehouses full of goods at Whampoa, waiting to go *down*-river.'

Luke was excited. 'The traders might back Killian's stand against the Chinese, but they'll not turn down the chance to cut their losses.'

'Killian's not going to be happy with you. He's sent a letter to the Provincial Governor telling him that, unless there's an official apology for the insult sustained by the British flag, it won't be seen flying on the Pearl River again.'

'All right, then humour him. You're an American – fly your own country's flag in *Black Swan*. But get the cargoes. Killian's pigheadedness has given us a wonderful opportunity to make some much-needed money for Gemmell Company. It won't last for ever, so let's make the most of it while we can. How long will each trip take?'

Gideon Pyke grinned happily. 'Under normal circumstances about three days each way. I'll make it in two. Tell Dan I'm back. I'll call in and see him next trip if you give me five minutes to spare. Right now I'm away to make sure those good-for-nothing coolies unload *Black Swan* in record time. See you around, Luke. . . . I think I'm going to enjoy working with you.'

Gideon Pyke's promise to cut down the time for the voyage between Macau and Canton was no idle boast. Five days later he paid another brief visit to the factory at Canton. In that time he had carried a full load to Macau, and returned to Whampoa with holds packed full of cargo and the decks of his ship piled so high it was in serious danger of capsizing. To speed up the voyage, the enterprising Yankee captain had taken on a dozen Chinese oarsmen. With their long sweep-oars, they defied wind and tide as they sweated to cut down the time spent on the river.

Dan Gemmell was overjoyed at the success of the venture and chortled happily as he learned that the traders who derided him for not dealing in opium were now desperately outbidding each other for cargo space in *Black Swan*.

'They've only themselves to blame for the state of things here, Luke,' he said. 'They've become too greedy. It wasn't enough to store opium in receiving ships and wait for buyers to come to them. They had to bring it up to Canton and rub the Tsotang's nose in what they were doing. They fooled themselves into thinking they were safe, hiding behind a flag the Chinese neither recognize nor give a damn for. There's a whole lot wrong with Chinese trading methods, Luke, but this is their country. They set the rules. We'd do well to abide by them.'

Luke felt uncomfortable at Dan Gemmell's words. He wondered what the merchant would say if he learned about Kuei. Dan Gemmell's health seemed much improved now. He spent long periods sitting out of bed. He was even talking of making the walk to his factory. If he walked in upon Luke and Kuei, their idyllic nights together would come to an abrupt end.

In sharp contrast to Dan Gemmell, Soo Fang was fighting a desperately painful battle with his addiction. At first, Abel Snow attempted a total cure, cutting the fisherman off entirely from the drug; but Soo Fang's spasms became so violent that the doctor feared for his life. He was now trying to wean Soo Fang away from the drug by easy stages, with indifferent success. Abel Snow had no doubt that the fisherman would one day return to his former ways, but he intended keeping him in the mission hospital while any hope remained.

Black Swan kept up her fast voyages between Macau and Whampoa, making a handsome profit for the Company, even though the American and Dutch traders were now operating their own boats between the two ports. Gradually the unsatisfactory method of trading became routine, as did the situation at the Canton factories. As Luke and Kuei's nights together stretched into weeks they were so happy that they allowed themselves to forget that one day their happiness would have to come to an end.

One night, long after the hour when the sounds of the walled city had usually ebbed away, Luke was awakened by the screaming of women and children. Through the screams he could hear the hungry crackling of flames as they consumed the tinder-dry bamboo frames of houses and shanties. Waking Kuei, who lay asleep in his arms, Luke leaped from the bed and ran to a window at the rear of the factory. From here he could see the flames climbing into the night sky above the suburbs, just across the creek to the east of the factories.

Hurrying back into the bedroom, he began dressing quickly, telling Kuei what he had seen.

'But why are you dressing? The creek will keep the fire from the factories.'

'The factories are safe enough, but listen to those screams, Kuei. There are women and children caught in the fire. The flames are jumping from house to house as fast as a man can run. Without help hundreds will die.'

'Wait. . . . I am coming, too.'

'No, you stay here. I'll be back as soon as I can.'

But, even as Luke ran from the room, Kuei was throwing on her clothes. She could think of a hundred reasons why Luke should not go into the Chinese suburbs of Canton, but she knew he would not stay to listen to any of them. Yet she was determined he would not venture out alone.

When Luke reached the hump-backed bridge that spanned the creek he had to battle against the tide of Chinese fleeing from the fire. It became easier when he reached the narrow streets on the far side, and soon he was on the fringe of the blaze. The heat was overwhelming here. Matting was smouldering on the walls of frame houses thirty feet from the fire. Coolies who lived in this poor quarter of the city were running this way and that in terror. All was utter chaos, with no effort being made to contain the blaze.

Luke grabbed one of the running men and shook him for a full minute before he became coherent enough to tell Luke where water could be obtained. Eventually, Luke's own calmness had its effect. His panic conquered, the Chinese did his best to help. With his aid, Luke organized a chain of men and women with buckets to fight the blaze. There was no hope of actually putting it out, but by constantly soaking the buildings ahead of the wind-driven flames they succeeded in halting its advance for a while. It was long enough for Luke and his helpers to pull down a whole row of matting-covered shanties and provide a firebreak.

As they worked, a mother and two children appeared at the heart of the fire. Surrounded by flames and smoke, they were miraculously unscathed and Luke plunged into the inferno to bring them to safety.

Wiping his streaming eyes, Luke was about to rejoin the bucket-wielding firefighters when he was confronted by a number of men who had no part in extinguishing the fires. They wore the yellow uniform of Canton's police. Behind them, seated in an open sedan chair, was the Tsotang of Canton.

The Tsotang's interest lay not with the fire, but with Luke. Two of his policemen took Luke by the arms. He shook them off angrily. Pointing to the blaze which roared hundreds of feet in the air, only a few yards from where they stood, Luke shouted for the Tsotang to put his men to fighting the fire.

It was doubtful if the Tsotang heard him, and Luke was not given the opportunity of repeating his words. One of the policemen raised the stout bamboo pole he carried and brought it crashing down upon Luke's head. As Luke stumbled, other policemen joined in and he was brutally beaten to the ground. The beating continued long after Luke fell still beneath their blows, a limp arm flung across his head in a vain attempt to protect it from their blows.

Beyond the policemen, Kuei stood at the edge of the small crowd that watched the incident. Fortunately, those about her believed her hysterical screams were a result of the fire that had razed a whole suburb to the ground. They would have been less tolerant had they known her fear was for the safety of the unconscious Fan Qui being carried into the walled city by the Tsotang's men.

Eight

LUKE regained consciousness, fighting against the water that hit his face and ran down his neck. He tried to brush it away, but his arms would not move to his will. He made two attempts to raise his head. When he eventually succeeded, the back of it struck hard against a stone wall. His eyes responded reluctantly, one not opening at all. The other did so painfully, and he peered at the world through a slit in the swollen flesh.

He looked into the grinning face of a yellow-uniformed Chinese, holding in his hand a bowl of none-too-clean water. Suddenly, memories of the fire and the Tsotang's men flooded back to Luke. He was in an uncomfortable sitting position and, still dazed, he struggled to rise to his feet without success. Turning his throbbing head, he quickly saw the the reason. His outstretched arms were chained to rings in the stone wall behind him, and heavy chains secured his ankles.

'What's the meaning of this? Why am I here?' he croaked, his tongue thick and his throat dry and sore from the smoke of the fire.

'Ah! You speak our language. That will make our questioning so much easier.'

Turning his head to bring his good eye into focus, Luke saw the Tsotang. The Chinese magistrate wore a silken skull-cap with a narrow saucer brim, on which was proudly displayed a gold badge, denoting that the wearer was a mandarin of the seventh grade. This was well down the Imperial social scale, but it was sufficient for him to wield considerable influence among the hundreds of million Chinese who would never achieve Imperial recognition.

Teng Ching, Tsotang of one of the largest cities in the great Chinese Empire, was a highly ambitious man. He intended that one day he should become a provincial governor. It was a precarious position, subject to the whim of the Imperial Emperor and the ambitions of fellow-officials. Few governors served for longer than a couple of years. But in that short time a clever man could become immensely wealthy by skilful misuse of his power and position. When he was eventually banished to obscurity, Teng Ching meant to have enough wealth to keep him in great comfort for the remainder of his life. His capture of Luke in a forbidden area of Canton should provide the means for advancement to the sixth or even the fifth grade of mandarin. The barbarians were in universal disfavour. It was a great opportunity to show everyone, barbarians and Chinese, that all men were subject to Imperial law. Such a lesson would not go unrewarded by the Emperor.

Lifting the hem of his silk robes clear of the dungeon's disgustingly filthy floor, Teng Ching advanced closer to Luke.

'Tonight a fire destroyed the homes of twenty thousand unfortunate people in the suburbs beyond the city wall. At least fifty beloved subjects of the Emperor were burned to death. The figure will be much higher when those who seek their families learn they will never meet them again in this sad world.' The Tsotang leaned closer to Luke. 'Why did you start the fire, barbarian? Why did you destroy the homes and possessions of His Imperial Majesty's subjects?'

Luke looked at the Tsotang in disbelief. 'You're mad. You know very well I was helping to put the fire out.'

His painfully rasped denial was cut short dramatically. One of the yellow-coated policemen hit him in the mouth with the back of his hand. 'You will speak to the Tsotang with more respect.' He struck out again, and Luke tasted the sweetness of his own blood as his tongue sought his lips.

'You lie,' said Tsotang Teng Ching. 'Only a barbarian would think of such a stupid lie. Here, in Canton, there are more than a million people. Would one man make any difference to the help that a million can give?'

'Your million were too busy running,' retorted Luke through thickening lips. 'You know I was helping fight the fire. You saw me yourself.'

Luke's head snapped back as he was struck from his blind side. This time the beating continued until he lost consciousness.

The Tsotang looked at Luke angrily. Extracting a confession from this barbarian would not be as easy as he had anticipated. However, with the passing of painful time, he would say whatever he was told to say. The Tsotang's prisoners always did – eventually. Teng had no doubt that a barbarian felt pain just as keenly as the Emperor's own subjects. He certainly bled as easily. Stepping back from Luke, Teng raised the hem of his robes higher and made his way from the stone-built cell, brushing aside the men of his police force as he went.

When Kuei saw Luke beaten to the ground by the Tsotang's police she screamed for them to stop. Her first instinct was to run to him and drag his assailants away. Common sense took over when the Tsotang and his men looked around for the source of the screams. Kuei could not understand why Luke was being arrested, but she realized that, whatever the reason, her interference would only make things worse for him.

At that moment, the burning roof of a nearby house fell in with a loud roar. As sparks and flames were flung to the sky, a number of women bystanders screamed and fled in terror. The Tsotang and his men returned to their task. Luke was beaten unconscious and, as the police dragged him away, Kuei followed.

It was no easy task to keep up with the yellow-clad men. It seemed the whole population of the suburbs was seeking refuge within the walled city. At the same time, thousands of the city dwellers were trying to push their way out through Canton's four main gates, eager to view the worst fire in the history of the city. The police cleared a path for themselves and the Tsotang with heavy and frequent blows from their long staves, but Kuei had to fight her way through as best she could.

She followed Luke and his captors as far as the city's high-walled prison. When the heavy iron-studded doors slammed shut Kuei stood outside for many minutes, not knowing what to do next.

After a while, Kuei found a spot in the shadows of a narrow alleyway from where she could see the prison gates. All water-people were terrified of prisons, and Kuei was no exception. Used to a free and unrestricted life on the rivers and oceans about China, a Hoklo did not survive long when confined to a narrow prison cell. Canton's prison in particular had acquired a frightening notoriety. Many Hoklo had been taken there over the years – but few had returned to tell of their experiences within the high grey walls. It was hardly surprising. The Chinese judiciary was sadly lacking in patience and regard for justice. Both prisoners and witnesses were tortured, often to death, in order that a case might be concluded in a manner already decided upon by the Tsotang. His decision was usually influenced by a substantial donation from one or other of the parties involved.

Kuei waited in her alleyway that night and all the next day, ignoring the kicks and irritable jostling of those who needed to pass along the narrow way. She saw the Tsotang leave the prison, and was there when he returned again the next evening.

Beside herself with worry, Kuei could think of no one to whom she could turn for advice. Then, when dusk had fallen again, she saw a company of Tartar bannermen marching off to assume night guard duty on the city gates. Suddenly, she knew where she must go. General Shengan, the officer commanding the Tartar army in Canton, was the uncle of her friend, Lo Asan. She would go to speak to him.

Kuei found General Shengan's house beside the barracks of the Tartar regiment. Shengan's own men mounted guard before the house and they refused to allow her to pass. Only after being subjected to a great many ribald comments did Kuei manage to persuade one of the soldiers to inform General Shengan that a friend of his niece wished to speak with him.

Looking quite as fierce as legend had painted him, General Shengan frowned at the grey-clad Hoklo girl as she went through the ritual obeisance demanded of a girl of the peasant classes when faced with an official of Shengan's high rank.

'You say you are a friend of Lo Asan? Do you carry a message from her?'

'No, your Excellency. I come to beg for your assistance.'

Shengan's frown deepened. There was always someone begging him to use his influence to solve a petty problem.

'You use the name of my niece and waste my valuable time to seek a personal favour?'

Shengan's anger caused Kuei to quake in fear, but she persisted. 'It is not for myself, Excellency. It is for a Fan Qui. He is known to Lo Asan. She asked me to take care of him. . . .'

'A Fan Qui? What manner of nonsense is this?'

Determined not to be overawed by the General's angry manner, Kuei told Shengan of Luke's arrest by the Tsotang's police.

By the time she ended her story, General Shengan was no longer angry, although his face registered concern.

'The Tsotang is a fool! Does he wish to start a war? You

did well to come to me, girl. No one else would be able to challenge the power of the Tsotang.'

'You will help him?' Kuei's joy was far more than that of someone who had been granted a favour for the sake of a friend.

'This Fan Qui, what is he to you?' General Shengan knew the answer before Kuei dropped her glance to the floor at her feet.

'This Fan Qui . . . he is Luke Trewarne?'

Kuei nodded without raising her eyes.

'Ah! Then it was you who brought him up-river from Hong Kong. You are Kuei, daughter of Soo Fang.'

Kuei looked up at him, startled.

'You thought it was a secret? So it might be to most people. But did you think the arrival of a Fan Qui in Canton would pass entirely without notice?'

General Shengan saw the natural beauty of the water-gipsy before him and he smiled inwardly. He had already met Luke Trewarne. A young girl and a young man together on a small boat for at least three days and nights . . . ! It mattered not that they came from vastly different backgrounds. Shengan sighed. He wished the differences between their two countries might be resolved as easily.

'This Fan Qui . . . you share his bed?'

Kuei met his gaze unashamedly. 'I share his bed.'

General Shengan acknowledged her frankness with a nod of his head. Who was he to criticize? His favourite mistress had been a black-skinned Orissa girl, captured from the harem of a dissident rebel leader in the eastern mountains. . . . Lo Asan, too, had been sold to a Fan Qui – and Luke Trewarne was a better man than Ezra McCulloch.

'I will help Luke Trewarne but *you* must leave Canton immediately.'

'But . . . my father is ill in the factory hospital.'

'I am aware of that. He is there because of the Fan Qui opium. He must go with you. It will be too dangerous for either of you to stay in Canton – and will put me in danger, too. I risk the displeasure of my Emperor by interfering with the duties of a Tsotang. I do it only because I believe it to be more important than you, me, or any Fan Qui. It is for the future of China. Should you or your father fall into the hands of Tsotang Teng, he will make you talk – and there are men at the court of the Emperor eager to attach other meanings to my actions. You will leave *immediately*. This is understood?'

After only a moment's hesitation, Kuei nodded. She had been successful. This was why she had come to see General Shengan. Luke would be taken from the prison and returned to the factory – even though she would not be there to welcome him, to be held in his arms and loved by him. . . . She blinked away the unwonted tears that blinded her, hoping futilely that Shengan had not seen them. It did not matter. When Luke was free he would come to Hong Kong and find her. She would wait for him there.

Kuei began to thank General Shengan, falling to her knees and bowing her forehead to the floor.

He waved her from him impatiently. 'You are wasting time. We both have much to do. Go! Take your father from the Fan Qui hospital and leave – and say nothing of this talk to anyone.'

The yellow-jacketed police 'questioned' Luke enthusiastically for twenty-four hours. Each of the Tsotang's men wanted to be the one to whom Luke would admit starting the fire that had gutted the Canton suburb. Because of their conviction that Luke would eventually break, the interrogation, though painful, was not as brutal as it otherwise might have been. Only when an interrogator became thoroughly exasperated with his continuing silence was Luke beaten into blissful unconsciousness.

When darkness once again hid the sky beyond the single barred window Tsotang returned to the cell. Standing over Luke, his clean scented silk robes contrasted sharply with Luke's smoke-grimed clothes, soaked by now with his own blood. The magistrate was in a happy mood.

'I am pleased to see that my police have not been too violent with you. It is good.'

The Tsotang signalled to one of his men, and Luke's head was pulled back so that he looked up at the Tsotang. Luke's head swam alarmingly and he saw the mandarin through a bloody haze.

Tsotang Teng Ching barked an order, and one of his policemen picked up a bucket of water from a corner of the cell. Half its contents were flung into Luke's face. While he was still gasping for breath, the chains about his wrists were unfastened from the wall and he was dragged to a rush sleeping-mat spread out on the floor. Groaning at the pain that the movement caused him, Luke was dumped upon the mat and propped up to enable one of the policemen to pour water down his throat. Luke choked but continued to swallow as much as he could. It was the first water he had tasted since being brought to the prison.

When he could drink no more, Luke was laid, gasping, on the sleeping-mat, his aching head dropping the last six inches to the hard surface.

'You will be fed tonight, and can have as much water as you wish,' the Tsotang beamed amiably. 'Eat well. I trust that when you wake tomorrow morning you will be restored to full strength.'

The policemen about the Tsotang smiled, too, and Luke felt more apprehension than he had during their ill-tempered questioning.

'You will be pleased to hear I accept your explanation concerning the events of last night. Indeed, I am told your conduct was praiseworthy. That you rescued a woman and her child from the fire.'

Relief surged through Luke. 'Then . . . I can go back to the factories?' He did not recognize his own voice.

'Yes . . . eventually.' Tsotang Teng Ching's face lost its smile, and Luke's heart sank as he realized his ordeal was not yet over. But he was totally unprepared for the Tsotang's next words. 'Unfortunately, another matter has come to my attention. A very serious allegation has been made against you. I am told you are guilty of raping a young Hoklo girl who was foolish enough to visit your factory.'

'That's a lie! I've raped no one.'

'Another denial? How sad. It means I will need to send my men to find this girl and hear *her* story. I believe her name is Soo Kuei and that her father is in the hospital of the American missionary. We will have them both brought here for questioning.' Tsotang Teng Ching was smiling broadly now. 'Is that what you wish, barbarian? Do you still say you are not guilty of raping this girl?'

Luke looked up at the smiling Tsotang, and from him to the brutal faces of the yellow-clad policemen. He had already experienced their methods of questioning. It was not difficult to imagine what they would do to Kuei.

90

'No.' Mumbling through swollen lips, he fought to gain control of his voice. 'No. . . . There is no need to bring her here. I raped her.'

'Ah!' A sigh of satisfaction escaped from the Tsotang. 'That is better, barbarian. Your confession will be written down and you will sign it. You are wise, barbarian. You give me an opportunity to show my mercy. For such a crime as this I could order you to be beheaded. Instead, as you saved lives in the fire, I shall give you a chance to save your own. Tomorrow you will be taken out and given two hundred strokes with a heavy bamboo. You are young and strong. You *may* survive.'

Nine

LUKE awoke from a long and deep sleep when his captors arrived to unfasten the chains that had been placed on his wrists and ankles again the previous evening. The Chinese police were in a good humour. Only when they began discussing the quality of his clothing and who would have each article did he understand why. They did not expect him to survive his judicial beating!

His limbs free, Luke was prodded to his feet, but when he stood swaying in the centre of the cell the stone walls began swimming about him. He would have fallen had not two of the guards caught him. His weak condition earned no postponement of the sentence passed upon him by the Tsotang. With two Chinese policemen supporting him, Luke stumbled from the cell and along a long dark corridor with heavy barred doors on either side. At the end of the corridor a flight of worn stone steps led upwards to an open courtyard. Luke's legs rebelled at the steps, and by the time he reached the courtyard he was being dragged along, the toes of his shoes leaving a double track in the dry dust on the ground.

The sight of the Fan Qui being dragged to the place of punishment brought howls of glee and derision from a huge crowd, assembled to witness the unique event. They were convinced that Luke was being brought out in this manner because he was afraid to face up to his punishment.

The wooden whipping-post was worn smooth by the writhing agony of decades of victims, and Luke's arms were secured to it with rope. Passed through a hole in the top of the eight-foot post, the rope was pulled until Luke's arms were stretched high above his head, his cheek resting against the post. When he rose to his toes in a futile bid to take some of the strain from his arms, Luke's legs were tied to the post. Tsotang Teng Ching was present and he walked around Luke slowly, satisfying himself that Luke was properly secured.

Next, Luke's shirt was ripped from his back and left hanging in tatters from his waist. Then a burly Chinese stepped forward, carrying a number of bamboo canes clutched in his arms. The canes were each at least six feet in length and the thickness of Luke's thumb. The man who held them was Canton's chief executioner. The muscular man's speciality was lopping the head off a kneeling man with a single flick of the heavy curved sword kept in the prison for this sole grisly purpose.

The executioner was a disappointed man. He had expected to be allowed to practise his expertise on this Fan Qui before an appreciative crowd. Instead, the Tsotang had decided upon the less satisfactory punishment of flogging. The only consolation the executioner gained was the certain knowledge that the end result would be the same. The executioner boasted he could kill a man with fifty blows of the bamboo. Two hundred put the outcome beyond dispute. He would place the first one hundred and fifty blows carefully, inflicting maximum pain, but with the minimum of damage to the internal organs. The final fifty strokes would rupture the Fan Qui's kidneys, leaving him to die an agonizing death.

The executioner selected his first bamboo rod, and Luke braced himself as the crowd fell silent in anticipation.

The bamboo sang through the air – and the blow exploded in a line of fire across Luke's back. The sigh that rose from the watching crowd was a strange mixture of satisfaction at the weight of the blow and instinctive sympathy with Luke.

The first ten blows left their bloody marks down one side of Luke's taut back, from his shoulder to the bottom of his rib-cage. Then the perspiring executioner walked to the other side of his helpless victim. With a skilled back-handed cut that brought applause from the crowd, he repeated the pattern on the other side of Luke's back. At each stroke, a teller counted the number of blows given, singing the number out in a monotonous voice.

After twenty strokes the executioner rested, drawing deep draughts of air into his lungs. At this juncture, Tsotang Teng Ching left his seat and crossed to the post to look into Luke's face. He said nothing, but Luke knew the magistrate was waiting for him to break.

Another twenty blows were delivered with equal sadistic skill, stripping the remaining skin from Luke's back. Although he had not uttered a sound, his breath was coming in uncontrolled sobs and he knew he would be unable to hold on much longer.

The Tsotang knew it, too, and he gave Luke a mocking smile when he crossed the courtyard for a second time. Luke's body jerked beneath the next blow, and the teller had called 'Sz Shap Yat' – 'forty-one' – when there came an unexpected commotion from the crowd. It rapidly grew louder, bringing the Tsotang to his feet. The executioner began his next stroke, but it fell without weight as the crowd parted and Tartar bannermen poured into the courtyard. Behind them rode General Shengan.

The teller was perplexed, not certain whether the last blow should be called or discounted. Never before had the skill of the executioner left room for such doubt.

Tsotang Teng Ching bowed deeply to Shengan. The General was an aloof man, as befitted a hero of the first grade and a Manchu. He had never before bothered with the magistrate. It was an exciting moment, a time to show unfamiliar humility.

'Welcome,' said Tsotang Teng Ching, still bending low. 'Had I known you wished to witness the flogging of the Fan Qui, I would have personally brought you an invitation, and sent my constables to escort you here. . . .'

'Does the unicorn need an escort of ducks when he leaves his house?' Shengan rasped scornfully. It was an oblique jibe at Teng's inferior rank. The badge of a military man of the first grade was a unicorn; that of a seventh-grade civil official a gaudy mandarin duck. 'I travel with fighting men, Tsotang – not with those who need to bind the limbs of enemies before they dare attack them.'

Tsotang Teng Ching flushed angrily. 'I wish it had been my good fortune to fight our Emperor's enemies in far-off places, General Shengan. However, I am proud to serve him as a humble magistrate, seeking out those enemies who are within our borders.'

'Is this how you serve the Emperor?' Shengan pointed a finger at Luke. 'By doing your best to bring the anger of this barbarian's people down upon China?'

'The barbarians are few, Lord General. Our people are like the stars in a summer sky. Our soldiers the bravest—'

'Enough! Not far from Canton are the Bogue forts. Not many weeks ago a single ship of the Fan Qui navy turned its guns on them. Go there, Tsotang. See what that one ship did to the forts. They have many such ships. We have none. Think of such things before you arrest another Fan Qui. Now, release the barbarian.'

The Tsotang's manner underwent an immediate change. General Shengan was an officer of the first grade — he was a Manchu and a famous general; but he, Tsotang Teng Ching, was the magistrate for Canton. He, and he alone, dealt with criminal matters.

'The Fan Qui has committed a serious crime against a girl of the Hoklo people. I have his signed confession.' The Tsotang waved the rolled document before General Shengan.

Shengan kneed his shaggy little pony forward. Before the magistrate could guess his intention, he snatched the confession from his hands.

Tsotang Teng Ching took a step forward to protest. His way was immediately blocked by one of Shengan's wary Tartars, and the Tsotang's mouth dropped open as Shengan opened out the confession and tore it into tiny pieces.

'This is the worth of your "confession", Tsotang.'

'I have a witness. . . . A servant from the Fan Qui factories. . . .'

'A liar,' declared Shengan. 'I, too, have a confession from your witness.'

'I don't believe it. . . .' Tsotang Teng Ching was stunned more by General Shengan's personal intercession on behalf of the Fan Qui than by the thought that his witness was a liar. The Tsotang knew only too well he had twisted the words of the witness to suit his own end. The factory servant had told him only that Kuei had been spending nights with Luke. 'I will bring him in and question him again.'

'You will need to be quick, Tsotang. When I left the barracks he was amusing my soldiers. Release the barbarian, or you will join your witness.'

Tsotang Teng Ching knew that his own official position meant nothing to the man before him. There was no doubt in his mind who was more important to the Emperor. China had thousands of magistrates, but only one General Shengan.

The Tsotang ordered Luke's release.

Swooning with pain, Luke had followed little of the conversation between General Shengan and the Tsotang. He knew only that the Tartar general had arrived on the scene and the beating had stopped. Released from the whipping-post and supported between two of the Tartar bannermen, Luke was dragged before Shengan.

Expressionless, the General looked from Luke's facial injuries to the blood that stained the waistband of his trousers.

'You have made enemies in China. It is well you have also made some good friends.'

To the soldiers who held Luke, General Shengan said, 'Take him to my quarters and dress his wounds.' Ignoring the Tsotang's deep bow, General Shengan kneed his horse from the courtyard.

The house General Shengan occupied reflected the status of China's greatest soldier, but the silks, velvet curtains and vases of great antiquity were not to Shengan's liking. The Tartar general had ordered most of the furniture to be removed from a whole section of the house. Here, in Spartan surroundings, he lived closely guarded by selected men of his regiment. In a land as large as China there were many men of ambition and treachery. Great and loyal soldiers had a historical record of blocking ambition.

Luke was given a room that still had many of the trappings of luxury, but the treatment of his wounds was of the standard meted out to Tartar bannermen on the field of battle. The wounds made by the bamboo were casually washed clean, and then raw salt was applied to them and bound in place with long strips of cotton cloth. This primitive dressing achieved more than the executioner's bamboo. Luke fainted.

He was lying on his face when he awoke. He moved, and immediately regretted it. The crust of blood and salt that had formed on his back split, and Luke groaned.

'You sleep as only a man with a clear conscience might. I wish I were able to do the same.'

Luke turned his head and saw General Shengan sprawled loosely in a chair beside the bed. Gritting his teeth against the pain, Luke struggled to sit up. Shengan sat impassively watching him, making no attempt to help. Eventually, Luke's panting and gasping brought a Tartar soldier hurrying into the room to help Luke to a sitting position.

The effort had drained much of the strength from Luke and, after brushing the perspiration from his eyes, he said, 'I owe you my life, General Shengan. Why did you do it? Why did you stop the beating and bring me here?'

Shengan came close to a smile. 'I imagine those questions are troubling the Tsotang more than they should you. You are safe; Teng is uncertain. As I told you before, you have friends – good friends.'

Luke was still puzzled. He could think of nobody of sufficient importance to influence a Chinese general – or, indeed, who knew he had been captured by the Tsotang.

He had left the factories alone. Only Kuei knew where he was going. . . . He looked at Shengan. 'Kuei? It was not possible. . . .'

Shengan was watching him closely. 'Do you doubt your own reasoning? Have you no faith in the charms of our simple Chinese girls? Ah! I see by your face that my words confuse you even more. Yes, Soo Kuei came to see me. She pleaded for me to help you . . . for the sake of my brother's daughter, Lo Asan. I believe you know her?'

Luke leaned back against the pillow with a sigh of relief. For a moment he had thought . . . ! He felt foolish at his wild imaginings. This proud man who sprawled in the chair beside him could have any girl in the vast kingdom of China – and beyond. He would not want a Hoklo girl, no matter how attractive she was.

'Lo Asan must mean a great deal to you. I am grateful to her and to Kuei – but most of all to you.'

'I was very fond of Lo Asan when she was a small girl, but I have not spoken to her or her father since she became the woman of a Fan Qui.'

Luke was startled. 'Then why did you help me? I am a Fan Qui.'

Again there was a near-smile from Shengan. 'No, you are a *barbarian*. There is not yet enough evil in you to be a Fan Qui.' Shengan's eyes glittered angrily. 'Lo Asan's man is a Fan Qui. He has done more than anyone else to ensure that the trade in opium continues. He is truly an enemy of China.'

Weakened as he was, Luke felt totally confused by what General Shengan had just told him. He could think of no reason why the Tartar general should help him escape from Canton's Tsotang. But Luke was about to learn that Shengan was more than a brilliant soldier.

'Unless men like McCulloch are stopped, they will one day deliberately provoke a war between our two countries. We would lose such a war, and in defeat be forced to take opium as a trading commodity.'

'I've spoken to McCulloch. I don't think he wants a war,' said Luke cautiously. 'He's expecting your Emperor to make the opium trade legal without that.'

'Never!' declared Shengan emphatically. 'Emperor Tao Kuang

knows too well the bad effect the drug has upon his people. It found its way into the Imperial Palace and poisoned his own son. He remembers, too, the army he sent against the Yao rebels. They suffered a humiliating defeat because more than half their number were made cowards by opium. Those who seek to allow opium into China would make eunuchs of our men. If any soldier in my own regiment is found smoking opium, he is immediately executed. The same punishment must be seen to be imposed upon those who sell opium to the people. That is why the two men were executed in the factory square where we first met.'

As he spoke, General Shengan rose to his feet and paced restlessly about the room. Pausing beside Luke's bed, he spoke with less vehemence. 'Lo Asan's father and some others hope the Emperor will have a change of heart. No doubt they tell McCulloch what he wants to hear – that the Emperor *will* one day allow opium to enter China. They wish to keep McCulloch happy while they grow rich on the opium he supplies. They are foolish. One day McCulloch must learn the truth, and I fear the heat of his anger will cause war to flare up between our countries. I dread the thought of such a war. Yes, I, Imperial General Shengan, *fear* a war. The fear is not for myself – or for my bannermen. Our lives count for nothing. We gave them to the Emperor on the day we joined his army. To die in his service is to bring great honour to our families. No, I am afraid for the land of my birth. A war with your country will be the end of China. We will not win. My Tartars are the bravest soldiers in the world, but bravery is not enough. Your ships have guns able to reduce a city to rubble in a matter of hours. The muskets of your soldiers can kill farther than a man can shout a warning. My men are skilled with arrows and spears. They have few muskets. Even if we had your weapons, it would probably change little. Soldiers win or lose only battles. The outcome of wars is decided by the men who rule our countries – and how can Emperor Tao Kuang learn new ideas? The officials in Peking who advise him still believe that it needs no more than the stamp of a foot in the Imperial Palace to make the whole world quake!'

'You do not agree with them?' Luke was so fascinated by this insight into General Shengan's mind that his pain and discomfort had been momentarily forgotten.

'I have fought on all China's borders. I have killed many

men who have never heard of Emperor Tao Kuang. They respected only the fighting qualities of my soldiers. I have watched your people. You are not like us. Each of you believes he is his own master. You are arrogant. You kowtow neither to our mandarins nor to your own. Times are changing rapidly. Your people are part of the changing world. We are not. It is necessary to tell the Emperor what is happening; to persuade him that China must take her place in the world. I am not alone in this thinking, Luke Trewarne. Other men also wish to bring this state of affairs to the attention of the Emperor – but we need more time. This is why McCulloch must not be allowed to cause trouble between our countries. It is why I need your help.'

'My help?' Luke was startled. 'I am only the head clerk in one of the smaller trading companies. What can I do?'

'You can do much. Tell McCulloch this is not a good time to try to change the Emperor's mind about the trade in opium. You speak our language. Tell him you have heard talk that Tao Kuang is angry with those who caused his favourite concubine to become addicted to opium. That no one dares to mention it in his presence.'

'Is this true?'

'Who knows?' The hint of a smile was on Shengan's lips again. 'I can think of no man who would dare ask the Emperor the truth of such a rumour.'

General Shengan sat down heavily in the chair once more and leaned well back, his legs stretched out before him. 'There is one more thing you can do. It is well known that Gemmell Company does not sell opium. Make a success of your trading. Let others point to you and say, "See! There is Gemmell Company. They grow rich without selling opium." That is an example that traders will understand.'

Luke gave Shengan a wry smile. 'I doubt if I'll be able to help you on that count.'

Shengan looked at him sharply. 'Why? Has your beating made you angry with the Chinese people? Do you wish to have revenge upon the Tsotang? I will invent an excuse to have him executed. It will not be difficult. . . .'

'No. . . .' Luke did not doubt for one moment that General Shengan could deal swiftly and ruthlessly with the magistrate, but Luke would prefer not to have the death of Tsotang Teng Ching on his conscience. 'What I mean is that I probably won't see Ezra McCulloch for many months, even if the situation here returns to normal. McCulloch is forbidden to come up-river to Canton. Then, as far as trading is concerned, I doubt whether Gemmell Company will amount to much for a very long time. We might make a small profit this year, but that's all.'

'Then increase your trading.'

'That's easier said than done – for many reasons. The main one is lack of money. We have only one ship of our own. It's small, so we can bring in only a limited amount of trade goods, and take out only what can be carried as far as India. That rules out the most profitable line – tea. The market for China tea is in England, and the biggest profits for those whose tea is first on the market each season. That requires a fast purpose-built clipper – or the money to buy cargo space in one. Both cost more than Gemmell Company can find.'

'How much would one of these "clippers" cost?' asked Shengan, almost casually.

'At least fifty thousand silver dollars.'

A Spanish silver dollar, the accepted unit of exchange in Chinese trading circles, was worth about one-fifth of a pound.

Shengan nodded. 'Yes, that is a lot of money. How many voyages would it have to make before such a sum is earned?'

Luke's mind worked hard on the figures he remembered from his East India Company trading days. 'If the ship beat all the others with tea to England, and found the right return load, it could pay for itself on a single round trip . . . but first Gemmell Company would need to find the money to buy such a ship.'

'What would you say if I told you there was one of these clippers for sale at Macau for less than half the price you quote? It is owned by a man who has lost his love of trading because of Killian's foolishness.'

Luke shrugged – and wished he hadn't. The movement cracked the salt crust on his back again and caused him to gasp in pain. When he recovered he said breathlessly, 'At that price the ship is a bargain, but Gemmell Company can afford neither the ship nor the tea to fill it.'

'Would you buy this ship if you had the money – and a cargo of tea?'

'Of course! Anyone who didn't would be a fool.'

General Shengan stood up. 'When you are well enough to leave my house you will go to see your Hong. He will loan you the money for the clipper – interest-free. You will go at once to Macau to buy it. I will visit the ship when you bring it back to Whampoa. I wish to see inside a Fan Qui ship.'

Luke was not sure he had heard Shengan correctly, it was such an incredible offer. But Luke worked for Gemmell Company, not for Imperial General Shengan. 'I'll have to talk this over with Dan Gemmell. I'm only an employee of the Company. . . .'

'Talking about it will not be necessary. You will go to Macau,' Shengan said imperiously. 'I spoke to the Fan Qui doctor from the missionary hospital today. He disobeyed the Tsotang's orders and entered the city looking for you. He was arrested, of course, but on this occasion Tsotang Teng thought it best to send him to me. Before he was returned to the factories I learned that the barbarian Gemmell is now well enough to look after the factory until you bring your ship to Whampoa – and the doctor will accompany you to Macau.'

'There is still the cost of a cargo of tea. . . .' Luke made the statement knowing full well that Shengan would have the answer. He felt as though he were caught in a riptide that would carry him with it no matter what he did.

'Did I not mention that? Your Hong, Lien Ling, will give you a full cargo of prime Pekoe tea – on credit. It will be paid for when your ship returns laden with trade goods.' This time there could be no doubt about General Shengan's smile. 'It is well that Lien Ling is a wealthy man. You are pleased?'

'I . . . I'm overwhelmed. . . .' Luke meant it. Suddenly his future was bright once more. Such an opportunity as this rarely came a man's way. He was pleased, too, for Dan Gemmell. This would do much to repay him for the lean years, caused by his refusal to trade in opium.

'Does my offer make the pain in your back easier to bear?'

Luke grinned ruefully. 'I'd hate to have had to pay the executioner for two ships. I'm greatly in your debt, General Shengan.'

'If you can persuade the other Fan Qui traders to follow your Company's example, and war is averted, I will be in *your* debt. So, too, will Lien Ling, however much he may complain at parting with his money.'

Luke leaned back cautiously on to his pillows. 'I owe Kuei much, too. It must have taken great courage for her to come to see you. When I return to the factory I'll—'

'When you return to your factory you will find she has gone,' Shengan said matter-of-factly.

'Gone? You mean back to Hong Kong? But what of her father?'

'If she has good sense, she will go farther from Canton than the island of Hong Kong. You must realize that neither Tsotang Teng nor myself are playing games, Luke Trewarne. If Teng took the Hoklo girl prisoner, she would be made to confess her association with you. Teng would use such a confession to embarrass me at the court of the Emperor in Peking. I told her to take her father and leave Canton immediately.'

Luke was dismayed. He had fallen deeply in love with Kuei, and believed she loved him, too. She would be very unhappy. He had to see her again – and soon. In his agitation, Luke moved his body too quickly and immediately cried out in pain.

Shengan stood up to leave the room. 'If there is anything you need, you have only to call. A servant will be within hearing at all times. One thing more. You have an enemy in the factories, but I doubt if he will trouble you again. He should be gone by the time you return. I fancy he may be on his way at this very moment.'

'An enemy? I haven't been in Canton long enough to make enemies.'

'Nevertheless, this man is one. He is a Fan Qui who was friendly with the two men you turned out of your factory. He sent his servant to tell the Tsotang that your Hoklo girl was spending nights with you.'

'Hans Moller did that –' Luke gritted his teeth against both pain and anger. 'He'd *better* be gone by the time I return. . . .'

'I made quite certain he would be. The servant who gave the statement to Tsotang Teng told my men everything – but not until he had been held over a fire for rather longer than was good for him. I sent his head to the Fan Qui as a gift. My messenger reported that this Moller was violently ill, and I understand he left on the next boat bound for Macau.'

Ten

EZRA MCCULLOCH'S ship *The Two Brothers* limped into the sheltered waters of Hong Kong harbour with twenty feet of her foremast snapped off and the bilge pumps fighting a losing battle with three feet of rising water. The Chinese villagers crowded the foreshore, loud-voiced and excited, only to scatter hastily when Captain Obadiah Innes maintained his shoreward course and beached his ship on the shingle of the cove, immediately below McCulloch's hillside house.

It had been a disastrous voyage. Trading north as far as the mouth of the Yangtze Kiang, *The Two Brothers* had been harried by junks of the Imperial Navy, eager to avenge the defeat of their colleagues in the Pearl River. The fast merchantman scornfully outpaced the lugsailed vessels, but no sooner had one junk disappeared over the horizon than another appeared to take its place. Then, sailing up the wide estuary of the Yangtze, *The Two Brothers* had been engaged by three Imperial junks and Obadiah Innes had had to fight his way out to sea, losing two seamen in the ensuing battle.

In a desperate bid to evade the Imperial war-junks, and still anxious to sell the opium he carried in the ship's holds, Obadiah Innes headed for the island of Formosa, a hundred miles off the coast of mainland China. Here, in a deep-water bay, he anchored his ship and sent word to neighbouring villages that he wished to trade.

The response was poor, and Obadiah Innes soon learned the reason. *The Two Brothers* had anchored on a coast that abounded with pirates. The rapacious sea-marauders had little interest in trade. If a ship carried anything they wanted, they took it. Only sheer luck saved *The Two Brothers* from falling into their hands. A seaman, unable to sleep in the hot and stuffy crew-quarters, made his way on deck in the early hours of the morning. The moon was casting a magic silver light on the distant mountains of the island, polishing the sea with a soft silver sheen. As the seaman took in this idyllic scene, the incautious sound of a creaking oar was thrown across the water. It came from the shadows beneath the high stone cliff off the far beam of the ship. Curious, the seaman crossed the deck of the merchantman and peered across the stretch of moonlit water. He frowned as he searched the dark shadows, seeing nothing at first. Suddenly, two long narrow boats leaped into moonlit water. Each was propelled by at least sixty long oars. The craft, known locally as 'scrambling dragons', cleaved the phosphorescent sea water, heading straight for *The Two Brothers* and her prize cargo of opium.

The seaman leaped to the ship's bell and sounded an urgent warning that brought seamen tumbling from their hammocks and desperately running out the ship's cannon.

Minutes later, as the seamen on the forecastle struggled to raise the anchor under a barrage of ill-aimed musket-fire, Captain Obadiah Innes led his men in a fight for their lives.

Cannon-shots were exchanged at pointblank range, and one pirate craft came close enough to send grappling hooks flying through the air to land on the deck of *The Two Brothers* and slither across the planking seeking a hold. Obadiah Innes hacked through two of the ropes with his naval officer's sword, while seamen used axes to cut away the remainder.

Fortunately for the British seamen, there was a fresh breeze blowing, and as the sails were shaken out *The Two Brothers* got under way. Now she was no longer a sitting target for the pirates.

The battle was not yet ended. *The Two Brothers* crowded on full sail, but the pirate vessels had oars to supplement their smaller sails and managed to keep pace with the merchantman. The chase lasted for three days. Whenever the wind dropped, the long boats moved in and engaged *The Two Brothers* in a fierce and determined action. Fortunately, the wind never dropped long enough for the tenacious pirates to make another boarding attempt.

On the third night, the sun set over the rim of the ocean in a blaze of gaudy colour. The pirate vessels dropped away and turned in towards the coast, their oars snatching the surface of the sea like the legs of huge departing spiders. Watching them go, Obadiah Innes knew full well that he had little cause for celebration. The sun had set in a typhoon sky, and *The Two Brothers* was a long way from Hong Kong. In a bid to shake off the pirates, Obadiah Innes had headed his ship out into the vast expanse of the China Sea. The typhoon would hit them long before they reached Hong Kong harbour.

That night the winds increased, and the seamen were constantly being called out of their hammocks to clamber aloft and reduce the spread of sail as the wind sang a raucous song in the taut rigging and the yardarms danced to its tune.

Shortly before the arrival of a squally dawn, the barometer dropped dramatically and the wind's song changed to a maniacal scream. For thirty-six hours Captain Obadiah Innes called upon all his years of sea-going experience to keep his ship afloat. Wave after mountainous wave bore down upon *The Two Brothers* as the sea was whipped into a frenzy about the vessel.

When the storm eventually exhausted itself *The Two Brothers* was leaking from a number of strained joints. The foremast had gone, and much of her canvas had disappeared overboard – together with three more of Obadiah Innes's crewmen.

As he sat in the lounge of his Hong Kong home, listening to a weary Captain Innes tell his story, Ezra McCulloch arrived at an important decision. Coupled with the cessation of trade at Canton, the failure of *The Two Brothers'* trading voyage meant that this was likely to prove a disastrous trading year. It was time that his investment in Lo Asan paid him a dividend. Ezra McCulloch decided to send her on a visit to Peking to see her parents.

He told her of his decision later that night, when they were alone in his bedroom. The thought of seeing her parents again should have filled Lo Asan with delight, but at the moment she had something else on her mind.

'Please, Hau-ye, I do not wish to go until Kuei has returned from Canton. She has been gone too long. I worry for her.'

'Worry about what? We know she got Trewarne to Canton safely; there's nothing else to worry about. You'll travel as far as you can in my ship *Cygnet*. She's been lying in the harbour doing nothing for long enough. Feeding her crew is costing me good money. She'll take you to Tsing-tao, the home of your grandfather. From there you can go overland to Peking. I'll provide you with enough money to travel in style. You'll be the envy of your sisters.'

'What am I to do there, Hau-ye?'

'Just look happy. Tell everyone how well I look after you. You'll also deliver a letter from me to your father. I'll have it written in the morning.'

The letter would call upon Lo Asan's father to make good the promise he had made when he gave his daughter to McCulloch: to bring all his influence to bear upon his friends at the Imperial Court, in a bid to make trading in opium legal.

'And you, Hau-ye? What will you do while I am away? You will stay here, in Hong Kong?'

'No, I'll be going to Macau for a couple of months. I have business to discuss with James Killian. I'm doing my bit to improve trade and get him his knighthood. I'll expect him to swallow his pride and get back up-river to Canton. If he doesn't, we'll get rid of him and put someone in his place who will.'

Lo Asan was more unhappy than ever. McCulloch's wife and daughter were in Macau. Lo Asan had always feared that he would one day go to his family and never return to Hong Kong again. Ezra McCulloch was a hard man — at times a cruel man — but Lo Asan loved him. He had taken her from the narrow and lonely existence of a high-class Manchu girl and given her a life that was comparatively free, and occasionally exciting. She was the mistress of a Far Eastern merchant king who was the Hau-ye of an island where there was no law but McCulloch's. Lo Asan had told Kuei that one day he would give up his trade in opium, for her sake. He never would, and in her heart Lo Asan knew this, but she still believed in miracles. Every night she made an offering to Kwan Yin, the Goddess of Mercy. Lo Asan begged forgiveness for McCulloch, and asked the Goddess to turn him away from his trade in opium.

Luke journeyed to Macau in *Black Swan* three weeks after his whipping. His back was almost healed, although he had to be careful not to bend or to turn too quickly, for fear of splitting the newly formed skin. He would carry the crisscrossed scars of his beating to his dying day. Abel Snow travelled with him, ordered to make the voyage by the autocratic General Shengan.

Luke had spent fourteen days in the city of Canton, in Shengan's house. Each night they had talked together for three or four hours. Although many of Shengan's attitudes were barbaric by Western standards, Luke learned both to like and to respect the Tartar general. In his turn, Shengan showed a genuine affection for 'Luke Trewarne'. Although Luke was not aware of it, he came closer to being a real friend to Shengan than any man the General had ever known. Fighting China's enemies on all her borders did not give a man time to make lasting friendships.

Before Luke set off on the voyage, he and Dan Gemmell discussed their future trading plans in the light of Shengan's offer. One result of the discussions was that Gideon Pyke was offered the captaincy of the new clipper. Luke made the offer on his way down-river. Much to his surprise, it was turned down. When pressed for an explanation, the American captain drawled, 'Well, if you put me in charge of a ship like that, you'll expect me to wear a blue and gold cap, and behave like a regular skipper. I'll be shuttling between Whampoa and London with the devil on my back. That's not for me, Luke. I'm a lazy man. I like to enjoy my life, feeling my way slowly around coasts that haven't been charted. I guess I'm just a sea-going vagabond.'

Gideon Pyke gave Luke a sideways glance. 'Is there still room for such a man with the new Gemmell Company?'

'There is as long as I'm with the Company. But I wouldn't set any time on that. By staying at Canton I've upset the Superintendent of Trade and our fellow-traders. They aren't going to be pleased that we're making money while they sit counting their losses in Macau.'

'They need neither sit nor sulk,' Abel Snow joined in the conversation. 'If they announce that they're giving up trading in opium, all Chinese harassment will cease.'

'And India's economy will collapse,' said Luke. 'I've had a lot of time to think about this problem during the last few weeks, and I've discussed it with General Shengan time after time. Until recently, I naïvely believed that the British Government was unaware of the scale of the opium trade between India and China. I don't believe this anymore. The amount of tea bought from China would lead to a shortage of silver in Britain if opium wasn't used to balance the trade. The British Government must know this.'

'Oh, they know all right,' agreed Abel Snow. 'We've had a couple of Superintendents of Trade in Canton who spelled it out to them. Both men were quickly replaced. Now we have the Honourable James Killian. He comes to life only when the British flag is insulted, turning a Nelsonian blind eye to the flagrant disregard of China's laws on opium smuggling. Administrators like Killian, determined to keep their heads down, come what may, lost America for Britain. One day they'll cost you the whole of your empire.'

'General Shengan is more concerned that Killian is looking for an excuse to bring about a war between Britain and China,' said Luke.

'Whether or not Killian is looking for war, he might well cause one,' replied Abel Snow grimly. 'If he does, Great Britain will never have fought for a more dishonourable cause. The consequences may well be far-reaching enough to give even your government a nightmare. The Chinese Emperor rules his country using a finely balanced mixture of fantasy, deception, corruption and suppression. His dynasty will survive only for as long as it can defeat all its enemies. When the Emperor's army begins losing battles the whole administration will collapse like a paper house in a storm. The ensuing chaos and bloodshed will shock the whole civilized world. I would hate to have such a disaster on my conscience when I stand before the Lord on Judgement Day.'

'Amen to that,' commented Gideon Pyke. 'Hopefully, Judgement Day is still some way off – Macau isn't. That's it dead ahead, Luke. A man can find anything he wants there. Women, drink, horse-racing. . . .' Gideon Pyke grinned at Abel Snow's frown of disapproval.

'You could also visit the place where St Francis Xavier died. He was one of the first medical missionaries,' Abel Snow explained. Then his natural good humour returned. 'But Gideon is right. Before you've been here a week you'll be caught up in the social life of Macau and have forgotten all else.'

Luke had other ideas. He missed Kuei desperately and wanted to complete his business in the Portuguese colony as quickly as possible, then leave for Hong Kong. He was convinced he would find Kuei there. When he had . . . ? Luke's thinking had not moved that far ahead. He just needed to see her again. All else would then fall into place. To Abel Snow he said, 'I'm here to buy a ship, not to dance attendance on James Killian and his social circle.'

In spite of his good intentions, Luke found it impossible to remain aloof from the English community in Macau. The merchants, chafing at their self-imposed exile from the Canton factories, were hungry for news of the new season's trading prospects. In a couple of months' time China's all-important tea crop would be harvested on the slopes of the hills inland from Canton. Competition was always dagger-keen for the first of the teas – and no trader wanted to be left out of the bidding. It was evident to Luke that the overwhelming weight of opinion would soon force Killian to return to Canton and resume trading operations.

But not all the trading companies would accompany the Superintendent of Trade up-river. The disillusioned owner of the fast tea-clipper *China Wind* was so anxious to wind up his affairs and return to Europe that he did not haggle about the price of the superb craft. Luke's opening offer of twenty thousand dollars was promptly accepted.

Archibald Wheeler was the captain of *China Wind* and he received news of the sale of his ship to Luke with some apprehension. He was fast approaching an age when he would be called upon to retire. He would never get another ship. He was greatly relieved when Luke asked him to remain in command – and even happier when he learned he would not be carrying opium. A rendezvous with an opium dealer in some uncharted and secluded cove was not for Captain Wheeler. He was the antithesis of his fellow Company captain, Gideon Pyke. Unimaginative, safe and reliable, Captain Wheeler would set no records on the run between China and England. But, if Luke could get *China Wind* loaded with tea and on her way before her competitors, Captain Wheeler would ensure that his ship kept the lead.

Three days after Luke purchased *China Wind*, the ship was on her way up-river to Whampoa to take on a cargo of silk. She was a fast vessel and could deliver the silk in Calcutta, take on a return cargo, and still be back at Whampoa in time to load the first consignment of tea. Such a ship was not to be wasted swinging at anchor in Macau harbour.

During those three days, Luke spent most of his time with Captain Wheeler on board *China Wind*, working day and night to prepare the documents for her trading voyage. Not until *China Wind*'s canvas sails were shaken out and the clipper slipped neatly out into the brown waters of the Pearl River estuary did Luke have time to learn what the Macau social life had to offer. To his surprise and embarrassment, he discovered that he was a much-sought-after celebrity in the tiny Portuguese colony.

The story of Luke's trip up-river to join a dying company

at a time when the factories were under siege had been re-peated many times and exaggerated into a heroic feat of daring. Rumours were also circulating that he had spent some time inside the walled city of Canton as a guest of the Tartar general, Shengan. Now, after weeks spent running the only British company still trading – and making a handsome profit – he had arrived in Macau to purchase a fast clipper. Luke went ashore from *China Wind* to find that the hosts and hostesses of Macau were fighting to be first to have him as a guest at their functions.

It would have been churlish to refuse all the offers that came his way, and Luke eventually accepted an invitation to a dinner-party at the lavish home of Lancelot Fox, a prominent merchant who ran his Canton factory from the comfort of his Macau home. One of the first traders to realize the potential of the opium market in China, Fox had made more money in his first year of trading than he would ever spend. His profits had increased every year since. This was to be Fox's last year in Macau. Leaving the company in the capable hands of one of his family, he was returning to England. Eventually, the talents of Lancelot Fox would take him to the House of Commons, a post as Far Eastern adviser to Britain's Foreign Secretary, and subsequent elevation to the peerage.

It was at Fox's party that Luke met Ezra McCulloch once more. Lancelot Fox's wife began to introduce them, but McCulloch interrupted her rudely. He had been drinking, but the cold eyes he turned upon Luke were the eyes of a sober man.

'We've met before. You've come up in the world since you travelled from India in my ship, Trewarne.'

Luke nodded. 'As you say, Mr McCulloch, things have im-proved for Gemmell Company – and we've done it without selling a single chest of opium.'

'Then you're a fool! Your *Black Swan* has been the only British ship working between Macau and Whampoa. Had you traded opium, you'd have been able to buy Dan Gemmell a whole fleet of clippers.'

'Had I put opium aboard *Black Swan*, she'd have been at the bottom of the Pearl River by now.' Luke saw James Killian making his way across the room towards them and raised his voice so that it would carry to the Superintendent of Trade. 'China intends to stop the trade in opium, Ezra. I've proved there's money to be made in legitimate trading. The sooner you do the same, the sooner you'll be back up-river.'

Ezra McCulloch flushed angrily. 'The day will never dawn when you've been in China long enough to give me advice, laddie; but I'll give you some. If you and Dan Gemmell want to stay in business, you'll open an opium account with the East India Company – now. Before the end of this year the Chinese Government will announce that the ban on opium has been lifted. Take my word for it.'

Luke heard the buzz of excitement in the room as traders crowded around to listen to Ezra McCulloch's loud words. 'You can forget all your other trade goods.' Ezra McCulloch's finger prodded Luke's chest. 'The Hongs won't want to know them. They'll be working full-time to move opium, and they won't need to tout for business. There's a line of eager customers stretching all the way to Peking.'

Ezra McCulloch had been seriously misled by Lo Asan's father. He really *believed* the ban would be lifted when his letter reached Peking. But Shengan's words were fresh in Luke's mind. This was a good opportunity to impress upon the trading community the strength of Chinese feeling on the subject.

'You're wrong, Ezra. Emperor Tao Kuang has first-hand experience of the effects of opium on his people. He'll *never* allow it to be traded openly in China. Most of his government are behind his stand. So, too, is General Shengan.'

'I suppose Shengan told you this himself?' The question, only half serious, came from one of the traders standing nearby.

'Yes, as a matter of fact, he did.'

Luke's reply provoked a mixed reaction. Many of his listeners were hostile, a few amused. Only one or two of them took his words seriously.

'Why would General Shengan confide in such a junior member of the trading community, Trewarne?' James Killian joined in the discussion.

Luke hesitated; he dared not tell Killian of his arrest and beating. The Superintendent of Trade would regard it as a further example of China's growing contempt for Britain and her subjects. 'Partly because I speak Chinese, but mainly because I was there when he wanted to talk about it.'

Luke told Killian of the fire, and of being taken to General Shengan's house when he was 'hurt'. He thought this would explain the bruising that was still in evidence on his face. He mentioned nothing of Tsotang Teng Ching, or of his experiences in Canton's prison.

Ezra McCulloch listened impatiently to Luke's explanation. 'Shengan told his cock-and-bull story to you because you haven't been here long enough to know different. Any one of us who has been here for any time at all would have pointed out that the mandarins who shout loudest against open trading are those who are making a fortune out of opium smuggling. They'll never find an easier way to earn a dishonest living. For all we know, Shengan is mixed up in the business himself. If he knows that free opium trading isn't far off, he's cunning enough to try to frighten us into paying more "squeeze", while he can.'

'General Shengan's only concern is the effect opium is having on his people,' Luke retorted hotly.

'If Shengan wanted to, he could use his soldiers to make it damned difficult for opium smugglers to operate in Kwangtung Province,' said Ezra McCulloch. 'I doubt if he wants to. The Chinese were taking opium before anyone in Europe had heard of their country. No one's going to stamp it out now.'

'Ezra is right,' said James Killian, smiling at Luke in a patronizing manner that Luke found infuriating. 'You're a resourceful young man, Luke. One day you'll be a trader to rival anyone in this room, but at the moment you lack experience in dealing with the Chinese. They're a wily lot, make no mistake. Take a tip from me. When a Chinese tells you something – anything – ask yourself, "What is he going to gain from this?" When you think you know the answer you'll be halfway to getting near the truth of what he's told you.'

There was a murmur of agreement from the men about them, and Luke fought hard to control his rising anger. Not one of the merchants spoke the language of the land where they lived and earned a living. Few had ever held a long conversation with a Chinese. They conducted business with the Hongs and gave orders to their Chinese servants. In their eyes, this made them experts on China, its people and its problems. But Luke suppressed an overwhelming urge to put his thoughts into words. Convincing the traders that General Shengan was telling the truth was of far more importance than Luke's opinions.

'General Shengan has nothing to gain from lying to me. He's a soldier. He hasn't been in Canton long enough to get mixed up in opium smuggling – and tomorrow he could be sent three thousand miles away to a remote border area where he can forget all about opium, if he wants to. He spoke from a genuine concern for his people. I believe we should take him seriously.'

'No one doubts *your* sincerity, Luke,' said James Killian, still smiling benevolently. 'But as Her Britannic Majesty's Superintendent of Trade I have a great responsibility. When men with the experience of Ezra McCulloch express an opinion, I listen. Indeed, I must tell you that I wholeheartedly agree with his view of the situation.'

James Killian beamed benignly at the merchants crowding about him. 'Gentlemen, I think this is a splendid opportunity to tell you of an important decision I have made. In anticipation of a general relaxing of the laws governing the opium trade, I believe we should show our own willingness to forgive past differences with the Chinese authorities. It is my intention to return to Canton and raise the Union Jack in the factory square, on the first day of September. From that day, normal trading will be resumed – but, of course, the carrying of opium will remain illegal until we hear to the contrary.'

The cheer that went up from the house of Lancelot Fox was mixed with laughter at Killian's tongue-in-cheek proviso. No one had ever taken the Chinese laws seriously. Before the echoes of the traders' jubilation had died away in the farthermost narrow streets of Macau, they were crowding around Killian, offering him their congratulations as though he had won a magnificent victory for them. In fact, he had done no more than retreat from the absurd stand he had taken two months before.

When the hullabaloo died away the merchants and their families drifted away to enjoy the party and eagerly discuss the prospects of the coming trading season. James Killian smiled triumphantly at Luke, but the smile was not returned.

'Do you *honestly* believe the Emperor will allow opium to be brought to China?'

'I do. What's more, I have told Lord Palmerston so in a letter I despatched to him a week ago. I have no doubt at all that, by the time the letter reaches the Foreign Office in London, a new era of understanding between Great Britain and China will have begun.'

Having made this statement of his beliefs, James Killian allowed himself to be led away and fêted for his diplomatic skill, leaving Luke dejected and frustrated behind him.

Luke walked to a window and gazed out across the crowded harbour to the estuary beyond. He had done his best to put Shengan's views to the traders, but it had not been enough. He did not believe their refusal to face the truth would actually lead to war, but there was certain to be serious trouble ahead. Luke was determined that, when it came, the advantage gained by Gemmell Company would not slip away because of the traders' pigheadedness.

During the time he had been a guest of General Shengan, Luke had given a lot of thought to the trading situation at Canton. Deep-sea ships were not allowed to come closer to Canton than Whampoa — twelve miles away. It made supervision of cargoes and communication between traders and their captains very difficult. Also, in times of trouble it was far too easy for either side to blockade the river. Luke realized that to guarantee continuing trade Gemmell Company needed a safe warehouse, well clear of Canton. Somewhere like Hong Kong island. Trade goods could be taken to Hong Kong from Canton when business was slack and, when relations with China were strained, Gemmell Company's ships could deliver and land at Hong Kong. Besides . . . Kuei was there.

'I wouldn't let them get you down. If you told them the house was on fire, they wouldn't believe you until Killian had confirmed it — or until their socks burned off. Do you really know General Shengan?'

The voice had the faint trace of a pleasant west Scotland accent. Turning, Luke saw a tall girl of about twenty standing beside him. Her fair hair was curled in loose ringlets and piled high on her head, accentuating her above-average height. For the Fox party she wore an off-the-shoulder dress of blue that matched her eyes and showed off her attractive shoulders to advantage.

'Have you met General Shengan?' she repeated.

'Yes. You've heard of him?'

'Of course. I nurse in the hospital, here in Macau. He's the hero of every Chinese patient I deal with. They regard him as the Duke of Wellington, Admiral Nelson and Robin Hood, all rolled into one.'

Luke smiled. 'Perhaps they're right. He's certainly a remarkable man.'

The girl grimaced. 'I wish I could meet him . . . but here a girl is nobody. Even if I were allowed to go to Canton I'd never get near him. For all the excitement I've found in Macau, I might as well have stayed at Miss Kilbride's School for Gentlewomen, in Edinburgh. You could at least be certain of getting a kiss from the grocer's boy if you were near the bushes by the back door when he arrived. More, if you didn't run fast enough afterwards.'

Luke laughed. The few European women he had met in India had been prim and aloof. This girl was neither.

Their hostess passed by at that moment and paused to give the girl a smile, and Luke a sympathetic pat on the arm. 'I'm glad to see you don't bear grudges, Luke. Although, of course, Morna has none of her father's preoccupation with trading. To Ezra it's everything in the world.' Leaning towards Morna McCulloch, Mrs Fox gave her an envious smile. 'Look after Luke well, my dear. He's the handsomest young man we've seen in Macau for many years.'

As Mrs Fox walked away to rejoin her friends, Morna McCulloch said ruefully, 'Why do hostesses have the knack of always saying the wrong thing, at the wrong time? I was hoping to charm you with my personality before you learned my name. If I tell you in advance that I share few of my father's views, will you stay here and talk to me, Luke?'

'I'll be happy to talk to you — but shall we have a wager on how long it will be before your father finds an excuse to take you away?'

'He wouldn't dare,' Morna McCulloch flared angrily. As her chin came up, Luke saw it had the same determined set to it as Ezra's. 'Not that he'd care, anyway. I'm his daughter, but Mother and I mean very little to him. We give him respectability in the community, that's all. If it weren't for that, we'd still be back in Scotland. I often wish to God we were. At least Mother was happy there.'

Luke remembered seeing Mrs McCulloch. She had been standing with her husband when Luke arrived at the Fox house. A small plump woman with an unhealthy pallor, there had been perspiration on her upper lip and chin, and damp patches around her armpits. He thought Mrs McCulloch would be perfectly at home in a small Scottish village. Spending her mornings making pastry and bread, she would delight in gossiping with neighbours she had known for a lifetime. Instead, she was condemned to making meaningless small-talk at a social gathering in Macau, a Portuguese enclave clinging like a tick to the underbelly of China.

'My father lives his life in a world he has set apart from ours,' Morna broke into Luke's thoughts. 'He spends most of his time on Hong Kong island. Have you been there?'

Luke nodded. He hoped she would not ask too many questions about her father's life on the island of 'The Fragrant Harbour'.

But Morna McCulloch was not a girl who evaded delicate issues. Her next question rocked Luke.

'Really! Apart from Father you're the only person I've met who admits to having been there. Did you meet my father's mistress?'

When Luke began mouthing like a hungry goldfish Morna said, 'I see you did. Is she very beautiful? Do you have a Chinese mistress?'

Luke was beginning to flounder helplessly under Morna's direct questioning, when succour arrived from a most unexpected quarter.

Captain Obadiah Innes, his ship high on the shore of Hong Kong island, was enjoying the rare pleasure of a few days ashore in Macau. With few Britons in the colony, he had automatically been placed on Lancelot Fox's guest-list.

The Captain had drunk as much as any man at the party — and more than most. It accentuated his mariner's gait as he pushed his way across the room to where Luke stood with Morna McCulloch.

'Well! If it isn't Luke Trewarne, late of the Honourable East India Company! I hear you've been making quite a name for yourself since I brought you to China in *The Two Brothers*.' He nodded to Morna. 'You mind what you say to him, Miss Morna. This young man intends being the number one man in these parts. Don't get passing on any of your father's secrets.'

'I'm far more interested in how many of my father's secrets Luke can tell *me*, Captain Innes. But he seems to have a closer mouth than most. Perhaps *you* can tell me something of my father's life in Hong Kong?'

Startled, Obadiah Innes made a mighty effort to pull his thoughts together. 'Your father will have told you all you need to know about Hong Kong, Miss Morna. He works hard there,

I *can* tell you that. Next to Jardine Matheson, he's the top trader in these parts. One day he'll be a mighty influential man. You can be sure of that.'

Captain Obadiah Innes shifted his intention back to Luke. 'You remember that, too, laddie. One day Ezra McCulloch will call the tune on the China station. You'll do well to stay on the right side of him.'

The seaman leaned forward and leered into Luke's face. 'But I can see you're making a start by being nice to his daughter. Good luck to you. Marrying into the family is the only way you'll ever take any of Ezra's trade from him.'

Before Luke could guess his attention, Captain Obadiah Innes gave him a mighty thump on the back. Then, chortling at his own wit, he swayed away to where a Chinese steward presided over the drinks table.

'Obadiah Innes is just the sort of man I would expect my father to employ. No doubt he enjoys standing on the deck of his ship, bellowing at the top of his voice for the sailors— Why, what's the matter?'

Morna looked at Luke in wide-eyed concern as he slumped back against the wall, a grimace of agony on his blood-drained face.

'What is it? What's happened?'

'Nothing. . . . I need to get out of here, that's all.'

Biting back a grunt of pain, Luke pushed himself away from the wall – and Morna McCulloch gasped.

Behind him, at shoulder height, a red stain the size of a man's hand discoloured the wall. Captain Innes's hearty thump had ruptured the barely healed skin on Luke's back.

'Come with me.' Morna McCulloch gripped Luke's arm and, as he leaned on her, she edged her way from the room, trying to hide the rapidly spreading bloodstain on Luke's back from his fellow-guests.

'I must get to Dan Gemmell's house. Help me there, then send for Abel Snow. He's the American missionary who came from Canton with me. No one else must know . . . do you understand?'

Morna McCulloch swallowed the questions that were on her tongue. Gripping his arm more tightly, she bent her head to his and tried to smile. To anyone watching them, it looked as though they were deep in an intimate conversation. In this manner, Morna got him outside the house and into the street. Here she called up a carrying-cart. Almost swooning with pain and the loss of blood, Luke was hurried to the house where he was staying.

Eleven

IT WAS three days before Luke was well enough to leave Dan Gemmell's Macau house. During that time he was tended by Abel Snow, with the help of Morna McCulloch. Morna had to fight back her tears when she first saw the brutal pattern of scars on Luke's back, but she asked no questions until the day Luke was able to take his first brief stroll along the waterfront, a light dressing protecting the broken scars.

Macau's waterfront was a wide flagstoned walk encircling the bay where ships of all nations rode gently at anchor. The commercial quays were situated on the far side of the half-moon harbour. Where Luke and Morna were, it was almost deserted. The only other people were a few Chinese who stopped and stared unashamedly at Morna McCulloch's long blonde hair, which she wore about her shoulders today.

They had stopped to look out across the harbour, when Morna asked, 'Are you going to tell me about your back now?'

Luke would have preferred not to discuss the events that followed on the Canton fire, but he owed Morna an explanation. He told her of the fire, his arrest and torture, the beating, of Shengan's intercession – and he told her of Kuei.

Morna was strangely silent for a very long time after Luke ended his story. He could read nothing of her thoughts from her face, but when she eventually spoke it was to ask him about Kuei.

'How did you meet this . . . this Chinese girl?'

Luke told her of the trip up the Pearl River in the sampan.

Morna choked on an attempted laugh. 'How can any European girl be expected to compete with such a romantic introduction as that?' More fiercely, she asked, 'What is it about Chinese girls that makes them so attractive to men, Luke? My father . . . you . . . no doubt every other man who has ever lived·and worked here has kept a Chinese mistress.'

Luke saw the unhappiness in her and thought it was caused by her father's involvement with Lo Asan. 'It's probably because they are attractive people. A man gets lonely. . . .'

'Is that why you took your Chinese mistress, Luke? Because you were lonely? Is that what you are telling me?'

Luke was reluctant to discuss Kuei here, but Morna was awaiting a more detailed explanation from him. 'No. Kuei is something special. She's like no other girl I've ever met — not that I've met many.'

Morna turned away from him, but not before he had seen the tears glistening in her eyes. As she stood staring silently out across the crowded harbour, he took her arm, but she shook his hand away fiercely.

'Damn you, Luke Trewarne! Why can't you have stayed in Canton with your Chinese girl? Why did you have to come to Macau at all?'

Luke was completely at a loss for words. 'I'm sorry, Morna,' he apologized, although he was not sure what he had done. 'I'm sorry. . . .'

She walked a few paces away from him, still looking out across the water. Luke saw her shoulders heaving as she gulped air into her lungs in a bid to gain control of herself once more. Blowing her nose noisily, she turned to face Luke once more. She was in command of herself again, and only her pink-tinged eyes showed any sign of the emotional battle she had just fought with herself.

'That was silly of me, Luke. I've always despised women who resort to tears when they are not getting what they want.'

'What is it you want, Morna? I thought at first I'd upset you by talking about Lo Asan . . . your father's . . . the girl on Hong Kong island. But it wasn't that, was it? It was what I told you about Kuei. Would you rather I had lied to you?'

For a moment Luke thought she was going to lose control of herself again, then she shook her head sadly. 'No, Luke. I wouldn't want you to lie to me — about anything. It's just. . . . Oh! You're too damned honest, Luke. Far too honest for *my* good.'

She took his arm, and as they began to walk again Morna looked up in his face and astonished him by giving him a happy smile.

Seeing his confusion, she hissed, through barely parted teeth, 'Smile back at me, Luke Trewarne. A girl I know is coming towards us and I am not as honest as you. I want her to believe I'm the happiest girl in Macau.'

Confused though he was, Luke gave Morna the semblance

of a smile and inclined his head to the girl who called a greeting to Morna, as she passed by in the company of an elderly severe-looking woman. The other woman did not acknowledge their presence, but passed on, wearing an expression of deep disapproval.

'Have you offended that woman at some time?' Luke asked when they were beyond hearing. 'She was determined not to speak to you.'

Morna snorted. 'I am offending her – and others like her – all the time, Luke. *Their* daughters leave the house only when accompanied by a chaperon. They are always telling my mother that I am given too much freedom. Perhaps they are right. If my whole life was arranged for me, I wouldn't go around making such a fool of myself. As it is. . . . But no matter; you've put up with me for long enough. You can take me home now.'

'Couldn't we walk up to the far end of the harbour? I thought I saw *Black Swan* coming a short while ago. I'd like to see what Gideon Pyke's brought in this time. I also enjoy your company and want to keep you with me for a while longer.'

Morna looked up at him quickly and saw no guile in his expression. Squeezing his arm, she said, 'Thank you for that, Luke. But I want to go home. You won't forget I am having a party tonight? You are my guest of honour. You *will* be there?'

'Of course . . . thank you. I really don't know what I'd have done without you.'

'Don't humour me, Luke. I made a fool of myself back there – as we both know – but I've faced up to it and we are still walking arm-in-arm together. Now, let's change the subject. Tell me about your General Shengan. *All* about him. He must be a fascinating man. . . .'

Luke arrived at Morna's party accompanied by Gideon Pyke. The American had brought *Black Swan* down-river that day. To Luke's great relief, he reported that Dan Gemmell was coping with things well in Canton. His health seemed much improved and he was enjoying running his company once more.

Luke had found it hard going to persuade the young American captain to attend Morna McCulloch's party. At the helm of his ship, Gideon Pyke was an intrepid seaman, at home in any weather conditions, but he admitted to Luke that the thought of facing the cream of Macau society at a social function terrified him.

'Goddamit, Luke!' he said for the dozenth time, as he slowly and reluctantly dressed in Dan Gemmell's house. 'It'll only take some fancy-footed popinjay to tread on my toe as he prances past in one of these new dances and I'll either drive his teeth down his throat or use swear words that'll send every lady running for the door.'

'Nonsense,' Luke grinned. 'You'll be the most interesting man at the party. The ladies will love you. There's another reason I want you there. I have something to say to Ezra McCulloch and I may have need of your support.'

Luke had made up his mind to build a warehouse on Hong Kong island and intended telling Ezra McCulloch what he was doing. He and the older man had very different ideas about trading, but Luke had no wish to make Ezra McCulloch an enemy as well as a business rival.

The party was a much grander affair than Luke had been expecting, but there was never any question of Gideon Pyke being out of place there. His easy charm and knowledge of the social graces told Luke that his young captain was no stranger to the society soirées he claimed to dislike so much.

The party had been under way for a couple of hours before Luke was able to corner Ezra McCulloch and tell him of his plans. Luke had anticipated opposition from the Scots trader but, to his surprise, Ezra McCulloch seemed highly delighted. Morna came across the room at that moment, escorted by Gideon Pyke, and her father said, 'Do you know what this young man has just told me? He's going to build himself a godown on Hong Kong island. It shows good sense. Only a fool would stay bottled up in Canton, subject to the whims of Chinese officialdom. You've got brains, laddie.'

'Then you don't mind?'

'Mind . . . ? I'm pleased. One day every trader in China will build himself a godown there. We'll have houses, too — and schools and churches. It will become a town — a British town. Any Chinese who want to trade will be able to come there and buy from us direct. There will be no Hongs dictating prices, and no mandarins taking most of our profits in "squeeze". Good luck to you, boy. You can stay in my place while you're building. My servants will look after you.'

'It seems you're eager for everyone to go to Hong Kong except your own family, Father. When are you going to let me go there to see this magnificent house and godown I keep hearing about? Or do you have some deep dark secret hidden away there?'

Luke held his breath for the explosion he thought was about to come. He was wrong yet again. Ezra McCulloch looked from his daughter to Luke, and back again. 'Now, what secrets would I have from you? All right, if you want to visit Hong Kong, then go with Luke.' Looking Luke in the eyes, he said, 'My Chinese housekeeper is away at the moment. I've got someone staying there, but you could chase up the servants for me. I'll arrange a boat to take you both. When do you want to go?'

'I'm going in *Black Swan* tomorrow,' said Luke. 'Morna is welcome to come with us.' He said it without conviction. Ezra McCulloch had made it clear that Lo Asan was not at the house on the island, but Luke had some enquiries of his own to pursue. Morna's presence might prove embarrassing.

'You might say it as though you meant it,' said Morna in mock indignation. She knew Luke was going to seek Kuei, and the thought cut into her like a knife, but Luke would never be aware of it. 'I'll swim alongside your damn boat if you don't want me on board – but I'm going to Hong Kong. I've been waiting for this opportunity for too long to lose it now.'

'You'll come in *Black Swan*,' promised Gideon Pyke. 'Or Luke will sail his own ship. Now, Morna, will you show me a room where I can smoke my pipe without choking everyone?'

As Morna led Gideon Pyke away, Luke turned to follow them. Ezra McCulloch called him back.

'Morna is fond of you, Luke. Where do you stand?'

The manner in which the question was asked made Luke's hackles rise.

'That's my business. It wasn't my idea that she should travel to Hong Kong with me.'

'True,' Ezra McCulloch conceded. 'But she's going anyway. You're too damn touchy, boy. I'm not saying that's a bad thing. I've always gone my own way, and to hell with the next man; but your path and mine are running a mite close at the moment. If you've serious intentions towards Morna, I've no objection. None at all. You've got a head on your shoulders. One day Gemmell Company will amount to something; and it will be yours by then – Dan Gemmell is not long for this life. Put McCulloch's and Gemmell's together and we'd have a company to push Jardine Matheson and Lancelot Fox out of the Far East. Think about it, Luke.'

Ezra McCulloch lowered his voice, but it carried with it all the menace of a man who meant every word. 'In case you've got other ideas about Morna, I'll give you something else to think about. Eunuchs! The Emperor has hundreds of them in his palace. They've learned the lesson of "look but don't touch", the hard way. So far I've shown you the generous side of my nature. Play about with Morna and you'll see the Ezra McCulloch that other men have known – only *you* won't be a man anymore.'

Twelve

WHEN Kuei hurried back to the factories after leaving General Shengan's house, she had great difficulty in persuading Abel Snow that Soo Fang must be released from the hospital. The missionary argued that if Soo Fang left now he would slip back into his old ways in a matter of days. By remaining in hospital, the fisherman had at least an outside chance of learning to cope with his addiction.

Kuei knew that, if she told Abel Snow the reason for the urgency, he would release her father immediately — but he would then go into the walled city and demand to see the Tsotang. She wanted nothing to interfere with Luke's release.

Eventually, Abel Snow had to give in to Kuei's demand, but it was with a sense of failure that he watched Kuei lead her father off into the darkness. He knew he was watching a doomed man. But Soo Fang was not the first opium addict to leave hospital prematurely. Neither would he be the last. Shaking his head sadly, the medical missionary went back inside his hospital to tend to the needs of his other patients.

Kuei took her father to their sampan where Tik-wei already waited. In the warm drizzle of a late summer night, they began a long and unhappy voyage down-river. Expecting the Tsotang to send his men after her, Kuei took a tortuous route among the narrow and shallower waterways that threaded their way southwards from Canton.

Throughout the voyage, Soo Fang behaved as a man who had lost his grip on life. Huddled in the sampan's shelter, he reminded the unhappy Kuei of a helpless animal. Neither speaking nor eating, he spent the entire day staring vacantly out into the distance. Kuei doubted whether he saw anything, and he gave no indication that he heard her or Tik-wei when they spoke to him. Nevertheless, Kuei held many one-sided conversations with him, in the hope that he would eventually respond. Once, when Tik-wei was startled into a shout by a silver pheasant that took noisily and ponderously to the air from the river-bank beside them, Soo Fang looked round at her.

Kuei held her breath, praying he might speak, but a moment later Soo Fang had forgotten what had attracted his attention. He retreated once more into the lonely place to which only he held the key.

By the time they reached Hong Kong, Kuei was convinced Soo Fang no longer had a mind capable of thought. It was for this reason she took no special precautions when she and Tik-wei went to McCulloch's house to seek Lo Asan, leaving Soo Fang in the sampan.

At the house, a servant told her that Lo Asan had gone to Peking. It was a cruel blow to Kuei's hopes. With Lo Asan gone there was no one with whom she could discuss her problems, or who could learn what had happened to Luke in Canton. But worse was to come. While she stood outside the house, wondering what to do, a Fan Qui man came to the door and ordered her from the house. Kuei was quite certain she had never seen him before, but the Fan Qui was beside himself with rage – and obviously knew her. He threatened to send word to the Tsotang of Canton, informing him of her whereabouts. Thoroughly frightened, Kuei took Tik-wei's hand and fled back to the sampan.

Scrambling across the other boats in the floating village, the two girls reached their sampan – and found it was empty. Soo Fang had gone.

Fearing he might have fallen overboard, Kuei called to the occupants of the neighbouring sampans, asking if anyone had seen her father. One old woman had. Bent almost double with pain, Soo Fang had made his way across the moored vessels to the shore and headed along the muddy coastal path to a nearby fishing village.

Ordering the protesting Tik-wei to remain behind, Kuei ran to the village. Long before she arrived at the first of the bamboo and matting houses, she heard the shouts and cries of excited people and knew it had something to do with her father.

Reaching the centre of the village, she pushed her way through a noisy crowd gathered before a small decrepit hut. Here she saw her father cowering on the ground, trying to protect himself from two men wielding heavy sticks. The sympathies of the crowd were divided between the man on the ground and his attackers, some urging them to beat Soo Fang harder, others calling upon them to stop. No one attempted to interfere.

Kuei leaped from the crowd with a loud screech of anger. Arms flailing, she fell upon the the two attackers. 'Leave my father alone! He is a sick man. Do you want to kill him?'

The two men fell back before her onslaught, but one of them said, 'He is a thief. He should be punished.'

Kneeling beside her father, who had now collapsed to the ground, Kuei saw that he was hardly breathing. His mouth hung open, and his eyes were staring up into his own head. She knew immediately what Soo Fang had stolen.

She screamed at the two men, 'You call my father a thief? He took opium because he cannot live without it. It is you who are the thieves. You rob a man of honour, self-respect – yes, and even of life itself! Look at him . . . look!'

Emotion robbed Kuei of her voice. With tears streaming down her cheeks, she slumped down until her head was resting on her father's chest. She knew what had happened. Soo Fang had swallowed the opium he had stolen from the den operated by the two men. It was a well-known method of committing suicide. Whether that had been Soo Fang's intention, she would never know. It was possible he had been so desperate for opium he did not realize what he was doing. Either way, Soo Fang was very close to death.

Around Kuei, the mood of the crowd had swung overwhelmingly in her favour and, as Soo Fang's two attackers backed inside the hut that housed their opium 'divan', someone threw a stone at them. Others followed the example, and as the two men darted out of sight the crowd surged forward and began beating at the flimsy structure. Within minutes the small hut was reduced to a fragile framework. As the two divan keepers escaped through the rear 'wall', a number of confused opium smokers crawled to safety. Moments later, the hut was battered to the ground.

During this enthusiastic exhibition of the crowd's sympathy, Kuei had been trying to protect Soo Fang as people milled around and trampled over them. By the time the mob began to disperse, laughing and calling to each other, Soo Fang was dead.

Kuei quickly learned that the sympathy of the villagers was not great enough to help her to carry Soo Fang's body back to the floating village. She was forced to leave her father lying in the mud of the village street and return to the floating village of the Hoklos to fetch help.

Soo Fang's body was committed to the Goddess of the Sea that same day, in the hope that the fickle deity would show more compassion for the fisherman in death than she had in life.

With Lo Asan away, there was now nothing for Kuei in Hong Kong. If the Fan Qui in McCulloch's house carried out his threat, it might even be dangerous for her to stay, but she could not leave until she learned what had happened to Luke — and only Lo Asan could ascertain that for her.

Kuei remained in the boat village, putting to sea each day with Tik-wei, catching fish in order that they might live. Then one day, as she brought the sampan back to the floating village, she saw Gemmell Company's ship *Black Swan* sailing into the harbour.

Overcome with excitement at the unexpected sight, Kuei worked frenziedly at the stern oar, trying to beat the hordes of sampans which always swarmed about a Fan Qui ship entering the anchorage. Now she would learn something of her Luke. He might be on board — coming to Hong Kong to find her!

Kuei was almost within hailing distance of the ship when suddenly her arms went limp and the oar stilled in her hands. As the sampan lost way, the blood drained from Kuei's face and her whole world collapsed about her.

Luke *was* on board *Black Swan*. He stood in the bows of his ship, looking up at the hill towards the McCulloch house. Standing close behind him, her hand on his arm and long blonde hair blowing in the wind, was a Fan Qui woman.

As *Black Swan* sailed past the small island guarding the entrance to Hong Kong's sheltered harbour, Luke saw immediately where he would build his house and warehouse. The spot was only a few hundred yards from Ezra McCulloch's property. Like his, the house would nestle beneath a section of the steep hillside that formed a sheer cliff. The godown would be between the house and the sea, on more gently sloping ground. There was no shingle beach, but as they drew nearer Luke could see that the water was deep right up to the edge of the rocky shore. He would build a quay. His ships would be able to tie up alongside, close to the godown. It would eliminate the need to use sampans to ferry trade goods ashore.

'Dreaming of the future, Luke?' Morna came to stand quietly beside him. Full of enthusiasm for the trip when they had set out, she had become more and more subdued as they sailed closer to the Hong Kong anchorage.

Luke nodded and pointed to where the white house amidst the trees gleamed in the bright afternoon sunshine. 'That's your father's place.'

Morna nodded. 'It's impressive.'

'Wait until you see inside. It's superb,' said Luke enthusiastically. He was happy. Here he was going to find Kuei again — but there was more than that to his feeling of well-being. In Macau and in the factories of Canton he always felt vaguely harassed — hemmed in by houses and people. Here, on Hong Kong island, man had made very little impact on nature. The great peak towered over slopes occupied only by scrub and trees, lush and green in this season of heat and high humidity. McCulloch had declared that one day this would be a thriving trading community, but that was still in the future. For the moment . . . ? Luke looked to where the Hoklo boats were moored, row upon row, at the edge of the fishing village, close to McCulloch's beach.

'I'm not so sure this is such a good idea after all,' Morna declared hesitantly.

'Why?' Luke looked at her in surprise, then immediately felt guilty. He had been so engrossed in his own hopes and ideas that he had not thought of Morna at all.

'I'm an interloper here. I don't belong, somehow. In that house is a part of my father's life that has nothing to do with my mother or me. It makes me feel the way I did once as a girl. I walked into my father's bedroom and saw him lying asleep . . . naked. I felt so guilty I couldn't speak to him for weeks. That's just the way I feel now. As though I'll be peeping at his nakedness — only this time it will be deliberate, and not an accident.'

'You'll see nothing your father doesn't want you to see. He was quite happy to have you come here, remember? Perhaps he's ready to share this part of his life with you now.'

Morna was silent for some minutes, staring across the shrinking strip of water dividing boat from land. Then she said, 'No, it's because she's not at the house.'

'Your father said he has someone at the house . . .' Luke began cautiously.

Morna interrupted impatiently. 'You know who I'm talking

about. Father told you his "housekeeper" was not at the house. He said it in such a way that only an idiot wouldn't have known he was talking about his mistress. I'm not an idiot, Luke. You've met . . . what's her name? Lo Asan? Is she very attractive?'

Morna knew of Lo Asan's existence; to lie to her would be childish. Far better to tell her what he knew of Lo Asan. 'She is probably the loveliest woman I've ever met – and she has a nature that goes with her looks.'

'My father has never settled for less than the very best.' Morna sounded disappointed.

'She is also a Manchu,' Luke added. He felt somehow obliged to justify her father's life on Hong Kong island to Morna. 'Her family holds high positions in China.'

'Oh? Is that supposed to make everything all right? Am I to believe my father and his Manchu girl spend their nights in bed together discussing trade? That sickens me more than anything else I've heard. Had she been some . . . some boat-girl, I could have accepted that he had fallen in love. I might even have admired him for it . . . a little. But he married my mother for her money, and used it to start his trading business. Now he's taken an influential mistress to further that same business. I wonder what reason he had for begetting me? There must have been one. No doubt he'll try to marry me off to whoever comes up with the best offer. . . .'

Morna looked at Luke in sudden dismay as enlightenment came to her. 'My God . . . ! He's already done that, hasn't he? In Macau it's being said you've got the best head for trading in this part of the world. That when you find your feet you'll leave everyone else behind. That's why Father let me come here. He wants to marry me off to you – for the good of the McCulloch Trading Company! What did he offer you, Luke? Forty-nine per cent of the Company? It wouldn't be more. He won't allow control to pass out of his own hands. . . .'

'You're jumping to too many conclusions,' Luke lied. 'If you really want to know, your father warned me that, if I step out of line with you, he'll emasculate me and pack me off to a eunuch's life in Peking.'

For a moment Luke feared Morna would pursue the matter farther, then her shoulders sagged and the aggression left her. She gave Luke a rueful grin. 'I'm sorry, Luke. I got carried away. God! What an awful thing it is to doubt every word and action of one's own father.'

She reached out and touched his arm momentarily. 'I'll try not to burden you with my problems. I know you have enough of your own. Neither will I let Father pack you off to Peking. You've suffered enough already for the women in your life.'

Behind them, Gideon Pyke called an order and the sails were quickly furled. The speed of the brigantine dropped away and an anchor splashed into the water, pursued by six fathoms of clattering chain.

As a small boat was lowered to the water, Gideon Pyke puffed thoughtfully on his pipe. He looked from the line of hills on the island to the nine peaks of the range that rose to the horizon northwards of the natural harbour. 'So this is to be home?' He spoke past the stem of his pipe to Morna. 'Your father knew what he was doing when he settled here. This is the best anchorage for miles – with a whole lot of potential.'

To Luke he said, 'You get to building, Luke. This place has a future. I can smell it in the air . . . and that's not all.' He wrinkled his nose and jerked his head in the direction of the nearby fishing village. ' "Fragrant Harbour", be damned! The place stinks. Do you reckon you can move that place a couple of miles around the bay?'

'That village will provide us with food, as well as labour for building and for unloading our cargoes. Now, let's get ashore and see what's going on.'

Luke, Gideon and Morna landed on Ezra McCulloch's beach, and Gideon and Morna went on to the house, leaving Luke to examine the place where he intended building a quay. He was well satisfied with his choice. Gemmell Company could build a quay to take at least three ships, leaving ample room to turn them at their moorings when they sailed away fully laden. Luke could already visualize the scene. A busy quay, a good road to a stout godown – and his own house, looking down upon the Gemmell empire.

It was in this happy frame of mind that Luke reached the McCulloch house and walked inside. He could hear Gideon and Morna talking in the lounge. There was another voice, too, a deep voice. Luke thought he had heard it before, but it was too indistinct to identify. Pushing open the lounge door Luke came face to face with Hans Moller.

Holding a bottle of brandy and two empty glasses in his hands, Moller was as surprised as Luke, but Luke recovered first. His first punch landed in Moller's face. As bottle and glasses smashed on the floor, the German staggered backwards. Luke hit him again before he recovered his balance, and Moller fell over a small table crowded with priceless bric-à-brac. Twice more Luke's fist slammed into Moller's face. Another punch sank deep into his stomach, and Hans Moller dropped slowly to the floor. Before Luke could pull him to his feet and hit again, he was seized from behind and dragged away from the other man.

'Luke! Luke! What the hell's got into you? What are you doing?' Gideon Pyke's voice penetrated the thick red blanket of anger as Morna darted past the two struggling men and kneeled beside Hans Moller.

'All right, you can release me now.' Luke shrugged Gideon Pyke away from him and pointed to the German, who sat on the floor, gasping in pain. 'But get him out of my sight.'

Morna looked up at him in bewilderment. 'He's employed by my father to look after things here. Who is he? What has he done?'

'His name is Hans Moller. He worked for Dan Gemmell until I threw him out for smoking opium with his Chinese friends. He got his own back by sending someone into Canton to tell the Tsotang about me and Kuei.'

Morna recoiled from Hans Moller, all sympathy for him gone. 'What do you intend doing with him?'

'If I have to look at his face for long, I'll end up killing him.' Breathing heavily, Luke glared down at Hans Moller. His back hurt as a result of his exertions, and that did not help.

'You'd better get out – now.' Placing himself between the two men, Gideon Pyke spoke to Hans Moller.

Hans Moller got to his feet slowly and painfully. 'What can I do? Where can I go?' Dabbing at a badly bruised eye, he edged along the wall away from Luke.

'Go anywhere . . . back to Macau. Get a fisherman to take you there – but be off this island by nightfall.'

Hans Moller made a break for safety. Thrusting Morna to one side, he ran to the door. Pausing there, he looked at Luke with undisguised hatred. 'I will leave the island, but you have not seen the last of me.' Anger thickened his accent to such an extent that his words were barely intelligible. 'You might as well leave, too. You will not find what you seek here. I have made certain of that.'

The German turned and fled, and it was some seconds before the full import of his broken English came home to Luke. Hans Moller must have been talking about Kuei! Luke ran outside, only to see the older man running recklessly down the slope towards the shore. Luke began to run after him but, long before he came anywhere near him, Moller leaped into a sampan and ordered the startled Tanka girl to pull away from the shore.

Far from fit, Luke collapsed helplessly on a rock halfway along the path and gasped in rasping lungfuls of air. He still had a dressing on his back, and the pain from his partly healed scars was making itself felt. He could have cried with frustration. Hans Moller had known something important about Kuei. Now he was gone.

By the time Gideon Pyke and Morna reached him Luke had his feelings under control. He allowed them to lead him back to the house and took a large glass of brandy from Morna's hands gratefully.

While Luke recovered, Gideon Pyke went down to the beach where he learned that Moller had sailed to Macau in the sampan. It would soon be dusk, and the captain of *Black Swan* announced his intention of spending the night on board his ship. Pirates abounded around the offshore islands, and Gideon would take no chances with *Black Swan*.

When Luke said he would accompany him to the beach, Gideon Pyke protested that Luke was not yet fit enough for such a walk, but he withdrew his objection when Morna said she would come with them. Luke would have preferred not to have her company. It was his intention to go to the floating village and ask for Kuei, but Morna informed him curtly that she knew very well what he wanted to do and would not get in his way.

When Gideon Pyke was well on his way back to the ship Luke and Morna walked together in silence until they came to the first of the sampans comprising the floating village. Here Morna paused. 'What will you do if Kuei is here? If you find her tonight?'

Luke shook his head. 'I don't know. I haven't dared allow my thoughts to get that far ahead.'

Morna said no more, and she stood back as Luke questioned anyone who would stay long enough to listen to him. Luke's task was not easy. The Hoklo were a shy and reticent people. One after another, they denied any knowledge of Soo Fang and his daughter Kuei. No one had heard of either of them. Before long, Luke became thoroughly exasperated. He was convinced they were lying. Kuei and her family had lived here for years before taking Luke to Canton. They must have been known to the whole floating community.

It was Morna who finally broke the deadlock. Calling to Luke, she pointed out an old Hoklo woman with a face as wrinkled as a Christmas apple. 'Ask her, Luke. She knows something. She just mentioned the Soo family.'

Seeing Luke's doubt, Morna said, in Cantonese equal to his own, 'I had more time on my hands than I knew what to do with when I first arrived in Macau, so I learned Cantonese – Mandarin, too.'

To the old woman she had pointed out to Luke, she called, 'You, mo ts'an – mother – what do you know of the Soo family?'

There were chuckles from some of the listening boat-dwellers at Morna's use of the word 'mother'. The old woman herself was so surprised that the blonde barbarian girl spoke her own language that she made no attempt to evade the question. 'Soo Fang's spirit has gone to live with those of his ancestors.'

'When? How did he die?' Luke demanded.

The old lady stared at him disdainfully before spitting a stream of betel juice through uneven red-stained teeth. 'He took too much "foreign medicine".' She used the common Chinese description of opium. 'Many others die of the same.'

Luke ignored the old lady's unconcealed contempt for him. 'Where are his daughters – Kuei and Tik-wei?'

The old lady shrugged her shoulders and looked about her with exaggerated disinterest. 'Perhaps they have gone back to Fu-kien. If you need a woman, find yourself a Tanka girl. They sell their bodies to sailors for a few taels of silver. You are young and strong; they will not make you pay so much.' She cackled noisily at her own ribaldry.

'I don't want a Tanka girl. I want to find Kuei and Tik-wei. Do you know where they went?'

Apparently bored with the conversation, the old lady shifted her position and looked out across the harbour, away from Luke. 'I have not seen them since they returned from the Fan Qui house on the hill. Tik-wei was crying. A Fan Qui had said she and Kuei must go. He said he would send men looking for them, to take Kuei to Canton for a flogging. Perhaps that is why you seek them?'

For one angry moment, Luke thought of baring his back to this irritating old woman, but he doubted whether such a melodramatic act would move her to tell the truth.

'Since when have Europeans done the Tsotang's work?' he asked, wishing he had not allowed Hans Moller to escape so easily. 'I want to find Kuei to help her. That is the truth; you must believe me.'

'I once thought I knew what truth was,' retorted the old lady. 'That was before the Fan Qui came here. You have one truth for yourselves, another for us. Neither is the same as the truth we teach our children. Go. If Soo Kuei needs you, she will find you.'

Until the old lady spoke the last few words, Luke was ready to believe Kuei must have gone from Hong Kong. Now he knew she was still here, somewhere close by. But he would learn no more from this old Hoklo woman. Tomorrow he would begin making enquiries farther afield.

They were on their way back to the house when Morna looked over her shoulder and halted suddenly. 'There's a ship coming into the harbour.'

The sun had disappeared behind the great island peak behind the McCulloch house and dusk was falling fast, but Luke could just make out the triple tier of dark gun-ports along the side of the ship as she rounded the farthermost point of the bay.

'It's a man-o'-war, a big one. Carrying seventy-four guns unless I'm mistaken. What's it doing here?'

They both stood watching the warship in the gathering darkness as it sailed slowly into the anchorage. When it reached a point off the McCulloch beach there was the clatter of an anchor chain and the man-of-war rode gently at anchor a hundred yards offshore.

Luke and Morna hurried back to the beach where a number of curious Chinese villagers had already gathered. By now it was too dark to see more than the faint outline of the ship, but the sound of a boat being rowed ashore carried across the water to them. Minutes later, the boat crunched upon the gravel beach and a British sailor jumped ashore to hold it in. A number of Chinese then jumped from the boat and were followed by a midshipman, carrying a bundle.

Luke moved forward to speak to the midshipman, Morna a few paces behind. 'What's happening? Why are you here?'

Before the midshipman could reply, the bundle in his arms

squirmed into life and a figure wriggled free. Splashing into the water, it rushed up the beach, shouting, 'Luke . . . is that you?'

It was Lo Asan.

Reaching Luke, she flung her arms about his neck and hugged him excitedly. Then she stood back a pace and flapped the loose arms of an outsize shirt in front of his face. 'Look at me, Luke. Do you think my new clothes are beautiful? They belong to sailor.' She pirouetted in front of him, chattering happily all the while. 'I was shipwrecked, Luke. On an island. It was very lucky I did not die. My clothes were torn on the rocks.' She shook a hand free from the shirt and spread her long fingers wide. 'Five days we waited, with no food. We were very hungry. Sometimes the men looked at me and I know what they are thinking. They think: If no ship comes tomorrow, we eat Lo Asan. Very tasty young girl.'

Lo Asan giggled happily. 'Then along comes a ship. It belongs to very important man. An admiral. He say, "Hello, Lo Asan. We send boat to take you home. Back to McCulloch Hau-ye." Where is McCulloch, Luke? He has not gone to Macau yet? He is at the house?'

Lo Asan went to push past Luke, then stopped short. One of the sailors from the boat had lit a pitch torch. The light from its crackling flames fell upon the golden hair of Morna McCulloch.

Wishing he could have spared her this moment, Luke said, 'Lo Asan, this is Morna McCulloch . . . Ezra's daughter. She's staying at the house for a few days. Ezra is not here. He's in Macau.'

As Luke talked, all the gaiety drained from Lo Asan. She became just a frightened little Chinese girl in clothes several sizes too large for her.

Turning a stricken face towards Luke, Lo Asan whispered in Cantonese, 'Does she know about McCulloch Hau-ye and me?'

'Yes, Lo Asan . . . and she also speaks Cantonese.'

'Oh!' Lo Asan's face crumbled, but she bowed low to Morna. 'I am sorry. . . . I go now.' Hitching the ill-fitting clothes about her, Lo Asan fled into the night. Luke would have followed her, but the midshipman was speaking to him.

'I hope we did the right thing, sir. The ship foundered on the Maku Islands, about three hundred and fifty miles from here. We found half a dozen survivors clinging to an island that was little more than a barren rock. They were lucky; few ships normally pass that close. I understand that some other survivors, including the ship's master, were picked up farther east by one of our frigates. They should reach Macau within the week.'

The midshipman grinned. 'We have Admiral Sir Charles Blunt on board, and the young lady captivated him. We should be well on our way to Manila now, but the young lady insisted we bring her here first. She says she belongs to McCulloch – "a very important man". She promised he would make plenty of trouble for the Admiral if he didn't do as she asked – so the Admiral did as he was told!'

'Yes . . . well, thank the Admiral very much. Er . . . will you come to the house?'

'No, thank you, sir. My orders are to repair on board as quickly as possible. When the moon comes up we'll set sail for Manila.'

A few minutes later, the boat creaked away in the darkness and the Chinese onlookers returned to their homes. Luke turned to Morna. 'We'd better be getting back now.'

'Yes.' Suddenly, Morna's hand found his. 'Hold my hand, please, Luke.'

As they walked up the hill towards the house, Morna squeezed his hand so tightly that Luke winced, but Morna was far too wrapped up in her own thoughts to notice. While Luke was still trying to think of something to say that would ease the turmoil he knew was inside her, Morna stopped and stamped her foot angrily and futilely on the ground. 'Damn! Damn! Damn!'

Looking up at Luke, she pleaded, 'Why did I have to meet up with Lo Asan in this way, Luke? Why couldn't I have caught her in my father's bed and tongue-lashed her to hell and gone? It isn't fair that I should see her after she's been shipwrecked, wearing ridiculous clothes – and hilariously happy. I've been hating her ever since I first learned about her. Now I've met her . . . and I can't hate her anymore. When she saw me back there on the beach and you told her who I was, she nearly fell apart. I've never seen anyone look so vulnerable. I . . . I wanted to hug her to me and say that it didn't matter. I could almost have loved the girl. Isn't that ridiculous, Luke? Isn't that so damned ridiculous?'

Although it was dark, Luke could see the tears glistening on Morna's face. He leaned closer and kissed her gently.

'You're a very special girl, Morna. Your father is a very lucky man. Luckier than he deserves to be.'

With Morna fiercely clutching his hand, they walked in silence the remainder of the way to the house, engrossed in their own thoughts.

Thirteen

LO ASAN did not put in an appearance that night. When Luke went looking for her he found she had locked herself in a room in the servants' quarters. She refused to let him in, and finally Luke returned to his own room and wrote a hasty letter to Ezra McCulloch. Gideon Pyke could take it to Macau in the morning. Luke felt the trader should know of Lo Asan's return – and the fate of the voyage upon which so many of his hopes had been pinned.

To Luke's relief, Lo Asan was in the kitchen when he came downstairs to breakfast the next morning. She was dressed in the unfamiliar grey trousers and shapeless grey jacket worn by Chinese servants, but only a puffiness about her eyes gave any hint of the unhappiness of the night before. She was ordering the servants about their various tasks in the manner of a ship's boatswain, tut-tutting about the state the house had been allowed to get into during her brief absence.

Morna had not come down yet, and Luke followed Lo Asan about the room, trying to have a conversation with her. But although Lo Asan was impeccably polite, inclining her head and saying 'Yes, Master Luke,' or 'No, Master Luke,' she refused to say more. Eventually, exasperated by her uncharacteristically servile manner, Luke took her firmly by the arm and propelled her from the kitchen into the large lounge.

'Hey! What you do? You let me go,' she said in English.

Luke observed with satisfaction that Lo Asan's servility had disappeared in her indignation.

'I want to talk to you . . . and I can't do it while you're behaving like every man's perfect servant. You're not a servant – and Morna knows that. Behaving like one isn't going to work, Lo Asan. If that's the game you want to play, then go ahead – but, first, what can you tell me about Kuei? Have you any idea where she is?'

'Why you want Kuei?' Again, Lo Asan spoke her own unique form of English. 'One barbarian girl not enough for you? Why you bring McCulloch daughter to father's house, anyway, eh? You no need bring her here. You no have bed in Macau, maybe?

Or you want Lo Asan to see what barbarian girl like? To be unhappy because I no have skin like milk, or hair touched by sun? All right, I see. Now you take her away.'

'She is *not* my girl, Lo Asan.'

Lo Asan called up a loud sniff.

Reaching out a hand, Luke turned her face towards him. 'You're going to listen to me, Lo Asan. If I have to take you outside, tie you to a tree and gag you . . . you're going to listen.'

Lo Asan looked at him defiantly, but remained silent.

'Morna McCulloch was not brought here to embarrass you. Ezra thought you were well on your way to Peking. Neither did she come because she and I need a place to go to bed together. Morna wanted to see this house, and Ezra thought it would be a good idea — with you away. I came to Hong Kong because I'm going to build a house and godown of my own here. When I do I want Kuei to share it with me. Morna McCulloch knows all about it — and now you do, too. But first I must find Kuei. Do you know where she is?'

Lo Asan's face had lit up with pleasure while Luke was talking. Now she darted at him and hugged him warmly. 'What I tell you, eh? I say when you know Kuei as I do you love her, too. I so happy, Luke. She is good girl. She will be very special for you.'

'Am I interrupting something?'

The cold voice of Morna McCulloch came from the doorway. Lo Asan slipped quickly away from Luke and bowed quickly to Morna. Then she said to Luke, 'I will go now. Perhaps I learn something at Chai Wan.'

'Just a moment. . . .' Morna came into the room and the deep shadows beneath her eyes betrayed the fact that she had not slept well. 'Are you here to run errands . . . or to run my father's house?'

Taken aback by Morna's stiff abrasive manner, Luke said quietly, 'Lo Asan is going somewhere for me, Morna. To find out about Kuei.'

'To hell with you and your Chinese . . . doxy! I don't want to hear about Chinese women. Yours or my father's. She's dressed like a servant — let her behave like one. Lo Asan, I want my breakfast.'

Lo Asan bowed very low again, but as she went towards the kitchen Luke called for her to stop and turned angrily on

Morna. 'Just because you've had a bad night, there's no need to—'

'Luke, please . . . !' Lo Asan's voice interrupted him. 'She is right. McCulloch Hau-ye pay much money for me. He treat me very good. Trust me for very important business in Peking. Instead, I come back to Hong Kong. He will be very angry. Perhaps if I am good servant for his family, he let me stay here. Not send me away in bad disgrace. I make happy servant . . . you see.'

'Oh, for Christ's sake!' The shout came from Morna. Startled, Luke looked at her and saw her face contorted in anguish. 'Damn you, Lo Asan. Why can't you behave like some smug Chinese bitch, or something . . . anything! I want to *hate* you, don't you understand? I want to hate you!'

Morna let out a strangled howl and fled from the room. Luke moved to follow her, but Lo Asan stopped him, speaking in Cantonese again. 'Leave her, Luke. I will go to see her. This is between her and me. You go to Chai Wan. It is a fishing village not far from here. Find Ah Mang, one of the servants. He will take you. I have learned that Kuei went there yesterday — after she saw you and McCulloch's daughter talking to the Hoklo woman.'

'Kuei saw me yesterday?'

'Yes. She thought, as I did, that McCulloch's daughter is your woman.'

'She saw me! God Almighty, she should know better! After what we were to each other at Canton. . . . Why does she think I'm looking for her?'

'Go, Luke,' Lo Asan laid a hand gently on his arm. 'When you find her everything will be all right. You will see. Now I go to McCulloch's daughter. She is very unhappy, too.'

The tiny fishing village of Chai Wan was more than five miles away, in a small bay in the north-west corner of the island. There were no more than thirty houses in the village, and only a few sampans, but anchored close to the shore was a very large junk flying a blood-red flag edged with gold.

At sight of the junk, Ah Mang began muttering nervously to himself, but he would not tell Luke what was disturbing him and soon they reached the first of the houses. To Luke's surprise, the small bamboo and reed house was empty, as was the next —

and the next. By the time they arrived at the fourth house, Ah Mang was a trembling wreck.

When he received no reply to his call at this house Luke went inside cautiously. It was in chaos. The few small items of furniture had been overturned and broken. Cooking-utensils and smaller belongings were strewn over the floor, and the shelving around the flimsy walls was cleared of all ornamentation.

While Luke stood puzzling over the scene, there came a cry from outside the hut. When Luke reached the door he saw Ah Mang being held by two men, while a third searched through his clothing. When Luke stepped through the door he was surrounded by a dozen more. The men were like no Chinese Luke had seen before. Not one of them had the shaven forehead and plaited 'pigtail' that was an outward sign of Chinese subservience to their Manchu overlords. These men had long matted hair, held back in some cases by a narrow band of cloth tied about the forehead – and each of them was heavily armed. Most carried a long curved sword and a few were armed with ancient muskets. All had knives tucked in their waistbands.

'What's the meaning of this? Who are you?' Luke demanded of the men.

'Ah! A Chinese-speaking barbarian. We have made a most unusual catch.'

The speaker elbowed his way through the men about him and confronted Luke. His face immediately attracted attention, and Luke had to fight against an instinct to recoil in horror. The man's face was horribly pock-marked, some of the scars eating deep into his skin. They extended to his eyelids and lips, distorting his face into a permanent sardonic grimace.

'Who are you? What's happening here?' Luke repeated.

'We are going about our daily business, barbarian. I think you Fan Qui call us "pirates". It is a good word – a strong word. I like it. My name is Ping Chuan.'

At the mention of the name, Ah Mang let out a loud wail and dropped to his knees. Whether it was from a sudden weakness, or in homage to their captor, Luke did not know, but the pirate chief bowed mockingly in his direction. 'I am honoured to know that my name is not unknown on this island.'

Taking a pace towards the unfortunate Ah Mang, the pirate chief kicked him savagely in the ribs. 'Tell your master of me, groveller in the dirt.'

Unable to control his trembling, Ah Mang looked up at Luke

with undisguised fear in his eyes. 'Ping Chuan is a pirate, master – the greatest of all pirates. He is known and feared by every man who sails the seas, or who lives within marching distance of the sea.'

Ping Chuan nodded his acknowledgement of Ah Mang's introduction before facing Luke once more. 'The groveller might also have told you that I have five hundred junks and fifty thousand fighting men under my command – and that I am a Christian with the Lord at my shoulder as I sweep the seas of unbelievers. You are a Christian, barbarian?'

'I like to think so. . . .'

'Good. I know you are telling the truth. The Lord has just spoken to me and told me so. I am pleased. Now I will not have to kill you; but you must, of course, reward my mercy. It is blessed to give, you know.'

Luke felt his stomach knot inside him as he watched Ping Chuan's eyes glittering behind the tattered lids. The man was mad. Any hope of making a rational appeal to him would be futile.

'You can have all the money I have with me, but it is only a couple of dollars.' Luke felt in his pocket, pulled out the money and passed it to Ping Chuan.

The pirate chief looked at the two silver Maria Theresa dollars and frowned. 'These will not even buy the life of your miserable servant.'

Luke shrugged, doing his best to appear nonchalant. 'It's all the money I am carrying – and Ah Mang is not my servant. He belongs to Ezra McCulloch.'

The mention of McCulloch's name brought an immediate response from Ping Chuan, and murmurs of interest from some of his followers. Ping Chuan gave Luke a twisted smile. 'So you are a friend of the barbarian McCulloch? That is lucky for you. We, too, are friends of McCulloch. He pays us much opium. In return, we allow him to stay on Hong Kong and give him our protection. That is good, eh? We Christians have to help each other. But what are you doing here, in Chai Wan?'

Luke shrugged off the sudden change of direction of Ping Chuan's questioning. 'I'm staying at Ezra McCulloch's house. I just took a walk this way.'

Behind Luke, Ah Mang rolled his eyes in terror, for fear that the lie might anger the pirate. Seeing this, Ping Chuan called to one of his men. The pirate advanced upon Ah Mang with drawn knife.

Ah Mang trembled violently, but when Ping Chuan repeated his question the servant looked first at Luke before babbling, 'I came only to keep master company.'

Ping Chuan nodded almost imperceptibly. The pirate with the knife seized Ah Mang's hair and the knife flashed through the air.

The movement was so sudden that Ah Mang did not begin to scream until a bloody ear was thrown to the ground in front of him.

'Shut up!' Ping Chuan's foot took Ah Mang in the ribs again. 'Now answer my question truthfully, or you will go back to McCulloch with a pair of ears stuffed down your throat.'

'We come seeking Soo Kuei,' blubbered the near-hysterical servant. 'She is a Hoklo girl. A friend of the young barbarian trader.'

Ping Chuan nodded. 'Thank you. Now you may pick up your ear.'

The unfortunate servant grabbed at the severed appendage with one hand, clutching the bloody side of his head with the other and crying with pain and fright.

To Luke, Ping Chuan said, 'This girl must be important to you.'

'She helped me when I was in trouble,' declared Luke. 'I want to thank her.'

'Very commendable.' Ping Chuan gave Luke another horrific mocking smile. 'I like a man who does not forget favours. Return to McCulloch's house, trader. *I* will find this Soo Kuei for you, as an act of brotherly love. No doubt you will be suitably grateful – and I will be pleased to accept a gift of opium.'

Luke went cold at the thought of Kuei being in the hands of these cut-throats. He hoped she was already halfway to Fu-kien. Better to lose her altogether than have her taken by this madman and his men. He silently cursed Ah Mang for talking, but he could hardly blame the servant.

'I don't want her that badly,' he lied. 'Besides, I don't deal in opium.'

Ping Chuan shrugged. 'We will think of something else I need. First I find the girl. Then we will agree on the form your gratitude should take. Amen, trader.'

The pirate chief turned away, and his men moved off after

him. Luke bent down to Ah Mang, believing the brief ordeal to be over, but Ping Chuan called to him.

'Trader, I will show you something to help speed your gratitude when I find the girl.'

He spoke to two of his men and they hurried inside a nearby hut. When they came out moments later they were dragging a naked woman between them. They threw her to the ground at Luke's feet and she lay face downwards, without moving. She made no sound when one of the two men kicked her. Cursing, he dragged her to a nearby hut and propped her in a sitting position against the wall. Her face was bruised and swollen and blood glistened on her thighs.

She was not a young woman and her breasts were empty flaps of skin, hanging to her flabby paunch. The pirate lifted one of the empty breasts and called to Luke, using a dialect Luke did not understand. His words brought a roar of laughter from his unkempt companions.

'He says it would make a good purse for barbarian silver,' explained Ping Chuan. 'If you care to sample what little pleasure she has to offer, he will cut it off for you to take as a reminder. No? Perhaps you would like to see how she comes to life in the hands of my lieutenant, Cheyen.' He waved towards a giant of a man who stood grinning at the edge of the pirate band. 'He spent many years breaking in new girls for the most celebrated whorehouse in Shang-hai. They still call for his services when he is available. Ah! But he is a master at his chosen craft. . . .'

Sickened, Luke helped Ah Mang to his feet.

'Remember what you have seen here, trader,' called Ping Chuan. 'This one is an aged worn-out woman who could not run away as fast as the other villagers. Cheyen much prefers young strong girls.'

Releasing Ah Mang, Luke swung around to face the pirate chief. 'If any harm comes to Kuei, I will hunt you down and kill you – and ten times your number of men won't save you.'

'Why should I wish to harm the girl?' said Ping Chuan, grinning broadly. 'Does the farmer slit the throat of his most valuable sow before he offers her for sale? No, trader, we are Christians, you and I. It will be good to do business together.'

By the time Luke reached McCulloch's house, Ah Mang was swooning from pain and the loss of blood. But sufficient strength remained in his cries to bring Lo Asan and Morna running from the house. The two women seemed to have come to an understanding and they exchanged horrified glances when Luke related the events of the day to them. When the name of Ping Chuan was mentioned, Lo Asan reacted as though Luke had just met the Devil himself. She whispered, 'Ping Chuan is a bad man. A *very* bad man. He has a sick mind. For many years he has gathered the scum of China about him. He now has so many men and junks that no one dares to fight with him. Oh, Luke! I wish you had not met him here.'

'Yet he professes to be a Christian.'

'Perhaps he is,' said Lo Asan. 'There are many stories about him. Some say he was an orphan child, brought up in a mission school in Macau. Others that his father was one of the Catholic missionaries who preach along the coast. McCulloch Hau-ye says he once sailed in an English ship, but was whipped and sent home for stealing.'

'Ping Chuan told me he has some sort of arrangement with Ezra.'

'I do not know. But if Ping Chuan sees the chance to make more money than McCulloch Hau-ye pays him, then he will forget all "arrangements".' To Morna she said, 'He must not know you are here. If he took you, he could ask for much silver.'

Luke cursed himself for sending Gideon Pyke to Macau with *Black Swan*. He told Morna that, as soon as the ship returned, he was sending her to Macau.

He expected her to argue. Instead, she said, 'You'll be staying here, of course, in case this pirate finds Kuei?'

'Yes. I'd be no use to Dan Gemmell if I went to Macau with you. I'd be too worried about Kuei....'

'I understand, Luke. I understand a great many things now. I'm ready to go home again.'

Luke wondered what had passed between Morna and Lo Asan during his absence, but he would have to wait to learn the answer to that question.

Black Swan returned to Hong Kong late that afternoon. Gideon Pyke had delivered Luke's letter to Ezra McCulloch. After reading it, the trader had instructed Gideon Pyke to tell Morna to return to Macau immediately. Of the blow to his plans for free trade in opium, Ezra McCulloch said nothing. Luke followed his example by saying nothing to Morna of her father's order.

146

Knowing her independent nature, he was afraid it might change her mind about leaving Hong Kong.

When Luke informed Gideon Pyke that he was to return to Macau again, the young captain complained bitterly that he was no more than a cross-river ferry-boat captain. His grumbling ceased when Luke explained about Ping Chuan, giving the American more details than he had given to Lo Asan and Morna.

'I think you should come with us, Luke. I've heard a great deal about this character. He's a sadistic lunatic who kills and tortures for amusement. You can't rely on anything he says. If he does find this girl of yours, he's quite likely to demand some ridiculous ransom for her. If you can't raise it immediately, he'll kill both of you.'

'I'll worry about that *if* he finds her,' declared Luke. 'But I want to be right here for as long as he's searching for her. In the meantime, I want you to remain in Macau until the arrival of the British man-o'-war carrying the survivors of McCulloch's ship. Speak to the naval captain. Tell him about the pirates and the raid on Chai Wan. Ask him to come across here and deal with Ping Chuan. If he can kill or capture him, he'll make a lasting name for himself and leave China in Britain's debt. That should be enough to bring any red-blooded naval man here post-haste.'

Fourteen

FOR three days Luke went about his business on Hong Kong island, expecting at any moment to have Ping Chuan and his pirates descend upon him. It was not a comfortable feeling, yet during these few days Luke managed to survey the site of his proposed house and godown, and put together a team of Chinese to carry out the building for him.

On the third day, Luke was on McCulloch's beach to meet *Black Swan*, at that moment heading into the anchorage, when a Chinese came along the path towards him. The man had long tangled hair hanging down as far as his shoulders.

A confused mixture of emotions exploded inside Luke. The appearance of one of Ping Chuan's men moving so openly could mean only one thing. He had found Kuei.

Luke hurried to meet the pirate and was greeted by a smile that revealed a mouthful of blackened teeth as the man bobbed him a brief bow.

'We have found the girl.'

'Where is she? Take me to her.'

'She is in our junk. Before you can see her, Ping Chuan says you must pay ten thousand dollars.'

'That's ridiculous. Take me to Ping Chuan.'

'I am certain he will be pleased to accept five thousand dollars.'

The speed with which the pirate halved the amount told Luke that Ping Chuan had actually demanded the latter sum. Doubling the ransom had been the messenger's own idea – a bid to make himself a rich man.

Luke was busy thinking on a plan that had just sprung to mind. 'I'll have to see if the captain of my ship has brought any money from Macau for me. Wait here.'

There were two Tanka girls seated in their sampans at the water's edge. Leaping on board the nearest boat, Luke ordered the girl to put off to meet *Black Swan*.

When Luke reached the brigantine he wasted no time on greetings. To Gideon Pyke he said, 'How many cannon do you carry on board?'

'Two – both twelve-pounders. Why?'

'Can you outsail a junk?' snapped Luke, ignoring the question.

'Outsail a . . . ? *Black Swan* can give any junk a mile start and win a two-mile race. But I don't think you've got a race in mind.'

'Not exactly. I'm out to sink a pirate junk. Send a boat ashore to wait for me. While I'm gone check those cannon. I'm off to make a deal with Ping Chuan.'

Luke swung himself back into the sampan and the Tanka girl took him back to the beach, where the pirate waited uneasily.

'I can't get the money – but I might be able to get opium instead.'

The pirate hesitated. He had been told by Ping Chuan not to return until Luke had agreed to pay the ransom – in silver. But opium was short, and the pirates smoked it to a man. He signalled for Luke to follow and set off along the track.

The Chinese pirate junk was anchored a hundred yards offshore, about a mile from McCulloch's beach, but Ping Chuan and a few of his men were lounging on the shore.

When the pirate chief saw Luke he grinned broadly, and called, 'Welcome, trader, welcome! You agree that five thousand dollars is a fair exchange for such a lovely girl as your Kuei? Such spirit. She drew blood from two of my men with her teeth. Had we not agreed to trade, I might have kept her for myself . . . for a while.'

Luke's throat felt dry as he said, 'I haven't got five thousand dollars, Ping Chuan.'

'You haven't . . . ?' Ping Chuan's smile disappeared. He climbed slowly to his feet and glared fiercely at his pirate messenger.

'He said he could not get the money,' said the pirate hurriedly. 'But he has opium. He said so.'

Ping Chuan glared at Luke. 'You lie. I know all about you. You work with the barbarian Gemmell. He does not trade in opium. Do you think you can trick Ping Chuan?'

'I'm not trying to trick you. I have a chest of East India Company opium at McCulloch's house. It's yours in exchange for the girl.'

'*One* chest? Is the girl worth so little?' Ping Chuan cupped his hands to his mouth and hailed the junk. A big man stood up from the deck, and Luke recognized the one-time Shang-hai brothel employee.

'Bring the girl up on deck. The barbarian needs to be reminded of her beauty.'

A few minutes later both Kuei and Tik-wei were pushed into view on the open deck. They had their hands tied behind their backs, but Kuei stood tall and unbending as she gazed about her uncertainly. She said something to Tik-wei. Even at this distance, Luke could see that the little girl was dusty and dishevelled, her hair as untidy as it had been on the first occasion he had seen her. His heart went out to both girls but, at a signal from Ping Chuan, Kuei and Tik-wei were pushed below deck again.

'All right, *two* chests of opium – for both girls.'

'*Both* girls? You said nothing about the young one, trader. Besides, we have all taken a fancy to her. My lieutenant, Cheyen, would like to keep her and bring her up to our ways. He swears she has great promise.'

'Damn you, Ping Chuan. I ought to knife you, not barter with you. Two chests are all I have – and I've taken them from McCulloch. There's enough opium there to keep a thousand men supplied for six months. They can be yours within the hour. Wait for your money, or more opium, and you might have to wait for days, or weeks. I want the girls, yes. But you can't take more than I've got. What's it to be, opium for your men *now*, or the promise of something for the future?'

The pirates lounging nearby had been following the conversation closely. Now they began muttering among themselves. Ping Chuan frowned angrily. He did not like being backed into a corner.

'That is all the opium you have? You give me your word as a Christian?'

'Yes.'

'Then I will accept your offer, but you will lose much face when the Hoklo girl learns you could afford only two chests of opium to buy her release.'

'I'll have to put up with that. Bring the girls ashore, then you and your men can come with me for the opium.'

'Oh, no, trader! You trust me – because you have no choice. I do not trust you. Go back to McCulloch's house and have the opium taken to the water's edge. My junk will then come for it. When it is safely on board you may have your gipsy-girl back.'

Luke hated the idea of Kuei and Tik-wei remaining in the hands of the pirates for one second longer than was necessary, but he had no choice in the matter.

'The opium will be on the beach waiting for you – and so will I.'

Luke strode away before Ping Chuan could think of a reason to delay the handover. Behind him, as he went, he heard the laughter of the pirates as they crowded around their leader, happy that their supply of opium was assured for the foreseeable future.

Now that he had completed the negotiations, Luke found his excitement building up at the thought of having Kuei with him again. He had gone over the words he would say to her many times in his mind – but first he had to get her back safely.

At McCulloch's beach everything went according to plan, but it all happened so fast that Luke found no time for explanations. The pirate junk arrived while Luke was bringing the two chests of opium down the hill from McCulloch's godown, and the sailors from *Black Swan* helped to load the chests into the brigantine's dinghy.

Once alongside the junk, the chests were hoisted aboard, and not until then were Kuei and Tik-wei brought up on deck.

When she first looked down into the dinghy, Kuei's joy at seeing Luke was evident and Luke's heart lifted. But when he swung her down from the junk and tried to hold her to him she quickly turned aside, remembering Morna McCulloch. There was no time to explain. Tik-wei was being dangled over the side of the junk, squealing like a frightened piglet. Luke caught her as she was dropped by a pirate, and her delight at seeing him contrasted greatly with her sister's constraint.

Tik-wei clung to him so tightly that he had great difficulty disentangling himself. When he eventually succeeded, he set her down and urged the sailors to pull hard for the shore. The pirate junk was already under way, cutting through the choppy waters of the anchorage.

'When you get ashore go straight to McCulloch's house. Lo Asan is waiting for you there. Everything will be all right now – everything. I'm going to build a house here on Hong Kong. You're going to live here with me, Kuei.'

There was not a spark of enthusiasm, and Luke suddenly felt sick as a thought crossed his mind. 'What did they do to you on the junk, Kuei? Did Ping Chuan's men harm you?'

She looked at him then. A direct pain-filled look. 'They did not hurt me much – but why did you send *them* to find me? Why?'

The men in the boat put up their oars as the boat bounced in towards the beach and Lo Asan was running down the path to meet them.

'Lo Asan will explain everything. Anything she misses out I'll tell you when we get back. I love you, Kuei.'

The two girls were bundled over the side, and Luke leaped into the water to push the boat out again. He floundered chest deep before he was hauled back into the dinghy.

From the shore Lo Asan called, 'Luke! Where are you going . . . ?'

Luke waved to her. 'I'll be back soon. We're going after Ping Chuan.'

Black Swan was already under way, and the dinghy and the men in it were scooped up neatly as the brigantine swept past them, gathering speed.

Gideon Pyke had boasted to Luke that his ship would easily outsail Ping Chuan's junk, but the pirate vessel showed a surprising turn of speed, matching *Black Swan*'s pace in the sheltered waters between Hong Kong and the mainland. It was only when both vessels sailed into open water beyond the neighbouring island of Tung Lung Chau that *Black Swan* began to gain on the Chinese craft.

Luke fretted at the slow progress being made. He was determind that Ping Chuan should not escape.

'If only you had brought the naval frigate with you,' he commented to Gideon Pyke. 'Her guns would have sunk the junk at this range. Had the man-o'-war still not arrived when you left Macau?'

'The frigate was there,' said Gideon Pyke. 'But her cap'n has no intention of making any sort of name for himself – unless it's "Captain Cautious". I told him everything, just as you gave it to me. I could see right away that he was looking for a way to do nothing – with "honour", of course. He must have stroked his chin for five minutes before he said, "Well, Mr Pyke, I have only your word for what has gone on . . . and you are not a British citizen, are you now?" ' Gideon gave a passable imitation of a somewhat nasal English accent. ' "You tell this Mr Trewarne of yours to come and see me himself," he said. "But I don't promise anything. As I see it, these depredations have been carried out by Chinese – upon Chinese. Hardly a sound reason for putting British lives and one of Her Majesty's ships at risk, would you say?" Goddamit, Luke! If all your captains were like that one, you'd have no battle of Trafalgar to look back upon with pride. But stand by! It looks as though Ping Chuan is going to stand and fight!'

The master of the pirate vessels had no intention of taking on the brigantine in battle. He could see that the merchantman was gaining on him in the open sea and was turning to seek refuge among a cluster of offshore islands. It was a fatal mistake. By turning, the pirate gave *Black Swan* full advantage of the stiff breeze. Minutes later the junk was within range of *Black Swan*'s cannon.

The shot from the first gun dropped harmlessly behind the junk, but the second smashed a hole through one of the junk's two triangular bamboo sails.

The junk fired back immediately, but her small brass cannon, hastily shifted from its usual forward-facing position, was not even pointing at *Black Swan*. The brigantine's second salvo struck home in the body of the junk, and the third brought the Chinese vessel slewing around out of control.

To Luke, it seemed that the twelve-pound cannonballs were making no impression on the stout wooden hull of the pirate junk, but he learned otherwise when the fifth salvo was fired off at a point-blank range. There was a sudden muffled roar and flames leaped upwards from the heart of the junk, enveloping her masts and sails. Pirates began tumbling from hatchways and hidden parts of the junk. Shouting in terror, they ran to the side of the vessel and plunged into the sea.

'Spin that wheel! Get the hell out of here!' Gideon Pyke matched his words with actions. Bounding to the wheel, he spun it frantically. The brigantine heeled over and sliced through the water, away from the junk. They were just in time. The junk's cannons had proved ineffectual but, as Gideon knew, all pirate junks carried a great store of gunpowder on board. When the spreading flames touched it, the gunpowder exploded with a deafening roar that tore the junk apart, engulfing *Black Swan* in a blast of hot air that sent her perspiring crew staggering about the deck, gasping for oxygen.

Gideon Pyke held the wheel of his ship hard over, and the vessel scratched a wide circle on the surface of the ocean. The junk was settling fast, and no more than half a dozen Chinese could be seen floundering in the water. Gideon Pyke brought *Black Swan* into the wind, close to the survivors.

One of the pirates raised his hand for help, and Luke recognized Cheyen, the pirate leader's giant lieutenant.

'Where's Ping Chuan?'

The big pirate coughed water. 'Hong Kong . . . he went across the island.'

'Damn! We've missed him.' Luke was bitterly disappointed. He had been determined to capture the pirate chief.

'We'd better hurry if we're going to pick up these men — look!' Gideon Pyke pointed over the side of *Black Swan*. Not more than twenty yards away, a glistening black dorsal fin cut through the water as a shark circled the struggling survivors. Even as Luke watched, it was joined by a second shark, attracted by the boom of the explosion and the noise of the screaming pirates. Soon the whole area would be infested with marauding sharks.

Luke hesitated, then saw Cheyen — and remembered the woman in the village of Chai Wan.

'Head back for Hong Kong.'

The crew, ready to throw ropes over the side for the swimming pirates, looked at Luke in surprise — and then to Gideon Pyke for his orders.

'Let's go,' Luke repeated. The sharks would ensure that none of the pirates survived to tell their chief what had happened to their junk. With Ping Chuan still alive, it was better that the disappearance of his vessel remained a mystery.

Gideon Pyke nodded to his helmsman. *Black Swan* caught the wind, and as Luke went below to Gideon Pyke's cabin he heard the screams of the pirates as the first shark raced in to the attack. Cheyen would perform no more duties for the brothel-keepers of Shang-hai.

It was dark by the time *Black Swan* returned to the anchorage at Hong Kong island and Luke was rowed ashore in silence by one of Gideon Pyke's crew. The seaman disapproved of Luke's actions in leaving the pirates to the sharks. Luke was in no mood to offer explanations and he jumped on to the beach and pushed the boat away – then dropped into a defensive crouch as someone rushed at him across the shingle of the beach.

It was not an attack by some of Ping Chuan's men. It was Kuei, and he was almost overwhelmed by her enthusiastic welcome. Her voice muffled against his chest, she said, 'I am sorry, Luke. I gave you much trouble. If I had come to you when you asked for me among the Hoklo people, you would not have had to fight with Ping Chuan. But I saw you with the barbarian woman. . . . I thought. . . . .'

'It doesn't matter now. You're with me again. . . . Nothing else matters. We'll have no more misunderstandings. I'm going to build you a fine house right here and fill it with nice things. You'll stay and look after it for me and I'll always know where you are.'

'You will have the best-run house in China,' Kuei promised. 'Lo Asan will teach me what to do. I will cook for you and make you fat and happy. When important men come visiting, I will call you "master" and kowtow to you many times. They will see what a great man you are.'

'I am Luke Trewarne – not Ezra McCulloch. You will never kowtow to me, and you will not call me "Master", "Hau-ye" or anything else but "Luke". You'll be mistress of my house, and I'll be proud to show you off to anyone who comes visiting. Why, I might even marry you.'

'Oh, no, Luke!' Kuei was genuinely horrified. 'You cannot marry me. If you did, you would lose much face. I am a poor Hoklo girl. I have nothing but a sampan to bring with me in marriage. You are a very important man. When you take a wife it must be someone from a good family. Someone very rich. A girl like . . . McCulloch's daughter. But please do not marry her too soon. I have so much love to give to you . . . and I think you have love for me, too. Let us enjoy that for a while. You will be staying at McCulloch's house for a long time?'

'No, Kuei,' Luke replied. 'I must go to Canton tomorrow with *Black Swan*. Dan Gemmell has sent word that he has cargoes for Manila for both our ships. He needs me in Canton to help him.'

'Then we have already wasted too much time talking, my Luke. Tonight I must love you so much you will not look at another girl while you are away in Canton being a very important man.'

That night, after Kuei had wept bitter tears for Luke's scarred and ridged back, she came to him with a fierce hunger. It carried them both far from the troubles that were about to descend upon China.

Fifteen

THE HONOURABLE JAMES KILLIAN, Her Britannic Majesty's Superintendent of Trade, hoped to regain some of his lost prestige by returning in style to Canton. On the last day of August 1838, he, and all the merchants travelling with him, embarked in the British frigate *Pincher*, recently arrived at Macau on a routine visit. In keeping with so many of Killian's actions, it was a woeful mistake.

Killian knew the Chinese authorities did not allow foreign warships to proceed farther up the Pearl River than the Chuenpi forts, at the entrance to the Bogue, but he gambled that they would be so eager to resume trade they would not molest the frigate.

Killian was wrong.

The Chinese forts were situated on either side of the river, at the point where it left behind the high hills on either side and flowed into the wide Pearl River estuary. The moment *Pincher* came within range of the cannon in the first fort, a single shot was fired. It was in marked contrast to the usually appalling Chinese gunnery. Passing through *Pincher*'s rigging, it punched a hole in one of the taut sails and severed a number of halyards.

The shot was the signal for all the guns in both forts to commence firing. It was immediately apparent that the first shot had been a lucky accident. The most accurate pieces of Chinese ordnance were the cannons dedicated to Christian Saints by Father Verbiest, the Jesuit missionary who had cast them for the then Emperor, two centuries before. Fortunately for Killian and his travelling companions, Father Verbiest's ancient artillery had been securely set in position, unable to swivel or elevate.

Nevertheless, this was not the kind of return the Superintendent of Trade had planned. *Pincher* was quite capable of fighting her way up-river to Whampoa island, but the Chinese would block the river against the man-of-war's return – and trade at Canton would once again come to a standstill.

Two heavily laden junks had followed closely in *Pincher*'s

wake up the wide Pearl River estuary, protected against pirates by her presence. When the guns of the Chuenpi forts opened fire they quickly turned tail. Coaxing them back again, Killian called upon their assistance.

After prolonged negotiations, the junkmasters agreed to convey the barbarians to Canton for a considerable amount of silver. Not until he had climbed on board the first of the junks did the last vestige of dignity desert James Killian. Her Britannic Majesty's Superintendent of Trade had booked his passage to Canton on a Chinese pig-boat!

Followed at some distance by *Pincher*'s cutter, laden with their luggage, the returning traders made a slow and far-from-triumphant voyage up-river. Somehow, word of their ignominious return reached Canton ahead of them. Thousands of the city's residents turned out to line the river-banks and crowd the factory square to witness the arrival of the Fan Qui traders and their Superintendent.

Ignoring the taunts of the jeering crowds, James Killian stood on the jetty until the naval cutter edged into the shore. With six perspiring sailors standing to attention at the foot of the tall flagpole, Killian gathered the shreds of his pride about him and the Union Jack was raised to the top of the pole. The Superintendent of Trade was once more in residence at Canton.

Luke reached Canton on the day that Killian gave a party for the factory residents and the Chinese Hongs. He received a cool reception from the other traders, but it did not upset him. Gemmell Company's books were showing a healthy profit for the first time in years. Accompanied by Dan Gemmell, Luke was in high spirits.

Killian greeted them by expressing his displeasure that they had continued to trade when most of the other merchants had left Canton with him.

'I hardly expected the Americans to agree to cease trading,' Killian said to Dan Gemmell. 'But in this heathen country I am the representative of Her Majesty the Queen. As such, I am entitled to the support of her subjects.'

'I was in a sickbed in the mission hospital when you took off down-river in a huff,' retorted Dan Gemmell bluntly. 'Had I gone with you, I'd have died, likely as not. Would my death have set the Chinese back on their heels and had them crying for you to return and trade with them? No, you know damned well it wouldn't. Lord Napier's death achieved nothing. Neither mine nor yours will make one scrap of difference.'

Dan Gemmell was reminding Killian of Lord Napier, an earlier Superintendent of Trade. Napier had arrived in China expecting to be accorded all the pomp and deference due to a titled representative of Great Britain. He received a rude awakening. The Chinese had no diplomatic links with Britain – or, indeed, with any other European country. They refused to recognize Napier, and he was ignored. When he persisted in demanding recognition the Chinese humiliated him and curtailed their trade with Britain. In a disastrous attempt to bring the Chinese to heel, Napier ordered two warships up-river, blasting the Chinese forts into silence along the way. The Chinese retaliated by blocking the river, cutting off all trade with the factories and isolating the two men-of-war. Finally, after only four months in China, the distinguished career of Lord Napier, a once great British naval commander, was brought to an ignominious end. Escorted by jeering crowds beating gongs, a sick and deeply humiliated Lord Napier was taken to Macau by the Chinese and died a few days afterwards.

There were a great many parallels between Lord Napier's fiasco and Killian's own voyage to Canton, but the Superintendent of Trade pushed such uncomfortable thoughts behind him.

'I am not suggesting you should have *died* in order to show your support for my stand, but it *was* made on your behalf, Mr Gemmell. Yourself, and every other trader at Canton. We are all exiles in a strange and uncertain land. Only if the Chinese see us acting as one will they begin to rethink their policies towards us.'

'Act as one, Mr Killian?' Luke broke in upon the conversation. 'Are you saying that we should trade in opium, along with the rest of those who support you? How many traders who accompanied you down-river called back the boats selling opium up and down China's coast? No, don't bother to reply. I'll tell you – none! Yes, we live in an uncertain land, but it would be less uncertain if we honoured the laws of the land. Gemmell Company doesn't import opium. If the other traders followed our example, relations between Britain and China would improve dramatically. Think about it the next time you go off in a huff because the Chinese won't dance to your tune.'

'We'll *all* be dancing to a different tune before long.' Killian somehow managed to produce the semblance of a smile. 'When trading in opium becomes legal I doubt if Gemmell Company will be lagging behind.'

'There is more to my life than making profits,' declared Dan Gemmell. 'One day soon I hope to come face to face with my Maker. No man who trades in opium will ever do that.'

Someone crossed the room with a message for the Superintendent of Trade, and the conversation came to an end.

In truth, James Killian found himself in an impossible position. Officially, he was in Canton to help smooth out any troubles the merchants might have. At the same time he was responsible to the Chinese Government for the good behaviour of the foreign community, ensuring they did not bring opium into the country.

Unofficially, Killian had been instructed by the British Government to do nothing to hinder 'free trade'. By 'free trade' they meant, of course, opium.

Opium was grown in India and sold in China. Tea was grown in China and sold in England. The Indian economy was dependent upon opium. That of Great Britain was heavily subsidized by the tax on tea. The traders in the middle grew fat on the profits they reaped from both products. Only the Emperor of China was unhappy. Hundreds of thousands of his people had become opium addicts. Its poisonous fumes demoralized both rich and poor and its effect was being felt in the huge Civil Service and in China's army. The silver that should have been flowing into the country's coffers from the vast exports of tea was leaving the country at an alarming rate to pay for opium. In some coastal provinces they were having to mint coins in various base metals because of the silver shortage.

But true greatness is rarely achieved by considering others, and Great Britain was on the brink of the most remarkable epoch in its long history. The young Queen Victoria was in the first year of a reign that would make her ruler of half the world. What was happening in China mattered little. Only Great Britain's needs were of any importance.

The Honourable James Killian was no more than a pawn in the game being played out by his country and he would ultimately please no one. The policies of Great Britain were predetermined. Killian would be manipulated to provide the excuse needed for carrying them through.

Yet James Killian still nurtured the belief that he was in com-

160

mand of events at Canton. He was also convinced that he was of some importance to China. The Hongs, relieved to know they would still be in business when the tea arrived from the hills, encouraged his illusions. Bobbing and smiling politely, they agreed with all he said, declining to express any opinion of their own.

General Shengan sent one of his Tartar officers to fetch Luke from the Gemmell factory in the dead of night. Luke accompanied the soldier through the streets of the walled city as unseen beggars coughed and snored in shadowed doorways. Around every corner, the coolie women, gathering night-soil, clip-clopped along on wooden sandals, laden buckets hanging from the sagging bamboo poles they carried across their shoulders.

Shengan greeted Luke warmly, then waved him to a seat while he paced the room like a caged tiger. A servant brought in rice wine and cakes, but Shengan sent him scurrying from the room as soon as the food had been placed upon a low table.

Luke had observed before that General Shengan was inclined to cut short the exaggerated ritual politeness that so exasperated European visitors to China. Tonight, Shengan got down to business with an abruptness that might have been considered rude, had Luke not known him so well.

'This man Killian – does he return to Canton in a spirit of contrition? Has he given the traders orders not to bring opium to China?'

Luke matched Shengan's forthright manner. 'No. On the contrary, he's convinced that your government will soon make the trade in opium legal. Nothing I tell him will convince him otherwise.'

'Ahhh!' A long sigh escaped from Shengan's lips. 'I thought this was so. It is bad. Bad for your people – and for mine. Very bad.'

General Shengan picked up a small bowl of wine from the table and tipped the contents down his throat. Swinging a chair to the table, he straddled it, resting his arms on top of the high back.

'Killian's thinking could not be farther from the truth. Far from changing his policy, the Emperor has resolved to stamp out the trade in opium once and for all. A new edict orders all opium smokers to be arrested and beaten. Any who deal in opium are to be summarily executed. It is a total defeat for those who sought to have the drug sold freely in China. Indeed, many of their number have already been arrested – Lo Asan's father among them. They will be degraded and banished to far parts of the land. You see, the scheming of this man McCulloch has not gone unnoticed. He is already forbidden to enter the Canton factories. Should he be found here he will be taken prisoner by the Tsotang and sent to Peking for trial. He will have no Superintendent of Trade to raise a weak voice in protest there. McCulloch will be sentenced to death – and die he will. The Emperor himself will be happy to witness his execution.'

'But McCulloch is in the factories right now . . . !'

So convinced was Ezra McCulloch that the opium trade would soon be legal that he had defied the order forbidding him to enter the factories and had travelled up-river with Killian. Luke had spoken to the Scots trader only that day, to explain about the two chests of opium he had taken to ransom Kuei. Ezra McCulloch had smugly commented that opium had its uses, even for those opposed to its sale. When Luke pointed out that he had sent the opium to the bottom of the China Sea the trader had shrugged indifferently. It would make no difference to the price Luke would be charged.

The two men had little in common, but Luke would not allow Ezra McCulloch to be taken prisoner by the Tsotang. He told Shengan he intended warning the trader.

'Good – but you must do it tonight. Tsotang Teng will send his men to arrest McCulloch tomorrow. If they are successful, it will cause great trouble. McCulloch is an influential man among your people. Tell him to return to Hong Kong before daylight. He will be safe enough there for the time being.'

Resting his chin upon his hands, Shengan's black eyes studied Luke. Abruptly he stood up and resumed his pacing. 'I also have news for your Superintendent of Trade. The Emperor is so concerned by the amount of opium reaching China that he is sending a commissioner to Canton with special powers to deal with the problem. He has chosen Lin Tse-hsu for the task, and he has chosen well. Imperial Commissioner Lin is a man well able to solve such problems. He is totally opposed to opium and will employ drastic measures to stamp out its use. Warn Killian and your fellow-traders of the coming of Commissioner Lin, although it will be common knowledge before many days have passed. Make them give up this trade before his arrival. They can become rich enough by carrying on honest trading.'

Luke started to protest that the traders were in no mood to listen to him, but Shengan interrupted him abruptly.

'They *must* listen to you. If they do not, they will be closing the door on peaceful trade between your country and mine. The consequences will be tragic for us all. Your country is young and forceful, proud of its strength and eager for every nation to recognize its power. My country is ancient and wise, but the wisdom is that of a hermit, one who has remained aloof from the world for too many years. Unfortunately, Commissioner Lin belongs to the group of officials who are disdainful of anything that does not originate within China's borders. They would like to break off all outside trade and ignore the rest of the world. They cannot see that it is already too late. Their policies have made China impotent – a eunuch among the nations of the world. True, we have great thinkers and poets, but the thinkers seek their wisdom within themselves, instead of looking outwards – and the words of a poet cannot kill an enemy. While Lin and his fellow-officials produce only words, I hear of great inventions made by those we like to call "barbarians". Of ships without sails that belch smoke and flail the water with great paddles, defying wind and tide. I am told that in your own country these same ships can crawl over land, pulling great loads after them. I have seen for myself that your cannons are far superior to any that I can get for my men. We can learn much from your people, yet men like Commissioner Lin, our greatest "thinkers", refuse to accept this.'

General Shengan stopped in front of Luke and shook his head sadly. 'I think war between our countries is inevitable. It will be brought about by men of closed minds among my countrymen – and men of greed among yours. Your country will win such a war, but the victory will bring no peace, and it will not be an honourable victory. Honour is for men who fight for ideals. Your country will be fighting to force mine to buy opium from your traders. I know there are other issues on which we disagree, but take away opium and all other misunderstandings might be quickly resolved. Your country's determination to sell opium to China is an insurmountable obstacle in the path of those of us who seek to take China into the modern world.'

General Shengan reached for the wine on the table and filled his wine-bowl to overflowing. 'Now I have bared my heart to you. I have spoken such thoughts to no other man.'

He carried the bowl to his lips and drank until it was empty, but the alcohol did nothing to take away the sadness that was in him. 'I fear all our efforts are already too late, my friend. War is in the air all around us. I have breathed such tainted air in the hills of Tibet and in the sands of the Shamo desert. Now I smell it here, in Canton.'

Shengan filled his wine-bowl yet again, and Luke suspected it had been filled many times prior to his arrival. 'It is sad. We have become friends too late, you and I. We could each have learned much about the country of the other. But you will still learn – from your Hoklo girl, in the palace you build in Hong Kong.'

Luke expressed no surprise that Shengan knew of his building venture. Instead, he said, 'I'll do my best to convince Killian to stop the trade in opium, Shengan, but I'll make no promises. Far from fearing a war, I feel that many of the traders would welcome it. They believe it will throw open a vast new market for their goods.'

'Perhaps they speak the truth. I know little of trading. I know only that war will bring suffering and humiliation to my country and its people. Many men will die. I and my soldiers must be among the first. It will bring unhappiness for you, too, and an end to many of your dreams and ambitions.'

General Shengan slammed his wine-bowl down upon the table and glared at Luke. 'I am a general of the Emperor's Tartar army – an army never defeated in battle. Yet now I speak of an unfought war as though it were already lost. It bodes ill. Yet I say only what is true for all with the will to see clearly. Before the first man is killed, you and I must fight many battles with words and not swords. I wish you good luck. Now I must return you safely to your factory. I think much will happen before we meet again. Goodbye, my young barbarian friend.'

That night, Luke was able to warn Ezra McCulloch and discharge a debt he felt he owed to him. The Scots trader left Canton before dawn and at Whampoa transferred from a sampan to one of his own armed merchantmen. Later that morning the Tsotang's men left the factories empty-handed, James Killian's protests ringing in their ears. The fact that the Chinese were prepared to arrest such a prominent merchant shook the European trading community and added to their apprehension about the forthcoming arrival of Commissioner Lin. Even so, Luke found few of them ready to discuss opium-free trading.

The tea season was almost upon them. They would take full advantage of the opportunity it afforded them to make a large profit. Then they would sit back and allow events to take their course.

Sixteen

GEMMELL COMPANY'S fast clipper, *China Wind*, was at Whampoa, ready and waiting, when the first consignment of tea arrived from the tea slopes. The season began two weeks earlier than anticipated. As a result, *China Wind* was loaded and in the open sea while other tea-clippers were still straggling up-river to the island anchorage.

China Wind was as fast as any other clipper engaged in the tea trade. Barring accident or unforeseen ill-fortune, she would reach England during the first few days of 1839, well ahead of her rivals. General Shengan had kept his word to Luke, and the loan from Lien Ling, the Chinese Hong, would be repaid on the ship's return.

For Luke, the departure of the clipper meant that he was able to return to Hong Kong once more. Luke intended bringing prime trading goods to Hong Kong, thus ensuring that *China Wind* would have a full and profitable cargo awaiting her upon her return in the spring — whatever the situation might be at Canton.

Work on the buildings had progressed much faster than Luke had anticipated. The house was completed, and most of the furnishings already installed. Luke thought some of them looked familiar, and a proud and excited Kuei confessed that, with Lo Asan's connivance, Chinese carpenters had copied much of the furniture in Ezra McCulloch's house. Kuei's pride swelled to bursting-point when she took Luke upstairs and led him by the hand into the main bedroom of the impressive granite-built house.

Here, in the centre of the room, stood a huge, elaborately carved wooden bed. It must have been at least seven feet long, and almost as wide.

'There!' said Kuei. 'Lo Asan says McCulloch is very proud of his bed. I decided you must have a bigger and better bed than his. You like it?'

'I like it very much, Kuei.'

Luke's inclination was to smile, but he knew that if he did he would upset Kuei. He kept his face as straight as he could manage as he leaned forward to look more closely at the carvings on the woodwork. To his amazement, he saw that each carving depicted a man and woman making love in a different position.

'Ah, you see!' burbled Kuei happily. 'Lo Asan says that when McCulloch drinks too much he always tells Lo Asan, "My bed shows fifty different ways to make love. *I* am best at every one of them." '

Kuei's voice had dropped low as she attempted to imitate the deep voice of Ezra McCulloch. She beamed at Luke. '*This* bed shows *eighty* ways of making love – and you and I will make love better than Lo Asan and her McCulloch.'

Kuei sat on the edge of the bed and bounced up and down gleefully. 'You see, Luke? This is a truly splendid bed. We will make many babies here together. No . . . not now. . . .'

Luke's lips cut off her protests, and minutes later Kuei was responding to him with an abandonment that no erotic carving could ever capture.

For the next few months, Luke relaxed in Hong Kong. Both Canton and Macau might have been a thousand miles away. Luke met Ezra McCulloch only twice during this time. On both occasions Luke was supervising the construction of the quay. McCulloch merely passed the time of day and grunted at the progress being made. That was all. The two men might have been acquaintances meeting in a busy town street, instead of the only two Europeans on an island no more than a few miles long.

Luke and Kuei saw far more of Lo Asan. When Ezra McCulloch was away, she spent most of the day at the house with Luke and Kuei. She often stayed until late in the night, teaching Luke centuries-old Chinese games that were incredibly complicated. Some of them were Manchu games with origins at the court of the Emperor, where skills at such innocent pastimes were highly acclaimed.

One evening, during his early weeks on the island, Kuei took Luke up the steep slope of the hill behind the house after dark. He stumbled after her along a narrow path until they reached a rocky shoulder, a couple of hundred feet above the house. Here Kuei allowed Luke to rest, and snuggled against him in the darkness.

'Are you happy to be here with me, Luke?'

'I'm happy to be with you anywhere.' He slid an arm about her and hugged her to him. 'But have you brought me all the way up here just to make love? We could have sent Tik-wei to bed and done that in our own house – and I wouldn't have been worn out from climbing a mountain.'

'It would take more than a gentle walk up a hill to tire you too much, my Luke; but I did not bring you up here for that. Tonight is very special. There, you see that . . . ?'

She pointed excitedly to the east, where the rim of a full moon put in a first appearance above a line of hills on the mainland. It was a full harvest moon. Caught in the unseen rays of the sun that were bringing daylight to the far side of the earth, the moon was as plump and colourful as a soft ripe peach.

Kuei opened a linen-wrapped package and handed Luke a large flat cake. 'This is a moon cake, my Luke. Tik-wei and I made it specially for you. You must eat it as the moon rises.'

Kuei was as full of fidgety excitement as a young girl, and as soon as she saw Luke sink his teeth into the cake she began to eat a similar one.

'You like it?'

'Umm!' He had his mouth full of sweet and highly spiced meat, with which the cake was filled. 'It's delicious.'

'Now it is necessary for you to kiss me.'

As he hastily swallowed the mouthful of cake, Kuei threw her arms about his neck and brought her mouth hard down upon his.

When he felt he would burst for want of breath, Luke held her away from him. 'Hey! What's all this?'

'Luke . . . I love you very, very much. You make me . . . very happy girl.'

Kuei spoke the words carefully and deliberately in English, and Luke knew she must have practised them for many long hours. From the highly original pronunciation of some of the words, he knew she could only have learned them from Lo Asan.

'Soo Kuei, I love you very, very much, too. You make me happier than I could ever hope to tell you,' he replied in Cantonese. 'But how long have you been able to speak English so perfectly . . . and what is the occasion?'

Kuei squirmed happily in his arms. 'Tonight is our moon festival. It is very lucky to be in a high place with the one you love, and to watch the moon rise together. If the Moon Goddess sees that two people are very much in love, she will bless them; then they will never be parted from each other. I would like that, my Luke. I would like that very much.'

Luke hugged her to him. 'I would like that, too,' he murmured. 'I want to be able to enjoy moments like this with you for ever.'

But 'for ever' were words all too easily lost in the uncertainty of the times. In the Canton factories, in particular, there was an air of unease. Trade went on smoothly enough, and the tea exports seemed set to break new records, but tension mounted as the traders waited for the arrival of Commissioner Lin.

Each day added to the long list of rumours reaching Canton. The screw was tightening inexorably on China's opium users. Three princes of the Imperial blood were publicly admonished for smoking opium. Men of lesser rank were either degraded or publicly whipped. Lo Asan's father, banished to the borders, had been brought back to Peking, but given a much lower rank. Men agreed that his reinstatement was due entirely to the influence of his brother, General Shengan. Opium smokers with no rank that might be stripped from them forfeited their lives. Some travellers claimed that hundreds of men were being strangled and decapitated daily in Peking.

In less populated areas of the Emperor's 'Heavenly Kingdom', justice was tempered with sound common sense. Opium smoking was widespread here. Such large-scale arrests and executions would have led to a serious shortage of labour – but the peasants could not be allowed to escape the Emperor's punishment. The problem was solved with typical Chinese simplicity – and barbarity. Provincial magistrates cut out a portion of the upper lip of offenders. The disfigured peasant could still work, but had great difficulty in sucking smoke from an opium pipe.

Initially, such tactics had the desired effect upon the opium trade. The demand for the drug dropped off dramatically. But the larger European traders took the setback philosophically. When the enthusiasm for reform had waned, financial considerations would ensure that the demand would return stronger than ever. The traders cut back their orders from the East India Company, storing the opium they already had in receiving ships, anchored off Lin-tin and Hong Kong islands.

The smaller traders could not afford to be so casual about the state of affairs. Suddenly, Gemmell Company was no longer the pariah of the China traders. On the occasions when Luke left Hong Kong to attend to business matters in Macau or Canton his advice was sought eagerly by fellow-traders. The Gemmell Company brigantine, *Black Swan*, was followed closely by the ships of other trading houses, all eager to share in the profits being reaped by Dan Gemmell and Luke – profits that increased with every telling.

Then, in February 1839, Luke's brief idyllic way of life came to an abrupt end. A tired Tanka girl brought her sampan into the anchorage with a letter from Canton. It came from Abel Snow. Dan Gemmell had collapsed and was seriously ill. The American missionary wrote that there was nothing he could do for the trader at Canton. After despatch of the letter, he was taking Dan Gemmell to Macau. He asked Luke to be there to meet them.

Luke set off for Macau, leaving Kuei behind, filled with a great many forebodings. If Dan Gemmell was as seriously ill as Abel Snow thought, the future for himself and Kuei was uncertain, to say the very least. A great many of the established traders would be eager to buy Dan Gemmell's half of the prospering company. Luke hoped that Abel Snow had been unduly pessimistic, and that Dan Gemmell would improve in the more congenial atmosphere of Macau.

Dan Gemmell's lungs had failed him once again – but this time there were further complications. Luke learned that the trader had suffered a heart attack at Canton, and another on the voyage down-river. In spite of the gravity of his illness, Dan Gemmell insisted on seeing Luke as soon as he reached the Macau hospital.

'You're tired, Dan,' protested Abel Snow. 'You've had a long journey from Canton. It's time to rest.'

'Can you promise me that, if I do, I'll not have another heart attack?'

Abel Snow shook his head. 'Only the Lord can make a promise like that, Dan.'

'God has already given me two very clear warnings of what's to become of me, Abel. If I don't set my affairs in order now, I'll be disregarding Him. You wouldn't suggest I do that, would you? Leave Luke and me alone for a while. There are some things I need to say to him.'

Abel Snow looked towards Luke and spread his hands wide in a gesture of resignation. 'Try to keep it brief, Luke. Dan may be a tough old China hand, but he's not immortal.'

When the missionary had left the room, Dan Gemmell gave Luke a weary smile. 'Abel has been a good friend, Luke. Sometimes a man stands too close to his own problems to see them clearly. It's at such times that I've learned the value of Abel's opinions. I hope you'll keep his friendship when I've gone. . . .'

'What sort of talk is this? You're good for a great many years yet, Dan. Once you're well again. . . .'

'I'm dying, Luke. It's all right; I don't mind. I die a satisfied man. After years of struggling, I can see the company I started begin to amount to something. You know, the fact that it's all been done without selling opium pleases me more than the success itself. Now I look forward to being reunited with my dear wife and our son.'

Memories brought sadness to Dan Gemmell's face. 'My son would have been about your age now, Luke. I like to think he would have been much like you.'

Closing his eyes, Dan Gemmell lay back on his pillow and breathed deeply for a few minutes. With his eyes still closed, he said in a tired voice, 'I've made a will, Luke. Abel has it. I've left the company to you – with a ten-per-cent share for Gideon Pyke.'

Taken aback, Luke protested. Dan Gemmell opened his eyes wearily. 'I'm not sure I'm doing you any great favour, Luke. I'm confident you'll continue my policy of not trading in opium, and because of it you'll be despised by all those who do. It's a lonely life when you follow your conscience through life. There were many times when I might have exchanged all my principles for the friendship of those who shunned me for them.'

'Gemmell Company will never sell opium, Dan; and one day the world will honour you for your stand. But enough of this gloomy talk. We'll take Gemmell Company to even greater things, you and I together. Every other company will follow our example before we're through.'

Dan Gemmell gave Luke a wan smile. 'Bless you, Luke. I'll pray that time proves you right . . . but I won't be here to see it happen. Leave me now, Luke, I'm tired . . . so very tired.' He raised his hand and let it linger on Luke's arm for a few moments. 'Thank you, Luke. Thank you for everything.'

Dan Gemmell died in his sleep early the next morning and was buried beside wife and son in the little Macau cemetery. The trader had complained often to Luke that his stand against opium had set him apart from his fellow-merchants, but it was true to say they respected him as an honest man. Every trader in the tiny colony attended his funeral, led by the Superintendent of Trade himself.

When the ceremony was over, the mourners were supplied with refreshment at the Gemmell Company house that now belonged to Luke. Such social gatherings followed the same inevitable pattern here in Macau and, as drinks flowed freely, voices grew louder. Occasionally an unthinking laugh rang through the house where the blinds were still drawn in a gesture of respect for its late owner.

Morna McCulloch was there, and when she came across the room to offer condolences to Luke she had to shout to make herself heard above the Babel. Looking about them in disgust, Luke took Morna's arm and led her from the house. When the door closed behind them, he said, 'I feel in need of some air. Half the "mourners" have forgotten why they are there. They won't miss me until the drink runs out. By then it will be time they went home. Do you feel like a walk?'

Morna nodded. As she fell into step beside Luke she said, 'You mustn't be too hard on them, Luke. They really did respect him, you know.'

'It's a pity they didn't show him some of their respect while he was alive,' replied Luke bitterly. 'Their lack of understanding made Dan a lonely man for all of his life.'

Morna took his arm as they turned the corner to the waterfront where they had walked together once before. 'He was a happy man at the end, Luke. I met him off the boat and went to the hospital with him. He was very proud of you.'

'He was a good friend. I'll miss him.'

'Talking of friends. . . . Do you know that General Shengan is here, in Macau? He and some of his soldiers are camped by the barrier gate. Everyone who is anyone in Macau has paid him a visit.'

The 'barrier' was the wall built across the narrow isthmus, isolating the six square miles of Macau from the mainland.

'Shengan and his soldiers recently destroyed a pirate base along the coast. My maidservant spends hours at the gate every day, hoping to get a glimpse of him.'

Luke had not seen Shengan since he had given Luke the news of the coming of Commissioner Lin. This was an opportunity not to be missed. Apologizing to Morna, Luke said he would escort her home and then go to find the Tartar general.

Morna gripped Luke's arm tight and pulled him to a halt. 'Let me come with you, Luke.'

'You . . . ? I can't take a woman with me to meet a Tartar general.'

'Why not?' Morna was too excited to express true indignation. 'What you are really saying is that no one has ever done it before – but no European has ever made a friend of a Chinese general before. Please, Luke! If he's as great a man as you and everyone else say he is, he'll probably welcome the opportunity to meet a European woman.'

Luke looked at Morna doubtfully, but there might be some truth in what she said. Shengan *was* a man who enjoyed cutting through unnecessary barriers. On the other hand, he might be greatly offended. Luke made a decision.

'All right, but we'll need to wait until after dark – and you'll have to come to his camp in a covered carrying-cart. I'll speak to Shengan while you wait outside. He might not want to meet you.'

Morna bit back her objections to the conditions Luke had imposed. If she was able to meet the hero of China, they would be worth while.

On the way to Shengan's camp that evening, Morna was less reticent about the comfort of the curtained carrying-cart, borne on the shoulders of four men. When they were almost at the barrier gate, Luke looked inside to check that she was all right. He found her quietly fuming. In answer to his question, she snapped, 'No, I'm *not* all right. I'm hot and uncomfortable. I feel like a pig going to market. This form of transport may be all right for Chinese women who can't totter around on bound feet; *I* would rather walk.'

'Hush! We're close to the gate now.' Luke closed the curtains with a quick grin. It was not often anyone was able to tell Morna McCulloch to keep quiet without fear of instant retribution.

Luke was recognized by Shengan's guards and escorted to the tent which served as the General's campaign headquarters and his living quarters.

'It is good to see you again,' Shengan greeted Luke warmly,

genuinely pleased to see him. 'I thought you were on your island hideaway with your gipsy-girl. What has brought you to Macau?'

Luke told him of Dan Gemmell's death, and the expression of pleasure left Shengan's face. 'That is sad, very sad. He was a good man. An example to the others. Will you continue to trade?'

'Yes.' Luke told Shengan of Dan Gemmell's will.

Shengan nodded in satisfaction. 'Good. Then the example he set will continue. Things are going our way at last, my friend. There is little opium being sold. Only Jardine Matheson, Fox and McCulloch are known to be still trading, and they are not having everything their own way. Junks of the Imperial Navy follow them wherever they sail. . . . Is something wrong?'

Shengan's mention of McCulloch had reminded Luke of Morna, waiting outside in the carrying-chair, and he quickly told Shengan about her.

General Shengan looked first puzzled and then angry. 'You bring McCulloch's daughter here and ask me to speak to her? Have you gone mad? Far better had you brought her father to me. No, I will not see her.'

'I think you have made a bad decision, Shengan. She is a friend of your country and she speaks the language well. She is bitterly opposed to the opium trade and looks upon you as a great hero, fighting for the rights of your people. Who knows, she might one day influence her father where all other means have failed.'

Shengan frowned suspiciously at Luke. 'What is this girl to you? Has she taken the place of your water-gipsy?'

Luke shook his head. 'No, but she has helped me in the past. She is a nurse who tends your people and her own. She learned of my beating at the hands of the Tsotang but told no one.'

'A woman of any country who knows how to keep a still tongue is exceptional.' General Shengan nodded. 'All right, I will see her . . . as a favour to you.'

General Shengan ordered the carrying-cart to be brought to the tent entrance, in order that Morna might enter without being seen by too many of his inquisitive Tartar soldiers.

Inside the cramped carrying-cart, Morna was hot and felt devoid of all dignity. She was also angry. When the cart was lifted and carried to Shengan's tent, the sudden movement caught her off balance and she fell to the floor of the curtained vehicle in a tangle of arms and legs. When Luke pulled back the curtain and called for her to come out, she emerged like a cork from a champagne-bottle. Morna had groomed herself with extra care to meet the famous general, but her efforts had been in vain. She had wilted inside the stuffy carrying-cart, and the final tumble destroyed her last hope of appearing before the hero of China looking cool and elegant.

'That's the last time I travel in one of those things,' she hissed at Luke as she tried to push ringlets back into place before passing ahead of him into the tent. 'They are designed for midgets with a sense of balance and numb backsides. I *hate* you, Luke Trewarne!' She spat the last comment at him as he gave her a wide grin.

Luke held the tent flap open for her and she went inside, her chin thrust out beligerently. This was not the way she had intended such a meeting would begin. Through her maid, Morna had learned the fact and the legend of General Shengan. In her mind she had already built him into one of the greatest generals of all time – a fighting soldier. Macau was garrisoned by Portuguese soldiers who had never fought a battle, yet they strutted about the tiny enclave in gaudy uniforms, preening themselves before any girl who had the time to stand and watch. They reminded a scornful Morna of displaying peacocks. Shengan, on the other hand, had fought and won so many battles his name was known to every man, woman and child in 'The Heavenly Kingdom'. Yet he avoided all attempts to lionize him. Few outside his regiment of Tartars would recognize him if they passed him in a city street.

Inside the big tent, Morna saw her hero squatting on a cushion on the floor, putting the final inked characters to a document stretched on the thin writing-board he held expertly on his knees.

Her first reaction was one of disappointment. The broad figure of General Shengan seemed smaller than she had imagined he would be, and his clothes were hardly impressive. Instead of silken robes, Shengan had long ago adopted the dress of the Tartar horse-warriors of Manchuria. His uniform was of soft beaten leather, edged with fur, unrelieved by any artificial colouring. Suddenly, Shengan raised his eyes to hers and Morna's disappointment was forgotten. She no longer doubted that she was in the presence of a truly great man.

Shengan put aside the writing-board and slowly stood up.

Without saying a word, he walked around Morna, viewing her from every angle. He was particularly fascinated by her long blonde hair, and once he put a hand up to touch it, but stopped when his fingers were only inches away.

Remembering Morna's outburst of a few moments before, Luke held his breath as Shengan completed his inspection. He might have been examining a horse at a market. But Morna's anger had gone, dissipated by a single look from the Tartar general.

'So you are the daughter of the trader McCulloch,' Shengan said without preamble. 'Why does a man with so much beauty at home go out and spread evil among my people?'

'A daughter does not choose her father's way of life, General Shengan. He has always gone his own way – and no doubt he always will.'

Shengan inclined his head. 'That is the way of a Chinese family, too; but *you* are a bringer of comfort to the sick and diseased. You did not know it, but you treated two of my sick soldiers recently. They are both improving. I thank you. I wish we had one of your hospitals in Canton. Tell me about your work.'

General Shengan had departed from accepted Chinese practice by agreeing to meet Morna. He could not immediately shake off the age-old attitude that women should be entirely subservient to men – but he was trying very hard.

Morna told him of her work at the Macau hospital.

A great many of her patients were opium addicts, and it was obvious that Morna deeply deplored the trade in opium.

Shengan looked from Morna to Luke. 'How many of your people think as do you?'

'Our people are the same as yours, Shengan,' replied Luke. 'Most of them are totally ignorant of anything that happens beyond their own borders – in most cases, beyond their own towns or villages. Neither do they really care.'

'But there *are* caring people,' Morna said. 'The leaders of our churches condemn the sale of opium.'

'Ah, yes . . . your "Christians",' General Shengan smiled without humour. 'China has seen many of them. A hundred years ago they were causing so much trouble in the country that they were expelled and banned for ever; but still they came, calling themselves "missionaries". More recently they have been travelling the coasts of China in the ships of Jardine

Matheson and' — he nodded to Morna — 'in ships belonging to your father. They sell opium and give away free tracts from your Christian Bible with each sale. Do the leaders of your Christians condemn this? No, they are interested only in sending more people to this "heaven" of which they speak, jealously counting the numbers who enter through the doors marked "Roman Catholic" or "Protestant". They run the religions they represent as though they were rival trading houses. I care little for your religions . . . or for those who seek to bring their teachings to my people.'

Morna's face registered a protest, but Shengan held up a hand before she could speak. 'Listen to me. I have not finished talking about Christians. I have just returned from leading my troops against a village occupied by a man who calls himself a Christian. He is one of our people, but is the product of one of your mission schools. I will spare you the details of the horrors we found in the village. It will be sufficient to tell you, Luke Trewarne, that this Christian was Ping Chuan.'

Luke's interest quickened. 'Did you kill Ping Chuan?' he asked eagerly.

'No. Just as you found when you sank his junk, Ping Chuan was elsewhere; but he lost five hundred of his followers. I take no pirate prisoners.'

Morna had not heard of Luke's exploit against the pirates in *Black Swan*. She was torn between an overwhelming curiosity to learn about that incident and horror that General Shengan could speak so matter-of-factly about executing five hundred of his fellow-men.

Shengan had been watching her closely and he said, 'The deaths of enemies of the Emperor are of little consequence to anyone. We will have a drink of wine and talk of happier things. Trade is still good for you, Luke Trewarne?'

'Excellent. The other traders are doing well, too — even though they are finding it well-nigh impossible to sell their opium.'

'This is what I hear. I am pleased.' Handing small bowls of wine to Luke and Morna, Shengan added, 'Perhaps they will learn new methods of trading before Commissioner Lin arrives. That would be to everyone's advantage. . . .'

They chatted together for another half-hour before Luke, not wishing to outstay his welcome, declared that he had accounts to check before going to bed and must leave.

Following Luke's lead, Morna rose reluctantly to her feet, but General Shengan waved for her to be seated again. 'I will allow Luke Trewarne to leave because I know he and I will meet again. I may never have another opportunity to enjoy the company of one of his countrywomen.'

'Perhaps you should take her hostage. It might persuade her father to stop selling opium.'

'If I thought that, I would be a willing hostage,' Morna said quietly — too quietly, Luke thought.

General Shengan inclined his head to her. 'Thank you . . . but you need have no fear for her. She is a guest, not a hostage. I will have her escorted safely home. Go happily back to your work.'

The Tartar general smiled at Morna. 'I believe you met my niece during your brief visit to Hong Kong. It must have been a most interesting encounter. Tell me how she is keeping. . . .'

Luke was uneasy at leaving Morna in the Tartar camp. He told himself he was being foolish. Shengan was an honourable man. But still the feeling persisted.

It was not until much later, working at his desk on Gemmell Company's accounts, that Luke realized why he was troubled. Shengan and Morna were completely at ease in each other's company — and that in itself was most unexpected. But there was more. Both were inclined to shrug off convention. Both cut their own paths through life. They had the same attitudes and standards. They could almost have been made for each other. . . .

Seventeen

LUKE worked most of the night on the accounts of his newly acquired company. When he finally closed the book he was well satisfied. Gemmell Company was now in a sound financial state. Luke had made enough profit with *Black Swan* alone to repay the loan for the purchase of the clipper *China Wind* at once, if he wished. When the clipper returned in cargo to Canton he would be able to pay for the tea she had carried to England. *China Wind* would then make two or three trading runs between Canton and India before coming out of the water at Hong Kong to scrape the barnacles from her hull and add a few knots to her speed for the next season's tea run to England.

Things were working out well. It was sad that Dan Gemmell had died before he could enjoy the best years of the company he had founded. He would have been well able to afford to return to England for a year or two, had he wished. With a jolt of surprise, Luke realized that, given another year of profitable trading, he, too, would be able to make the voyage to England – and take Kuei with him. A few more years and he could sell up and return to his native Cornwall, never needing to work again. It was an incredible thought! For the first time in many months, Luke thought about his mother and the small farm where he had spent his childhood.

It was in this happy frame of mind that Luke set off to return to Hong Kong later that morning, making the voyage in a junk laden with silks to store in his new godown. Before setting off, Luke went to the McCulloch house, hoping to see Morna and receive an account of the time she had spent with General Shengan.

Luke was told curtly by Ezra McCulloch that she was still in bed, having been kept out until ungodly hours of the morning by Luke himself. Luke did not enlighten the Scots trader. On his way to the Macau waterfront he wondered what Ezra McCulloch would have done had he learned she had spent those hours with a Tartar general! Fortunately, Ezra McCulloch had not pursued the matter. He, too, was going to Hong Kong later that morning, aboard one of his own armed merchant vessels.

McCulloch was removing the opium from his godown and the Hong Kong receiving hulk, prior to the arrival of Commissioner Lin. Together with most of his fellow-traders, he was sending the opium to Lin-tin island. Although it was more exposed in bad weather, the anchorage there was small enough to be successfully defended, should Commissioner Lin send the Chinese Navy against the opium-receiving ships.

The junk in which Luke was taking passage was more than half the distance across the Pearl River estuary when Luke went up on deck. He had slept for a couple of hours in the tiny cabin usually occupied by the junkmaster. They were sailing quite close to the large island of Lan-tau. Shading his eyes against the sun to view the monastery perched on one of the island's highest hills, Luke's attention was distracted by the sight of two large junks putting out from a nearby bay. They took a course which would bring them close to the cargo-carrying junk and, as they drew nearer, he saw they were both flying large flags.

A chill went through Luke when he saw the colours of the flags. They were a fiery red with gold edging. The colours of Ping Chuan!

'Pirates! Pirates!' Luke shouted the warning to the master of the merchant junk as he ran towards the tiny brass cannon mounted upon wheels in the blunt bows of the junk. The cannon was heavy, but Luke succeeded in rolling it backwards and swinging it around to face the two pirate vessels bearing down on them.

'Is this loaded?' Luke shouted the question at one of the seamen who ran past him, but the man was in a blind panic and gave no answer. Luke had given warning of the pirates in expectation that some action would be taken to evade Ping Chuan's men. Instead, terror had robbed them of the ability to think clearly. Luke had to grab the junkmaster by the front of his jacket and bring him to a halt before he received an answer to his question.

'No, we have no gunpowder,' gasped the terrified Chinese. 'It is unwise to resist Ping Chuan. He will kill every man in the crew . . . and my wife is on board. . . .'

'Ping Chuan will kill us all anyway,' said Luke. 'And God help your wife.' Luke had seen the junkmaster's wife in the living-quarters. A young delicate-looking girl, she would survive no more than an hour of the pirates' attentions. 'What are you going to do? You can't just give up.'

'It is useless to try to fight Ping Chuan,' repeated the junkmaster helplessly. 'I will throw myself upon his mercy.' Shouting to his crew, he ordered them to lower the sail.

The halyards supporting the heavy sail were quickly unfastened and it crashed to the deck. Moments later, Ping Chuan showed his 'mercy'. As one of the pirate vessels dropped away, to come up on the far side of the wallowing merchant junk, pirates in the first vessel opened fire with a ragged volley from a dozen ancient muskets. Two of the unarmed crew of their prey dropped to the deck. One lay still where he fell, the other writhed and screamed in agony from a stomach wound.

Luke had seen enough. He was not staying to sample any more of the 'mercy' dished out by Ping Chuan. Shengan had learned that Luke was responsible for sinking one of Ping Chuan's junks. No doubt the pirates knew, too.

Luke clattered down the ladder to the junk's living-quarters and found the wife of the junkmaster in hysterics. She was fully aware of the fate awaiting her at the hands of Ping Chuan's men.

Luke was still trying to quieten her when he felt the crash and protesting squeal of timbers as the first of the pirate junks came heavily alongside. It was followed immediately by the screams of the men on deck, as Ping Chuan's men swarmed on board and began hacking at the unfortunate crew with their curved swords.

Luke wasted no more time. Grabbing the woman, he dragged her to the rear of the living-quarters with one hand over her mouth to stifle her screams. This was a river cargo-junk, much smaller than the sea-going junks of the pirates. Set into the stern was a small hatch, useful for throwing out rubbish on a cross-river trip, or for running out a gangplank when taking on cargo from a low-lying river-bank. Kicking open the hatch, Luke dragged the woman half through and was about to leap into the water with her when the second pirate junk crashed alongside with even more force than the first. Luke lost his footing and somersaulted into the river, leaving the woman hanging half out of the hatch, screaming hysterically at the top of her voice.

Luke plunged deep into the water before he was able to turn

and strike out for the dark shape of the junk, wallowing in the water above him. He hit the bottom of the junk harder than he had intended, grazing a shoulder against the barnacles encrusted there. Then he was treading water between the cargo-junk and one of the pirate vessels, with the screams of the junkmaster's wife ringing in his ears.

Luke dived again immediately and swam underwater to the large rudder at the rear of the cargo-junk. With no one at the helm, the rudder had swung hard over, forming a triangular-shaped refuge with the stern. Above him, the woman now struggled against the grip of one of the pirates. Suddenly, she broke free and fell through the hatch, striking the water only a few feet from Luke – only to be carried away by the tide. Luke flattened himself back against the stern of the junk, hidden from the view of the pirates by a slight overhang.

Above him a heated argument was taking place about who should dive in for the woman. Before a decision was reached, an ugly grey shape hurtled up from the depths and hit the woman so hard that she was thrown almost clear of the water. Then the streamlined shape of a shark's dorsal fin broke the surface. It turned in a tight circle . . . then disappeared as the shark rolled into the attack.

The woman vanished without a word, and a roar of disappointment went up from the pirates at the open hatch. It was now that Luke noticed blood oozing from a multi-furrowed gash in his shoulder. He immediately heaved himself as far out of the water as he dared, squeezing himself into the tight space between rudder and hull.

He clung to the precarious safety of his position, shivering with cold terror as more sharks arrived and began circling about the junks in search of food. Luke had heard of these sharks; the Chinese called them 'Ping Chuan's hounds'. It was said they waited outside the pirate stronghold at Mirs Bay, some of them following each pirate ship when it left, secure in the knowledge that Ping Chuan's men were a certain source of food. Once something bumped against the rudder beside Luke and he drew his legs up quickly, clinging desperately to the stern of the junk.

Luke's life was probably saved by the actions of Ping Chuan's men. They had slaughtered every man in the cargo-junk's crew and now they began to kick the bodies overboard as they prepared to sail the captured junk to Mirs Bay. The water around

Luke was churned into a bloody frothy maelstrom as shark fought shark for a share in a grisly meal.

Luke's next worry would be when the junk got under way. He could not hope to maintain his grip on the rudder when the vessel began to sail at speed.

Fortunately, Luke was not called upon to find a solution to his predicament. Not long after the last body had hit the water, he became aware of a great deal of activity on the two pirate junks. The shouting of their crews now carried an anxious note. First one junk and then the other cast off its grappling hooks and Luke heard a muffled boom from some distance away. As the cargo-junk drifted in a gentle circle on the current, Luke saw a large European merchantman bearing down upon the junk. It was McCulloch's ship, and puffs of black smoke belched from her open gun-ports as she sped the pirates on their way.

Unable to negotiate the overhang and get back through the hatch, Luke had to remain in his dangerous position until McCulloch's ship came alongside. Even then, it was a full fifteen minutes before his cries were heard and he was hauled back on board at the end of a rope.

Luke was the sole survivor of the pirate attack. As he sat in the dining-room on board the merchantman, surrounded by the ship's officers and gulping down good French brandy, he shivered as he related details of his narrow escape to his rescuers. Reaction to his ordeal had set in now, but his trembling was interpreted by the crew of the merchantman as the result of the time he had spent in the winter-cold waters of the Pearl River estuary and Luke's glass was quickly refilled.

Ezra McCulloch was less sympathetic as he studied Luke over the rim of his own brandy-glass.

'You're born lucky, Trewarne . . . but luck is an unreliable friend. She'll desert you when you need her most.'

'Then I'll . . . back her up . . . with a brace of pistols,' declared Luke, struggling hard to control his shivering. 'I've never felt so helpless in all my life. I had nothing with which . . . to defend myself . . . or anyone else.'

'Being armed would have put off the inevitable for no more than a matter of minutes. Think yourself lucky you *weren't* carrying a gun. What's needed is action to destroy the bases from which these pirates operate. But, if the Chinese Army can't do it, what hope do we have? They've just wiped out a pirate village along the coast; today we've seen the result. Ping Chuan's pirates are like hornets. Disturb their nests and they buzz around looking for someone to sting. No, Trewarne. You need to apply the principles of trade to the problem. You want something . . . so do they. Give them what they want and they'll leave you alone. I doubt if there's a trader out of Canton who isn't buying off Ping Chuan.'

'With opium, of course.'

'Why not? There's plenty of it around at the moment,' growled Ezra McCulloch. 'Look, laddie, face the facts of life out here. Opium is what these people want — not just the pirates, but thousands, *millions* of ordinary Chinese. Christ . . . ! You've seen how they live. The filth, the squalor and the poverty. If opium helps them forget all that for a while, then we're doing them a favour. You must agree with that?'

'Without opium they might have the will to get up and do something about the filth, the squalor and the poverty.'

'Never! They've lived like it for a couple of thousand years . . . since long before they discovered opium. They couldn't change if they wanted to. I'll tell you something else. There's a whole lot of talk about the Emperor wanting to do away with opium smoking. It's not true, Trewarne. If the people of China stopped using opium, they'd get to thinking of all the things that are wrong with China. Right at the top of the list would be the Emperor and his entourage of Manchu leeches. He knows that. He *must*. So, if you were him, what would you do? Stop opium coming in? No, you'd make damn sure the peasants got as much as they wanted.'

Ezra McCulloch pounded the table with his fist to emphasize his words, and Luke said quietly, 'You know, I really think you believe all that.'

'You're damn right, I do — and you'll believe it, too, if you've got any sense.'

Ezra McCulloch glared belligerently at Luke for a few moments; then his mood underwent a complete change. 'But what the hell are we arguing for, Trewarne? Like it or not, we're both on the same side — and we're here to make money. I made you an offer a while back and it still stands. It's a damn good offer, laddie. Marry Morna, merge McCulloch's and Gemmell's, and we'll build the biggest trading company in China. Within a couple of years we'll oust Jardine Matheson and the others, and have a trading empire that'll last for as long as China itself. When I die the whole lot will become yours — yours and Morna's. You'll be able to do anything you want. Go back to England and buy the largest estate in the land. Get yourself elected to Parliament. While you're doing all that, the company will go on making money faster than you can spend it.'

Ezra McCulloch's voice dropped to a low vibrant whisper. 'I'm offering you the world, Trewarne.' He held out his hand, palm uppermost. 'The whole bloody world, right there in your hand . . . and a good-looking girl to go with it.'

The trader had bared his soul to Luke, exposing both his strength and his weakness. Ezra McCulloch's great love was not his family, or Lo Asan. It was his trading company. For its sake he would sacrifice the lives of countless Chinese and give away his own daughter. McCulloch's biggest disappointment in life was not having a son to perpetuate the company. Morna hated the business of trading in opium; he knew that. Unless he could find the right husband for her, she would sell the company the moment it became hers. Ezra McCulloch wanted to be remembered by something more substantial than a weathered tombstone in a Macau churchyard. He intended extending his influence beyond the grave. His burning ambition was to make the company — his company — live for ever.

Luke felt sorry for McCulloch, but he felt an even greater sorrow for Morna. She had lived with the knowledge of her father's disappointment for many years.

'I'll not found *my* fortune on the misery of others, Ezra, and I suggest you consult Morna before dangling her out as bait to add to your own. She's a strong-minded girl. She won't be bought and sold as part of your trade.'

Ezra McCulloch shrugged his shoulders and stood up, his face expressionless. 'You're a fool, Trewarne . . . as most young men are fools. My offer still stands, but time is important to me. You're my first choice, but you're not the only one. That young captain of yours, Gideon Pyke, would make a son-in-law I could take to.'

Eighteen

A THIRD great pirate junk was sighted by the look-out on Ezra McCulloch's merchantman as she rounded the north-west point of Hong Kong island. The junk was anchored close inshore, near McCulloch's beach. But when the merchantman was still a mile away the pirate crew shook out their sails and, assisted by a bank of oars on either side, sped away in the opposite direction.

'What the devil were they doing here?' Ezra McCulloch scowled as he followed the progress of the junk through a telescope.

'Can I use that . . . ?' As McCulloch lowered the telescope, Luke took it from him and trained it upon his house on the slope above the beach. It was impossible to see the house properly because of the trees and shrubs surrounding it. The same was true of McCulloch's house, but as he swung the telescope between them Luke caught a glimpse of a large number of Chinese clambering up the slope behind both houses. The men were wearing their hair long.

'The junk has left some of Ping Chuan's men ashore. It's a large party, too. It looks as though they must have been to the houses. . . .'

'What? Here, give me that.' McCulloch snatched the telescope from Luke's hands, cursing when he discovered Luke had altered the focusing. 'Ah! I've got them now. . . .'

There was a long silence, then McCulloch lowered the telescope and turned to Luke. 'They're carrying a woman with them . . . but I couldn't see who it was.'

Luke leaped over the side of the longboat before it beached on the shingle. The landing-place was crowded with excited Chinese from the nearby village, all eager to tell of the landing of Ping Chuan's men. Not one of them was able to say what the pirates had done on the island.

Luke took off up the hill at a run, ignoring the calls of the seamen in the boat to wait for them to accompany him. Breathing hard, he stumbled over the body of a pirate on the pathway close to the house and he dreaded what he might find inside. But the house seemed intact, although there were the marks of an axe or a heavy sword on the woodwork of the door and the window-shutters. There were also a number of bullet-holes, splintering outwards, indicating that the shots had come from inside. It looked as though someone had seen the pirates arrive and had time to secure the windows and doors against them.

Luke gave silent thanks to the workmen who had carried out the work on his house, with just such a defence as this in mind.

'Kuei, are you there? It's me, Luke.' He shouted the word, but stood clear of doors and windows just in case the defenders were still feeling nervous. Three times he called without reply, his apprehension growing. Then there was the sound of bolts being drawn. The door was flung open, and Kuei rushed out of the house and into his arms.

'Luke! The Gods must have heard my prayers. I thought we would never meet again. . . .'

Luke held her to him. 'It's all right. It's over. Everything is all right now. . . .'

Then he remembered that Ezra McCulloch had seen the pirates carrying a girl away with them.

'Tik-wei . . . where is she?'

Kuei clung to him and turned a tragic face up to his. 'She is dead. Killed by Ping Chuan's men. . . .'

Kuei fought for control of her voice. After some minutes she had a grip on herself, but the story of the tragedy came out in jerky emotion-filled sentences.

'I thought she was safe with Lo Asan. Then we heard shots. . . . They came and threw her body on the path.'

Luke felt the pounding of blood in his head. 'Did they . . . ?' He could not bring himself to ask the question.

'No. She must have been running from them. She was shot in the back. . . .' Kuei clung to him fiercely for a while, then pushed him from her. 'I am better now.'

Luke asked softly, 'Where have you put Tik-wei?'

'In the house. I could not leave her lying here.' As she turned her face up to his, he saw a large bruise on her cheekbone.

Touching it with his finger, he asked, 'What's this?'

Kuei's hand went up to his. 'It is nothing. It happened when I fired the gun through the shutters. I have never used one before. It kept jumping up and hitting me. It. . . . Oh, Luke! If only I had been able to do something more to save Tik-wei.'

'You were lucky not to have lost your own life. Thank God you were in the house.'

They both heard a wail of anguish from the direction of McCulloch's house, and Luke knew who it was the pirates had been carrying away.

'Give me a loaded musket, Kuei. Then go back inside. Don't open the door to anyone until I return.'

'You are not going away again?'

'I must. I think Ping Chuan's men have taken Lo Asan.'

Kuei reeled back as though Luke had stuck her, eyes wide in horror. She fled inside the house but returned again carrying an ancient long-barrelled wheel-lock musket together with a pouch containing powder and shot.

'Find her, Luke. Find Lo Asan quickly.'

Luke set off for McCulloch's house at a run, calling upon two seamen who were coming along the path at a trot to follow him. It was apparent when he reached the house that the pirates had taken the inmates by surprise. The unshuttered windows were smashed and inside it was a shambles. The bodies of two of McCulloch's servants were draped over the furniture and bloodstains discoloured the pale carpet.

'Where's McCulloch?' Luke put the question to an English seaman who stood leaning carelessly on his musket.

'Down there.' The seaman nodded towards the godown. He could not see what all the fuss was about. It seemed the pirates had taken little apart from the Chinese girl. No doubt she was a good-looker – the traders' women usually were – but nobody got this excited over a Chinese girl. There were plenty more where this one came from. . . .

Luke found Ezra McCulloch prising the lid off a box on which was stencilled: 'Samuel Colt, Patterson, New Jersey'.

'You know they've taken Lo Asan?'

Luke nodded. 'They've murdered Tik-wei, too.'

Ezra McCulloch spoke through clenched teeth. 'I wish to God they'd killed Lo Asan. I'm going after her. Are you with me?'

'That's why I'm here. . . .'

The lid came off the box and crashed to the floor. McCulloch ripped through layers of oiled paper and pulled out a hand-gun unlike any Luke had seen before. Throwing it through the air to Luke, the trader said, 'Here! You said you wanted a gun. This is better than any brace of pistols. It's a five-shot revolver from America. You'll see no other like it hereabouts.'

'If it will kill Ping Chuan's pirates, it will do.'

Followed by Luke, Ezra McCulloch went outside the godown to speak to the half-dozen seamen who had brought them ashore.

'You all know what's happened. Ping Chuan's cut-throats have raided my house and carried off a Chinese girl. I'm going to get her back, and Luke Trewarne is coming with me. I'm asking you to come, too.'

To Luke's surprise, the men mumbled among themselves, looking down at their feet, at each other – anywhere but at Ezra McCulloch.

'Well, speak up. Are you coming with me, or not?'

'We're not paid to go chasing pirates halfway across some island, Mr McCulloch,' said one of the men hesitantly, gaining heart when the other seamen murmured their agreement. 'We'll fight well enough if we meet up with 'em at sea – and it'd be different if it was an English girl they had. But a Chinese . . . !'

Only one seaman, a young lad of no more than eighteen, disagreed with his shipmates. Stepping forward he said, 'Peter Jago, sir. If you think she's worth rescuing, then I'm with you, Mr McCulloch.'

'I'm not setting off on a crusade, son. My house and godown have been attacked by Ping Chuan and his men. They've gone off with something that belongs to me. If they get away with it this time, they'll do it again. D'you understand?'

'Ay.'

'Good, then help yourself to a gun. The rest of you men can wait here until we get back. You'll be paid off when the ship returns to Macau. I want no cowards crewing my ships.'

Having settled the future of the five seamen, Ezra McCulloch said to Luke, 'That leaves only three of us to go after at least twenty of Ping Chuan's men. Do you still want to go?'

'I'll go on my own, if need be,' retorted Luke. 'But I'm going to avenge Tik-wei and fetch Lo Asan back, not to save your face.'

Ezra McCulloch showed Luke and Peter Jago how to load the new-model revolvers, and all three men also carried muskets. Then, led by one of McCulloch's surviving servants who feared the trader more than he did the pirates, they set off up the hill, following the path taken by Ping Chuan's men.

Along the way, Ezra McCulloch explained that the path led to a small cove on the far side of the island. It was frequently used by pirates as a rendezvous and a place to beach their junks for repairs.

'So we're quite likely to find far more than twenty pirates there?' Luke put the question.

'No doubt of it,' agreed McCulloch. 'But by the time we arrive I'm counting on nine-tenths of them being stupid on opium – and half the remainder drunk. Now, save your breath – and mine. We've a steep climb ahead of us.'

It was dark by the time they scaled the slope, and then they stumbled along a narrow path in the darkness for almost two hours before the moon rose. Another hour and they reached the shadow of a small clump of trees. Here Ezra McCulloch told their Chinese guide to wait for them. The man's relief was evident. He had been trembling at the knees for the last half-mile, lest they meet up with some of Ping Chuan's pirates.

'The cove is no more than a quarter of a mile from here,' explained McCulloch in a low voice. 'We'll need to go cautiously in case they've set a guard.'

The three men edged their way forwards as silently as they were able, Luke doing his best to hide his impatience. He estimated that the pirates would have arrived here with Lo Asan at least three hours before. A great deal would have happened to her in that time.

When they reached the next bend in the path Luke could hear the sound of surf running up a shingle beach. Another fifty yards and he heard another sound – one that raised the hairs on the nape of his neck. It was the scream of a girl.

The scream died away, drowned by the laughter of many men. Luke ignored McCulloch's soft call for caution. Hurrying along the path, he reached the top of a steep grassy slope. From here the path zig-zagged downwards to the beach.

Had Luke not known who the men below him were, he would have thought there was a party going on in the small cove. A huge driftwood fire blazed on the sand, with most of the pirates gathered nearby. Luke counted more than forty of them. Many were lying beside their opium pipes, lost in a dream world, but McCulloch's estimate had been greatly optimistic.

Half the pirates were still on their feet and would have to be reckoned with in any fight.

The main group of men was to one side of the fire, and it was from here that all the noise was emanating. There was another bloodcurdling scream, and the pirates roared their approval. A moment later a pirate walked away from the group, grinning as he adjusted his trousers. The group parted briefly, and Luke saw the figure of a naked woman spreadeagled on the sand.

'Shall I shoot him? I can get him from here.'

Luke turned to see the young Peter Jago squinting along the barrel of his musket at the pirate who had just left the group.

'Don't be a fool! That will achieve nothing,' hissed McCulloch.

'It will make them leave her alone,' the young seaman whispered fiercely.

'Yes, and before we got anywhere near them they'd have Lo Asan on a boat and halfway to one of the junks.' Ezra McCulloch pointed to where three junks rode at anchor on the moonlit water. 'There are at least a hundred men on each of those boats. Is that what you want for her?'

'What we all want is to get her away from the pirates quickly,' declared Luke. 'We'll not do it from up here. Our only chance is to get down there and rush them, then carry Lo Asan away with us in the confusion.'

'You've got the idea,' agreed Ezra McCulloch. 'But we'll need to get as close as we can without being seen first. Then, when I give the signal, fire into the crowd and make as much hullaballoo as you can. They'll run for the boats. You make sure they keep running and leave me to get Lo Asan. I'll shout when I've got her, and you can cover me while I get her back up here. Have you got that?'

As Peter Jago nodded nervously, another roar of laughter rose from the pirates and Luke grated, 'We've talked enough. Let's go.'

The hastily conceived plans of the would-be rescuers almost came to nought – through the efforts of Lo Asan herself. The attention of the pirates was now directed at two of their number who disputed the right to be next in line for Lo Asan. The two men began fighting and others either tried to separate them or joined in, according to their mood.

Halfway down the cliff, Luke and his companions paused

momentarily as the uproar grew louder — and suddenly they saw Lo Asan. Taking advantage of the confusion, she made a desperate bid to escape. Crawling on hands and knees, she headed away from the firelight — but she was crawling towards the sea, putting the brawling pirates between herself and the three men waiting on the cliff.

As Luke watched in helpless anguish, Lo Asan collapsed, exhausted. She lay on the sand, as helpless as an abandoned kitten, and Luke mentally urged her on. Very slowly, she pushed herself up from the sand and renewed her desperate crawl once more. She had almost made the shadows beyond the firelight, when one of the quarrelling pirates saw her. With a shrill yell of triumph, he ran across the sand and fell on her at the edge of the firelight. The fight quickly broke up as more of the pirates saw what was happening. They hurried to shout encouragement to their victorious comrade, who took Lo Asan like a dog as she kneeled on the beach and wept her shame into the sand.

Luke had seen enough. Abandoning caution, he scrambled down the cliff and ran across the beach in a blind fury, with Ezra McCulloch and Peter Jago close behind him.

Engaged in their salacious entertainment, Ping Chuan's men were not aware of Luke's presence until he plunged among them. Yelling like a banshee, he fired off his musket from hip level and had the satisfaction of seeing two men fall to the single shot. Then Luke was using the musket as a club, and Ezra McCulloch and Peter Jago joined the fray, using their new revolvers.

The initial clash lasted a matter of seconds only before the pirates fled, convinced they were being attacked by a large well-armed rescue-party. Behind them, they left seven of their number wounded and dying on the sand.

The pirate who had prevented Lo Asan's escape was slower than his companions to comprehend what was happening. As he rose from Lo Asan, two bullets, fired simultaneously by Luke and Ezra McCulloch, knocked him backwards into the darkness.

Ezra McCulloch scooped up Lo Asan. As he ran with her to the shadows on the far side of the fire, Luke and Peter Jago began their retreat.

They were just in time. The pirates must have had muskets

stored in the boats at the water's edge. They now began a desultory fusillade, aimed in the general direction of the fire.

By the time Luke and the young seaman reached the cliff path, the pirates were beginning to organize themselves. The unexpected attack had taken them completely by surprise, but when it was not immediately followed up they regained some of their confidence. They greatly overestimated the numbers of their attackers, but were not afraid of a fight. Already their comrades in the junks were tumbling into sampans to come ashore to their assistance. They began to advance up the beach as Luke and Peter Jago paused to reload their guns before taking to the shadows of the cliff path.

Above them, Luke could judge Ezra McCulloch's progress by the moans of his abused burden and the small avalanche of earth and stones dislodged by his feet. Once or twice, Luke thought he heard Lo Asan's voice raised in a tearful plea to McCulloch, but he could not make out her words.

This was the first time Peter Jago had seen any action. He had stood up well to the ordeal, but now a reaction was setting in. His hands trembled so much he was quite unable to pour a measured amount of black powder down the long barrel of his musket. Luke loaded the young seaman's gun for him, then they began a slow climb to the top of the cliff.

They had reached no more than halfway when Ping Chuan's men reached the foot of the cliff, but a well-aimed shot from Luke dropped one of the pirates and sent the others diving for cover. The time so gained enabled Luke and Peter Jago to scramble to the top of the cliff – and safety.

'We're all right now,' said Luke. 'Leave your musket with me and go and help McCulloch with Lo Asan. I'll stay here for a while and discourage anyone from following.'

Without a word, Peter Jago handed his loaded musket to Luke. He turned to go. Then, from some distance along the path, there came the sound of a single shot.

Lo Asan had been in the kitchen of Ezra McCulloch's house showing Tik-wei how to make a cake when the pirates struck. Forty strong, they had landed farther along the coast and taken a circuitous route along the slopes behind the house to avoid detection by the fishermen in the villages along the shore. It was a well-timed operation, the large pirate junk not appearing in the anchorage until most of those who landed were already inside McCulloch's house and the remainder were hurrying towards Luke's new home.

The pirates fired no shots as they forced their way into McCulloch's house, using their curved swords to cut down the two servants they encountered in the first of the ground-floor rooms. Hearing their screams, Lo Asan ran from the kitchen and was immediately seized by two of Ping Chuan's long-haired pirates.

'What are you doing? Let me go! Ping Chuan will kill you for this. He has an arrangement with McCulloch Hau-ye. . . .'

A heavy fist crashed into Lo Asan's mouth and she tasted blood.

'Shut up, whore of the Fan Qui. Ping Chuan himself ordered this raid. Soon there will be no more Fan Qui in China. Ping Chuan says we should take what we want before the Emperor's thieving bannermen cross from the mainland and take it all for themselves.'

'You lie!' Lo Asan spat at the pirate. 'The Fan Qui will never leave. Never! More and more will come, and McCulloch will be the greatest of them all. He will kill you for what you are doing here today.' Behind the pirate, she saw a wide-eyed Tik-wei brought into the room from the kitchen.

The leader of the pirate raiding party drew back his hand to hit Lo Asan again, but as she stared at him defiantly he looked more closely at the heart shape of her face and the pale sheen of her smooth neck. Taking a grip on her collar, he ripped her cheung sam from neckline to waist.

Reaching out, he gripped her nakedness and squeezed until she cried out in pain. It was now, when all the pirates' eyes were turned on Lo Asan's naked body, that Tik-wei twisted from her captor's grasp and darted from the house.

'Run, Tik-wei,' screamed Lo Asan. 'Warn Kuei—'

The pirate leader's blow knocked her head back. To the man who had let Tik-wei escape, he spat, 'Kill the young girl.'

'No!' Lo Asan jumped at the pirate who was going after Tik-wei, but she was seized from behind by the pirate leader.

'The Fan Qui have tamed neither your body nor your tongue, little whore. It would have been different had you remained with your own kind. You will have forgotten what it is to enjoy one of your own people. I will remind you.'

There was the sound of a shot from outside, but Lo Asan was squirming desperately in the grip of the man who held her. She struggled in vain. The pirate leader raped her standing up, encouraged by the two men who held her and the jeers and shouts of the pirates crowding the room as Lo Asan gasped and struggled to bite back her cries.

When their leader grunted his satisfaction and stood back from her, it was the turn of the others, but no sooner had one of the pirates loosened his trousers than the boom of the pirate junk's cannon echoed over the island.

The pirates ran from the house to see what was happening and were in time to see the pirate junk slip her anchor and get under way. The reason was not far off. Ezra McCulloch's ship was heading for the anchorage.

Lo Asan's hopes rose when she heard the consternation among the pirates. She knew the ship would be McCulloch's. But when the pirate leader returned he said, 'We'll cross the island to the meeting-place. The other junks should be there by now.'

'What about the girl?' asked the pirate whose hopes had been dashed by the junk's warning signal.

The leader looked at her body, exposed by the torn dress. 'Bring her. She'll provide some amusement while we wait for Ping Chuan's instructions. Where is the little one?'

'Dead,' came the cryptic reply. 'We delivered her body to the house of the other Fan Qui.'

Lo Asan fought every inch of the way from the house. Finally, one of the pirates cracked her on the side of her head with the hilt of his sword. Half-unconscious, she was swung to the shoulder of one of her captors. Halfway up the hill behind the house, the pirates stopped to bind Lo Asan's hands with a tough vine, cut from a tree. From now on she either walked and kept up with them, or she was dragged along behind her impatient captor, the undergrowth tearing at her body.

When the pirates reached the tiny sheltered cove, shortly before dusk, there were three junks anchored just off the beach. Many of the pirates were ashore, building a fire to chase away the chills of the February night. They crowded about Lo Asan, and she was subjected to some rough and crude handling, until the leader of the small band responsible for her capture roared at them to leave her alone, knocking one man down with the flat of his sword to add emphasis to his words. When they fell back he growled, 'That's better.' Suddenly he grinned, exposing teeth stained with betel-nut juice. 'You can wait your turn with her – but I'm taking her again first.'

Then began a nightmare that went on without respite until Lo Asan lost all sense of time. Her mind became numb with pain and loathing for the men whose stench filled her nostrils with nausea.

The abuse of her body only ceased when two men quarrelled and fought over her and the fight became a battle. She seized the opportunity to escape, but did not have the strength to get clear.

The pirates fell upon her again – and then suddenly there was the sound of shooting, and pirates began dropping to the ground about her. She thought she saw Luke and another European, and believed her reason must have snapped – but then McCulloch was bending over her.

'Come, Lo Asan.'

She cringed away from him, ashamed that he should see her like this, lying naked on the sand where the pirates had left her.

McCulloch picked her up in his arms and carried her away in a jolting painful run. At the foot of the cliff he put her down. By bullying, cajoling and occasionally carrying her, he somehow got her to the top and then hurried with her along the path.

A few hundred yards farther on, he set her down and kneeled on one knee beside her, looking down at her with a strange expression in the moonlight.

'Well . . . ? Haven't you anything to say?' The words came out as fiercely as his breath.

'I am sorry, McCulloch, Hau-ye,' she whispered.

From behind them in the darkness there was an exchange of musket-fire, but McCulloch seemed not to hear it as he stared down at her.

'I have brought you shame.' She reached out her hand and found his, but he shook it away quickly. He had rescued her and made the point that no one could do as they liked with what was his. But he would lose all the 'face' he had gained if he kept her. The pirates had not only raped Lo Asan. They had stripped her of all honour. If she remained in McCulloch's household, every Chinese he met would look at him with derision. He would be the Fan Qui whose mistress had been enjoyed by God alone knew how many filthy long-haired pirates. Many of them would wonder whether she had secretly enjoyed the experience. If he kept her, Ezra McCulloch knew he would sometimes ask himself the same question. . . .

Lo Asan was looking up into his face aware of the battle going on inside him. She thought she had no tears left inside her, but they came now, silently carving clean furrows down her cheeks.

She knew she must not look at him again. He would not be able to do what had to be done if she did. Closing her eyes, she rested her head against his knee. 'It's all right, McCulloch, Hau-ye. I love you. I love you. I love you. . . .'

When Luke reached Ezra McCulloch, the trader was standing over the still form of Lo Asan, the revolver held in his hand.

Luke did not want to believe what he saw. There had to be another explanation. . . .

There was not. Raising his eyes from Lo Asan as though waking from a bad dream, Ezra McCulloch stuck the revolver in his waistband and looked at Luke, his face devoid of all recognizable emotion.

'She's dead. It was the only way. She knew that. Her father will thank me for what I've done when I write and tell him.'

'You put her down as though she were an injured dog,' Luke whispered hoarsely. 'With your help she could have got over what happened today. She would have lived . . . for you.'

'I've told you before, you'll need to be in China for more years than God will give you before you tell me anything about the damned Chinese.'

Ezra McCulloch reeled back as Luke's fist struck him in the face.

'I'm not a religious man, McCulloch, but God's name doesn't belong on your lips.' Luke struggled to keep control of an anger such as he had never known before.

'Why, you . . . !' Ezra McCulloch reached for the gun tucked inside his waistband.

'Don't do it, Mr McCulloch. I'll be obliged to kill you if you touch that gun.'

It was the tremulous voice of Peter Jago at Luke's elbow. The musket-barrel he levelled at Ezra McCulloch's stomach compensated for the uncertainty in his voice, and the click of the hammer being drawn back sounded loud in the darkness.

Ezra McCulloch hesitated, then his hand dropped to his side.

'I'll not forget that blow, laddie. The day will come when you'll remember you once struck Ezra McCulloch.'

With this parting threat hanging on the air, the burly trader strode away along the path, leaving the two men with the body of Lo Asan.

Luke kneeled down by Lo Asan. The light of the moon was sufficient for him to see the powder-burned wound on her left temple where a shot from McCulloch's revolver had ended her life.

'Why did he do it? It doesn't make sense. He risked his life — all our lives — to save her. And then he killed her. Why, Mr Trewarne?' Peter Jago's whispered question cut through Luke's anguish.

'You'll need to ask McCulloch that — but I doubt if he'll give you an answer to satisfy you. Whatever his reason, you can be sure it benefited Ezra McCulloch. You'll find yourself in need of another ship on your return to Macau. Find Captain Pyke of the *Black Swan*; he'll take you on. Now get on back. I'll follow in my own time.'

Picking up the body of Lo Asan, Luke set off along the path. Behind him the pirates reached the cliff top but came no farther. Firing off a few shots to vent their feelings, they filed back to the beach again. None of them had the stomach to follow a well-armed foe any farther in the darkness.

Nineteen

IMPERIAL HIGH COMMISSIONER Lin Tse-hsu, Viceroy of Han-kow, Director of the Board of War, and trusted favourite of the Emperor of China, arrived in Canton on the tenth day of March, in the year 1839. His journey overland from Peking had taken two and a half months. Lin's mandate was clear and succinct: to stamp out the opium trade in the maritime province of Kwang-tung, of which Canton was the provincial capital. Rumours travelling ahead of the Commissioner had it that he saw his mission as a test of his devotion to the Emperor.

Lin was an ambitious and arrogant man with a stern manner. The son of a Fu-kien teacher, he had risen fast through the ranks of the Imperial Civil Service, by dint of his academic ability and determined character. They were allied to a fearlessness that impressed even his enemies. He had once put down a revolt single-handed, by going to the rebel camp alone and discussing their demands with them. He was certainly no stranger to the problems associated with opium. In his home province of Fu-kien, it was estimated that more than half the population used the drug. He had, more recently, largely eliminiated opium smoking in the inland provinces of Hu-peh and Hu-nan.

Commissioner Lin arrived in the walled city of Canton borne on the shoulders of twenty men and preceded by criers and men beating gongs. His state litter bore the insignia of a mandarin of the first grade.

He was met by every high official of the province, led by the Viceroy. Lin Tse-hsu had been given authority over each one of them – with a notable exception. Although he had invested his High Commissioner with more power than any other man in the kingdom possessed, the Emperor had sounded one cautionary note. The Tartar army in Canton would obey only General Shengan – and through him the Emperor himself.

The pomp and ceremony over, everyone in and about the city waited to see what the opening shots in his war against opium would be.

They waited for eight days before Commissioner Lin issued the first of many edicts. Addressed to all foreigners resident in the Canton factories, it ordered them to surrender all the opium they owned within three days — wherever it might be. Once this was completed, they would be required to sign bonds declaring they would never again engage in carrying opium to China. They would also sign an acknowledgement that, *should* opium be discovered on a ship, the trader who owned it would suffer execution!

Lin also published new laws for the Chinese. Smugglers, dealers and owners of opium dens were to be put to death. For the moment, opium smokers would be dealt with leniently — once they had handed in their pipes and promised to give up their pernicious habit. However, such lenience would be of short duration. At a date in the very near future, smokers who had not taken advantage of Commssioner Lin's amnesty would suffer the same fate as dealers and smugglers.

On the same day, Lin sent an order to the Hong merchants of Canton. To them was passed the responsibility of extracting the bonds of good behaviour from the foreigners. They were also to apply pressure to obtain their opium.

Should the Hongs fail to carry out Commissioner Lin's orders, he declared he would hang some of their number as an example to the others.

Luke found an atmosphere of anger and apprehension in the factories when he arrived there in the wake of Lin's edict. He had left Gideon Pyke in Macau, with orders to stay away from Canton until it became clear how Lin's arrival would affect trading. Meanwhile, on Hong Kong island, Luke had strengthened still farther the defences of his property. Kuei and the servants had been instructed in the use of firearms and had been left with enough powder and shot to withstand a siege, should Ping Chuan take it into his head to attack again.

In Canton, the traders held a number of inconclusive meetings to decide their future action. It was eventually decided to send a delegation to put the case to James Killian. The Superintendent of Trade was currently in Macau, peeved at not being invited to meet the incoming Commissioner.

But the Canton traders had made their decision too late. Another order had already been issued by Commissioner Lin. None of the traders would be allowed to leave the factories until all the opium had been handed over. The traders were isolated from the rest of the world.

Alarmed, they played for time, sending a message to Commissioner Lin, through the Hongs, informing him that such important matters as these needed time for discussion – and the freedom to seek advice.

The matter of the bonds pledging good behaviour, in particular, carried far-reaching implications for them all. The Europeans had hitherto refused to subject themselves to Chinese law – and with very good reason. On two occasions in the previous fifty years offenders against Chinese law had been handed over for 'questioning'. Both had been summarily executed. By signing such a bond as Lin had in mind, the traders acknowledged that they, too, were subject to the same Chinese 'justice'.

Lin's reply was swift. Chinese bannermen began to assemble in the suburbs, and armed militia in boats blocked the river in front of the factories. As dusk fell upon the uneasy community, the Hong merchants came to the factories, sagging beneath the weight of shackles and chains. They begged the traders to do something immediately. Lin had told them that if the *impasse* remained at ten o'clock the next morning two of their number would be beheaded in the factory square.

Such executions would hit the traders hard, as Lin knew well. Trading at Canton was such a complicated business that the Hong merchants were always heavily in debt to the foreign traders and there was no Chinese law which made next of kin liable for their debts. If the Hongs died, their debts died with them.

Galvanized into action, the traders cast around for a quick solution, and Abel Snow suggested that they ask Luke to help. His suggestion was greeted with scepticism by some traders, but the Hong merchants seized on the idea eagerly. They had heard rumours that Luke had influential friends within the walled city and they insisted that the traders seek his help.

Luke doubted whether Shengan would be willing to do anything in the present delicate situation, but he sent one of his servants with a message, asking Shengan if he would speak to him.

Luke expected Shengan to send soldiers to escort Luke to his house, but he waited until after midnight in vain. Then, when he had given up waiting, an awestruck servant came into the room to tell Luke he had a visitor. The 'visitor' entered the room close on the heels of the servant. It was Shengan. Outside, his escort of only six Tartar warriors kept discreetly to the shadows. No one would enter or leave the Gemmell factory while their general was inside.

Shengan dropped heavily into a wooden-armed chair and leaned back, stretching his legs out before him. 'You wanted to see me, my friend. I have no doubt the subject of your concern is Commissioner Lin?'

'You know he's ordered the traders to hand over their opium and sign bonds agreeing never again to deal in opium?'

Shengan nodded. 'Reasonable demands, I think. You disagree?'

'Not with the handing over of opium. It won't hurt any one of the traders to take a loss on that. Making ourselves subject to Chinese law is a very different matter. It doesn't work the same as our own. We have little faith in its justice.'

Shengan sat upright in the chair and leaned closer to Luke. 'Why should Chinese law conform with Fan Qui law? This is not yet your country. This is China. Those who make the laws live here. If my people obey them, then why not yours also? Could we come to your land and say, "No, I will not obey your laws because I am Chinese"?'

'In my land you would be free to go where you wished and enjoy the benefits those laws bring. Here we have to stay in the factories – and in the factories we run our own affairs.'

Shengan shrugged. 'No trader is forced to stay in China. Is it for this you wished to speak to me?'

'Not entirely. Lin has said that, if all opium isn't given up and bonds signed by ten tomorrow morning, he'll behead two of the Hong merchants.'

'So? The Hongs are the greatest rogues in all China. Many less cunning men have died for doing no more wrong than a Hong merchant.'

In spite of the extreme seriousness of the situation, Luke could not hide a quick smile at Shengan's words. 'No doubt many traders would agree with you, but they stand to lose fortunes if the Hongs are executed. The Superintendent of Trade will ask my government to intervene and demand compensation. We both know what that will mean.'

'Yes. War.'

Shengan sank lower in his chair and lapsed into thought. When he raised his head it was to look at the brass clock on the wall. It showed one o'clock. 'It is now the hour of the fourth drum, but the moon sees Commissioner Lin working as hard as does the sun. I will go to see him now. I feel confident

I can save the lives of the totally unworthy Hong merchants, but Lin has a reputation to uphold. He will want something in return. That something can only be opium, my young friend — and it will take a great deal of opium to satisfy His Excellency the Commissioner.'

'It's a fair exchange,' agreed Luke. 'The lives of the Hong merchants for opium.'

'Talking of lives. . . . I have been told you put your own at great risk in a bid to rescue my niece from Ping Chuan's men.'

Shengan had taken Luke off guard. The sudden memory of that night came back to Luke as sharp as a sword-thrust.

'She *was* rescued . . . but I couldn't save her from those she loved. You know she's dead?'

'I know. It is best. Life would have held no honour for her.'

'But she'd done nothing wrong, Shengan. Had such a thing happened to a European girl she would have been given sympathy and understanding by her family and friends.'

'Sympathy and understanding would not undo what had happened, or erase it from men's minds. No, my friend, I owe you a debt for not leaving Lo Asan to die at the hands of Ping Chuan's criminals. I thank you. I thank you also for bringing the daughter of the trader McCulloch to see me. We met again before I left Macau. She has an independent and original mind. It makes me wonder whether I might have misjudged her father. What manner of man is he?'

'He's an opium smuggler with nothing but contempt for China and its people,' Luke replied curtly.

Shengan looked at Luke strangely. 'I see. I wonder whether you are angry with me, with McCulloch . . . or with his daughter. It matters not. We will remain friends, you and I.'

Luke sent out messengers as soon as Shengan had left the factories, and a meeting of tousle-haired traders and shivering Hongs began at three o'clock that morning.

Without mentioning Shengan's name, Luke put forward the General's proposals. Some of the traders saw it as giving in to Lin's demands and declared they could not afford to lose their opium. Not until Abel Snow suggested the Hong merchants might be prepared to compensate the traders for any opium handed over on their behalf was an agreement reached. When the meeting broke up at dawn, a thousand chests of opium were promised, for which the Hong merchants would pay the traders their purchase price.

As soon as it was a reasonable hour, the Hong merchants hurried to Commissioner Lin's office. On their knees they told him of their success in squeezing opium from the Fan Qui traders. To their great relief, he agreed that the quantity was sufficient to save their lives. But he wanted still more opium. Much more. For the time being, the senior Hongs, Lien Ling and his brother, would continue to wear chains about their necks to remind them and the Fan Qui of Commissioner Lin's displeasure.

Meanwhile, in Macau, James Killian had received only vague rumours of what was happening at Canton. But they were serious enough for him to order all British ships at the various anchorages to assemble in a place where they might be safe from harm, and defended against a seaborne attack. The place he chose was the Hong Kong anchorage.

Not until almost a week after the night meeting at the factories did James Killian receive detailed news from Canton. It arrived in the form of a letter, smuggled out of Canton and brought to Macau by sampan from Whampoa.

The Superintendent of Trade's reactions were exactly those anticipated by Luke. Killian sent a despatch to Lord Palmerston in London, setting out in exaggerated detail the humiliations and provocation suffered by the residents of the Canton factories in recent months. He quoted the threatening language used by Commissioner Lin and declared it was no longer possible to continue peaceful relations with the Chinese. He stated his intention of calling on Lin to allow all Europeans to leave Canton immediately and promised to prepare a list of all losses suffered as a result of the Commissioner's actions, urging that they be lodged against China by the British Government. Killian ended his letter by saying that Lin's actions, if not actually a declaration of war against the European countries, must be construed as an inevitable preparation for war.

A copy of this letter was sent to Commissioner Lin and another by fast clipper to the Governor-General of India, with a covering note requesting naval assistance immediately.

When these letters had gone, the Honourable James Killian called for a cutter from a British frigate currently visiting Macau. Rowed by British sailors, he set off up-river to Canton. He was prepared to martyr himself in the cause of his country.

To his chagrin, the Chinese allowed him to travel to Canton without hindrance, as though everything were normal.

Killian's arrival at Canton was far more satisfying to his ego. He stepped ashore to the cheers and wild applause of the factory residents. Luke was amazed. They were behaving as though Killian had arrived at the head of a force to relieve the beleaguered factories. Intent on furthering this impression, Killian had the sailors from the cutter form a guard of honour while he hoisted the Union Jack from the mast in the square.

Later that same day, the Chinese sent in workmen to build walls and seal off all lanes and alleyways from the factory square, leaving only a single entrance. Here they erected barriers and posted a strong guard. Next, they sent a ragged motley of peasant militia to perform appallingly bad drill in the shadow of the British flag. When dusk fell, the militia was withdrawn and replaced by a 'band'. Equipped with trumpets and gongs, the so-called 'musicians' kept up a deafening din until dawn.

Although he was maintaining an unrelenting pressure on the traders, Commissioner Lin was concerned at the tone of Killian's letter. He had refused to accept it, as a matter of course, but had ensured that a copy was made before the letter was sent back. He dismissed most of the contents as mere posturing, but was not happy at the thought of the Fan Qui leaving Canton *en masse*, blaming him for the rupture in relations. An important factor in the elimination of opium smuggling was the serious drain upon China's silver currency. It would not help the Emperor's treasury if Lin destroyed *all* trade.

Late the next night, when the Chinese instrumentalists were once more entertaining the long-suffering traders, Shengan and his small escort returned to the Gemmell factory. Shengan had brought with him a spare uniform of a Tartar soldier. He threw it down on the desk in front of Luke. 'Put this on. Tonight you are to be doubly honoured. The first is that you are to become one of my Tartar warriors for a few hours.'

'And the second?'

'You will meet Commissioner Lin Tse-hsu and discuss with him the problems of your fellow-traders.'

'Me meet Lin? I'm not the man for this, Shengan. If there's any talking to be done, it should be with the Superintendent of Trade.'

'Your Superintendent of Trade's tongue is tied by pride and self-importance. *I* told Lin he should speak to you. Are you questioning my judgement?'

'Yes, Shengan . . . but I'll come. I'd like to see this man who has Killian by the tail.'

Lin Tse-hsu was a large man with a fleshy face that rested upon a nest of flabby chins. He had a long down-curving moustache and a straggly goatee beard, but the only hair to be seen upon his head was a thin greased queue hanging from beneath his saucer-brimmed hat. He wore a dark-blue silk robe embellished with a crane, the symbol of a civilian mandarin of the first grade. Around his neck hung a necklace of jade beads that reached to his waist, and he fondled these during the whole time Luke was with him.

It was evident when Luke entered the room that Commissioner Lin was waiting for the elaborate ritual of obeisance accorded to a man of his rank. Luke responded by giving the Commissioner a shallow bow, then stood back, waiting for him to speak.

Lin frowned briefly, but when he spoke to Luke he was civil enough. 'So you are the barbarian General Shengan has befriended?'

There was no invitation for Luke to be seated, although General Shengan strode a few feet away across the room and adopted his usual sprawling position on one of the chairs set around a large table.

'Life must be very difficult for you and your friends in the factories?'

Luke shrugged non-committally. 'We eat and drink – and listen to the music of your nightly band.'

Again there was a frown. 'Ah, yes! A regrettable inconvenience, but it seems that it is necessary to remind your people that they are living in China and are totally dependent upon the goodwill of the servants of the Emperor.'

'I don't think anyone needs to be reminded of that, but if relations between us get any worse you'll have China to yourselves pretty soon.'

'There are many who think that greatly to be desired, Luke Trewarne, but our illustrious Emperor has a far more generous nature. It pains him to see the distress of the barbarians who have enjoyed the hospitality of our country for so many years. Because of his warm feelings towards you all he has sent me here. I am to point out gently the error of your present ways and guide you back to the benefit of his full favour.'

Luke decided he did not particularly like Commissioner Lin. He was pompous and condescending. Unless he came to the point quickly, Luke would be here all night without settling anything.

'The traders in the factories wouldn't agree with your idea of hospitality, Commissioner. You've made us all prisoners and stopped trade. That's a peculiar way of guiding anyone anywhere.'

'The restrictions on trade will remain in force only until every ounce of opium is handed over and bonds for future good behaviour signed.'

'Then you can expect to have British warships fighting their way up to Canton to rescue us. I couldn't care less what happens to the opium. My company has never brought it to China and I have no time for those who do, but I'm damned if I'll sign anything that makes me subject to your so-called Chinese justice. I've sampled some of it myself and will carry the scars to my grave. Signing your bond puts every trader at the mercy of the Tsotang – or anyone else who stands to gain by his arrest and execution. That means Hong merchants, disgruntled servants – even unscrupulous fellow-traders. No, such a bond is out of the question.'

Turning his back on Commissioner Lin, Luke said to Shengan, 'I'll go back to the factory now. I thought I was coming here to discuss my opinion, not to listen to Commissioner Lin repeat his ridiculous demands. He could have done that to Killian.'

Shengan stood up. 'As you wish. . . .'

'Wait!' Commissioner Lin was scowling angrily. He was unused to being spoken to in such a disdainful manner, but he had need of Luke's knowledge of James Killian and the traders. 'You are a good example of why young men should never be sent on missions of diplomacy. Matters of importance should not be dismissed in haste, or anger. Sit. We will have tea.'

Clapping his hands, Commissioner Lin summoned a servant and waved Luke to a seat at the table. Shengan, too, sat down again, his booted legs extended before him, apparently enjoying the stormy meeting.

Commissioner Lin sat in silent thought until tea was brought to the room. Then he came to the table and sat down facing Luke. 'I can see the reason for your fears, Luke Trewarne. I do not agree with them, but I can understand that a man far from home needs reassurance. I will think again about the bond. However, I have sworn a sacred oath to the Emperor and will not leave Canton until this vile trade in opium has been stamped out, once and for all.'

'So what will you do?'

'There is much I *can* do. China has a vast population, with every man ready to fight for his Emperor. An invading army would be quickly overwhelmed.'

Commissioner Lin was trying to impress upon Luke that he spoke from a position of strength.

'However, as my Emperor is kindly disposed towards those who come from far across the seas to trade with China, how can I, his servant, find it in my heart to be less understanding? Give me every chest of opium from your ships and I will not insist upon the bond. The edict will not be withdrawn, but no one will be required to sign anything.'

'And our imprisonment in the factories?'

'It is not an "imprisonment". But, for the moment, I regret that all barbarians must remain in their factories . . . for their own safety. There will be no shortage of food and water. I will have it sent in to you – as a gesture of goodwill. When half the total opium has been delivered to me, I will allow the passage of boats between Canton and Macau once more. Then, when all the opium has been surrendered, you will once again enjoy trade with my country.'

Luke realized this was a major breakthrough in the confrontation between Commissioner Lin and the European traders.

'This is a firm agreement? You will put it in writing?'

'It is a firm agreement, Luke Trewarne, but there must be no record of this meeting . . . for many reasons. However, if your Superintendent of Trade surrenders all the opium held in Fan Qui ships without further prevarication, he will learn the value of my word.'

Luke knew he could ask for no more concessions and he had expected to achieve much less from such an unprecedented meeting.

'Thank you, Commissioner Lin. You will get your opium.'

Hiding his own jubilation, Lin nodded. 'Thank you, Luke Trewarne.'

When Luke had set off on the return journey to the factories, escorted by Tartar soldiers, Commissioner Lin relaxed and smiled at Shengan. The General was his only social equal in the whole province, and Lin felt able to drop some of his official aloofness.

'I find your friendship with this young barbarian surprising,' he said. 'He is no respecter of rank or authority.'

'I am a soldier. In the Army a man has to *earn* the respect of his companions. What is more important to me is that Trewarne is a respecter of the truth. Other men tell me what they think I wish to hear. He tells me the truth, however uppalatable it may be.'

'An honest and truthful friend is a gem of inestimable value,' murmured Lin blandly.

Shengan looked at the Commissioner sharply. He did not trust him. He did not trust any high government administrator. He hoped Lin was not going to try to be devious with the Fan Qui at Canton.

Commissioner Lin gave Shengan another disarming smile. He liked the sound of his last observation. It rolled easily off the tongue. He must remember to use it in one of his poems. Lin considered himself one of the country's foremost poets, and his efforts had been graciously received by the Emperor himself.

Then Lin thought of his meeting with the barbarian friend of General Shengan, and his moment of pleasure turned sour. It was bad enough having to discuss trade at all. That was a subject for lesser men – for the despised Hong merchants. When the discussion was with a bad-mannered Fan Qui it became even more distasteful. General Shengan must be mad to have formed such an ill-conceived friendship.

He gave Shengan a sidelong glance. Mad, or traitorous? He would think of a discreet way to bring the matter to the attention of the Emperor without criticism of himself; but Lin would bide his time. Shengan's influence was not to be underestimated. As for future relations with the Fan Qui. . . . Trade would resume when he was satisfied that all their opium had been handed over – but it would be on terms dictated by Commissioner Lin himself.

The Fan Qui needed reminding that they were inferior beings.

Their trade with China was dependent upon the benevolence of the Emperor. Never again must they be allowed to disrupt China's economic and social life as they had in recent years. They *would* be brought under the restraining influence of Chinese law.

Twenty

JAMES KILLIAN was indignant that Luke had been able to arrange a meeting with Commissioner Lin, where he had failed, and he was scornful of Lin's concessions.

'Commissioner Lin knows full well he is not bound by anything he says to you. If he wishes to negotiate on the present situation, he should speak to me.'

'I think he already has,' retorted Luke. 'He's cut off trade and is holding us as hostages until he's got all the opium in Chinese waters. He needn't say any more.'

It was in the early hours of the morning. On his return to the factories, Luke had woken Abel Snow and together they had come to see the Superintendent of Trade in the former East India Company factory.

'Commissioner Lin can't enter into direct negotiations with you,' said Abel Snow. 'He's issued an edict in the Emperor's name. All he's expected to do now is sit back and wait for the opium to come in – or watch everyone in the factories starve to death.'

'He wouldn't dare allow the situation to deteriorate to that extent . . . !' Killian rose to his feet and began pacing the room, his official starchiness out of keeping with the striped cotton nightdress, beneath which his bare feet occasionally showed themselves. 'There would be an international outcry.'

'It would come too late to help us here,' said Luke. 'And I doubt whether Lord Palmerston will be happy to have the opium question made an international issue.'

'How do I know I can trust this man?' James Killian put the abrupt question to Luke.

Luke shrugged. 'You don't. But I'm convinced Lin will get hold of the bulk of the opium, sooner or later. Whether anyone dies in the process is up to you.'

James Killian came to a sudden decision. 'All right, Trewarne. I'll order the traders to surrender their opium. I realized soon after my arrival here that I could do little else. Of course, by issuing such an order I am rendering the Government of Great Britain responsible for compensating the traders, but these are exceptional circumstances. However, I am going to need more time than Commissioner Lin has given to me. I must send someone from Canton to locate the opium ships and arrange the handover. Lin will have to agree to this.'

The next few days saw scenes of feverish activity in the Canton factories. James Killian called the traders to meeting after meeting. Twice Luke was sent into the walled city after dark for meetings with Commissioner Lin and Shengan. At the end of four days, the traders had submitted to the Superintendent of Trade details of the opium held by them in receiving ships and warehouses. The total was staggering. Between them, the traders had 20,283 chests of opium waiting to be poured into China – 1268 *tons*. This total did not include the opium held by Ezra McCulloch and those few traders who were not held captive at Canton.

Commissioner Lin found it difficult to conceal his delight. Such a huge amount of opium provided overwhelming justification for the stand he had taken against the Fan Qui. When word of his success reached the Emperor, no honour would be too great. The highest office in the land would be his for the asking.

In spite of the magnitude of his victory, Lin was not prepared to loosen his stranglehold on the Canton factories until the opium was in his hands. He would allow only one man to leave Canton and arrange for the opium to be surrendered. That man was Luke. James Killian would have preferred to send out one of his own assistants. There were a number of face-saving 'arrangements' that might have been possible, but Killian was forced to bide his time.

Commissioner Lin looked upon the surrender of the traders' opium as the ultimate victory. James Killian knew this was no more the first round in a long battle – the round that Great Britain traditionally gave to its opponents.

In benevolent mood, Lin sent in pigs, chickens and eggs to feed the Fan Qui. Taking advantage of Commissioner Lin's euphoria, Killian sent a letter to him. In it he stated that each of the traders at Canton had given his word to him not to deal in opium hereafter. It was a shrewd and cleverly worded document, forestalling any future demand that they be required to enter into a bond for their good conduct. Giving no mention of Chinese jurisdiction over foreign traders, Killian's letter declared that they had all given their word to *him*. To demand more would imply a lack of trust on the part of Commissioner Lin.

James Killian was well pleased with his latest move. It was an important letter to refer to, should there be more trouble in the future. Commissioner Lin was less enthusiastic. He returned the document, declaring it had not been submitted through 'official channels'. As there were no official means of communication between Lin and the Superintendent of Trade, it meant there would be no record of the letter in official Chinese files. The exchange boded ill for future relations between Commissioner Lin and Superintendent of Trade James Killian.

Luke left Canton armed with instructions from each trader to the captains of the ships in which his opium was stored. The opium was to be taken to Chuenpi island, just below the first of the Bogue forts, and there Lin would arrange for its destruction.

Not all European ships in Chinese waters had gone to Hong Kong, and on his way down-river Luke called in at the Lin-tin and Lan-tau island anchorages. Here Luke learned that it was not going to be easy to assure the captains that the instructions he carried to them had not been written under duress. It was natural that the captains should be wary of taking their opium cargoes up-river and handing them over to the Chinese. Convincing them of the necessity of such a course of action took time, but Luke went on to Macau satisfied that they would carry out their instructions.

In Macau, Luke had an even more difficult task. Armed with a letter of explanation from Killian, he had to persuade the traders living in the safety of the Portuguese colony to give up their opium. If he failed, Luke knew that Commissioner Lin would have a loophole through which he could withdraw from the agreement he had made. Lin wanted *all* the opium held by the traders.

Once again, Luke was successful. But it was not compassion for their fellow-traders that convinced the Macau-based merchants. It was the reality of the situation in which they found themselves. The area around Canton was reeling under Commissioner Lin's attack on the opium smokers and their suppliers. There was no market in opium for the present. All the traders agreed to give up at least a percentage of their stocks.

One of the largest single consignments was handed over by the company of Lancelot Fox, but it was no quixotic gesture.

For years the continually expanding company had exerted pressure on the British Government, urging them to take action to have the ports of China thrown open to trade. More recently, Lancelot Fox had returned to England to take a seat in Parliament, leaving a nephew in charge of the company. This was too good an opportunity to be missed. As a 'victim' of Commissioner Lin's unprecedented seizure of British property, Lancelot Fox could roar indignantly during parliamentary debates on the situation in China. He would be called upon as an expert on Chinese affairs, and as such be able to influence Great Britain's future policy in the area. By demanding that the traders hand over opium to him, Commissioner Lin had presented the pro-opium faction in Britain with a powerful weapon. It would be used against China with devastating effect.

Before leaving Macau for Hong Kong, Luke paid Morna McCulloch a visit. She greeted him enthusiastically and, after he had made polite conversation with her mother, led him away to her own drawing-room. Luke was flattered by her pleasure at seeing him, but soon discovered that her real interest lay elsewhere. No sooner had the door to her room closed behind them than she asked eagerly after General Shengan.

When Luke told her that Shengan was largely responsible for agreement being reached between Lin and the traders, she sat on a window-seat and hugged herself in delight. 'I knew it! As soon as I heard what was happening I knew that Shengan had used his influence with Lin. He promised me he would.'

'Shengan promised you? Morna . . . what is there between you and Shengan?'

Morna jumped up from the window-seat and kissed Luke affectionately. 'Don't tell me you're becoming stuffy, Luke? As a matter of fact there is *nothing* between Shengan and me – but that's his fault, not mine. I think he's the most exciting man I've ever met in my life.'

Handing him a drink, she saw his expression and stiffened defensively. 'Does it surprise you so much that I find a Chinese attractive, Luke? I wonder why. You've made it quite clear to everyone how you feel about Kuei. No doubt my father loves Lo Asan, too – as much as he's capable of loving anyone. How is she? Have you seen her lately?'

Luke had not realized that Morna knew nothing of the tragic episode on Hong Kong island. Her mention of Lo Asan took him by surprise. It was as though Morna had dealt him a physical blow.

Morna had raised a glass to her lips: now she lowered it quickly. 'What is it, Luke? Has something happened to Lo Asan?'

'You . . . you'd better ask your father that question.'

Luke put down his glass, the brandy untouched, and stood up to leave.

Morna was too quick for him. She reached the door and put her back to it as he reached for the handle.

'My father isn't here, Luke. . . . I'm asking you. What happened to Lo Asan?'

Luke would have liked to leave the house and forget the question, but Morna would not allow him to go until she had received an answer.

'Lo Asan was taken by pirates. They . . . they treated her very badly. We . . . your father and I, got her back. She didn't live.'

Her hand gripped his arm fiercely. 'That isn't the whole story, is it, Luke? He killed her. My father killed Lo Asan.'

'It wasn't as simple as that, Morna. She *wanted* to die. It had to do with this stupid Chinese interpretation of "honour" – the need to save face.'

'But *he* killed her. You don't have to say any more, Luke. I've lived with him long enough to know what he would do. If he hadn't killed her, he'd have broken her heart. Lo Asan would have known that. Someone else had possessed her. He would never have gone near her again. Poor Lo Asan.'

Morna began to cry, and Luke led her to a chair. Filling her glass from his, he handed it to her, murmuring sympathetically.

Suddenly, she rounded on him. 'God! Why are men such hypocrites? They go whoring about as they please, but if a woman is touched by another man – even if it's rape – she becomes an outcast.'

Luke thought of the number of pirates who had raped Lo Asan, but he said nothing. In an effort to find some excuse for Ezra McCulloch's action, he had gone over the incident time and time again in his mind, wondering what he would have done had it happened to Kuei. Each time he had come up with the same answer – and it was not McCulloch's way.

He said quietly, 'The pirates killed little Tik-wei, too.'

Morna's expression became one of horror, and she repeated, 'Poor Tik-wei. . . . Poor Tik-wei,' over and over again.

Morna slowly regained control of herself and, after pouring herself another brandy and drinking it down without a pause, she threw up her chin aggressively. 'I've forgiven my father for many things, Luke – but not this time. I'll never forgive him for this.'

'He did what he thought was best, Morna. There are many who agree with his actions. Shengan is one.'

Morna took a deep breath; the brandy was beginning to take effect. 'I don't want to talk about it anymore, Luke. I'd like you to leave me now. Tell Kuei how deeply sorry I am about Tik-wei. . . .'

Lo Asan's death had helped Morna to make up her mind about something she had been toying with ever since General Shengan had suggested it to her. It was an intriguing offer – but one which would appal her father. She intended telling him before mentioning it to anyone else.

Luke arrived in the Hong Kong anchorage on board *Black Swan* the next day. There were almost fifty ships crowding the harbour and, rather than have to explain his mission fifty times, Luke passed the word that he was calling a meeting of the ships' masters in his house that evening. Then he went home.

Kuei was overjoyed to have Luke home with her so unexpectedly, but she seemed quieter, more reserved than usual. When he questioned her she assured him all was well, and he put her mood down to the recent loss of Tik-wei.

Kuei clucked happily enough over him, declaring he had lost weight since leaving her, and sat him down to a hurriedly prepared meal before saying, 'The daughter of McCulloch is here, on the island.'

Luke dropped the piece of fish he had been holding between two chopsticks and looked at Kuei stupidly. 'What do you mean . . . here? I spoke to her only yesterday – in Macau.'

'She arrived on the island this morning and came here before going to McCulloch's house.'

'She came here?' Luke had thought Kuei must be mistaken; now he knew she was not.

'Yes. She asked me to show her Lo Asan's grave. I took her there. . . . She wept.' Kuei kneeled beside Luke and rested her head in his lap. He saw that she, too, was very close to tears. He stroked her hair gently as she said, 'She is a very nice girl.'

'She was very fond of Lo Asan.'

Kuei raised her head and looked up at him. 'She is very fond of you, too. I know. I watch her closely when she speaks of you. I saw her fear when I told her how bravely you fought the pirates for Lo Asan. I would be very happy for you to marry her, my Luke. She would be a good wife for you.'

The unhappiness had returned, and Luke knew she was feeling unsure of herself. He had been away too long. Lifting her, Luke held her close. 'Kuei, you're the only woman I want. One day you'll be my wife.'

'No!' Kuei struggled against him for some moments before she accepted that he was not going to release her. Resting her face against his shirt front, she said, in a muffled voice, 'You cannot marry me, my Luke. I am not a Fan Qui girl. You must marry one of your own kind, or your people will laugh at you. I am a girl for the night-time, when other eyes cannot see us together. I will stay here for as long as you want me – but you cannot marry me.'

'Now, what's all this about?' Luke pushed back his chair and held her at arm's length in order to look at her. He had never seen her so unhappy. 'I'll have no more of such foolish talk, do you hear me?'

Kuei nodded her head vigorously, but would not look up into his face. Neither would she give him any indication of what had happened to upset her so much. Luke thought it was probably the sudden arrival of Morna and the visit with her to the graves of Lo Asan and Tik-wei, buried side by side in a cleared patch of ground on the hillside. He wished he could stay with her for a while. But he would be home for no more than a night or two. There was important business to be attended to.

Later that afternoon, before the meeting with the captains of the ships in the anchorage, Luke walked to Ezra McCulloch's house. He went alone; Kuei declaring she had much to do before the meeting could begin.

He found Morna alone in the huge lounge of her father's house. She was seated at Ezra's desk, writing a long letter. When Luke was shown into the room, she smiled at him. 'I wondered how long it would be before you came to find out what I'm doing here.'

'What *are* you doing here? If you needed to come to Hong Kong, why didn't you travel in *Black Swan* with me?'

'I had to see my father, Luke, and I thought you might try to put me off.'

'Do you want to tell him about you and Shengan and watch him squirm?'

'That was my intention at first, but I changed my mind, even before I set off. I wanted to see Lo Asan's grave. I felt I . . . a McCulloch owed her at least a prayer. A prayer and a posy of flowers – it's not much, is it? That's all she's got to show that a girl named Lo Asan once lived and loved, laughed and cried on this island. It's so sad.'

Morna gave Luke a watery smile, but kept tight control on herself. 'I had another reason for coming here. When Shengan came from his battle with Ping Chuan's pirates some of his men were wounded. I treated them at his camp and later he visited the hospital where I work. He was impressed. Before he left Macau he asked me if I would set up a similar hospital in Canton.'

'But Abel Snow already has a hospital there . . . and women are not allowed in the factory area.'

'Shengan wasn't talking about a hospital in the factories. He wants me to open one in the Tartar quarter of the walled city, to treat his soldiers and their families. He says a recent epidemic killed dozens of children, and Chinese medical methods couldn't cope with it.'

Luke remembered the primitive application of salt to his back after his beating by the Tsotang's executioner. He shuddered involuntarily, but Morna's words alarmed him.

'You can't possibly consider such a thing at the present time, Morna. Commissioner Lin has stirred up so much anti-European feeling among the Chinese you'd be risking your life.'

Morna smiled. 'You're Shengan's friend, Luke. Surely you have more faith in him than that? Besides, the anger is against you traders. This could possibly be one of the few occasions when being a woman is an advantage. Anyway, my mind is made up.'

She picked up the almost completed letter from Ezra McCulloch's desk. 'I've told my father all about it in here. I don't expect him to understand my reasons . . . but I thought you might. I have a *feeling* for these people, Luke. You have it, too, I know you do. I am at home among them . . . contented.'

'Is this feeling for the Chinese people, Morna . . . or is it for Shengan?' Luke asked the question quietly.

'I don't know the answer to that yet, Luke. That's another reason why I must go to Canton.'

'I hope you've set things out very clearly for your father, Morna. If you haven't, he'll be calling for British troops to come to rescue you.'

Luke would have liked to prolong this discussion, but the ship's clock on the wall of the lounge showed him he had less than half an hour before the meeting with the captains of the merchant ships.

When he informed Morna, she said, 'Kuei will need some help in the house. I'll come with you. I want to talk to you about Kuei before we get there.'

Luke thought he might have been right to assume Morna had upset Kuei earlier, but the Scots girl soon put him right. She told him the seamen from the ships in the anchorage — and the wives of some of the captains — had been giving Kuei a hard time.

'Nobody expects anything more from the seamen,' snorted Morna scornfully. 'Once ashore they set their caps at any girl, black, white or yellow — and Kuei is more attractive than most. But the seamen have been no more than a nuisance; it's the women who have really hurt her. Some of the ships' captains have their wives on board with them and they've been coming ashore and walking through your house as though it were a public building. Not only that; they've been treating Kuei as a servant, expecting her to jump whenever they call.'

'So that's why Kuei is so upset.' Luke was relieved it had nothing to do with Morna. Well, we'll soon put that right.'

Some of the wives came ashore with their husbands for the meeting, and the largest room in Luke's house was uncomfortably crowded. Kuei, helped by Morna, kept the servants busy serving tea and small Chinese cakes, while Luke related the happenings at Canton. He handed out letters from the traders, ordering the captains to take their ships to Chuenpi and deliver up the opium to Commissioner Lin's men.

There was much resentment on the part of the captains about the traders' decision, for they shared in the trading profits from each voyage. Handing over the opium without payment meant they would make nothing at all.

'This is hitting the small traders harder than the others,' grumbled one of the captains. 'What about Jardine Matheson and Lancelot Fox? I see none of their captains here.'

Luke had already noticed the absence of the blue flag with the white St Andrew's cross from the yardarms of ships in the anchorage, but it meant nothing. The well-armed Jardine Matheson ships went their own way. No doubt they had a secret anchorage where they felt more secure than here. They, like the Fox Company, had promised to hand over opium.

Luke was unaware that, while they were handing over opium in Chinese waters – and filing a claim for its retail value against the British government – Jardine Matheson were buying elsewhere. Lin's actions in China had so alarmed the opium dealers that the price of opium had dropped to a record low. Jardine Matheson were buying all they could lay their hands on, in readiness for the day when things returned to normal and they could sell at an enormous profit.

'I've heard no mention of Ezra McCulloch's company giving up anything.' The comment came from the same man who had queried Jardine Matheson's participation.

'Then you'll hear it now.' Morna's voice rang out. 'There's upwards of a thousand chests stored in my father's warehouse. You can take them on board your ship tonight and deliver them to Commissioner Lin yourself.'

Morna's declaration effectively silenced the dissenters, and Luke breathed a sigh of relief. He had anticipated great opposition to the plan by Ezra McCulloch. Without his opium, it was doubtful whether Commissioner Lin would have considered any agreement satisfactorily concluded. Ezra McCulloch's armed opium cutters were notorious for opening fire at the slightest provocation. They had earned for McCulloch a notoriety unequalled by any other trader. What he would say when he learned his daughter had given away his opium reserve was another matter!

The remainder of the business was speedily dispensed with and the meeting broke up as the captains formed loud-voiced groups, arguing for and against Killian's action. Before drinking dulled their brains too much, Luke called for silence. He had something more to say to the captains.

'Gentlemen, before this meeting breaks up I have a matter of a more personal nature to bring to your attention. Some of your sailors have been allowed ashore and a few have come to this house – my house – and made a nuisance of themselves. . . .'

Half the men and all the women in the room looked to where

Kuei stood with Morna. She was the subject of a great deal of interest in the ships of the assembled merchant fleet anchored off-shore.

'This is private property, gentlemen. I built it – and I'll protect it. There are arms in the house and my servants have been trained to use them. In the past they've used them well against Ping Chuan and his pirates. From today they'll have orders to shoot anyone else who comes here without permission and refuses to leave when told to do so. I hope I make myself clear.'

There was a stunned silence amongst the assembled captains. It was quickly replaced by an aggrieved muttering that continued for some time. Such a warning would have been accepted without question had it been given by Ezra McCulloch, James Matheson or the ageing but respected William Jardine. All these men had fought, bullied and traded their way to the respect they now enjoyed. Luke had built up a considerable reputation for himself since his arrival in the trading world of China, but he was still an untried newcomer. The captains commanded some of the toughest crews in the world and they resented his ultimatum.

Before they returned to their ships, Luke gave the captains and their ladies more cause for indignation.

Kuei was making a valiant attempt at hostessing, and her ready smile made up for her lack of English. Luke, helped by Morna, took care to see that she was not overawed by the assembled 'Fan Qui'. Gradually, the wives of the sea captains gathered in one corner of the room, their guarded conversation punctuated by knowing glances in the direction of Luke and Kuei whenever they talked together. Luke successfully avoided that corner of the room, but his generous supply of brandy loosened tongues and eventually overcame the discretion of one of the captain's wives. She accosted him as he crossed the room to open another keg.

'Mr Trewarne, all the ladies here are dying to meet you. I do declare you seem to be avoiding us!'

'Such a thought never entered my head,' lied Luke, allowing himself to be led to the corner where the women all fell silent in anticipation at his arrival.

'We've all been saying how lucky you are to have Morna McCulloch here with you,' said the woman who had brought him to the corner. 'Such a capable girl. So attractive, too.'

'Yes,' agreed Luke easily, waiting for what he knew would come next.

'But even Morna's beauty pales beside that of your Chinese hostess, Mr Trewarne. Such a lovely girl. With such a treasure in the house I can quite understand your concern about the sailors. Tell me, is she one of your servants . . . or have you bought the girl?'

Every woman in the group held her breath. Passing nearby, Morna paused, to hear Luke's reply to the blunt question. Slavery had been officially abolished in the British territories six years before, but it still existed here — for specific purposes. It was well known that in China a European employed a servant — but bought a mistress.

Luke accepted the woman's challenge. Looking her in the eyes, he smiled. 'Not only is Kuei a very lovely girl, but she has also had an interesting life. She saved my life once — and her father died as a result of the opium your husbands bring into China. She's neither my servant nor my property; but, if I have my way, she'll soon be my wife and the mistress of this house.'

During the stunned silence that followed his words, Luke turned and walked away from the captains' ladies. He had shocked and appalled them. Among the Europeans living and working in the Far East, only the Portuguese married local women — and they were despised for doing so. Englishmen had Chinese mistresses — discreetly, of course — but marriage! If such unions ever became socially acceptable, it would shake the very foundation of the European women's existence here. There was not a woman in the room who could match Kuei's beauty or natural grace.

Morna caught up with Luke outside the room. Flinging her arms about his neck, she kissed him enthusiastically.

'Luke Trewarne, I'm proud of you. Some of the old biddies in there with unmarried daughters will have nightmares about such a heresy becoming popular. Personally, I think Kuei is worth ten of any other woman you're likely to find out here. . . .'

At that moment Kuei herself came from the room behind them and looked with dismay at Luke standing with Morna in his arms.

Morna was the first to recover. Slipping away from Luke, she hugged and kissed the surprised Kuei in the same enthusiastic manner.

'Congratulations, Kuei. Luke has just told a roomful of people that he is going to marry you.'

As Kuei's dismay turned to disbelief, Luke said softly, 'You can't refuse to marry me now, Kuei. You couldn't let me lose face in the eyes of so many of my own people.'

Twenty-one

LUKE'S hopes of an early solution to the opium problem were dashed by a series of acrimonious letters that passed between Commissioner Lin and James Killian. Accusation and counter-accusation were made and refuted as opium trickled in slowly from reluctant ships' captains. March passed, and most of April. Not until the twentieth of the month was the halfway mark of the promised opium reached. Then Lin refused to honour his word and allow river traffic to resume between Macau and Canton. He claimed to have learned of a European plot to leave Canton *en masse* and so avoid giving up the remainder of their opium.

Travelling incessantly between Lin-tin, and Lan-tau, Macau and Hong Kong, Luke had no doubt at all that the Commissioner's accusation was fully justified. But he succeeded in increasing the trickle of opium reaching Chuenpi into a flow and, early in May, all the armed boats guarding the approaches to Canton were withdrawn. The siege of the Canton factories was over. The arrival of the first boat up-river from Macau, loaded with mail and supplies, was celebrated with wild enthusiasm.

The jubilation was shortlived. Four days later the Tsotang of Canton posted a notice in the factory square. It listed the names of a number of traders who would not be allowed to leave the factories until the last chest of opium had been delivered and destroyed by Imperial Commissioner Lin. The notice also drew the traders' attention to a new law. *Anyone* apprehended for trading in opium faced summary execution. On the same day, all Chinese shops in the tight little lanes leading from the factory square were closed by the Tsotang's police and the occupants moved into the suburbs close to the city wall. The shops were on the other side of the wall from the factories, but the shop-keepers were accused of illicit trading with the Fan Qui. It was Lin's evident intention to force the factory occupants into even farther isolation.

James Killian fumed at what he considered was Lin's double-dealing. He wrote a long angry letter, accusing the Emperor's

224

Commissioner of breaking every promise he had made to the traders, and of deliberately provoking a situation that might only be settled by force of arms.

The letter, sent through the Hong merchants, was returned unopened. This time the reason given was that Killian had not marked the outside of his letter with the Chinese word 'Pin', signifying that the letter came from an inferior being to one who had passed the Imperial examinations. This was the age-old rock upon which diplomatic relations between China and European countries had foundered on numerous occasions over the years. No European country was prepared to declare publicly that its representatives were in any way inferior to Chinese officials.

Once more the flow of opium into Lin's heavily guarded compound at Chuenpi showed signs of drying up. With all his efforts in danger of failure, Luke tried to see Commissioner Lin, but it proved impossible. As in previous times of crisis, the Chinese servants had been withdrawn. There was no one to deliver a message. Luke tried to get word to Shengan, but there was still only one gate open between the suburbs and the factories and it was heavily guarded by undisciplined Chinese militia. When Luke attempted to persuade them to take a message to Shengan, he was badly manhandled. Had some of the factory residents not come to his aid, he would have been seriously injured.

Fortunately, Shengan's remarkable system of intelligence carried news of the incident to the Tartar general. That same night, a small party of Shengan's soldiers entered the beleaguered factory area and Luke was taken into the city. Here he brought Shengan up to date on the faltering negotiations between the two sides, and told of Killian's bitterness at Lin's actions.

'Lin has proved himself to be a dishonourable man,' concluded Luke. 'Killian deeply regrets ordering the traders to hand their opium over to him.'

'The Superintendent of Trade had little choice in the matter,' retorted Shengan. 'Lin set a neat trap and Killian leaped into it with all the eagerness of a man who seeks glory. By coming to Canton he has put himself entirely in Commissioner Lin's hands. Lin is cunning – and I doubt if he sees anything dishonourable in his actions. He agreed the traders need not sign a bond, but he did *not* say they were exempt from the laws made by the Emperor. The conduct of a few traders has been so bad in the past that Lin feels they should give additional assurances never again to trade in opium. I am inclined to agree with his thinking. It is his actions that cause me concern. But many Chinese have already been executed for trading in opium. Their families ask why the Fan Qui go unpunished for the same crimes. They say your barbarians laugh at the Emperor. Commissioner Lin must prove that the Emperor's law is the same for all men. Tell your people to take care, my friend. Lin would enjoy taking a barbarian head to quieten those who complain.'

Shengan stood up and clapped a hand on Luke's shoulder. 'Come, I have something to show you.'

Shengan took Luke along dark and narrow alleyways to the back door of one of Canton's many great civic halls. It was guarded by two bannermen who jumped to open the door to the Tartar general. Inside, the hall was lit by a number of oil-lanterns. In their light, Luke saw thousands upon thousands of opium pipes laid out in rows along the length of the hall.

'Commissioner Lin has been a busy man since he came to Canton,' explained Shengan. 'Almost a thousand men have been beheaded. Here we see the result of the fear he has spread among the opium smokers. Under a cover of a brief amnesty, fifty thousand have given their pipes to Lin . . . rather than their heads. It means there are fifty thousand unhappy and resentful men, all waiting for Lin to make a mistake or show weakness. It is the same story in every town and village throughout China. Commissioner Lin *must* show strength and firmness, or risk a revolution. These are difficult times, but your Superintendent of Trade must master his pride for a while longer. Persuade him to do what *your* heart tells you is right. Commissioner Lin will not be here for long. He has been made Governor of the Liao Kiang. It is the second most important post in the land. He will leave for Nanking as soon as the opium is destroyed and lawful trade between our two countries is resumed. He is anxious that this should be as soon as possible . . . and so am I. I am a fighting man, and Commissioners are never in evidence when battles are being fought. Having an Emperor's man close enough to watch my every move makes me uneasy. Help Lin to leave Canton quickly and next year all will be as it was before – but without opium.'

When they left the civic hall, Shengan walked with Luke back towards the factories. The moon was high, its light illuminating the wide main streets, but the two men walked in the shadow of the raised sidewalks. Covered in by the considerable overhang of the buildings on either side they provided shelter from the heavy rains of summer. The bulk of the population was sleeping, but Canton was not a silent city. From behind shuttered shop-fronts there came the clatter and swish of ivory mah-jong pieces being shuffled on wooden table-tops, as the night was gambled away. Coolies in loose black tunics shuffled along in a wooden-soled rhythm, heavily laden buckets dangling from poles that bit into their scrawny shoulders. In doorways of deeper shadow, the homeless and destitute coughed their discomfort to an uncaring world.

One young girl sat with her back to a supporting pillar, clutching both hands to her stomach and moaning softly. Shengan stopped by the child and asked her gruffly what was wrong. The girl's reply was to offer herself to him for a sum that would do no more than provide her with a single good meal. Grunting in disapproval, Shengan dropped a coin into her eager hand.

'Take this and buy food. In the morning go to the Tartar quarter and ask for the hospital. There you will find a barbarian woman. Tell her you have been sent by Shengan. She will give you something to ease the pain in your belly.'

'Morna is here, in the city?' Luke took up Shengan's words.

'She opened a hospital a month ago and has already proved that it was long overdue. Every morning the wives and children of my soldiers line up before dawn to be treated.'

'Why did nobody tell me before? Can I see her?'

'Not tonight. She works very hard all day and earns the few hours of sleep she takes. If either of us were to disturb her, we would be torn apart by my soldiers. She does not spare herself for their children and, in return, they would die for her. She gives orders to my officers as though they are Chinese coolies. They call her "the Empress of Canton", but she has their love and respect.'

'Does she have your love and respect, too, Shengan?' Luke expressed the concern he felt about the undefined relationship between General Shengan and Morna McCulloch.

'She has my respect, my gratitude and my . . . affection, Luke Trewarne. All that an honourable man can give to an excellent nurse who is also a fine woman.'

Luke left the walled city happy in the knowledge that Morna was as safe in Canton as she would be anywhere else in the world — but he wondered what Ezra McCulloch would make of the situation.

Luke had a difficult meeting with James Killian, the day after his visit to Shengan. A number of the traders were present, and opinion was divided about the action they should now take. Killian was in favour of halting the handover of opium until Commissioner Lin removed all his petty restrictions and made it clear that European and American traders were not subject to the harsh new opium laws.

Luke pointed out that the laws had been issued by the Emperor, not by Lin. Furthermore, Killian was in no position to dictate terms. The senior traders were inclined to agree with Luke. Most of them were on Lin's list of those banned from leaving until all the opium had been given up. Lin's intransigence alarmed them. They would not feel safe until they could see the comforting sight of British sails and the open sea through the windows of their Macau homes.

When Luke told Killian of Commissioner Lin's promotion to the Liao Kiang, the Superintendent of Trade reluctantly agreed to order the ships' captains to speed up their efforts. But he did it with such bad grace that Luke prayed nothing else would happen to damage Killian's pride farther. If it did, Luke feared he would throw his reluctant restraint to the winds.

Luke left Canton that same day to round up the remaining opium ships and bring them to Chuenpi. He found most of them at the Hong Kong anchorage and learned from one of their captains the reason for their tardiness. When Luke handed him the letter from the Superintendent of Trade, the sailor shrugged his shoulders in disappointment.

'That's that, then, I reckon. Nothing I can do about a direct order from the Superintendent of Trade. All the same, it's a big disappointment that Ezra's been proved wrong.'

'Ezra McCulloch? What's he got to do with anything?'

'He told a few of us to bide our time. Said this new Commissioner was collecting the opium to sell for himself, when the trade was made legal. He assured us that if we held on to our opium until then we'd make a killing.'

'The only "killing" will be made by the Chinese,' declared Luke soberly. He told the captain of the public notice posted in the factory square, forbidding certain traders from leaving until all the opium had been handed over and destroyed.

'That the way things stood when I left,' added Luke. 'But Commissioner Lin is out to add to his reputation. If things don't go his way, he's likely to send troops to the factories and execute those he thinks are guilty of opium offences. Lin's taken a big gamble – and he has no intention of losing.'

'I'll get under way within the hour,' declared the captain. Luke received similar promises from the other captains.

Ezra McCulloch was less reasonable.

That evening, Kuei was teaching Luke a Chinese gambling game, played with numerous coloured counters on a board marked out with a complicated pattern, when the big Scots trader burst in upon them.

'I want you, Trewarne,' he roared by way of greeting. When he moved closer, Luke could smell the alcohol on his breath. Behind McCulloch, two of Luke's servants hovered in uncertain apology. Kuei ushered them from the room and gave Luke a questioning glance. He nodded for her to go with them.

Swaying before Luke, Ezra McCulloch was beside himself with rage. He waved a number of sheets of crumpled paper at Luke. 'I've been waiting for you to come back to Hong Kong, Trewarne. What d'you know of this? It's a letter from Morna. She blames me for what happened to Lo Asan and gives me some cock-and-bull story about giving away my opium and going off to work in a hospital in Canton.'

'Is your concern for your daughter . . . or for your opium, Ezra? As for Lo Asan, Morna feels as I do. There was no need for her to die. She'd tell you so herself, but she's already in Canton. She's made her decision and I've no doubt she'll abide by it. Now I'll bid you goodnight and thank you not to enter my house unannounced again.'

'Not . . . ? You bloody young pup! Less than a year ago you'd never heard of Hong Kong and couldn't have raised enough money to pitch a tent here. Now you've the nerve to tell me what to do. . . .'

'I learn fast, Ezra. I suggest you do the same. Times have changed. Commissioner Lin came from Peking with orders to destroy the opium trade – and he's doing it. At the moment he's got his boot against Killian's neck and he'll not be afraid of stamping down – hard. Killian's *ordered* all opium to be given up. That makes it official, so you can lodge any complaint with the British Government. If you've got any other ideas, keep them to yourself until the traders at Canton are beyond Lin's reach.'

'Times might have changed, laddie, but the day will never dawn when a Chinese dictates to me. I don't care whether he's a commissioner, governor . . . or the Emperor himself. I'll get Morna back, too, you'll see.'

'How? Go to Canton to fetch her? Lin would love that. There's been a price of fifteen thousand dollars on your head since *The Two Brothers* opened fire on the Chinese Navy, and Lin is looking for a European to sacrifice to his critics. Leave Morna to live her own life. She's as safe in Canton as anywhere. General Shengan is giving her his personal protection. Apart from anything else, Shengan feels he's in your debt. He's usually a forward-thinking man, but he agrees with the action you took with Lo Asan. As her uncle. . . .'

'General Shengan was related to Lo Asan? She never told me. . . .' Ezra McCulloch blinked drunkenly before suspicion penetrated the alcoholic mist. 'Yet she told you? I always thought there was more between you two than I knew about. No wonder you were so eager to help me rescue her, and so upset when she died. I should have known. . . .'

'The last time I knocked you down you were standing over Lo Asan's body, Ezra. I'll be happy to do the same now, for her memory. You've a foul mouth.'

With fists clenched, Luke took a step towards the Scots trader. Then he stopped, his hands falling to his sides.

'This is ridiculous. There are more urgent matters to concern us all at the moment. Nearly one hundred traders are trapped at Canton at the mercy of a man with less regard for life than you. On behalf of the Superintendent of Trade, I'm calling on you to stop trading in opium – at least until all the traders are released.'

'I'll stop – around Canton – but only for as long as Jardine Matheson do the same. I'll not have them stealing a march on me.'

Luke breathed a sigh of relief. Jardine Matheson had already agreed to cease trading in opium until all the threatened traders were safely out of Canton. Now there should be no reason for Commissioner Lin to place more difficulties in the path of normal trade. To Ezra, he said, 'Take this opportunity to find yourself some legitimate trade goods, Ezra. Commissioner Lin is in deadly earnest. He's broken the opium trade, once and for all.'

Ezra McCulloch looked scornfully at Luke. 'I've told you before, you're still wet behind the ears when it comes to trading, laddie. Far from putting a stop to it, this Commissioner Lin could hardly have done better if he had shares in the opium business. Not only has he overstepped the mark by holding British subjects to ransom, but he's also confiscated their property . . . and made the British Government liable for compensation to the tune of about ten million dollars! Countries have gone to war for less – and war it will be this time, you mark my words. Lin will have his edicts rammed down his throat and opium will be on sale in the open market before he's finished choking. In the meantime, the shortage he's created will raise the value of opium threefold.'

Ezra McCulloch laughed. 'If you doubt me, you come down to my beach tomorrow and meet a man who'll be boarding *The Two Brothers* for a very interesting voyage. He's a missionary – a German missionary. The Reverend Charles Moller, brother to the man you forced to leave China. You did me a favour, Trewarne. Charles Moller came to me on his brother's recommendation. He's been preaching in Siam, awaiting an opportunity to convert the heathen Chinese to Christianity. Moller speaks their language as well as you. Tomorrow we set off to the northern coasts – well away from the problem of Commissioner Lin. We'll be delivering religious tracts – and selling opium – with a percentage going to the Church, of course. Doesn't that appeal to you, Trewarne? Not that it matters, whether it does, or not. It shows that the Church has seen which way the wind is blowing and has jumped in on our side. Have you ever known Mother Church back a loser?'

Ezra was distorting the truth only a little. The Reverend Charles Moller *was* all the trader claimed him to be. He *was* going on a combined mission and trading voyage along the northern coast of China in *The Two Brothers*. Whether his mission society would have approved of it was another matter. It was certain that Charles Moller was not being taken on the ship from any religious convictions on Ezra McCulloch's part. The missionary spoke most of the Chinese dialects and would earn his share of the profits.

Moller was also zealous to the verge of insanity. To gain a

single soul for the Church, he would happily sacrifice the lives of a thousand irredeemable opium-smoking pagans.

Satisfied he had succeeded in startling Luke, Ezra McCulloch turned to leave. At the door he paused. 'You've been treading on my toes ever since you arrived, Trewarne. You'll do it once too often one day, and I'll kick you right back where you belong. In the meantime you can tell Morna, through your Chinese friends, that she's doing no one any favours by staying in Canton. I'll get her back – and all those who persuaded her to go in the first place will wish they'd never heard of the McCulloch family.'

Ezra McCulloch crashed his way from the house, leaving Luke with a great deal to think about.

Luke's latest efforts to speed up the delivery of opium were quick to bear fruit. Within a week all the opium had been delivered at Chuenpi. Commissioner Lin was overjoyed, believing he had succeeded in his mission. He was convinced that the illegal trade would never recover from such a blow. He had justified his Emperor's faith in him.

Lin realized that the barbarians were saying he intended amassing a fortune from the opium he had obtained from them. To show how wrong they were, Lin turned the destruction of the opium into a great show. Huge trenches were dug, with sluice gates leading to the open waters of the Pearl estuary. Five hundred coolies were employed to carry opium to the trenches and pound it into a pulp before mixing it with quicklime. When Lin was personally satisfied it was beyond redemption, each sluice gate was raised and the whole foul mixture washed to the sea.

Lin had thought of everything. Before the destruction commenced he had gone to the site and there, on the shore, sacrificed to the Sea Gods, explaining what he was about to do, and warning them to remove the creatures of the sea to a safer place. The Sea Gods seemed to have allowed his warning to pass unheeded. For weeks the sea was polluted for a mile offshore with the bodies of dead and dying sea life, victims of Lin's foul concoction.

On land, Lin met with more success. Around the pits he erected a series of great pavilions. To these Lin invited all the officials from Canton and the surrounding provinces. They would bear witness to the extent of the Commissioner's great victory over the Fan Qui traders. Some of the barbarians were also present, a number of Portuguese and American dignitaries eagerly accepting the invitation to travel from Macau and meet the man who was so close to the Emperor.

Luke was the only Englishman, invited as a reward for his part in the whole operation. He attended, hoping to learn that Lin was now prepared to forget the past and allow trading to resume more or less normally. When Luke was able to put the question to the all-powerful Commissioner, it provoked a characteristic reaction.

Lin first scowled at Luke angrily, then he said, 'You are asking me to make a gesture to your fellow-traders? Very well, Luke Trewarne, you shall have it.'

Lin barked out orders to the officers supervising the destruction of the opium. The orders were given in Manchu so Luke had no idea what to expect. A few minutes later two coolies were dragged before the pavilion where Luke and Lin sat and forced to kneel with downcast eyes.

Their arrival was so unexpected that all conversation in the pavilion ceased. Even the hard-working coolies in the trenches paused in their task of destruction.

Luke looked at Lin questioningly. Eyes glittering angrily, Lin said, 'These two creatures thought to deceive me. They filled their mouths with opium and hoped to carry it past my guards. Look well!'

Lin nodded his head to the officer guarding the two kneeling men. Without more ado, the officer took a great sword from one of his soldiers. Raising the weapon above his head, he brought it down with all his strength. The sword whistled through the air and moments later a decapitated body fell twitching to the ground. The second coolie let out a howl of terror and raised his head, begging Lin for mercy. But the Chinese officer was an expert swordsman. Dulled with the blood of the first victim, the sword was whirled about the officer's head and brought across in a powerful horizontal cut. The unfortunate coolie's head fell to the grass in front of the pavilion and the wide-open eyes seemed to be staring at Luke in rapidly dulling reproach.

'There you have Commissioner Lin's gesture to the traders, Luke Trewarne,' said Lin. The words were accompanied by a look which expressed all Lin's contempt for the Fan Qui. 'These men were poor ignorant peasants. Can the punishment be less for men of learning and knowledge? Go back to your traders, Luke Trewarne. They may resume their trade once more – but be sure you give them my message. They will have no second warning.'

Twenty-two

JAMES KILLIAN heard of the executions through one of the Hong merchants, and Luke made no attempt to deny the incident when Killian taxed him with it. Luke had hoped the matter might remain a secret from Killian until normal trade got under way. Then the Superintendent of Trade might have been able to swallow his pride and wait for Commissioner Lin to leave Canton for his new appointment. As it was, Killian felt obliged to take action to express in the strongest terms his disapproval of all that had happened since Lin's arrival in Canton.

Killian had swallowed so much pride in recent months it was threatening to choke him. The complete success of Commissioner Lin's campaign, coupled with this final macabre gesture, was just too much to take. The time had come to reassert his authority.

Taking everyone by surprise, Killian declared that Commissioner Lin's action, coupled with the numerous edicts he had issued, rendered normal trade between the Europeans and China impossible. Traders could not carry on their business subject daily to the unpredictable whims of the Commissioner. As the British Government would no doubt soon be taking appropriate action to recover the money due to the traders by way of compensation for their lost opium, he recommended that all Europeans should leave Canton immediately. Killian warned that anyone who stayed could expect to be taken hostage by Lin, in a bid to inhibit the government of Great Britain.

Commissioner Lin looked upon Killian's declaration as a foolish act of bravado. There was not a single British warship in Chinese waters, and it was unthinkable that one country should make war on another because a few traders had been disciplined for illegal activities.

The traders themselves were in a quandary. The way was open for them to resume trading, but their only hope of obtaining compensation for their opium losses was through the British Government. The latter consideration won the day. They prepared to evacuate Canton yet again.

As before, Luke and the Americans refused to leave. The

235

Americans shrugged off all Killian's arguments. They were in China to trade – and trade they would. If the going was too tough for the British, they were right to get out. The Americans were there to make money, not to enjoy a soft life.

Secretly, the Americans were delighted with the turn events had taken. They remembered the earlier absence of the other traders from Canton. Following Luke's example then, they had made a fortune carrying cargoes between Canton and Macau, at the same time keeping the cream of the trade for themselves.

James Killian made a strong plea for Luke to pull out of the Canton factories with the others, but commented coldly that he did not expect Luke to stand with them.

'Why should I?' demanded Luke. 'Your quarrel with Lin began with opium. I've always believed that selling opium is wrong. I always will.'

'There is more at stake here now than opium, Luke. I am making a stand for the whole concept of trading. The recognition of basic rights, in accordance with accepted international law.'

Luke found Killian's hypocrisy difficult to swallow. 'The recognition of whose rights? Ours? Certainly not those of the Chinese. They've told us time and time again that they don't want opium brought to their country. Had we bothered to listen to them, we might have found they were more ready to accept our ways of trading.'

Killian was not prepared to argue on matters of policy. Luke's reasoning came uncomfortably close to the thoughts that invaded his conscience during those quieter moments when he was his own man and not governed by ambition, politics or expediency.

'You haven't been here long enough to appreciate the need for a show of solidarity against the Chinese, Luke. No doubt your judgement has also been coloured by your acquaintance with General Shengan and the Chinese girl who shares your house on Hong Kong island. For your own good I suggest you keep such relationships in perspective. You are an Englishman. Your place is with your fellow-countrymen. There is an ugly word for men who side with enemies of their country in times of crisis.'

'Is there a word for men who allow greed and ambition to override moral right? I'm not forcing anything upon the Chinese, Mr Killian. They, in their turn, will allow me to trade in a way that satisfies me and gives me an honest profit. I'll stay at Canton for as long as it suits me, and my ships will continue to trade with the Chinese. When you come to your senses you'll be grateful to me because there will be someone here to negotiate with the Chinese for your return.'

In spite of his words, Luke watched the evacuation of the European factories with sadness and some misgivings. There had been breaks in trade before, but Luke believed it would take more than a cooling of the Superintendent of Trade's anger to bring the traders back again this time. Both sides had called the other's bluff once too often.

But, while the other traders cooled their heels in Macau, Gemmell Company had a busy time. *China Wind* had returned from England, where Luke's tea had fetched top prices, and Luke promptly turned the ship around with a cargo for India. *Black Swan* was once more ferrying goods between Canton and Macau for the frustrated British traders, and Luke travelled freely between his house on Hong Kong island and the other two trading ports. He also made the occasional night visit inside the walls of Canton to visit Shengan and Morna.

There was now an easy intimacy between Morna and the Tartar general that became more apparent to Luke with every visit. It would have sent Ezra McCulloch into a paroxysm of fury — yet Luke remained puzzled over the relationship of his two friends. He had no doubts about Morna's feelings for Shengan, and it was obvious that the Tartar general regarded Morna with much affection; but Luke never saw them so much as touch each other, and he was convinced from his unexpected visits that both Morna and Shengan slept in their own lonely quarters.

Meanwhile, James Killian sat in Macau, apparently waiting for some miracle, or at least word, from the government in England. One was as long in coming as the other.

Finally Commissioner Lin lost his patience. He was eager to take up his new post, but had been ordered by the Emperor to remain in Canton until trading resumed. In a bid to force Killian's hand, Lin issued an ultimatum to the ships in the Hong Kong anchorage: 'Resume trading — or leave Chinese territorial waters.'

The only immediate result of Lin's message was that the ships were redeployed into a tighter defensive formation. Angry at their refusal to obey him, Commissioner Lin ordered the

Portuguese Governor of Macau to expel all the remaining Britons from the tiny Portuguese enclave. He added weight to his order by manning the barrier wall between Macau and China with General Shengan's Tartar troops. Less effective, but impressive by their very numbers, he had regiments of bannermen, reinforced by local militia, set up camp on the narrow peninsula beyond the wall, clearly visible from Macau.

Alarmed at what was happening, Luke tried first to see Shengan, and then Commissioner Lin, but neither was in Canton. Lin was inspecting the garrison at the Macau barrier. Shengan was supervising the strengthening of the Bogue forts. War was in the air.

This feeling was heightened when Luke travelled down the river to Hong Kong. There were sixty ships in the anchorage now, many of them crowded with women and children, hastily evacuated from Macau. Running short of food and on the verge of panic, they awoke one morning to find their access to the food markets of Kowloon blocked by three Imperial war-junks, ordered to the harbour by Commissioner Lin.

Luke released all the rice he had in his godown on the island, but there was little else. With more than two thousand mouths to be fed on board the anchored ships, the rice lasted only nine days. Then, just when it seemed Killian must capitulate to Commissioner Lin, salvation arrived in the form of two frigates of Her Britannic Majesty's Navy.

After having an urgent discussion with the commanders of the two naval craft, Killian deployed the men-of-war to positions opposing the war-junks. Then he went ashore in a pinnace belonging to one of the frigates to buy food. Flanked by a party of armed ratings, Killian found the merchants ready enough to do business — until a company of bannermen moved in and forced their countrymen to flee.

Angry at being thwarted in his attempt to obtain food, Killian returned to the pinnace and headed for the frigates. When one of the junks set out, apparently to intercept the pinnace, Killian ordered his crew to open fire on the Chinese sailors.

It was the signal for which the frigates' commanders had been waiting. As the pinnace headed towards them, the two warships ran out their cannons and opened fire on the war-junks, pouring broadside after withering broadside into their stout-timbered sides. The fire was returned with less effect by the junks and by a shore battery set up in Kowloon itself.

The battle was inconclusive and warranted no more than a brief mention in the logbooks of the two frigates. But the devastating fire-power of the British ships so impressed the Chinese that they withdrew their war-junks and bannermen, leaving the food markets of Kowloon open to the merchantmen.

The incident was greatly magnified in the despatches rushed off to London the next day by Killian and would reverberate through the capitals of Europe. The first serious shots had been exchanged in the war between Great Britain and China.

PART TWO

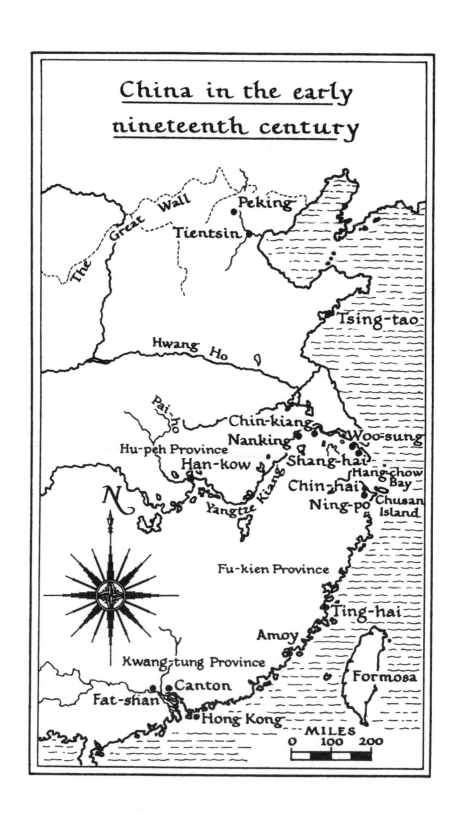

China in the early nineteenth century

The Great Wall

Peking

Tientsin

Tsing-tao

Hwang Ho

Pai-

Chin-kiang

Nanking

Woo-sung

Hu-peh Province

Han-kow

Shang-hai

Hang-chow Bay

N

Chin-hai

Ning-po

Chusan Island

Yangtze Kiang

Fu-kien Province

Ting-hai

Amoy

Kwang-tung Province

Formosa

Fat-shan

Canton

Hong Kong

MILES

0   100   200

One

IN THE YEAR 1839, news from China was slow in reaching London. A fast voyage via the Cape of Good Hope took eighty-five days. This time could be cut if a letter were sent with an intrepid messenger. Sailing to the head of the Red Sea, he could then journey overland to the Egyptian port of Alexandria and take advantage of one of the many Mediterranean routes to England.

The Honourable James Killian sent his urgent plea for help via this latter route. But by the time details of Lin's seizure of British opium reached London the 'battle' of Kowloon had already been fought.

Lord Palmerston, Great Britain's Foreign Secretary, was well aware of the justice of Lin's campaign against opium. He also knew that the opium trade was absolutely vital to the economies of both India and Great Britain. He denounced Lin's 'outrages' with an almost indecent eagerness. It was an unexpected gift with which to smother the voice of the parliamentary minority, which urged an end to the sale of opium.

Lord Palmerston appealed to the patriotism of his fellow-countrymen. Britons had been humiliated, Great Britain demeaned – and Queen Victoria herself insulted. Before the mighty roar of indignation died away, Palmerston consulted Lancelot Fox.

It was the moment for which this Chinese expert – and opium smuggler *par excellence* – had been waiting. His plans had been laid meticulously. Even as he travelled to meet Palmerston, petitions were being handed in at the Foreign Office from manufacturers as far apart as London, Manchester and Leeds. Their demands were the same. Unless the vast market of China was opened up to their goods, hundreds of businesses would fail and tens of thousands of employees be thrown out of work. Parish poor-houses would be unable to cope with the enormous burden thrust upon them and the vital economy of the Midlands would collapse.

There were other important factors for Lord Palmerston to consider. Thanks to James Killian's pledge to the Canton traders, Britain had been landed with a debt of two million pounds. It was a colossal sum – one Britain could ill afford, especially if trade with China were completely severed. The tax on tea imports alone had poured three million pounds into the British Treasury the previous year. Taken over all, the trade with China provided one-sixth of the total revenues for both Great Britain and India. But, if the already tottering government tried to evade its responsibility towards Britain's hard-pressed subjects in Canton, it would fall.

Lord Palmerston set the problem before the Cabinet and a decision was quickly reached. China was responsible for the debt. China must pay. Palmerston penned a secret letter to Killian. An expeditionary force would be sent out to teach the Chinese a salutary lesson. The force, of at least four thousand experienced soldiers, with ample naval support, would be assembled in India, but it would take a considerable time to muster. Killian should not expect it to arrive in China until mid-1840. Until then he must endure every insult hurled at him by Lin. Indeed, it might be easier to silence Palmerston's critics if Killian were surreptitiously to provoke the Chinese. It would help neither Palmerston nor the Canton traders if the idea ever took hold that Great Britain was going to war because a handful of opium smugglers had lost their wares.

The laurels of victory were already being woven for Ezra McCulloch and those men who shared his views on trading.

Luke was married to Kuei in their house on Hong Kong island, on 3 February 1840 – the first day of the Chinese New Year. The day's proceedings were marred by only one sad note. The marriage service was conducted by the Reverend Abel Snow, as his last official function in China. His mission hospital at Canton had been closed by Commissioner Lin and the medical missionary was returning home to America.

Lin had closed the factory hospital on the grounds that the number of European residents no longer warranted such an establishment. This, of course, was true, and since Lin had also forbidden sick Chinese from attending the hospital there was little work for Abel Snow.

The wedding was a quiet but happy affair. Gideon Pyke was there and so, too, was Peter Jago, now one of *Black Swan's* crew. Among the other guests, looking ill at ease in such unfamiliar surroundings, were half a dozen Hoklos, close friends of the late Soo Fang.

Through the window of the room in which Abel Snow conducted the simple ceremony, Luke could see untidy lines ·of ships in the anchorage, swinging with the tide. There were fewer of them now. Some disillusioned captains had sailed for markets plagued less by politics. Others were on their way to England, loaded with tea brought down from Canton by *Black Swan* or the American ships operating the lucrative ferry service. More recently, two British captains had ignored Killian's boycott and sailed their ships up-river, signing an innocuous declaration that they were not carrying opium.

'I pronounce you man and wife. You may kiss the bride.'

Abel Snow closed his prayer-book and everyone in the room beamed as Luke took Kuei in his arms and kissed her.

'I love you, Mrs Trewarne,' he whispered, his lips close to her ear.

Kuei hugged him to her fiercely. She was happier than she could ever remember. She had argued against the marriage from a genuine fear that it would harm Luke's business, but now it was done – and this was *her* day. She would resume her worrying tomorrow – as Kuei Trewarne.

When she and Luke took drinks to the small group of water-gipsies, they all bobbed politely, wide grins on their faces. One of the women asked Kuei a question in the Hoklo tongue and Kuei blushed, giving a short reply which could only have been a firm 'No'.

It was not until much later that night, as the last guests, Gideon Pyke and Peter Jago, were singing their way back to the jetty, that Luke remembered the Hoklo woman's question and asked Kuei what had been said.

'It was nothing,' replied Kuei. She always spoke to him in English now, determined he should not lose face among his own people because of her ignorance. 'She spoke of something my people do when a Hoklo girl marries. It is too silly !'

'Tell me about it.'

'No. We go to bed now. Not speak of foolish Hoklo custom.'

In the bedroom Luke watched Kuei undress, enjoying the same thrill at seeing her body as he had experienced when he saw it for the first time. But now the mud island on the Pearl River seemed a million miles away from the luxury of their bedroom.

Luke grabbed Kuei and pulled her down to the bed before she could slip into the nightdress bought for her by Gideon Pyke from a Japanese trader.

She put up a token struggle, then relaxed in his arms as he kissed her. 'Now tell me about this marriage custom,' he demanded gently.

'It is called "Inspect the Bride". The girl must sit in a room while all the men come to look at her, and husband says, "See. . . . She is so beautiful. Hands . . . face . . . feet. All are so lovely." Then husband and his friends leave, and the women come to see the bride. They are not so kind. They say, "Look, her arms are too thin. No good for work. These" ' — Kuei cupped her hands beneath her breasts — ' "too small. They will not feed many sons. . . ." '

Kuei's chin went up. 'I tell Hoklo women my husband will not play such games.'

'Why?'

As Luke grinned down at Kuei, they both heard the crackle of fireworks from the village on the waterfront. The villagers were saluting the New Year. 'The women could find no fault with you, Kuei. I have a perfect wife . . . and just think what I could tell the men! Never again would they be satisfied with their own wives.'

'You will tell nobody of our secrets, my Luke . . . ah!' Kuei gasped as Luke's hand moved down her body and caressed her. She pulled him to her and whispered, 'Love me, my husband . . . love me.'

The next few months were happy ones for Luke and Kuei. Luke made only an occasional voyage up-river to Canton, being happy to leave Gideon Pyke to negotiate all but the most important business with the Hong merchants. Gideon Pyke enjoyed haggling with the wily Chinese traders, but he was becoming bored. He grumbled that he was little more than the captain of a cargo-ferry, plying between Canton and Hong Kong.

When a small schooner, marooned for months at Whampoa, came up for sale, Gideon Pyke urged Luke to buy the vessel. 'It's ideal for the the river trade, Luke. Give the vessel to Peter Jago; he'll make a first-class skipper. Sure, I know he's young — but he's a damned good seaman and he knows the river. I was taking a fishing-boat from Nantucket to the Newfoundland fishing banks when I was younger than Peter. He'll do, take my word for it. He's brought *Black Swan* down-river for me on more than one occasion.'

Luke looked at Gideon Pyke thoughtfully. It would be a gamble, but he had learned to trust his American captain's judgement.

'All right, we'll buy the vessel, and Peter Jago can take command. He'll start on half the pay you were receiving when I arrived here – plus five per cent of all we make on his cargoes. Now tell me what you'll be doing while Peter Jago is getting thoroughly sick of the Pearl River mud-banks?'

Gideon Pyke grinned. 'I'll be finding new business for Gemmell Company. There's a group of islands to the south of the Philippines well worth a visit. They have a stone there that's indistinguishable from Chinese jade. . . .'

Luke put up no argument. Gideon Pyke would take *Black Swan* off more to satisfy his own sense of adventure than anything else. But the American had trading in his blood. He would come back showing a substantial profit from the voyage.

Meanwhile, in the anchorage at Hong Kong, James Killian still held fast to his principles – and followed the instructions he had received from Lord Palmerston. When things became too relaxed, the Superintendent of Trade sent the two naval frigates at his disposal on a foray up-river. On one of these brief voyages, the frigates clashed with a large fleet of Imperial war-junks, off Chuenpi. In the ensuing battle, three junks were sunk and a number of others damaged.

Lin's reply to Killian's provocation was to bombard the assembled merchant fleet from the gun positions he had set up at Kowloon. Although much ammunition was expended, there was not a single European casualty. Nevertheless, Chinese 'face' had been restored.

Further provocation by the two frigates resulted in yet another edict from Lin. This time he declared that trade with Great Britain was now ended 'for evermore'. Only Luke and the two traders whose ships had defied Killian's orders were exempted from Lin's ban. Events were moving exactly as Palmerston hoped they would – and as Lancelot Fox had planned.

There were now a number of small houses on Hong Kong island, built by traders weary of life on board the merchant ships. Strung out between the two fortified houses belonging to Luke and Ezra McCulloch, they provided a focal point for the other ship-bound families when they exercised ashore. Life on board ship was both boring and uncomfortable and, as summer approached, Luke twice invited the families of traders to visit his house and stay for a day or two. He quickly learned that such friendly gestures were not successful. In the presence of the Europeans, Kuei adopted the exaggerated self-effacement that was traditional among Chinese women. For their part, the wives of the other traders maintained a stiff-backed frigidity towards Kuei, unable to look upon a Chinese woman as anything other than a house-servant.

Both these attitudes infuriated Luke. He was determined to have Kuei accepted by the European community as Kuei Trewarne – his *wife*. He hit upon the idea of taking Kuei to the temporary church, newly built on the shore, close to his jetty, and attended each Sunday by the seaman and traders.

Kuei attracted a great deal of attention from fellow-worshippers, but most of it came from the single traders and the women-starved sailors from the merchant vessels. Kuei was a strikingly attractive girl, and the lonely men found Kuei more to their liking than the guttural interpretation of the Lord's Word provided for them by the Reverend Charles Moller. Perhaps it was for this reason that Moller preached a sizzling diatribe against 'the heathen enemies of Christian men and women who cared nothing for the brotherhood of men and put themselves beyond the mercy of human understanding'.

After the service, Moller stood outside the church shaking hands briefly with his temporary parishioners. Ignoring Kuei, he held out his hand in a formal gesture to Luke. Not until the hand was angrily brushed aside did the German missionary look into Luke's face. He wore an expression Luke had seen once before – when he had met Ping Chuan.

At best, Charles Moller was a religious zealot. At worst, he was mad.

Two

IN THE July of 1840, Luke decided to take Kuei on a trip up-river, away from the heat and tensions of Hong Kong. They travelled as far as Whampoa with Peter Jago, in the new Gemmell Company schooner, renamed *China Trader*. She was an excellent little craft, and her young captain handled her skilfully. She carried a crew of twenty-five. It was far more than was needed for shipboard tasks, but necessary to deter pirates. Ping Chuan's men had become increasingly trouble-some of late, owing to the preoccupation of Imperial war-junks with opium smugglers — and their defeats at the hands of British men-of-war.

Whampoa had always been the farthest point up-river to which the Chinese would allow Fan Qui women, but Luke intended getting Kuei to Canton. He wanted her to meet Morna McCulloch once more. Morna was the only European woman he knew who would accept Kuei without reservation. In view of Kuei's recent experiences in Hong Kong, Luke realized this was very important to her.

He had worked out a number of possible schemes for travel-ling from Whampoa to the Chinese factories without arousing the suspicions of the Chinese authorities, but it was not necessary to put any of them into operation. With the vast majority of European traders gone, Chinese supervision had be-come very lax. No officials were waiting to board *China Trader* at Whampoa, and Kuei merely hailed a fellow Hoklo woman in a nearby sampan. The woman was quite willing to convey the party the few miles to the Canton factories, and Kuei attracted no attention. Sitting in the stern of the sampan, she chatted happily to the owner in her native language, occasion-ally taking a turn at the stern oar.

It was dusk when they arrived off Canton, and Kuei was put ashore to make her way to the hospital in the Tartar quarter of the city, while Luke went on to Gemmell Company's factory.

In spite of the ease with which Kuei had been able to land, Luke worried about her until an escort of Tartar soldiers arrived to take him to the house of General Shengan. Then he knew Kuei must have reached her destination safely.

Luke found Morna and Kuei with Shengan at his quarters, and it was immediately evident that the relationship between Morna and Shengan had grown much closer since Luke's last visit. Morna anticipated many of Shengan's needs, and the softness in his voice when he spoke to her would have astounded friend and foe alike. It was this unexpected gentleness, coupled with Morna's delight at having Luke and Kuei in Canton, that helped Kuei to overcome her awe of China's greatest general. They spent a happy few hours together, exchanging news and views. Luke was not surprised to learn that the Chinese knew all about Ezra McCulloch's repeated opium venture along China's northern coast. Commissioner Lin had recently raised the reward for his capture to a staggering fifty thousand dollars.

Then, halfway through the evening, Morna insisted on taking Luke to look round her hospital, while Kuei stayed to give Shengan a Chinese viewpoint of life on Hong Kong island.

The Tartar hospital was clean and well equipped, and there was an air of well-run efficiency about it. Luke was surprised to learn that Gideon Pyke and, more recently, Peter Jago were in the habit of carrying supplies of herbs and medicines up-river for the hospital.

As Morna showed Luke around, her enthusiasm was so plain to see that it was unnecessary for him to ask whether she was happy. It showed in her every word and gesture. Her success was also beyond question. It was reflected in the respect she received from staff and patients alike as she walked through each ward.

The tour of inspection over, Morna said, 'There! Now you've seen what an enlightened general can achieve for his soldiers and their families. Shengan really cares for them, Luke. They are his family, his whole life, and they worship him.'

'He's a lucky man, Morna — especially now he has you to run his hospital for him. . . .' Luke hesitated. 'You have no regrets about making this hospital your mission in life?'

Morna smiled wryly at him. 'What you are really asking is . . . do I regret coming to Canton to be near Shengan? The answer is an emphatic "No".'

Morna took Luke's arm and squeezed it happily as they stepped from the hospital into the dark streets outside. 'Shengan is a wonderful man, Luke. Before coming here I had a vague and highly romantic idea of General Shengan, the great warrior-hero and idol of the nation. Now I know the *real* Shengan. He's a greater man than his most ardent admirer could ever imagine. He's concerned not only for his soldiers, but also for his country and its people. They all matter to him. He realizes that China can no longer pretend the world ends at her borders. He says his country must learn from us . . . the despised "Fan Qui". It's a pity the Emperor won't allow Shengan to negotiate with James Killian. He might get us all out of the mess we're in now. He . . . he's just a fine man, Luke.'

Luke knew that the time for negotiation was long past. It would be Shengan's skill as a soldier that the Emperor was going to need in the next few years. But Luke did not spoil the happy moment for Morna by putting his thoughts into words. Instead, he said, 'Then I won't waste time asking you to return with Kuei and me when we go down-river.'

'I'll stay here, Luke . . . but thank you for caring. Perhaps common sense will eventually prevail. Shengan doesn't want war. . . . I don't believe anyone does.'

Luke did not share Morna's confidence and, despite Shengan's hope for peace, it was apparent that the Tartar general was preparing for war. Luke also noticed that the guards about Shengan's house were armed with brand-new muskets. Someone – probably an American trader – was bringing weapons and ammunition to Canton to rearm the Tartar army.

Luke had intended staying at Canton for only a few days, but the fringe of an offshore typhoon kept *China Trader* secured at Whampoa for almost a week while gale-force winds lashed the Pearl River estuary. Peter Jago protested that he had sailed less seaworthy vessels in far worse weather, but Luke kept the ship at Whampoa. The young captain was comparatively inexperienced, and an increase in wind strength in the narrows of the Bogue would render the ship unmanageable.

Kuei did not mind the enforced stay. She was happy to help Morna in the Tartar hospital, while Luke worked in the Gemmell factory and planned future cargoes with the Hong merchants.

On the seventh day at Canton, as daylight was fading, Luke was working at his desk when he heard the shouts of an angry crowd outside in the square. Moments later there came the sound of glass being smashed. Striding to the window, Luke saw a mob gathered in front of the East India Company factory, in which was the unoccupied office of the Superintendent of Trade. A barrage of missiles was being hurled at the windows and, as more and more Chinese spilled into the square, a group of militiamen brought up a stout piece of timber with which they began battering down the door.

Luke was alarmed. He had no idea what had provoked the riot but, at the rate the Chinese were pouring into the square, it could very soon spread to the whole of the factory area. Luke had no intention of waiting until there was an angry mob howling outside the Gemmell Company factory.

Taking a coolie's hat from the servants' quarters at the rear of the factory, Luke pulled it well down on his head and slipped out of the building. He hoped to take advantage of the rapidly approaching darkness and the preoccupation of the Chinese to make his way to Shengan's house, inside the city. There he would learn what had happened to provoke the residents of Canton.

Unfortunately for Luke, the gate from the factories to the suburbs, unmanned in recent days, had once again been taken over by the militia – and they were leading the rioting.

When Luke saw the guard he quickly turned away, moving back into the square with the crowd. But he had been seen in the light of one of the flaming torches held high by the guard. Before he could make his escape, he was seized by a group of militiamen and carried struggling to the gate. There he was pummelled to his knees by the shafts of the militiamen's pikes.

There was no mistaking the ugly mood of his captors. As Luke shielded his head against their blows, he remembered the nightmare of his earlier captivity in Canton and feared it was about to be repeated.

Fortunately, Shengan had sent a detachment of his Tartars to bring Luke to the safety of the walled city and they arrived before he was beaten into unconsciousness. Snatching him from the protesting militia, they hurried him into Canton. On the way, it was made clear to Luke that his rescuers were acting on instructions, and had not chosen to save his life.

General Shengan was dressed in full uniform, pacing the hall of his house impatiently and snapping questions in Manchu at a dust-stained Tartar officer. When he saw Luke, Shengan barked an order and sent the officer scurrying from his presence.

'What's going on? Has there been a rebellion?' Luke asked Shengan.

'Worse.' General Shengan's face wore a strained expression. 'What I have feared for so long has happened. Your country has sent an army to China. They have attacked my men at the Chuenpi forts.'

Luke was shocked. He looked at Shengan in disbelief. The sorrow on Shengan's face told him there could be no mistake.

'This . . . this is a sad day, Shengan. . . .'

'Sad, my friend? No, for me it is a disaster. Your ships of war bombarded the forts for more than an hour, using two hundred cannons. When the walls were reduced to dust your soldiers came ashore and stormed the forts. I am told my men died magnificently, but they saved only their honour. At the end of the day the forts were in the hands of your soldiers. It is the first defeat my army has ever suffered.'

Luke seized on a point in Shengan's story, hoping to prove the whole story was only a hideous rumour. 'Ships bombarded the forts? What of the typhoon? They couldn't have made it up-river.'

'Your ships with many guns were pulled through the water by others without sails. They belched smoke and thrashed the water with paddles like giant wheels. They, too, had guns. But what has been done is done. Your soldiers came only to destroy the forts. They left as swiftly as they came. Now I must go to the forts to see for myself what happened. I want you to take me and my officers down the river in your ship. It is the fastest at Whampoa.'

The winds were still strong, but Luke knew they would make it safely to Chuenpi. 'Of course . . . but Kuei and Morna? They'll not be safe here now.'

'Morna is as safe here as she would be in her own country. She will stay. She asks that Kuei be allowed to remain with her, to help with my wounded. I will return her to you safely when the need for her has gone. There are many wounded soldiers. My officers say as many as five hundred.'

'Where is Kuei now?'

'At the hospital with the first of my men to return. She wishes to stay – if it is your will.'

Luke nodded. Kuei could be subjected to no more criticism for nursing Tartar soldiers than he would be, should it be learned he was carrying their general to the scene of the recent battle.

With a stiff breeze behind her, *China Trader* went down-river at an alarming speed. Peter Jago stood at the wheel with Luke beside him to translate the rapid instructions of the Chinese pilot. Any doubts Luke might have had about Peter Jago's ability to handle the schooner were dispelled on this voyage. The thirty-five miles around sandbanks and through narrow mud-channels were covered in seven hours.

Shengan was landed at the lower of the two shattered forts. As he looked through a telescope at the shambles that had once been the fort, Luke felt sorry for his friend. Shengan suffered, with his men, for a war he had done his best to avoid. There would be many such heartbreaks for him in the future. Of that Luke was certain.

Once clear of the Bogue, *China Trader* was hailed by a British frigate and Luke asked to state his business. Luke replied that he was a trader, coming down-river from Whampoa and bound for Hong Kong. *China Trader* was allowed to proceed, after the captain of the man-of-war explained that the river was being blockaded by Great Britain. He added that Luke had been fortunate to escape from the Chinese. Luke wondered what the officer's reaction would have been had he known that China's foremost general had been on board *China Trader* only a short while before.

The anchorage at Hong Kong was crowded with ships of all types. In addition to the regular merchantmen, Luke counted three 74-gun ships of the line, a dozen other warships of various sizes and twenty-two troopships.

More ships were still arriving and, from ship to shore, boats and sampans crewed by enterprising Hoklo and Tanka women scuttled back and forth. On the island, patches of bright reds, greens and blues showed where the various regiments of soldiers had made temporary camps.

As *China Trader* came alongside Gemmell Company's jetty, Luke could hear the shouted accents of Ireland and Scotland, and the high-pitched babble of dialects he had last heard in India.

James Killian was standing on the jetty with a number of senior army officers, full of his recently re-established importance. As the seamen on *China Trader* tossed mooring-ropes ashore to waiting Chinese, Killian hurried to the side of the ship and looked up to where Luke stood with Peter Jago.

'You can't tie your ship alongside here, Trewarne. This jetty is being used for military operations.'

Luke strode to the side of *China Trader* and glared down at Killian. 'This jetty belongs to Gemmell Company, Killian. I built it. The Army are welcome to use it if they wish — but tell me to move my ship again and I'll have it blown up.'

Allowing the Superintendent of Trade no time to reply, Luke clattered down the ladder to the master's cabin. When Peter Jago came down after him a few minutes later, Luke was looking out of the open porthole at the huge assembly of ships in the anchorage.

'It's an impressive sight right enough,' declared Peter Jago, looking over Luke's shoulder. 'It fires the blood to see so many fighting ships and men.'

Luke turned to look at him sadly. 'It will cool your blood down if you remind yourself they are only here to help sell opium.'

Three

TWO DAYS after Luke's return to Hong Kong, all the soldiers and most of the ships had gone. They had stayed only long enough to give Commissioner Lin a short sharp demonstration of their strength, close to Canton. Now, with the commanding general Sir Piers Tudely-Hext on board the flagship, they were heading northwards to flex their muscles closer to the heartland of China. It was Tudely-Hext's intention to impress the Emperor himself with the might of the nation he had offended by his unreasonable stand against opium.

He succeeded admirably. Less than a month later, the Union Jack flew over the island of Chusan, strategically placed eight hundred miles north of Hong Kong. On the island, two thousand dead Chinese soldiers bore mute witness to the over-whelming superiority of the Fan Qui army – and the word 'loot' had been added to the English language. While the soldiers filled their pockets with the valuables of the island's residents, the senior British officers marvelled at the workmanship put into the half-dozen brass cannons made by Father Verbiest two centuries before. With a miscellany of bows and arrows, pikes and a few ancient muskets, they had comprised the sole pitiful armament of the defending army.

Accompanying the victorious British army was the Reverend Charles Moller, acting as official interpreter. Tudely-Hext hoped he would also prove useful as a guide, having recently com-pleted an opium-selling voyage along that same coast with Ezra McCulloch.

Luke had not seen Ezra McCulloch for some months, and when he met him on Hong Kong island a few days later he thought the Scots trader looked ill and drawn. Usually, both men would have passed each other with little more than a grunt of acknowledgement but, acting on impulse, Luke stopped and spoke.

'I saw Morna in Canton recently. I thought you'd like to know she's well and happy.'

For a fleeting moment there was a softening of Ezra

McCulloch's naturally aggressive scowl, but it as quickly disappeared.

'Bring me news of the girl when she appreciates the company of decent civilized people, Trewarne. Until then I have no daughter.' With that, Ezra McCulloch stamped his way down the path to the shore, leaving Luke looking after him sorrowfully.

For the next few weeks, news reaching Hong Kong from the British expeditionary force was sketchy, but each scrap of information helped to build up a clearer picture. The combined might of Britain's army and navy was proving invincible in the war against Imperial China. Any coastal fort foolhardy enough to turn its ancient guns upon the invaders was blown out of existence, its surviving occupants fleeing, or finding death upon the long bayonets of Scots and Irish infantrymen.

Ships of Her Britannic Majesty's Navy maintained a blockade across the wide mouth of the Yangtze Kiang, stopping trade from reaching Shang-hai and effectively sealing off the great cities of Chin-kiang and Nanking, two hundred miles away up the wide river. Meanwhile, the bulk of the fleet and the accompanying troopships anchored at the mouth of the Pai-ho River.

Now only the defences of the city of Tientsin stood between the British troops and Peking, China's fabled capital. War was closing in upon the ruler of 'The Heavenly Kingdom'.

Kishen, the governor of Tientsin, anxious to buy time, sent out boatloads of food and gifts to the invading army. The gifts were distributed among the troops, already heavily burdened with loot from Chusan. Munching the Governor's food, they settled down in the shadow of the high-walled city. They were awaiting the results of a series of meetings arranged between James Killian, General Tudely-Hext and Governor Kishen.

Meanwhile, in Hong Kong, Luke was seriously concerned about Kuei. Two months had passed since he had left her in Canton. Vague rumours were circulating that the Tartar army in Canton had been increased and that there were now forty thousand troops stationed in the city. Unused to General Shengan's strict discipline, the newcomers were reported to have clashed violently with the Chinese bannermen and militiamen also garrisoned there. Luke was unable to confirm the rumours because the blockade of the Pearl River continued.

257

Luke's frustration was made worse by his enforced idleness. His fast clipper, *China Wind*, was lying in the anchorage with the other British ships. Luke had enough trading goods in his warehouse to make a round voyage to India worth while, but he was reluctant to commit the big ship, hoping that trade might be unexpectedly resumed with China and *China Wind* able to load the tea now waiting in the warehouses at Whampoa.

The smaller *China Trader* was also underemployed, making only an occasional voyage to Macau, to load stores for the anchored merchant fleet. Even this trade was banned by Commissioner Lin, but the Chinese mandarins in Macau were resentful of the large amount of trade already lost to them by Lin's quarrel with Killian. They were willing to defy the orders of the Imperial Commissioner — if the bribe were large enough.

Then, in early October, Gideon Pyke sailed *Black Swan* into the Hong Kong anchorage. He had heard of the arrival in China of the British expeditionary force and cut short his cruise among the lesser-known islands of the Philippines.

Having the bluff and buccaneering American with him was a great relief to Luke. During the unloading of *Black Swan*, Luke told Gideon Pyke of the events of recent months, and of his fears for Kuei. Later that evening, in the quiet of Luke's home, a plan was put forward by Gideon Pyke for rescuing Kuei. Only a man with his background would have thought of it — and Luke was certain no one else would be able to carry it through.

He and Gideon Pyke were rowed out to *China Wind* in the darkness, and the following day the ship and her owner were missing from Hong Kong. Two days later, proudly flying the Stars and Stripes of America, the fast clipper *Burma Wind* arrived at the entrance to the Bogue under full sail, the fresh paint of her name stained with tea and diluted tar.

Luck had favoured Gideon Pyke. Usually there were two British warships blockading the river: a sloop and a frigate. Today there was only the sloop. The frigate had intercepted a pirate junk the night before and after a sharp engagement had captured the vessel. The frigate was now on its way to Macau, with seventy pirates locked on board under heavy guard.

A warning shot from the sloop caused *Burma Wind* to reduce sail, but she still headed up the Pearl River. When the British sloop drew close alongside, her guns cleared for action, a loud

American voice bawled across the narrow strip of water separating the vessels, demanding to know 'What the hell is going
on?'

'Heave to!' came the shouted reply. 'Britain is at war with
China. Canton is a blockaded port.'

'Is it, be damned? Well, it may be blockaded but my ship is
going up-river. Sheer off and give me room to manoeuvre,
mister.'

'Come about, or I fire on you.'

'You do that and you'll have a fight on your hands. What's
more, you'll be committing an act of war against the United
States of America. Think about that, and ask your admiral *his*
views before you commit any act of aggression. You can tell
me what he says when I return down-river.'

The officer commanding the sloop was young and uncertain.
He had never experienced a shot fired in anger. His orders had
been to prevent merchantmen from passing up-river to Canton,
but Gideon Pyke's words raised international issues that could
not be decided by him. He wished the more senior officer commanding the frigate was here. He hesitated . . . and lost. *Burma
Wind* maintained her course, and the sloop had to veer away
before she went aground on the rocks at the entrance to the
Bogue. Gideon Pyke had succeeded in the first and most difficult part of his plan.

One week later a silent clipper slipped out of the Bogue in
the moonless hours of early morning, unseen by the sleepy
look-outs on the waiting British ships and guided by someone
who knew every rock and sandbank in the river. Kuei.

That same evening, her name gleaming white with newly
dried paint, *China Wind* sailed into the anchorage at Hong
Kong, low in the water. Kuei was home.

The appearance of Luke's ship so heavily laden aroused a
great deal of suspicion among his fellow-traders. They appealed to the Superintendent of Trade to find out what he had
been doing but, before he could take any action, *China Wind*
had sailed for the tea markets of London – and there was not
a ship in the anchorage capable of catching her.

Kuei brought home with her harrowing tales of the wounds
sustained by hundreds of Tartar soldiers in defence of the
Chuenpi forts. Most of the men had been victims of the bombardment, but there were also a few survivors of the savage

hand-to-hand battle that followed. Of the garrison of eight hundred, fewer than one hundred escaped unscathed. The final death toll was three hundred and fifty. Kuei reported that only Morna's skill had saved the lives of a great many more soldiers, establishing her even more securely in the affections of the Tartars.

Many miles away, along the coast, the victors on Chusan island were finding that the climate and environment were succeeding where the Chinese Army had failed so miserably. British and Indian soldiers began collapsing with dysentery and 'Chinese fever'. Before long, two-thirds of the whole expeditionary force was laid low.

The commanding officer was seriously alarmed. If the Chinese launched a determined counter-offensive, he doubted whether he could muster enough fighting men to repel them. When the soldiers began dying, the officer reached a decision. Sending for replacements from the army still patiently waiting before the city of Tientsin, the garrison officer evacuated his sick soldiers and sent them down the coast to Hong Kong island.

In Hong Kong, hospitals were set up on the hill above the houses. Every day sepoys toiled up the hill bearing sick men upon stretchers. All too often they returned equally laden, carrying a body for burial in the hillside cemetery where Lo Asan and Tik-wei were buried side by side.

After a few days spent watching the pitiful processions passing to and fro on the slope above the house, Kuei told Luke she wanted to help nurse the soldiers in their makeshift and comfortless hospitals.

Luke realized that Kuei was distressed at the sight of suffering on such a large scale, but her decision took him by surprise.

'You want to help nurse British soldiers? Why, Kuei? They've come here to force the Emperor to accept opium, and are killing your people. I don't understand. . . .'

'It is not soldiers who sell opium. They are paid to fight. I think they kill my people because they do not know us. I will go to help them and they will learn that not all Chinese are their enemies. Besides, you are my husband – and they are your people. It is right I should help them . . . just as Morna helps Shengan's soldiers.'

Luke doubted whether Kuei's high ideals would save the lives of any of her people. An enemy, viewed down the barrel of a musket, was a singularly anonymous being. All she would do was make them aware of the attractiveness of Chinese women. Nevertheless, Luke went to the senior army surgeon and told him of her offer.

The surgeon accepted it gratefully. With more and more sick men arriving every day, he and the ship's surgeons were hard pressed. From that day, Luke rarely saw Kuei during daylight hours. She was up with the sun and returned home in a state of exhaustion at dusk.

One evening, Kuei was later than usual and arrived home escorted by a senior army surgeon who introduced himself as Pelham Barclay.

'I'm on my way back to my sleeping-quarters on board ship,' he explained. 'I thought I'd see your wife safely home on my way. One can't be too careful. We've a mixed lot here at the moment – and they don't see many attractive women.'

Luke thanked the officer and saw the grey tiredness on his face. 'Won't you come in and have a drink? You look as though you have need of one.'

The surgeon hesitated for only a moment. 'Thank you. I'd be delighted.'

When Kuei left the room to clean up and change, the surgeon looked about the well-furnished room in some surprise. 'You have a splendid place here, Mr Trewarne. I've seen nothing like it since I left England. There's little comfort to be found on board a man-o'-war trimmed for battle.'

Luke smiled, pleased at the compliment. 'You'll have to re-peat your comments to Kuei. I had to leave her in charge of things during the building of the house. She made a home of it.'

The surgeon accepted a large brandy from Luke and, with a grateful sigh, sank back into a comfortable wide armchair. He sipped the brandy, rolling it around in his mouth, savouring the flavour for a few moments before speaking again.

'Your wife is a remarkable woman, Mr Trewarne. She's saved the lives of a great many British soldiers. If they couldn't look forward to seeing her each morning, I fear many of them would give up and die in the melancholy darkness of the night.'

'Kuei will be pleased to learn that. She thinks it is important for British soldiers to learn that the Chinese are not unlike themselves – men and women who feel happiness and sadness, joy and pain, just as they do.'

'She'll not find it difficult to convince the ordinary soldier;

he has a remarkable knack of getting on with people. But I fear she'll never convince some of the officers – or the ladies on the boats out there.' Surgeon Pelham Barclay waved a hand in the general direction of the anchorage. 'Your marriage is bitterly resented by the wives of your fellow-traders, Mr Trewarne.'

Luke shrugged. 'I could do little to please them, or their husbands, even if I wanted to, Mr Barclay. I came here little more than two years ago to take over an ailing company. Now I own the company and have three ships, one of them the fastest clipper in these parts. I've made money at a time when everyone else is losing it. What's more, I've done it peaceably – and without opium. I have the success these women feel is due to their husbands. Their opinion matters little to me. I'm a trader. I trade when and where I can, to my best advantage. As to my private life . . . when I close the door of my house the world is outside. I'm happy to have it remain there.'

'Ah! There you have the vain wish of every truly happy man, Mr Trewarne. Vain, because we are all part of this unsatisfactory world, whether we like it or not. We can't put it on the other side of a locked door and forget it exists. Rightly or wrongly, a war is being fought on behalf of the British traders – you and your colleagues. We shall win this war, Mr Trewarne, be in no doubt about that, but when the soldiers have played their part the terms of peace will be dictated by you traders. Be careful you are not on the wrong side of that locked door of yours when that time comes. . . . But I've taken up enough of your time, and that of your lovely wife.'

Pelham Barclay stood up reluctantly. 'I have a meeting on board *Terrible* with the senior naval surgeon tonight. The troops in my care are not recuperating as speedily as I would wish. The air on these Chinese islands is not as healthy as it might be. I want to send some of the men to sea for a period of convalescence.'

'I'll walk with you to the jetty and have my servants bring torches. The path is rough in parts.'

Luke and the surgeon made their way to the water's edge, preceded by two Chinese carrying pitch torches that sent aromatic flames leaping high into the night air.

As they walked, the surgeon told Luke something of Kuei's duties at the makeshift military hospital on the hill. It seemed she had learned well from Morna McCulloch, and could be trusted with any task that did not require a surgeon's skill and experience.

They were still talking when they reached the jetty. It was busy here. Men, stores and beasts were being ferried back and forth as though it were still daylight. A stentorian-voiced ship's boatswain bellowed across the anchorage for a boat to take the surgeon out to his ship as Luke watched a large cutter manoeuvre alongside the stone-walled jetty.

There were a number of army officers on board the cutter. With them were Ezra McCulloch and Charles Moller, the Chinese speaking German missionary. There were also a number of Chinese – with long hair hanging about their faces. At first, Luke thought it must be a captured band of pirates being brought to Hong Kong. Then he noticed that they were untied and chatting quite amiably with Charles Moller.

Puzzled, Luke moved closer to the edge of the jetty in an attempt to learn what was happening. He was no more than fifteen feet away when the passengers on board the cutter parted respectfully to allow one of their number to pass through. Not until he stepped ashore, into the light of a lantern held high by a sailor, did Luke recognize the man.

It was Ping Chuan, the pirate leader.

Ever since the night of the battle with Lo Asan's captors, Luke had kept the heavy revolver given to him by Ezra McCulloch tucked into his trouser-belt. Now he pulled it out and with an oath stepped forward to confront the startled pirate chief.

His action caused consternation among the men on board the cutter, and those waiting on shore to meet them.

Before Luke could cock the weapon, he was pounced upon by a colonel and a major of the Cameronian Regiment and the gun forced from his grasp. Only the hurried intervention of Surgeon Pelham Barclay prevented them from hauling Luke away and having him thrown into chains on board one of the men-of-war.

'What the devil's going on here?'

From the cutter, a small man jumped lithely ashore. He carried a sword in a scabbard at his waist and was wearing an ancient soft cap with faded silver adorning the peak. His 'uniform' was no more than a pair of linen trousers, over which he wore a short linen smock-coat.

'That is Ping Chuan . . . a pirate leader.' Luke threw off the hands of the men who held him and pointed a finger that shook with fury.

'Surgeon Barclay, do you know this man?' The soldier spoke with a clipped Irish accent that carried with it undoubted authority.

'Yes, General.' Luke looked at the small man in surprise. Anyone less like a general he could hardly have imagined, but the respect in Pelham Barclay's voice told him that this man was a very senior member of the expeditionary force. 'He is Luke Trewarne, a trader. His wife is helping to nurse the sick soldiers from Chusan.'

'I've heard of you, Trewarne.' The General's statement cut the surgeon's explanation short. 'You acted as an intermediary between James Killian and the Chinese.'

'I did.'

General Sir Piers Tudely-Hext snorted. 'Huh! Damned poor job you made of it, too, from what I hear. Let this damned Commissioner Lin wipe his feet on the Superintendent of Trade.'

'If Killian had a little more patience and a lot less pride, we would be trading normally now and your soldiers would be spending their winter leave in the Indian hills. But none of that explains away Ping Chuan.'

'There's nothing to explain. He has an army of fifty thousand armed men and he's allied himself with us. That's all.'

Luke listened to General Tudely-Hext's explanation in amazement. 'Ping Chuan is a thief, a kidnapper – and a murderer.' Over the head of the small general, Luke saw the others climbing ashore from the cutter. 'Ask Ezra McCulloch. He has cause to remember Ping Chuan.'

General Tudely-Hext raised a quizzical eyebrow at Luke. 'Has he now? It may interest you to know that it was Mr McCulloch and his interpreter, the Reverend Moller, who persuaded Ping Chuan to fight on our side. You find that surprising, Mr Trewarne?'

Luke clamped his mouth shut on a denunciation of Ezra McCulloch. 'No.'

He looked to where the trader and Ping Chuan were talking together with Charles Moller. 'No, I don't find it at all surprising. They're two of a kind. But using men like Ping Chuan to fight our wars will bring everlasting dishonour to Great Britain. The Chinese will never forgive us – and I can't blame them.'

'Since you pride yourself on knowing the Chinese so well, perhaps you'll tell me how much honour they'll accord Great Britain if I lose this war. I have a force of only four thousand men in China. At this precise moment, eighty per cent of them are suffering from dysentery, fever or cholera. This Ping Chuan has his own army. What would you do, Mr Trewarne?'

'Meet with Commissioner Lin and negotiate a peaceful solution,' Luke said tersely. Reaching out, he took his revolver from the Cameronian major and tucked it back inside his belt. 'You go ahead and play your games, General. But keep Ping Chuan away from me and mine. If I see him near my house, I'll kill him.'

As Luke strode angrily away, Charles Moller came running across the jetty to General Tudely-Hext. 'What are you thinking of, General? Ping Chuan insists that you arrest Trewarne. He tried to kill him.'

'I don't take my orders from any pirate, Mr Moller. Tell Ping Chuan that he's here to discuss the supply of arms to his men. That should not take longer than an hour. When the talks are over, Ping Chuan can put as many miles as he wishes between himself and Trewarne. I'll see him in my tent. Right away, if you please, Mr Moller; I'm a busy man.'

'Don't you think it would be wiser to arrest this Trewarne fellow, sir? Keep him in custody until Ping Chuan is well clear of the island?' The question came from a red-coated major, one of General Tudely-Hext's staff.

'Arrest him for what? Being young and becoming involved in what he sees happening about him? Or for telling the truth? You and I both know he's perfectly right. I like to feel that if I were in his shoes I'd have the courage to stand up and speak out for my convictions. Instead, we are soldiers, Major. We fight our country's wars because that's what we're paid to do. For men like us there's no such thing as right or wrong – only friend and foe. Now, bring Moller and that repulsive pirate to see me, before they cook up a religious war for us.'

four

GEMMELL COMPANY'S schooner, *China Trader*, went aground in a late typhoon, eighty miles to the west of Macau. Luke had allowed Peter Jago to take his ship on a trading jaunt to the Philippines, in company with *Black Swan*.

On the return voyage, both ships had been a mere fifty miles from Hong Kong when the typhoon struck. Forced to run before the storm, Gideon Pyke kept the two vessels within hailing distance of each other until rain moved across the broken surface of the sea in an almost solid wall of water. On the decks of their ships, the seamen crouched behind any shelter they could find, shielding their eyes against raindrops that struck with the force of pebbles. The rain lasted for two hours. When it moved on, heading out to sea, the two ships had lost all contact with each other.

Gideon Pyke was desperately concerned about the other vessel and the safety of its crew. He had persuaded Luke to give Peter Jago command of *China Trader*, and he had no doubts about Peter Jago's ability as a seaman, but he had no experience of such weather as they had just experienced. In all fairness, there were few ships' captains who had.

For eight hours Gideon Pyke fought the typhoon, battling against a sea and wind in constant conflict with each other. Occasionally, it seemed both elements called a temporary truce with each other and rounded on *Black Swan*, in a bid to send her to the bottom of the China Sea.

It was dark before the typhoon tired of playing with the ship and moved off to find fresh amusement. Gideon Pyke had no idea how far along the coast his ship had been driven, but from near at hand he could hear surf pounding against a rocky coast. He took *Black Swan* out into the open sea until the sun rose and soothed away the anger of the night.

All that day Gideon Pyke searched the inhospitable inlets and islands of Kwang-tung Province for *China Trader*. Not until evening did he find what he feared most, and he sent a boat off to check the two bodies seen lying on the beach in a small cove.

The bodies were quickly identified as crewmen from *China Trader* – but neither man had been killed by the storm. One had a hardwood pike thrust through his body; the throat of the other was slit from ear to ear. Hastily, Gideon Pyke's men leaped back into their boat and were halfway back to *Black Swan* before they heard a desperate cry for help from the steep slopes above the cove.

They returned cautiously to the shore and seven breathless seamen, half-hysterical with relief, scrambled down the cliff-side to the safety of *Black Swan*'s boat.

In the crew's mess on board *Black Swan*, they told their grim story and speculated on the fate of their fellows.

The violence of the storm that followed the torrential rain left *China Trader* dismasted and rudderless. She was no more than a drifting hulk. Between squalls, the crew could see that they were perilously close to land. They could also see a large crowd of Chinese peasants, shouting and gesticulating excitedly as they followed the progress of the stricken ship for mile after frustrating mile.

The end was inevitable. *China Trader* foundered on the rocks of the mainland in deep water, only yards from a cove that would have afforded them a safe anchorage had they been able to steer the ship.

Angry at being denied the cargo of the trading ship, the hostile crowd fell upon the first survivors to struggle ashore, beating them unmercifully and stripping them of their sodden clothing. Those sailors who offered any resistance were slain on the spot. A few of *China Trader*'s crew chose death on their ship rather than face the brutal crowd waiting on shore. Others struck out into the still-raging sea, hoping to make a landing away from the howling mob. Seven succeeded in reaching the safety of the surrounding hills.

The killing of the helpless survivors only ceased when one of the villagers remembered that on a recent visit to Canton he had read a notice offering rewards for the capture of Fan Qui men. Five seamen, stripped naked and with their hands bound behind them, were marched inland, heading for Canton, the provincial capital. Peter Jago was among them.

At each village, the hapless prisoners were spat upon and reviled. They also suffered painful indignities inflicted upon their naked bodies by peasant women possessed of a coarse sense of humour. At dusk they reached a larger village than any they had yet passed through. Here they were thrown into a stone temple with damp floors and water running down inside the walls. They were disturbed only once during that first night, when men came in and fastened heavy chains about their necks and ankles.

For the next two days and nights they remained in the village and were subjected to a form of questioning that would have been farcical had it not been accompanied by constant brutality. Their captors spoke no English and the seamen spoke only dockside Chinese. The futility of their efforts eventually got through to their captors, and once more the captured seamen were marched through the countryside, this time linked together by heavy chains.

It was now more than three days since any of the shipwrecked men had tasted food. The following morning one of them tried to snatch a handful of rice cooking over the fire of the peasants who had captured them. The seaman was beaten unmercifully by the Chinese, who screamed at him as though he had committed a murder.

Apparently as a punishment, the unfortunate seaman was made to stand in the sun in a courtyard for the whole of that day. The Chinese from the village laughed and jeered at him each time he fell to the ground, and he was hauled to his feet time and time again. Later that afternoon the other seamen were marched away, leaving their exhausted companion behind. Peter Jago pleaded for him to be allowed to accompany them, but his efforts brought him a beating with a heavy bamboo cane. The seaman was never seen again.

That night, more dead than alive, the four remaining survivors of *China Trader* were herded inside a small fort occupied by a couple of dozen Chinese bannermen. Here they were given food and each man supplied with a pair of Chinese trousers and a lightweight tunic. The clothes were many sizes too small, but they were better than nothing. That night they slept on moderately clean straw in a hut from which a dozen complaining Chinese pigs had been recently evicted.

Peter Jago hoped the change of circumstances heralded a change in the treatment so far meted out to them. It did, but the change was hardly an improvement. The following morning they were pulled from the pig-sty and crammed inside bamboo cages less than three feet square. When each man was inside, a pole was thrust through the bars and the cage hoisted on the shoulders of two coolies. There was little room inside the cage before the pole was inserted. With it in place the occupant faced a painful journey.

That evening, the survivors and their captors encountered a ragged band of militiamen and a heated argument broke out. The seamen were aware that it concerned them. What they did not know was that the militiamen were demanding that the captives be handed over to their care. None of them had been paid since taking up arms to defend Canton and they wanted to claim Lin's reward in lieu of payment.

The peasants were not impressed with the reasoning of the militiamen. They lifted their prisoners back on their shoulders but, before they could move off, the part-time soldiers let out a howl of anger and frustration. Lunging forward, they stabbed at the two nearest caged prisoners with their spears.

One seaman died instantly, his body pierced by four weapons. The second man had a miraculous escape. Dropped from the shoulders of two coolies as the militiamen attacked, one spear embedded itself in the pole that passed within inches of his head and another left a great gash across his back, laying bare his muscles. It was an ugly wound but would not prove fatal.

Determined not to allow their rewards to be lost to them in such a manner, the peasants set about the militia with their bamboo poles and sent them running. Minutes later the surviving prisoners were swung into the air on the shoulders of their captors and hurried off into the gathering gloom of night.

Sometime before midnight, the captive seamen were ferried across the Pearl River by sampan and an hour later they were tipped to the floor of the cell in Canton's gaol once occupied by Luke.

When *Black Swan* limped into the Hong Kong anchorage bearing the scars caused by the typhoon, there were many willing hands to help her berth. Another merchantman had left the Philippines on the same day as the two Gemmell Company ships but had beaten the typhoon to the anchorage. Gideon Pyke and Peter Jago had been given up for lost.

Hurrying to the jetty, Luke saw the exhausted Gideon Pyke and shook his hand warmly, congratulating him on his safe return.

'Don't give thanks yet, Luke. I lost Peter Jago and *China Trader*. I've got seven survivors on board.'

The news deeply distressed Luke. He was not so concerned about his ship. It could be replaced. Peter Jago could not. But Luke knew Gideon Pyke would be feeling the loss of the young captain far more deeply than himself.

'You couldn't skipper two boats, Gideon. You did well to bring *Black Swan* in safely. How did *China Trader* go?'

Gideon Pyke gave Luke the story told to him by *China Trader*'s survivors.

'So there are probably some of our crewmen alive in Chinese hands?'

'Yes, but there's a war on and prices on the heads of Englishmen— Where are you going?'

'To see Killian. Before a reward can be claimed Englishmen have to be handed over to the Tsotang in Canton – alive. Come on.'

Killian had been with the expeditionary force along the coast in the north until two days before. He had a great deal of paperwork to bring up to date and he frowned in annoyance when Luke burst into his office, brushing past his protesting secretary.

'Some of my crew from *China Trader* have been taken prisoner by the Chinese. I want a letter from you giving me permission to take *Black Swan* through the blockade to Canton and get them back.'

James Killian put his quill down carefully on the deskstand and gave out a deep sigh. Talking with Luke Trewarne always resulted in decisions having to be taken – usually difficult ones.

'I suggest you tell me the full story, Trewarne – and please start at the beginning.'

Luke allowed Gideon Pyke to tell the story of the storm, his search for *China Trader* and the rescue of the survivors.

Killian snorted. 'They killed some of the seamen. What makes you think the others are still alive?'

'The rewards,' retorted Luke. 'Someone must have heard about them.'

Killian frowned. 'You want me to allow you and your ship to go up-river because of some forlorn hope that the Chinese might have kept some shipwrecked sailors alive?' He shook his head doubtfully. 'I would simply be delivering more hostages to Commissioner Lin.'

'I've been held prisoner by the Chinese, Killian. I'll not rest while there's the chance that some of my men are in their hands. If you won't give me official clearance, I'll make my own way to Canton.'

Many rumours had circulated about *China Wind*'s audacious voyage up-river. Killian knew Luke was making no idle threat. He did not want to be made to look a fool again. Furthermore, if there *were* survivors in Chinese hands, and it was learned he had done nothing to help them . . . !

'The Chinese have a fleet of war-junks above the Chuenpi forts. The Navy can offer you no protection if you are attacked.'

'I'll let it be known that you've advised me against the trip and granted permission only on humanitarian grounds, Killian. I'll send someone for your letter. If the wind stays as it is now, we'll go up-river this evening. You'll have *Black Swan* ready by then, Gideon?'

Gideon Pyke was desperately weary, but he knew of the scars Luke carried beneath his shirt. He nodded. *Black Swan* would be ready for a fast voyage to Whampoa.

The commander of Her Britannic Majesty's frigate *Columbine* viewed the letter presented to him by Luke with suspicion. He examined the Superintendent of Trade's seal in great detail, convinced it must be a forgery, but eventually he had to allow them to proceed. He warned that if they were attacked by war-junks he was not prepared to put his ship at risk on their behalf.

It was with some trepidation that Luke saw the loose line of Imperial war-junks draw nearer as *Black Swan* bore down upon them. When they were still a few hundred yards distant, the Chinese sailors could be seen running to take up positions around the brass cannons that gleamed in the strong sunlight.

Then *Black Swan* was sliding easily between two of the moored junks, and some of the Chinese sailors waved to them as they passed! Luke waved back, and his shoulders sagged in relief. They were through. The way to Canton was open to them.

Black Swan anchored at Whampoa, and the delight on the faces of the Hong merchants who came out to greet them was evident. There had been little time to load the ship with trade goods, but she still carried her cargo from the Philippines and the Hong merchants were eager for anything that might give them a profit.

Leaving Gideon Pyke behind to deal with the Hongs, Luke made his way to the Canton factories in a sampan propelled by a buxom Tanka girl. She, too, was delighted to have a Fan Qui customer again. When Luke returned to Hong Kong, she told him, he was to find 'Bungy Cooper', one of *her* seamen, and tell him she had his clothes waiting, all beautifully washed.

The Tanka girls at Whampoa did washing, and performed other personal services for sailors who took their fancy. It seemed that 'Bungy Cooper' had been taken by surprise by the untimely exodus of the British merchant fleet. Luke promised solemnly to pass on the message.

Only two men remained in the Canton factories; both were Americans. They were greedy for news of the outside world and questioned Luke closely on the progress of Britain's war with China. They were happy to provide a servant to take a message to General Shengan.

As soon as he was able, Luke excused himself from the news-starved Americans and made his way to Gemmell Company's factory to await a reply from Shengan.

It came soon after dark. The door opened and, to Luke's surprise, Morna entered the room. Flinging her arms about him she greeted him with delighted warmth. When he broke free, Luke held her at arm's length and looked at her. There had been times recently when he had worried about her. It was quite apparent he had worried unnecessarily. Morna was fit and well — and radiantly happy.

'What are you doing here?' Luke said at last. 'Does Shengan allow you to roam the streets of Canton alone now?'

Morna crossed to the window and pulled back the curtain an inch or two. Some of the animation left her face. 'Twenty of Shengan's best men are out there in the shadows. They brought me here in a closed sedan.'

'Why you? Why didn't Shengan come here himself?'

'He's having to be careful. He and Lin have fallen out. Shengan told him he thought his actions since he came here as Commissioner have proved disastrous for China. In return, Lin accused Shengan of treachery — of having the interests of the Fan Qui at heart. Each is waiting for the other to make a wrong move. Shengan is right, of course. Lin's period of office has been catastrophic. Quite apart from his mishandling of the opium problem, he has instigated a reign of terror here in Canton. There's unrest everywhere. Now Lin wants to sink all the shipping in the Hong Kong anchorage and give orders for all Fan Qui prisoners to be executed. Shengan argues that, while he will do all he can to strengthen China's defences, Lin must parley with Killian. Because of their differences, Shengan sent me to see you instead of coming himself. You must leave immediately, Luke. If you don't, Shengan fears Lin will have you arrested and concoct a story that you and Shengan are plotting against the Emperor.'

'I can't leave yet, Morna.' Luke told her of the loss of *China Trader* and the capture of some of her crew. 'I won't go until I know what's happened to them. But what of you? If things are so bad, why don't you leave?'

'They need me at the hospital, Luke. Shengan needs me, too. He hasn't said so, but I *know* he does. There's no one else here he can talk to who understands what he's trying to do for his people. I've even heard it said that he's lost his stomach for fighting. It isn't true, Luke. I sometimes wish it were. I dread the thought of Shengan going into battle against British soldiers. China and its damned unworldly Emperor still mean everything to him, but he realizes how close to disaster they are. He's determined to prop them up somehow.'

Morna ran out of words. She half raised her arms, then dropped them again in a gesture of helplessness.

'I'm sorry, Morna. I don't want to add to Shengan's problems, but if my men are still alive they'll have been brought to Canton. I can't abandon them to Lin and the Tsotang.'

'No . . . of course not. I'll tell Shengan why you are here. He'll be able to learn something. Until you hear from him – or me – stay inside your factory.'

Taking Luke's hand, she looked down at it for a few moments before speaking. 'I wish things were different, Luke. That there was more understanding between our people and the Chinese. . . . No war, and no Commissioner Lin. I could be so happy here. I have all I want within the walls of Canton. . . .'

'I understand, Morna. I understand.' Luke squeezed her hand affectionately. Morna had no one in Canton with whom she could share her thoughts about Shengan. But there was nothing he could give to Morna McCulloch but sympathy. He himself had chosen a difficult path in life when he married Kuei. By coming to Canton in order to be near Shengan, Morna had left the path altogether.

As though deliberately scorning the cover of darkness, Shengan rode into the factory square at noon the following day, at the head of a hundred well-armed Tartar warriors. His manner was more brusque than it had ever been with Luke and was evidence of his displeasure.

'This is foolishness. You come here among my people as though these were normal times, yet at this very moment your ships, laden with troops, are gathering in the Pearl River estuary. The Tsotang could justify your arrest as a spy, sent here to search out the weakness of our defences.'

'He could,' agreed Luke. 'But you and I would know the accusation contained no truth. I'm here to learn the fate of my men, Shengan. That's all. The captain of my ship was a young man who came with me and McCulloch to rescue Lo Asan from Ping Chuan's pirates.'

As Luke had intended, by giving this information to Shengan he had put the Tartar general in Peter Jago's debt. 'It was Peter Jago who prevented Ezra McCulloch from shooting me when I struck him.'

'I see. Then I will see what I can do to help him – if he is still alive. The Fan Qui prisoners are held in the prison. I will order their release and have them brought here. You must be ready to leave immediately, or suffer the anger of the people.'

'*You* will order their release? What about Lin . . . ? You'll be playing right into his hands.'

Shengan allowed a fleeting expression of self-satisfaction to cross his face. 'Lin Tse-hsu will push no more thorns into barbarian flesh. He has been stripped of his honours and will soon return to Peking in disgrace.'

'But . . . but this could bring about the end of the war!' Luke lacked Shengan's self-control and could not hide his elation.

'I fear not, my friend. One cannot turn about the ship that is being driven by the typhoon. However, with Lin gone, men of honour and goodwill might now discuss a just solution, without ambition barring the way. But Lin will not be leaving Canton until a successor has been appointed. In the meantime he has many friends and still wields much power. I expect him to revenge himself on many of his enemies before he leaves. So go quickly when you have your men. Do not let Lin attack me through you.'

'What about Morna? If Lin should take her....'

'She will not be harmed. Lin is in disgrace now, but I doubt if ambition is dead within him. He is a clever man; one day he can expect to be restored to favour. Such a thing will never happen if he attempts to harm Morna . . . for I will kill him.'

Five

LUKE had not known how many of the crew of *China Trader* had been carried off by the Chinese peasants, but when only *two* litters arrived in the factory square, borne on the shoulders of Chinese coolies, he was appalled. Accompanied by Morna, they were escorted by a full company of armed Tartar soldiers who knocked inquisitive Chinese from their path on the way to Gemmell Company's factory.

Luke ran out to speak to his men, but Morna intercepted him. 'Luke . . . before you speak to them, I must tell you. . . . They've been brutally tortured.' Experienced though she was in witnessing human suffering, the strain of tending the two men showed on her face as she spoke.

'How bad are they?'

'One . . . he's had his tongue cut out. The other, your captain, will never walk again. They've crushed his ankle bones. . . .'

Morna shuddered. 'I went with Shengan and his men to get them, Luke. They had Peter Jago's ankles in huge vices, weighted with great blocks of stone. He was screaming. . . . There were other men there being tortured. . . . Chinese men. The appalling thing is that the Tsotang genuinely believes he is doing nothing wrong. He is merely exercising his right to "question" prisoners.'

'I have first-hand knowledge of the Tsotang's methods of questioning,' Luke reminded her grimly. 'It's as well I didn't go with Shengan to the prison.'

'You must get them down-river to Whampoa – now, Luke.'

'Yes.'

Luke gave orders to the coolies and they hurried to the waterfront. Looking along the line of touting sampans, Luke saw the Tanka girl who had brought him up-river. She had told him she would await his return, but she cast frightened eyes on the grim-visaged warriors of Shengan's army as the two tortured men were placed in her sampan.

'Will you come down-river with us . . . at least as far as Whampoa?' Luke asked Morna.

'No, Luke. I think Shengan is going to order Lin to remain in his house until it's time for him to return to Peking. Shengan expects trouble. He wants me where his men can guard me. But take this.' She thrust a large stone bottle into his hands. 'It's a painkiller . . . made from opium, so be careful how you use it. Goodbye, Luke.'

Luke kissed her quickly and jumped into the sampan. The Tanka girl had pushed off from the river-bank when Luke remembered something he had meant to tell Shengan. In English, he called, 'Morna . . . tell Shengan that Ping Chuan is fighting on the side of the British. He claims to have an army of fifty thousand men. Tell Shengan to take care – but to kill Ping Chuan if he can.'

'He knows. Ping Chuan and his "army" have landed some miles up the coast. He is calling himself, "the new Emperor", and his progress can be measured by the screams of the women his men are raping.'

By now the sampan had moved into midstream to catch the current. The gap between sampan and shore was rapidly becoming too wide for even a shouted conversation.

'Goodbye, Luke. . . . Take care.'

'Goodbye.'

Luke turned and looked down at the terror-stricken reproach in the eyes of the tongueless man. Seconds later, the seaman began choking on his own blood. Luke held him up until the coughing subsided, then gave him a hefty dose of the opium mixture before laying him down on his side to sleep.

Then Luke went to where Peter Jago lay, his legs and feet immobilized by bamboo splints and bandages that encased his feet and the whole of his legs below the knees. But it was at the young captain's face that Luke looked and controlled his anger with difficulty. Only one eye was open and the whole of his face was bruised and swollen.

'Hello, Peter. Are you in pain? I have something here for you to take. . . .'

'I'm sorry I lost your ship for you, Mr Trewarne. I did my best.' Peter Jago's voice left his throat as a hoarse and painful whisper.

'The ship doesn't matter a damn. You're all I'm concerned with.' Luke took Peter Jago's hand and forced a smile. 'Gideon's waiting for us with Black Swan at Whampoa. He'll have you back in Hong Kong in no time at all. We've some good surgeons there now. They'll soon have you back on your feet.'

Peter Jago knew that no surgeon in the world would be able

to make him walk again, but his face lit up in an expression of joy when Luke mentioned Gideon Pyke.

'*Black Swan* survived the typhoon? I wish I were half the seaman Gideon is. . . .'

Luke patted his hand. 'You'll do, Peter. You'll do.'

'How many of my men were saved?'

'Gideon picked up seven from the coast where you went aground. There may be more.'

Distressed, Peter Jago shook his head. 'There'll be no more. The rest died with the ship. Five of us were taken captive. One was killed by militiamen. Another died under torture in Canton prison. . . .' He turned his head away so Luke would not see the tears that streamed down his face. 'Nine men. . . . Nine from a crew of twenty-five.'

Luke gave Peter Jago some of Morna's medicine and stayed with him until he dropped into a deep sleep. Then he sat hunched in the blunt bow of the sampan, gazing unseeingly at the terraced hills along the banks of the Pearl River.

Peter Jago dropped into a coma a couple of hours before *Black Swan* cleared the Bogue narrows, and died as he was being transferred to the patrolling man-of-war. After examining his body, the ship's surgeon expressed an opinion that Peter Jago had died from internal injuries, caused by a severe beating.

When Luke reached home, Kuei saw the emotional strain he was under showing in every line in his face. She did her best to drive away thoughts of the Tsotang's inhumanity, giving him all the love that was in her. It took a long time. Not until he had poured out the bitterness and anguish that filled him did the hatred for Tsotang Teng begin to fade. When his mind was free of the thoughts that had tortured him, Kuei knew how to bring his body to hers and she loved him with a completeness that drove away every last vestige of his grief and anger.

Afterwards, Luke dropped into an exhausted sleep, unaware of the silent tears Kuei shed over him as her fingers traced the scars that ridged his back. She knew why Luke had been willing to put his own life at risk to rescue his men from the hell that was the Tsotang's gaol, and why he had suffered such agony of mind at their fate.

The story of the capture and torture of the crew of *China Trader* swept swiftly through the small community in Hong Kong, losing nothing with each telling. James Killian came to the house soon after Luke woke, to learn the truth of the incident.

'So far all I've heard is rumour,' he complained to Luke. 'No doubt it has been wildly exaggerated . . . although if there is only a fragment of truth in what is being said there should be a report made to Her Majesty's Government. It's time London knew how these heathens behave towards distressed men. Perhaps then they will begin to understand why it's impossible to negotiate with them and treat them as normal.'

Luke bit back the retort that came naturally to him. More patience on the part of the Superintendent of Trade might have borne fruit and prevented the tragedy that had followed the wrecking of *China Trader*. Instead, he repeated Peter Jago's story, and told James Killian of the condition of the two men when they were released from Canton gaol.

When Luke's narrative came to an end, Killian muttered angrily, 'I'll make Lin answer for this when we take Canton.'

Luke looked at Killian in surprise. Shengan had said there were troop-transports outside the Bogue, but on the way down-river Luke had seen only the blockading men-of-war. He wondered whether the troops were making their way overland to Canton, but immediately dismissed the idea. The British army would be overwhelmed by the sheer number of Chinese soldiers and militia, without the backing of the Navy's guns. But there could be no doubt that some move against the provincial capital was being planned. Luke hoped he was not too late to put a stop to it.

'Lin has already paid for his mistakes. While I was at Canton, news came through that Lin has been stripped of all his honours and ordered to return to Peking. It seems the Emperor blames him for forcing China into war with Britain.'

James Killian was stunned by Luke's news. 'Lin has been recalled?'

Luke nodded. 'General Shengan has placed him under open arrest, to keep him out of mischief until he actually leaves the city.'

James Killian lapsed into a long silence as he assimilated the importance of Luke's news. The time was fast approaching when the Foreign Ministry in London would begin to analyze the course of events in China. As Her Britannic Majesty's Superintendent of Trade in China, he would have to accept the blame for many disastrous mistakes that had been made. He might even be held responsible for the outbreak of hostilities, especially if the army scored no spectacular victory in battle. In politics, it was considered expedient to settle the blame for unpopular actions on the shoulders of a minor official.

Before the beginning of the war, Killian had entertained hopes of a knighthood for his services in China. Had this hope been fulfilled, he intended returning to Great Britain to take up a political career and, ultimately, bring a new peerage into the Killian family. Now, thanks to Commissioner Lin, he would be lucky if he escaped being made the scapegoat for this whole sorry business.

At least, that had been the situation before Luke gave Killian the news of Lin's disgrace. With Lin gone, a glimmer of hope had returned. Killian might have the opportunity to retrieve something from the ruins of the policy he had pursued for so long.

Watching the Superintendent of Trade, Luke guessed what was going through his mind and was quick to seize the opportunity it offered.

'I doubt if there will ever be a better time to sue for peace. Few Chinese officials want war. The destruction of the Chuenpi forts taught them a short sharp lesson. Now they know our troops are capable of beating their army. It would have been difficult for them to accept peace without losing face, before. Now Lin is in disgrace, and they'll be quite happy to blame him for everything that has happened and open negotiations again.'

'It's a pity they didn't dismiss Lin before things went this far,' commented Killian airily. 'But I'll not let it be said I allowed personal opinion to stand in the way of a just settlement. I must go and discuss this latest development with General Sir Tudely-Hext.'

James Killian hurried away, and two hours later he was on board a naval frigate *en route* to the headquarters of General Sir Piers Tudely-Hext on Chusan island.

Before he returned, the tongueless survivor from *China Trader* was dead, a victim of the cholera epidemic that swept through the army hospital in Hong Kong.

Six

CANTON was an unhappy and uneasy city. The people had been unsettled by the speed of Commissioner Lin's downfall. They also resented the ever-increasing Tartar garrison stationed in their city, taxing the city's resources and draining their food stocks.

For many years Canton had remained the only port in China open for trade with the Fan Qui merchants. Its populace had suffered all the pressures of an ancient but stagnant civilization in constant conflict with brash and abrasive barbarians. In the early days of trading, the Fan Qui had tried to understand the Chinese, convinced they must be able to learn something from such a long-established empire. That had been many years before, when the barbarians still respected Chinese customs and traditions. More recently, the Fan Qui had sent arrogant men like James Killian to conduct business with them. The people of Canton had watched opium being ferried ashore in lonely creeks close to the city, and seen the curl of barbarian lips as mandarins sold their loyalty to the Emperor for a handful of silver.

All such indignities had vanished with the arrival of Commissioner Lin. The gross blunt envoy from Peking had re-established China's supremacy over the Fan Qui traders. He had backed them into their tiny corner of the waterfront, seized their opium, and degraded them in a hundred ways that gladdened the hearts of the Cantonese.

Now Lin was in disgrace for these actions, and Tartar troops — foreign-speaking soldiers from the wild country, thousands of miles to the north — filled the city. The Tartar troops had taken over every barrack building, turning out Chinese bannermen and the militia, forcing them out to wander the countryside in unruly disgruntled bands, finding food and board as best they could.

It was almost two hundred years since the Chinese Ming dynasty had been overthrown by the Manchus, backed by their Tartar warriors, but Chinese memories were long. The domination of the Army and the vast Civil Service by the Manchus and the Tartars was bitterly resented. Every few years, some corner of the vast empire of China witnessed a rebellion against the Manchu overlords – and Canton was ripe for just such an uprising.

Each new day brought a clash between the Chinese militia, who supported Lin, and the Tartar soldiers. When the Tartars, acting upon General Shengan's instructions, remained on the defensive, the Chinese dissidents grew bolder and the casualties in Morna's hospital increased daily.

Then Emperor Tao Kuang performed an amazing about-face. After condemning the war and supporting an unofficial truce that had been maintained for some weeks, he issued a fiery edict, calling on his people to reject the peaceful overtures of the Fan Qui. His militiamen were urged to fall upon the enemies of the Heavenly Kingdom and throw them into the sea.

Shengan came to the hospital and gave Morna the news as she busied herself at a clinic she held for the children of the Tartar soldiers.

'Does this mean Lin will be reinstated?' Morna carefully smeared an ointment beneath the inflamed lids of a young boy's eyes and absent-mindedly gave him a gentle smack on the bottom as she sent him back to his mother.

'No, Lin's failure is too great. He led the Emperor to believe that by confiscating the traders' opium he would bring them to their knees. Instead, he brought war. He will not be forgiven for such a serious error of judgement. But we must expect the soldiers of your people to attack us again soon. I believe they will try to take Canton. I have sent troops to the barrier at Macau. I have also had the river beyond Whampoa blocked with stones and sunken junks, but it will not hold back your army for long. If an attack comes, I will send soldiers to take you to safety. . . .'

'You will do no such thing!' Morna now spoke fluent Manchu, and the women and children in the room looked in awe at this Fan Qui woman who spoke to General Shengan as though she were his equal. Morna shooed them all from the room before resuming her argument.

'I'm running a hospital here. I have just as much of a responsibility to my patients as you have to me. Send your men off to fight this idiotic war, if you must. I will be here to treat their wounds when they come back – but they will receive only treatment . . . not sympathy. When you were fighting to prevent the sale of opium to your people you were fighting a just war.

Resuming the fight when there is a real chance of peace is not.'

Shengan bowed to her, a glint of amusement in his eyes. 'I value your opinion beyond measure. I wish it were possible for my Emperor to benefit from your advice. I know he is deeply satisfied at the valuable work you are doing here, but he has not sent a request for your advice on how to rule his country.'

Morna thought Shengan was poking fun at her. Then she saw his expression and knew he was not.

'The Emperor knows I'm working here, in Canton? You told him?'

'Of course. Would you rather he had learned of it from the late Commissioner Lin? You now have the Imperial permission to live and work in Canton – and are therefore afforded the protection of the Emperor and his army. You will leave Canton if I believe it to be necessary.'

Shengan left the hospital while Morna was still speechless with indignation. He knew from experience that such a condition would not last long.

Shengan's Tartar troops reached the Macau barrier too late. The British forces had already reduced the defences to rubble. It had been a repetition of the attack on the Chuenpi forts. The naval men-of-war blasted the walls out of existence with their cannon; then the infantry moved in and slaughtered the dazed defenders with musket and bayonet.

Hurrying to the barrier, Shengan surveyed the scene of carnage with a feeling of deep sorrow. The defenders had not been Tartars, but they had not fled from the attacking army. He had his men seek out the survivors and convey them to the hospital in Canton.

On the night of his return, Morna went to Shengan's house and found him in a melancholy mood. It did not take her long to draw the reason from him. Looking out of a window at the busy street scene, illuminated by torches and lights from many houses, Shengan said, 'It sometimes worries me that I am responsible for the future of all these people . . . for you . . . and for my own men, too. Most of all I am concerned for my men. Each morning I wake and wonder whether this is to be the day when I must send them out to die. They are brave men who have no fear of death and they fight as well as any soldiers in the world . . . but with what? I have received a thousand muskets – but have none of the new ammunition to use with them. Meanwhile, many of your troops now have guns that can shoot twice as far as the best musket we have ever seen. The American Fan Qui are helping us to make cannon at Fat-shan, but they are too heavy, suitable only for use in forts or very large ships. Your army has guns that can be brought ashore and carried up hills. If I could choose my battlefields, I might still win; but it is your people who choose both the time and the place, and to fight a battle within range of the cannons of your ships is madness.'

Morna was distressed to see Shengan in such a mood. 'Perhaps there will be no more battles.'

'There will be *many* battles, some fought on the Pearl River, others elsewhere. I believe that the war will be lost or won on the Yangtze Kiang, the river that flows to the heart of China, but I am convinced Canton will be attacked first.'

Morna was glad that Shengan was at the window with his back to her. It made it easier for her to say what was in her heart.

'Wherever the war is being fought, I want to be with you, Shengan.'

He turned to face her instantly. 'Such a thing is out of the question.'

'No, it isn't. If the battles take place far from here, you won't be able to send your wounded back to a hospital – and they will need to be treated at the earliest opportunity.'

'Not even a Tartar woman would be allowed at a place of battle. . . .'

'I don't ask to go on a battlefield; it would sicken me. I just want to be wherever you are.'

'Morna, I am a soldier. My Emperor's servant. My life is his. I can offer you nothing. . . .'

'You have already given me much, Shengan. Fulfilment in my work . . . yes, and love. I ask nothing more. Only to be able to keep what I already have.'

'It is impossible. I am a Tartar general. What *I* wish does not matter. . . .'

His eyes told Morna a different story, and the next moment she was in his arms, clinging to him as he murmured words to her that no other woman had heard from his lips. Suddenly, there was a hammering at the door and the moment was gone. Dropping his arms from her, Shengan strode to his huge desk. 'Come in.'

The door opened and Shengan's aide entered, hurriedly

284

fastening his tunic at the neck. 'Commissioner Kishen has arrived in Canton and wishes to see you. He is here now.'

Shengan hid his surprise. Kishen had wasted no time in reaching Canton. Word had been received only that day that he had been appointed to take the place of Commissioner Lin. 'Give me a few moments before you show him in.'

At one side of the office was an ante-room, leading to a corridor. Pointing to the door, Shengan said, 'Through there. Wait until Kishen is in the room with me before you leave.'

Morna kissed Shengan quickly before hurrying from his office. Once in the ante-room, she heard Kishen enter the room behind her and a shrill voice said, 'General Shengan, my good friend! I trust I find you well?'

'I am in the best of health – but why has no one told me of your arrival?'

'I entered Canton only minutes ago and came immediately to your house. I wanted to speak to you before meeting the lesser mandarins of the city and making my first official statement. It will be for the ears of the Fan Qui invaders, my friend. Doubtless they have as many paid spies here as anywhere else. I intend beginning negotiations for a treaty of peace immediately. Naturally, such a treaty will take a very long time to complete. The soldiers of the Fan Qui are sick. If our negotiations last long enough, perhaps they will tire of our land and return home.'

'The Fan Qui have little patience, Commissioner Kishen, but they are stubborn and do not give up easily.'

'I see. . . .' Commissioner Kishen gave a long-drawn-out effeminate sigh. 'Nevertheless, every day that passes sees an increase in the strength of our army. I fear the details of my treaty will keep everyone very busy for many, many months. . . .'

The door at the far end of the ante-room clicked open quietly, and General Shengan's aide whispered that it was safe for Morna to leave.

The first meeting between Kishen and the British took place in Canton – with Luke acting as interpreter. His presence had been especially requested by General Sir Piers Tudely-Hext, commander-in-chief of the British expeditionary force. When Luke protested that he had a business to run, the General curtly told him that an opportunity had arisen to hold peace talks with Commissioner Kishen in Canton. The only interpreters were with the forces, spread out along the northern coast. It would take time to find one of them and bring him back. Meanwhile, there would be unavoidable skirmishes and men would die – Chinese and British. He asked Luke to choose which he thought was more important – Commerce or men's lives.

Luke went up-river with General Tudely-Hext and James Killian.

The peace negotiations dragged on for two weary months, as 1840 passed into history and the page was opened on 1841.

Killian led the British delegation and, towards the end of January, his patience finally ran out. After consultations with Luke and General Tudely-Hext, he announced at the next meeting that he would endure no more prevaricating on the part of the Imperial Commissioner. He declared that, unless some form of agreement were reached within three days, General Tudely-Hext's troops would mount an offensive.

Commissioner Kishen expressed shocked dismay, but secretly he was not surprised at Killian's decision. Indeed, he had anticipated such a move many days before. He was already impressed by the forbearance of the barbarian negotiators. Unfortunately, things had not gone well for Shengan's plans. The British had maintained their blockade, and Shengan had not been able to get more muskets and ammunition for his troops. There had been a setback, too, in the plans to cast cannon at Fat-shan. A huge explosion had wrecked the plant, killing many men. Among them were two American advisers.

Clearly, the time had come to bend a little before the strength of the Fan Qui. To the amazement of Killian, agreement was swiftly reached on the terms of a provisional treaty. The treaty gave the British Government a six-million-dollar indemnity, promised official intercourse between the two countries, on equal terms, and declared that trade would resume within ten days. But by far the most important long-term clause was one that ceded the island of Hong Kong to the British Crown!

To Kishen, the provisional document was simply one more move in the devious game he was playing. No signatures had been placed on the documents drawn up by Luke, and the Imperial assent had not been given to the treaty. As a legal and binding arrangement, he considered it worthless.

Luke was of the same opinion. It had all been too easy. Kishen was too experienced an official to give away so much after the weeks of protracted bargaining. He told Killian so, but the Superintendent of Trade was so elated he was already celebrating his great diplomatic victory. The war was over and trade would soon return to normal. He had been unable to gain approval for the opium trade, but neither had it been specifically banned – and Great Britain now owned an island off the Chinese coast, an important toehold for a trading assault on the mainland itself.

The jubilant Superintendent of Trade sat down and wrote a long letter to Lord Palmerston, sending it off via the speediest route to London.

When the letter was on its way, James Killian thought his future career was once more secure. He was doomed to suffer bitter disappointment.

When the letter reached the Foreign Office, Lord Palmerston was enraged at what he considered to be a paltry settlement. With a British army at Killian's disposal, he felt the Superintendent of Trade should have concluded a treaty that would have made Great Britain the envy of the trading world. Instead, he had accepted a few 'concessions', together with an unknown island that no one, not even the Chinese, wanted.

His Imperial Majesty, Emperor Tao Kuang, was equally angry with *his* country's negotiator. He would concede nothing to the barbarians. Such proposals as were embodied in the 'treaty' should never have been committed to paper, no matter how worthless the document.

But in January of that fateful year the Honourable James Killian knew nothing of such criticisms. In spite of Luke's warning that such a move was premature, he issued a proclamation officially taking possession of Hong Kong in the name of Her Majesty Queen Victoria, Sovereign of the United Kingdom and Great Britain and Ireland. Furthermore, pending Her Majesty's pleasure, Killian appointed himself Governor of the island.

The next meeting with Kishen was fixed for mid-February, and Luke returned to Kuei until then.

During this period, James Killian shuttled busily between Macau, Hong Kong and the Canton factories, trying to gain early diplomatic recognition for his position as Governor of Hong Kong and persuading the traders and their families to take up residence on the island. To calm the anxieties of those who were not convinced of the permanency of such a move, Killian began the construction of an impressive army barracks on the hillside beyond the houses, and had plans drawn up for the building of an official Governor's residence.

On the day appointed for the next session of the peace talks, Luke was with Killian in Canton. The meeting-place was the old East India Company factory. It got off to a bad start – and became progressively worse. First of all, Commissioner Kishen kept the British delegation waiting for him for two hours, always an ominous sign in negotiations with the Chinese.

When he did arrive, Kishen made only minimal apologies for his unpunctuality and spent an hour avoiding all questions put to him about the formal signing of the peace treaty. 'The time is not yet right,' he kept repeating ambiguously; and 'There are still many things to be decided'.

When Killian protested that the terms of the treaty had already been agreed, and were only waiting ratification, Kishen snapped that the matter was too important to be hurried – or to be taken for granted. He suggested that a period of three months should elapse, in order that his Emperor could carefully study all the implications of the proposed treaty.

Killian was both confused and dismayed by Kishen's attitude. It was in direct contrast to the previous meeting. Then the Commissioner had gone out of his way to be polite and helpful. He had cause to be seriously worried. He had taken so much for granted. He turned to Luke and asked him plaintively what was happening.

'I don't think Kishen has ever had any intention of signing a peace treaty,' said Luke bluntly. 'I said so after the last meeting. He's buying time. I don't know his reasons – and, if I did, I don't think you'd like them very much.'

Killian was in a desperate quandary. He had informed the Foreign Office of the treaty as though the signing of it were no more than a formality. He had also officially annexed Hong Kong in the Queen's name. James Killian wished General Sir Piers Tudely-Hext were here with him, but he had deliberately left him behind in Hong Kong, wanting all the anticipated glory of the moment for himself.

'What do I do . . . ? What happens now . . . ?' Killian was in such a state he was unable to think clearly.

'Either you believe Kishen, or you don't,' said Luke unhelpfully. 'If you think he's telling the truth, then you've got to go along with him. If you believe he's lying, then give *him* an ultimatum. Tell him he's got until the end of the month to sign the treaty.'

James Killian was reluctant to admit he had been made to

look a fool. Then he saw Kishen smile as one of his mandarins made a remark to him and Killian's short-fused temper flared into life.

'Tell Kishen I'm tired of his prevaricating. I came here to sign the peace treaty that was drawn up with his agreement. Unless I have his signature one week from today, the present ceasefire will be at an end and I will order the resumption of military operations.'

None of the Chinese could understand English, but the tone of Killian's voice carried its own meaning. When Luke repeated the Superintendent of Trade's words in Chinese, Kishen made no reply and allowed none of his own feelings to show.

Commissioner Kishen had expected to be involved in more hard bargaining, and at the end of the day he had hoped to have gained at least another six weeks. Anything more would have greatly enhanced his reputation as a skilful negotiator. One week was certainly not long enough to solve Shengan's armament problem.

But the talks were over. Brushing aside the lesser Chinese officials who stood between him and the door, James Killian swept from the room, his face set in anger.

Kishen sat motionless in his seat until Luke stood up and began gathering together the empty papers set in front of him.

'Your Superintendent of Trade is not skilled in the art of negotiation, barbarian. Anger has no place at the table when men talk of peace.'

'True,' agreed Luke. 'But the Superintendent of Trade came to this meeting believing he had peace in his grasp. You put it there, Commissioner Kishen – and you snatched it away again. Where do we go from here? Is it to be war or peace for our countries? There can be no in-between now.'

Luke left the room with the depressing feeling that he had witnessed yet again the irreconcilable differences between Great Britain and China. It seemed that, no matter what anyone did, at the end of every day war had moved another pace forward.

Seven

THE DEADLINE set by James Killian passed without any attempt being made by Commissioner Kishen to reopen peace talks, and the Superintendent of Trade found himself in another quandary. If he ordered the resumption of military operations, he might be criticized by his own government for breaking the uneasy truce that was still holding. Yet, if he did nothing, Commissioner Kishen would be convinced he had mouthed empty threats when he stalked out of the peace talks.

Killian compromised. Whilst not committing his land forces, he called upon the Navy to sail into the Bogue yet again and destroy the long-suffering forts, together with any Imperial war-junks they encountered there. The Navy carried out its task well, and once again the Chinese felt the weight of its guns.

Then, when Killian was wondering about his next move, General Sir Piers Tudely-Hext exerted his military authority. A bluff no-nonsense soldier, he cared little for the finer points of politics. He had been given a job to do, and James Killian had stood in his way for long enough.

For many months the British expeditionary force had been divided into three parts, each almost a thousand miles from the other. He now ordered the whole army back to Hong Kong — but he did not sit down doing nothing while he waited for them to assemble.

With well-armed steamers towing the troopships, General Tudely-Hext set off up the Pearl River with his available forces, clearing the banks of Chinese troops as he went.

Just one week later, British soldiers were encamped on the hills about Canton. On the river in front of the walled city the men-of-war formed a close line, their guns turned on Canton. Occasionally, one of the shallow-draught steamers moved off to explore a nearby creek and destroy all the junks found there.

Luke was once again acting as General Tudely-Hext's interpreter, the General settling for no one else.

Luke had travelled up-river with a heavy heart. He carried sad news to pass on to Morna. Her mother was dead. Evicted from Macau with the other British families, Mrs McCulloch had refused to leave the merchantman in the Hong Kong anchorage. She would not live in the house her husband had built for his Chinese mistress. She declared she would die first. Even when all the other families moved to houses built for them on the island, Mrs McCulloch remained on board. Eventually, the lonely and unnatural life she was leading began to affect her mind. Convinced her husband wanted her killed, she became hysterical whenever any of the seamen approached her. Finally, she locked herself in her cabin and refused to open the door, even when food was left outside for her.

When Ezra McCulloch was sent for, he first tried to reason with his deranged wife. When that failed, he had her forcibly removed from the ship and taken to his house on the island. The move failed to prolong her life. On only the second night there, the unfortunate Mrs McCulloch threw herself from her bedroom window, fracturing her skull on the stone courtyard below.

She was laid to rest in the island's churchyard, beside an unmarked grave that had been in the cemetery since before its recent consecration. It was ironic that, had she been able to extend a ghostly hand, she could have touched the long-dead body of Lo Asan.

The British soldiers took the Canton factories without a fight, and General Tudely-Hext and Luke were making an inspection of the factory premises when a delegation approached from the direction of the city, waving a huge white flag of truce.

They carried startling news. Commissioner Kishen's brief reign had been even shorter than Lin's. He had pleased the Emperor no more than had his predecessor. At that very moment Kishen was on his way to Peking in chains. A trio of Commissioners, appointed by the Emperor, were hurrying from the capital, empowered to negotiate a new treaty with the barbarians. The first of the Commissioners was expected any day. General Tudely-Hext was asked to raise his siege until his arrival. As a sign of Chinese good faith, merchant ships would be allowed up-river to Whampoa immediately, and trade with the Hong merchants could be resumed!

It was a ludicrous situation. The two countries were at war, the city surrounded by troops, and the ruins of the Bogue forts still smouldered . . . yet the Chinese were willing to resume trading with the British.

General Tudely-Hext was at first inclined to question Luke's interpretation of the delegation's offer. Then it became plain to see that the idea of a trade truce in the middle of a war amused him.

He agreed. Trading could be resumed immediately. There was another reason for Tudely-Hext's acceptance of the unprecedented offer. He had examined the walls of Canton. Forty-five feet high and twenty thick, they were well constructed of stone and brick. Their demolition would prove a formidable task, even for the exceptional gunnery of the Navy.

Immediately the news became known in Hong Kong, there was a scramble among the traders to get their ships to Whampoa. Luke's two vessels, *China Wind* and *Black Swan*, were among the first, but Jardine Matheson and Ezra McCulloch's vessels were not far behind – and Ezra McCulloch returned with them. There was no one to enforce the ban on him now.

Luke took advantage of the unexpected truce to go inside the city to see Morna and break the news of her mother's death to her.

He found her with a new-born baby in her arms, having just performed the unusual task of midwife to the young wife of one of Shengan's soldiers. Tartar women were traditionally as hardy as their warrior husbands. A woman was expected to produce her child squatting within a circle of close women friends and relatives, gripping a horizontal bamboo pole as she strained against her labour pains. Unfortunately, traditional methods had not worked for this particular young woman. For three days she had struggled and strained to produce her child, encouraged and at times bullied by her companions.

On the third day, she was too exhausted to work at childbirth any longer and, shaking their heads sadly, the other Tartar women filed from the house. The Gods did not intend this baby for the world of mortals. It would live on in the better world – and the mother would herself soon be carried off to tend to the child's needs in that unknown spiritual world.

Fortunately for her, the Tartar woman's soldier-husband was not prepared to surrender his young wife and unborn child to the Gods without a fight. He carried them in his arms to Morna's hospital and pleaded with her to help.

It did not take Morna long to realize that the baby was lying in such a way that no amount of straining would bring it into the world. She was able to turn the child, and only an hour later the Tartar soldier had a son. Three hours after that, just as Luke arrived, the woman was preparing to return to her own home. Tartar women, even those married to enlightened husbands, did not languish in bed when there was work to be done and a son to care for. Before passing the baby to the happy and grateful parents, Morna took a small enamelled locket on a chain from her own neck and slipped it over the baby's head.

For my first Tartar baby,' she explained to the surprised and grateful couple. Then Morna saw Luke and her happy smile faded. 'Is something wrong, Luke?'

'Yes. . . .' Guiding her to a more private place, Luke told her of the death of her mother.

Morna shed no tears at the news. Her mother had always been an insignificant quiet woman, vaguely unreal, even to her own daughter. 'Poor Mother. She never did see Scotland again. Now she's buried in the place she hated more than any other in the world. How is my father taking her death?'

'I haven't seen him, but I believe he's on his way up to the factories at this moment.'

'I'd like to speak to him when he arrives. Please let me know, Luke.'

A few days later, Luke took Morna to meet her father in the East India Company factory, where he was staying with James Killian. Ezra McCulloch sat with a number of fellow-traders, and Luke observed with some apprehension that he appeared to have been drinking heavily.

When he saw Morna, Ezra McCulloch started to his feet. Then, after a visible struggle with his emotions, he sat down again heavily.

'I'm very sorry to hear about Mother . . .' Morna began, her quiet words loud in the hushed room.

'So sorry that you couldn't be bothered to leave your Chinese friends and attend her funeral? She's been dead a month.'

'I didn't know until Luke brought the news to me.'

Morna had not seen her father for two years. She was shocked at the change in him. He was no longer the man who had single-handedly built up a Chinese trading empire second only to Jardine Matheson. Since the death of Lo Asan he had resorted to drink as an antidote to the loneliness that overwhelmed him whenever he entered his home on Hong Kong island. There had been a succession of mistresses, even when his wife was only a few hundred yards away in the anchorage, but none of them lasted longer than a few days. Morna knew nothing of this, but she could see he was an unhappy man and she blamed herself for much of his unhappiness.

'Is there somewhere we can talk . . . just the two of us?'

'Are you ready to come back to Hong Kong with me? Will you leave these Chinese savages and return to live with decent people again?'

Morna closed her eyes momentarily, as though she were in physical pain. It had been a mistake to come to see him. He could understand neither her actions nor her motives. Ezra McCulloch refused to accept that the Chinese were capable of normal feelings. If he once acknowledged that they had hopes and fears, loves and hates, he would have to accept them as fellow beings, who suffered because of his own greed. Opening her eyes, Morna looked at the other traders in the room. All of them owed such wealth as they possessed to opium. Did they all share her father's contempt for the Chinese? But he was speaking to her again.

'Don't you know a war is being fought between your country and China? Men from our own home town in Scotland are lying in hospital in Hong Kong, wounded by the Chinese. Why don't you come back there and nurse them?'

'Wounded by Chinese, Father? I treated more than five hundred Tartar soldiers after the attack on the Chuenpi forts — and others had already died. I've heard about the casualties of "our" soldiers. One died and nineteen were wounded. Are you telling me that's war? No, Father, that's *slaughter*!'

There had been a gasp from the other traders in the room when Morna quoted the Chinese casualty figures, but Ezra McCulloch shrugged his shoulders nonchalantly. 'If they can't fight, they shouldn't have started this war. . . .'

'The Chinese *didn't* start the war,' Morna flared up angrily. 'It was brought about by you and the other traders in this

294

room – you and your damned opium. If you'd ever cared for anything but easy money, there would be no war. Oh, yes, I've heard all your arguments about the market already being there – that you are merely satisfying the demand. I've heard them so many times that I'm sick of them. You don't believe them any more than I do. I saw the shock on your faces when I mentioned five hundred Tartars being wounded in the Chuenpi bombardment. I treat three times that number for opium addiction *every* week. Not fighting men, soldiers with guns or bows and arrows in their hands. Ordinary men and women, too bewildered to understand what is happening to them. If it weren't for men like Shengan. . . .'

'Ah! I wondered when you'd mention your Chinese general. I suppose he's still your "friend"?'

Luke could see the danger signs. Both Ezra McCulloch and Morna were angry. He took Morna's arm, but she shook it off irritably. 'Yes, Shengan is a friend – more than a friend. He's worth a hundred Englishmen . . . or Scotsmen. He's a *real* man. . . .'

Ezra McCulloch leaped to his feet. Before Luke could prevent him, he gave Morna a back-handed blow that knocked her across the room. As Luke grappled with him, two of the traders came to his assistance.

'Ezra . . . Ezra, man. Control yourself now. She's your daughter.' The speaker was a fellow Scots trader who had known Morna and her father for many years.

'Daughter? Daughter, did you say?' Fuming, Ezra McCulloch shook off the men who held him. 'I have no daughter. Get her out of my sight.' He strode to the table and sat down heavily, his back to Morna and Luke.

Outside the factory, Luke put his arm about Morna's shoulders as he led her away across the square. 'It was the drink talking, Morna. He didn't mean anything he said. . . .'

'Oh, yes, he did,' Morna whispered fiercely. 'He meant every word.'

She turned her face to him, her right cheek scarlet from Ezra McCulloch's blow. 'But I learned something very important today, Luke. I was proud to tell those men in there what Shengan means to me. Yet, if my patients were to learn that I am Ezra McCulloch's daughter, it would fill me with shame.'

The first of the new Imperial Commissioners to arrive was Yang

Fang. One of China's venerable old warriors, Yang Fang was now well over seventy years of age and so deaf that the only method of communicating with him was by writing. Yet, old and decrepit though he was, Yang Fang lacked none of the guile of his predecessor. He took a boat trip to Whampoa to look at the strange European vessels and, on his return, was carried around the factory square. There he had his first ever look at the Fan Qui as they obligingly left their factories to see the new Commissioner.

While all this was going on, the aged Imperial Commissioner was having newly cast cannon brought from Fat-shan and set in secret gun emplacements on the river-banks about Canton, side by side with cannon salvaged from the Bogue forts. The wily old soldier also drafted thousands of Chinese bannermen into the city.

Getting wind of what was happening, Killian went to Canton from Hong Kong to learn the facts for himself. So alarmed was he that he ordered the immediate evacuation of the factories. He was only just in time. Urged on by Yang Fang, the Chinese bannermen fell upon the factories, screaming 'Exterminate the Fan Qui'. At the same time, fireboats were launched against the small naval squadron anchored in the river off the city. In a show of support, all Yang Fang's new gun emplacements opened fire, regardless of whether or not they had a British target in sight.

This time, General Sir Piers Tudely-Hext did not need Luke to act as a mediator. The Chinese had deliberately broken the fragile truce that had existed for two months. They needed to be taught a salutary lesson. Outnumbered by at least fifteen to one, General Tudely-Hext's troops fought their way through the Canton suburbs, outside the wall, while a line of men-of-war lobbed shells into the city. The British forces reoccupied the surrounding hills they had evacuated only weeks before — but this time they were defended by Shengan's troops, and it was a costly victory. Eventually, as on earlier occasions, the guns of the warships won the day and the area around the walled city was in British hands.

As General Tudely-Hext contemplated the formidable city wall, Yang Fang sent out mandarins to parley with the besiegers.

General Tudely-Hext wanted to send them back again without any discussion, but he reckoned without the Superintendent of Trade. James Killian was quick to point out to him that, whilst waging war was indisputably the General's business, discussing peace terms was his.

While General Tudely-Hext and his troops chafed in exposed and uncomfortable positions outside the city walls, Killian and the Chinese talked. The rainy season had begun and rain was falling at the rate of two or more inches a day. The conditions soon became intolerable. In the hills beyond the city, not only were the soldiers lashed by torrential rain, but they also came under attack from a huge army of Chinese. Swarming up the hillsides, they overran the British outposts, disappearing into the mist and rain when the British troops counter-attacked.

At first it was believed the attackers were Yang Fang's bannermen, but then an ugly rumour began to circulate. The attackers were not on the side of Imperial China at all. They were Ping Chuan's men, part of his huge rabble army, on their way to create a massive diversion in the rich and fertile Yangtze valley, five hundred miles to the north.

Ping Chuan's men had deviated from their planned route, hoping to have a part in the plundering of Canton. Had Tudely-Hext's troops breached the walls of Canton, and Ping Chuan's men succeeded in their aim, the pirate chief would have lost the bulk of his 'army'. There was enough plunder in the huge city to last his greedy horde for years to come.

As it was, Ping Chuan's men had to be satisfied with seizing those Cantonese who had fled the city to escape the bombardment and the threat of a Fan Qui occupation. The British soldiers had been attacked because they were mistaken for Chinese refugees in the poor visibility of the rain-sodden hills.

Luke returned to the Canton factories on the day the talks between Killian and Yang Fang came to an end. Yet again, the Superintendent of Trade had chosen the path of appeasement. Yang Fang and the Canton mandarins had ransomed their city for six million dollars – and the release of all European prisoners held in Chinese gaols.

Tudely-Hext was both relieved and angry at the terms of the ceasefire agreed by Killian. His relief was at not having to fight for Canton. His small army was being depleted every day by fever, and it was rumoured that there were still twenty thousand Tartar soldiers in Canton. If he had to fight in the narrow city streets, without the advantage of supporting gun-fire, he faced a very real threat of defeat.

Tudely-Hext wanted that threat removed. Today the Chinese did not want to fight. Next week, or the week after, it would probably be war again. The fiery little general insisted that, before the truce document was signed, the Tartar army must leave Canton and not return.

When Killian demurred, General Tudely-Hext threatened to withdraw his troops from their positions about Canton, leaving the Superintendent of Trade to conclude his truce without them.

Killian quickly had a new clause added to the Canton peace treaty. General Shengan's army was to be out of Canton within six days. It was the same period of time allowed for payment of the ransom.

Hearing the details of the latest clause from General Tudely-Hext, Luke hurried into the city to find Morna. With Shengan gone, Canton would be in chaos. Morna would have no protec-tion – and Luke knew her presence was bitterly resented by many of the city's mandarins. His intention was to bring her out of the city with him, but Morna had other ideas.

Luke found her in a despondent yet defiant mood. The hospital was full to overflowing with wounded Tartars and civilians, victims of the naval bombardment.

Shengan had told Morna he would be taking all his wounded men with him, whatever their condition. The Tartars were both feared and hated by the Chinese. By the time Shengan was ready to leave they would have additional cause for resentment. Feeding his vast army on the march would take a prodigious amount of food. Shengan intended taking it from Canton's own reserve. He would leave no Tartar soldier behind to face the fury of the Chinese. When he left, every Tartar man, woman and child would go with him.

Morna protested that the move would kill some of the more seriously wounded soldiers, but as the logic of Shengan's argu-ment sank home her attitude changed. She agreed the wounded would have to go – but she would go with them.

Shengan made no attempt to stop her. She would be going where no barbarian woman had been before her, but Morna had already set many such precedents. His own troops had never been in any doubt that Morna would accompany them on their long trek northwards. Morna had heard some of them talking about it and she still felt the warm glow inside her at the words they had used to describe her.

They had called her 'the General's woman'.

Eight

WHEN Shengan set out along the river valley to the north of Canton, his column of twenty thousand warriors, their wives, families, possessions and stores stretched back for a distance of five miles. Later they would break up into smaller units, but for the moment they made an impressive sight, and Luke and the British soldiers watched in silence as the Tartars moved off into the distance.

On an almost parallel course, but secure in the fastness of the hills, Ping Chuan's less disciplined 'army' also headed inland. With him were a number of British army officers. Sent as 'advisers' to the so-called rebel army, they had quickly given up any hope of bringing discipline to the opium-smoking pirate rabble. Tacitly accepting their new role of 'observers', the British officers dropped to their knees with Ping Chuan's followers at the compulsory morning and evening prayer sessions, and kept their thoughts to themselves.

Also accompanying Ping Chuan was the Reverend Charles Moller. He was with the rebel army at his own request, and had agreed to carry out interpreting duties for the British officers. However, they quickly learned that Moller's interpretations could not be relied upon. They tended to contain his own views and beliefs, rather than those of the speakers.

The object of Ping Chuan's incursion so deep into China was to keep the Imperial Chinese troops in the Yangtze Kiang basin occupied. He had been told to draw them away from Shang-hai and the great city of Nanking. Both were possible targets for General Tudely-Hext's army.

Ping Chuan's earlier boast of fifty thousand followers had proved to be something of an exaggeration, but at least fifteen thousand pirates had chosen to leave their ships and follow him in a trail of plunder into their homeland. The pirates cut a wide swathe through the Chinese countryside, leaving neither man nor animal alive in their wake.

Gradually, reports of the ravages of Ping Chuan's army reached General Shengan, and he sent large detachments of Tartars in search of him. But it was not until both armies

300

reached the great central plains of China that the Tartars fought their first battle with the British-backed rebels.

Fought in countryside rich with forest and lakes, the battle proved inconclusive, the Tartar force being no more than five hundred strong. However, contact between the two armies had been made and it was never to be lost for very long. No matter how often Ping Chuan split his forces, whatever direction they took, there were always Tartar horsemen following them, harrying them at every opportunity.

In fact, Ping Chuan's operation was going exactly as General Sir Piers Tudely-Hext had planned. Shengan had intended taking his army to reinforce the garrison at Chin-kiang, the fortress town on the Yangtze River that guarded the great provincial city of Nanking. Now only the Tartar families, with a small escorting force, would go there. The remainder of Shengan's army was deployed over thousands of square miles, in pursuit of Ping Chuan and the bearded Fan Qui priest who led the Chinese rebels into battle. Sword in hand, and calling on his God to smite His enemies, the Reverend Charles Moller was building himself into a living legend.

Morna travelled with Shengan and the main body of the Tartar army. At first, their passage through the countryside was fairly leisurely, but as clashes with Ping Chuan became more frequent the pace quickened. Mounted messengers left Shengan's headquarters in a steady stream all day, and galloped their horses into the camp at all hours of the night. The night camps gradually became briefer as the units of Shengan's army formed a loosely linked chain across the flat Yangtze plains and began to sweep the rebels before them, in the direction of the sea.

Then, just when it seemed that Shengan had the situation well under control, the rains came. Driven inland by typhoon-force winds, they turned the country into a quagmire, and friend and foe were lost to each other in mist and rain.

At this critical point in the campaign, Shengan was struck down with malaria. He had not seemed well for days and at a dawn meal he looked tired and drawn, with a thin film of perspiration on his forehead and upper lip. Morna watched him anxiously for most of the day. As he rode his wiry little pony, head bowed against the rain and wind, it seemed to her he swayed once or twice, as though he were falling asleep. Then, in mid-afternoon, as they were splashing knee-deep through floodwater, Morna saw Shengan suddenly slump forward across the pommel of his saddle.

Shouting to the Tartars marching immediately behind her, Morna kneed her own pony forward and held Shengan in his saddle until some of his men ran forward and lifted him down. Shengan was conscious, but in a state of delirium.

It was impossible for Morna to treat him in the heavy rain that was falling, and it was twenty minutes before the soldiers located a small village. Here they commandeered the house occupied by the headman, and Shengan was carried inside.

Before Morna could begin to examine Shengan she had to drive out the Tartar officers who crowded into the room, filled with anxiety for their general. When the last of them had reluctantly left, Morna stripped the wet clothes from Shengan and dried him, assisted by the aged wife of the village headman.

It was not an easy task. Perspiration poured from Shengan's every pore and, in his delirium, he thrashed about and moaned as though trying to throw off an imaginary enemy.

The symptoms of malaria were unmistakable and Morna dosed Shengan heavily with quinine. Many of the Tartars had been struck down with the fever since the army had arrived in the low-lying Yangtze valley, and Morna was concerned because her supply of quinine was running low. Indeed, there was now a chronic shortage of every type of drug, with scant prospect of obtaining more. The Chinese had little knowledge of medicines. Their doctoring consisted of a dangerous mixture of folklore and mumbo-jumbo.

Morna stayed at Shengan's side for two days and nights, as the rain hammered down on the wooden-tiled roof of the house, and sodden and miserable Tartar troops crowded into whatever shelter they could find in and about the village.

For the first thirty-six hours, Morna was concerned for Shengan's life. The delirium quickly passed away, but then he sank into a deep coma, his pulse weak and irregular and every breath a shuddering painful hold on life. It was now that the sceptics on Shengan's staff began to cast doubts on Morna's treatment of their commander, advocating more traditional methods.

Morna's answer was to drive them all from the hut and refuse to allow anyone to return, while she continued to dose Shengan with quinine and as much liquid as she was able to force down his throat.

In the early hours of the second morning, as she sat by Shengan's sleeping-mat, Morna's head sank lower and lower, until her chin rested against her chest and she fell into a shallow sleep.

She woke with a start as a hand gently touched her face — and she looked down into the wan but smiling face of Shengan.

'I'm sorry I woke you,' Shengan said as Morna seized his hand and held it to her cheek. She was not a deeply religious girl, but during the long nights she had prayed for Shengan's recovery. In those dark lonely hours, even prayers seemed of little avail, but now they were answered. The fever had broken. Shengan had taken his first step along the path of recovery.

'I'll get you a drink. . . .'

'No. . . .' His grip tightened on her fingers. 'Stay here with me, Morna.'

This was a Shengan she had never seen before. He had always been strong, both mentally and physically, capable of inspiring his soldiers to great feats of endurance and achievement by his own example. He had proved time and time again that he could do everything he expected of them. Now, for the first time in his life, Shengan was lying ill . . . and he needed her.

'How long have I been ill?'

'Two days. . . . Do you feel like food? Some soup . . . ?'

His fingers tightened on hers once more. 'Have you been with me for all that time?'

'Yes.'

'My men . . . ?'

'We are in a village. Your soldiers are camped all about us. No doubt your officers will be here soon, to see how you are. There's hardly an hour, day or night, when they haven't.'

'They are good men. No general could wish for better. I have been fortunate . . . and now I have you, too.' He carried her hand down to his mouth and softly kissed her fingers. 'I want you with me always, Morna. I wish you to marry me.'

'Shengan . . . don't.' Morna choked on her admonition. She had dreamed of the day when he would say these words to her, but she wanted them to come from Shengan the general, not Shengan the sick man. He was feeling the sick man's gratitude to his nurse. 'I'll stay with you . . . for as long as you want me. As for marriage . . . we'll discuss it when you're well.'

Shengan looked surprised. 'What is there to discuss? Don't you love me?'

'Of course I do.' The words were out before Morna thought about them. 'But. . . .'

'Then it is settled.' Shengan smiled at her. 'This is not the rambling of a sick man, Morna. I knew you were the woman for me on the first day Luke Trewarne brought you to my tent and we found so much to talk about. Then I did not think that a marriage between us could ever be. But I have seen you achieve so many miracles that I know all things are possible with you. You are accepted by my men as my woman; now I want to make you my wife. Will you marry me? I warn you: if you refuse, I will have the Emperor issue a command *ordering* you to marry me.'

'Shengan . . . you know I will.' Morna kneeled beside him and rested her face against him.

'Then it is settled.' Shengan stroked her hair as she clung to him. 'I will send one of my officers ahead to make the necessary arrangements. We will be married in Nanking, the ancient capital of China. It is the most beautiful of my country's cities, perfect for a special wedding such as ours. We will choose a day when the wind will send the music of the White Pagoda bells to every corner of the city. It will be a wedding for the people to talk about for ever. . . .'

The door to the hut crashed open and one of the Tartar officers stood in the doorway. 'Quick! Ping Chuan's men are attacking the village. We must get the General away.'

Through the open doorway, Morna could hear shouts and screams above the howling of the wind.

Shengan struggled to sit up. 'We have six thousand men with us. That should be more than enough to fight off Ping Chuan's pirates.'

The Tartar officer looked apprehensively at General Shengan. 'The rebels were reported to be attacking Lu Kiang, ten miles away. I sent the army to their aid. We have only your personal bodyguard in the village.'

Morna gasped; they had only a hundred Tartar warriors to defend them against Ping Chuan's hordes.

Shengan's expression became one of absolute fury as the Tartar officer stuttered, '. . . You were in a fever. . . . I had to make a decision.'

'Fool! Even a Chinese yellow bannerman would not have left his headquarters unguarded. Help me to get dressed.'

'You'll do no such thing,' declared Morna firmly. To the

officer she snapped. 'General Shengan is sick. Get men to help him. You'll need a stretcher . . . or better still a carrying-cart.'

Thankful for an excuse to leave the hut, the officer did as Morna told him. Shengan was not so obliging. Ignoring Morna's protests, he began putting on his uniform. He quickly learned just how weak he was. By the time the Tartar officer returned to the hut with some of the soldiers, Shengan was still only half-dressed, and he had exhausted himself.

There was no time to wait for Shengan's strength to return. The sound of fighting was all about the hut. Shengan was bundled unceremoniously outside and placed in the only con- veyance available – the village bridal sedan chair. Four soldiers heaved it hurriedly on to their shoulders and set off into the rain-filled darkness at a bone-jolting trot, other soldiers running ahead of them as a scouting party.

Meanwhile, Morna snatched up the few medicines she had left and tied them in a bundle. Then she, too, fled from the hut, following the path taken by Shengan's bearers.

In the darkness it was impossible to see the narrow track, but she could hear the grunting of the Tartar soldiers carrying the weight of their general. Then she slipped and tumbled down a steep bank into a water-filled ricefield. She rose, muddy and angry, and fought her way back to the path, slipping and cursing the mud and rain. When she finally regained the path, she could hear nothing. She made her way in the direction she thought the Tartars had gone, but after she had fallen and retraced her footsteps another half-dozen times she had to admit to herself that she was hopelessly lost.

Once she heard the clash of steel upon steel, and in running from the sound she tumbled again and found herself floundering out of her depth in a water-filled irrigation ditch. Seconds later, a man splashed past, only feet from her, but she could not see whether it was a Tartar soldier or one of Ping Chuan's cut- throats.

It was foolish to thresh about in the darkness. Morna could hardly see a foot in front of her and was as likely to attract the attention of Ping Chuan as Shengan's soldiers. In the depths of despair, Morna found the scant shelter of a small tree and crawled beneath its dripping leaves to wait for daylight.

She was more worried about Shengan than herself. Even if he had escaped from Ping Chuan's men, he still had to fight his malaria. The fever had broken, but it was likely to recur if he was not given more quinine. There had been some left in her main medical stores, but she did not know whether the retreating soldiers had taken them.

In the early hours of the morning, the rain stopped, for the first time in three days. Dawn arrived swathed in a thin mist that hugged the ground, giving the surrounding countryside an unreal and incomplete beauty. But its ethereal beauty was wasted on Morna. Her only thought was to find Shengan as quickly as possible. But where had his soldiers taken him? Suddenly she recalled the words of the Tartar officer, during the last few minutes in the hut. He had sent the soldiers to Lu Kiang. Shengan would be taken to Lu Kiang, too. . . . But where *was* Lu Kiang?

It was light enough now for Morna to see that she had walked in a circle during the darkness. She was on the outskirts of the same village where she had spent the last few days with Shengan, but she could see no sign of Tartar or rebel. Morna decided to seek a villager and ask the way to Lu Kiang.

She approached the first house cautiously, but such caution seemed unnecessary now. The village was so quiet that the events of the night might have been no more than a vivid nightmare. Then Morna stumbled over the body of a young Tartar soldier, lying on his back and half-submerged in water. The torrential rain had not been able to wash away the blood that discoloured the whole of his tunic front.

Nearby were more bodies. Not soldiers this time, but two children . . . and a man . . . two old women. . . . Suddenly, it seemed, Morna was surrounded by bodies. They lay in grotesque postures in the trampled mud, or half-hidden by the low swirling mist.

In one of the huts someone coughed, and Morna froze in sudden panic. All thoughts of seeking directions to Lu Kiang were gone. Ping Chuan's men had made a thorough job of sacking the village. If there were someone alive in one of the huts, it would not be a villager.

Morna turned to hurry back the way she had come, just as the door of a nearby hut opened and a man came out. His long hair hung dirty and matted about his shoulders. At sight of her, he let out a great bellow of delight.

Morna ran — but she slipped and fell in the mud. Leaping to her feet again, she evaded the outstretched arms of the rebel and headed for the path, only to be confronted by another of Ping Chuan's men. She ran between two huts – and two more rebels barred her way.

It became a game for the pirates. No matter which way Morna turned, there was one of them barring her way. Finally, she was forced to admit defeat. Dishevelled and muddy, she stood in the middle of a large circle of jeering rebels, her bosom heaving, sick with fear and sheer exhaustion.

Morna waited for the rebels to close in and take her. She had no illusions about her fate. These were the men who had carved a wide swathe of shame and degradation through the heartland of China.

'Leave the girl alone.'

The jeering died away and there was a sullen silence as Ping Chuan pushed aside two of his men and stepped into the circle to face Morna.

'Well, now, what have we here?' Reaching forward, Ping Chuan scraped some of the mud from Morna's cheek with his finger. 'A Fan Qui girl – in China?'

Morna said nothing, doing her best to call up defiance as she stared back at Ping Chuan. Suddenly the hand that had touched her cheek flashed out again. This time it struck her a blow that rattled her teeth.

'I asked you a question. I want an answer.'

Ping Chuan struck her again, and as she staggered a shout of approval rose from his watching men.

Suddenly a new voice made itself heard. A voice that spoke Chinese with a thick German accent. 'What is happening here, Ping Chuan? That is a white woman. Leave her alone.'

Charles Moller strode fearlessly through the crowd of pirates to where Ping Chuan stood with Morna. Hollow-eyed, Moller was suffering from the exhaustion that always took over after the fierce ecstasy of battle. His presence struck awe into the hearts of the rebels. Charles Moller was cast in the mould of the fighting bishops of the Crusades. Always to be found in the forefront of every battle, he fought with a reckless courage, emerging unscathed while those about him died. The pirates believed he was immortal.

Ping Chuan eyed Charles Moller angrily. He was jealous of the violent missionary's growing reputation. One day he knew he would have to prove that it was he, Ping Chuan, who led the rebel army, not Moller.

'Are Fan Qui women so much more valuable than Chinese women?'

'Yes. They are Christian. . . . You *are* a Christian?' He snapped the question at Morna.

'More Christian than anyone here, I think,' replied Morna defiantly, looking about her at the men of Ping Chuan's army.

Charles Moller ignored the implications of her remark. 'Who are you? What are you doing here?'

'I'm Morna McCulloch. I was nursing in Canton until General Shengan's army was ordered out of the city. I left with him, to tend his sick and wounded.'

She spoke in English. Only Charles Moller and Ping Chuan understood her. Each picked on a different aspect of her reply.

'You are Ezra McCulloch's daughter? Of course . . . I have heard of you.' Charles Moller's manner suddenly became effusive. Ezra McCulloch had not mentioned his daughter to the missionary himself, but others had, and Moller and Ezra McCulloch were friends – partners, almost. He would see that Morna came to no harm.

Ping Chuan was less pleased. 'You were helping General Shengan's Tartars?'

'Only the sick and wounded. It's a Christian thing to do,' Morna replied.

'Now you are with Ping Chuan's army. We, too, have wounded men. Come, you can dress their wounds.'

'I'll do nothing until I've had time to rest and get cleaned up. Then, if you have salve and dressings, I'll treat anyone in need.'

'You can use the ointments and medicines we captured from the Tartars,' said Charles Moller, and Morna's already low spirits dropped even farther. The missionary's statement meant that Shengan would not have the quinine he needed.

'Some of your countrymen are with us. I think it will be better for you to remain close to them until we can arrange for you to return to Hong Kong. . . .'

As Charles Moller led her away, Ping Chuan's eyes followed Morna. His mind was already working on a plan to turn her unexpected arrival to his own advantage.

The daughter of McCulloch could help him. She *would* help him. After all, he was a great commander. Even the Fan Qui general acknowledged this. He had sent his own officers to learn from Ping Chuan's tactics. Although they called themselves 'advisers', Ping Chuan knew the real reason for their presence. Every day more men flocked to join him. By the time he reached the gates of Peking, his army would outnumber the forces of the Emperor. He, Ping Chuan, would topple the Manchu usurper who occupied the throne and blasphemed the Lord by calling China 'The Heavenly Kingdom'. Only under Ping Chuan's reign would the country truly become the Lord's Kingdom. For Ping Chuan was God's chosen . . . the new Messiah. . . .

Ping Chuan brought his lofty thoughts down to earth as Morna was led out of sight. In order to conquer China he would require more help from the Fan Qui general. He had guns on wheels, as fearsome as those carried on the ships. His soldiers used muskets that could be reloaded in a fraction of the time it took Ping Chuan's men – and they would fire in wet weather, when the flintlock and matchlock muskets were quite useless.

Ping Chuan knew he was neither liked nor trusted by the Fan Qui. They had not given him any of these modern weapons before he and his army had set off. But he thought their attitude would change if he took a Fan Qui wife – especially if she were the daughter of one of their most prominent traders. There would be other wives, of course, and many concubines. But, as his first wife, Morna McCulloch would have the title of Empress. It would be a great honour to her and her country – and should ensure his ultimate victory.

Ping Chuan was even more determined to carry out his plan when he saw Morna later that day. Bathed and dressed in borrowed Chinese clothes, she was not only an investment for the future, but also a very desirable woman.

That night Ping Chuan dictated a letter to one of his more educated followers. Addressed to Ezra McCulloch, it demanded the hand of his daughter in marriage. By way of a dowry, Ping Chuan suggested that the trader might supply him with a shipment of opium.

As an afterthought, Ping Chuan had his writer add that McCulloch should send him the opium anyway. It would ensure that McCulloch saw his daughter again.

Nine

THE HEAVY RAINS that flooded the Yangtze valley were caused by a typhoon. Inland, they experienced only the fringe of the great storm. The heart of it was centred fairly and squarely upon Hong Kong island. No one there had ever experienced such a violent storm before. Driven in from the east, it whipped up enormous waves that ignored beaches and swept inland through low-lying valleys. Where the waves encountered cliffs, spray was hurled more than a hundred and fifty feet into the air.

In the anchorage of Hong Kong, considered to be the most sheltered harbour on that coast, ten ships were lost. Six sank to the bottom of the anchorage, the other four were thrown ashore and left lying on their sides, a hundred yards from the beach. Of the ships that survived, not one was undamaged.

On land, whole villages no longer existed. Houses and possessions were sucked up by the wind, broken into tiny pieces and strewn along a hundred miles of coastline. The new hospital buildings on the hillside overlooking the harbour were devastated. Walls and roofs were sent crashing to the ground and sick men washed out of their beds by an avalanche of water that poured off the higher slopes of the great peak behind the hospital.

Kuei was alone in the house on the island when the storm struck, Luke being absent on yet another reluctant expedition as interpreter to General Tudely-Hext. Her first thought was for the sick soldiers on the hill. Ignoring her own safety, she defied the fury of the storm to supervize the evacuation of hospital patients to her house and to the stone-built godown belonging to Gemmell Company.

The typhoon reached its climax at three o'clock on a Wednesday afternoon. The skies darkened as though the winds had succeeded in extinguishing the sun. Sepoys of the Indian regiments ran amok in a terrified frenzy, convinced that were witnessing the dying throes of the world. Struck down by flying debris, their scarlet-uniformed bodies were soon washing backwards and forwards in the floodwater along the waterfront.

A section of the roof of the godown was blown away, but the remainder held. Although terrified herself, Kuei managed to appear outwardly calm and went among the sick soldiers, assuring them that the worst of the storm had passed, and that things would soon be back to normal.

By nightfall, it was apparent that Kuei's words, although uttered more in hope than in anticipation, were coming true. The storm moved slowly inland. Rain still fell in torrents, but the wind had decreased to no more than normal gale force.

When it became clear they had survived the holocaust, Army Surgeon Pelham Barclay both delighted and embarrassed Kuei. In front of the other patients, and survivors from nearby houses, he put his arms about her and kissed her, saying, 'Mrs Kuei Trewarne, you have been wonderful . . . an inspiration to us all.'

Beaming down at her, he said, with a great deal of feeling, 'By God, girl! If you had a sister only half as attractive, and with a quarter of your ability, I'd marry her on the spot. I hope your husband realizes what a lucky man he is.'

Kuei was just getting the house and godown back to normal after the storm when another blow fell. One that promised to be far more damaging to her and Luke than any typhoon.

When James Killian annexed Hong Kong on behalf of the British Government, he announced that all land belonged to the Crown. It meant nothing to Luke at the time – and even less to Kuei. Luke had built his house on the island when he and Ezra McCulloch were the only Europeans there. It had been defended against pirates and storm. It belonged to him.

But Killian drew up a map, dividing the land around the anchorage into numbered lots. A notice announcing an auction of these lots was posted on the government notice-board on the island. But, three days before, Luke had embarked with General Tudely-Hext for Amoy, to negotiate a peace with the mandarins of that area.

The day after the land auction, Ezra McCulloch came to Luke's house and nailed a notice to the door. It was written only in English. Although Kuei now spoke the language well, she had not learned to read it. Hesitantly, for she had never lost her fear of him, she asked McCulloch its meaning.

'It means that your upstart of a husband hasn't been clever enough, that's what it means, girl. There's been an auction of land and he wasn't here to bid for his own place. I've bought it on behalf of Charles Moller. Your house is to become Hong Kong's first permanent church. You should be proud of that — you and he with your unholy alliance.' McCulloch grinned at Kuei's dismay. 'This notice is a copy of the deed of sale, signed by the Governor, James Killian. You're to be out of the house with your goods and chattels by noon tomorrow.'

'No! I never leave this house. Never. You want me to go, you have to kill me. You try to take Luke's house — I kill you.'

With this threat, Kuei slammed the door shut and put the bolts across on the inside. She was terrified of Ezra McCulloch, and did not understand the mysterious workings of her husband's people, but no one was going to deprive Luke of his house.

Ezra McCulloch arrived at noon the next day and knocked loudly on the locked door. He was accompanied by a number of Chinese, recruits to Hong Kong's recently constituted police force. McCulloch first called on Kuei to open the door. When he received no reply, he gave the constables the signal to batter down the door. No sooner had they begun than a musket-ball drilled a hole through the woodwork of the door and hummed angrily away above their heads.

The Chinese policemen dropped the battering-ram and flattened themselves against the stone wall of the house to the accompaniment of cheers from the crowd that had quickly assembled nearby. Not all the onlookers were sympathetic with McCulloch.

At that moment, Surgeon Pelham Barclay pushed his way through them. He looked in astonishment from the battering-ram lying on the ground in front of the door to Ezra McCulloch and the policemen.

'What the devil is going on here?'

Ezra McCulloch recognized the surgeon. He was the senior medical man serving with the expeditionary force. Rumour had it he would one day be Surgeon-General to the whole British Army. Ezra McCulloch was not anxious to quarrel with him.

'This is none of your business, Mr Barclay. I'm executing the Governor's warrant. Trewarne's Chinese woman was warned to be out by noon. . . .'

'That "Chinese woman" is Mrs Trewarne. As for getting out of her own house . . . ! Show me your warrant.'

Ezra McCulloch handed over an impressive document, to

which was attached the official seal of the Superintendent of Trade – acting Governor of Hong Kong.

Reading it with increasing incredulity, Pelham Barclay reached the end and looked up sharply at the trader. 'For what it's worth, this document says possession of this land now rests with the Reverend Charles Moller. If my memory serves me right, he's the man who negotiated some sort of treaty with a bunch of cut-throats. Where is he – and how do you come into this?'

'Charles Moller is with the army of Ping Chuan, fighting the same enemies of the Queen as your own soldiers. I'm acting on Moller's behalf.'

'Are you, now? In that case I shall appoint myself to act on behalf of Mrs Trewarne – a task, I might add, that a great many officers and men of the expeditionary force would willingly take from me and pursue with some vigour.'

'This plot of land has been sold to Charles Moller,' growled Ezra McCulloch. 'There's nothing anyone can do about it. Everything is legal and above board.'

'Legal it *may* be,' retorted Pelham Barclay. 'Above board it most certainly is *not*. But I'll argue that point with a higher authority than you, McCulloch. In the meantime, I'll persuade Mrs Trewarne to leave. I would point out, however, that possession of this land does not entitle you, or anyone else, to interfere with the house or its contents. They are indisputably Mr Trewarne's property. When Mrs Trewarne leaves I will have the house securely locked. After that, as Mr Moller's "agent", the responsibility for protecting the property rests with you. Treat it seriously, Mr McCulloch. I am quite certain Luke Trewarne will. Now remove yourself and your so-called "policemen". I doubt if I will persuade Mrs Trewarne to open the door while you are here.'

Ezra McCulloch was angry at the army surgeon's interference, and not happy at being made responsible for the protection of Luke Trewarne's house. It had been his intention to have the building gutted and refurbished as a church before Luke's return. He would have to be content with getting Kuei out of the house . . . for the time being.

When she was quite certain that McCulloch and the policemen were gone, Kuei opened the door to Pelham Barclay. It took him more than an hour to persuade her to leave peacefully. She had been determined to die in defence of Luke's house, if necessary. The army surgeon eventually managed to convince her nothing would be touched by anyone, and that a spirited defence would only cause damage to the house and unnecessary trouble for Luke. Until everything was resolved, Kuei would stay at the hospital.

As he closed the door behind her, Pelham Barclay said, 'McCulloch and his friends have secured a hollow victory, Kuei. We'll get the house and land back for you – if I have to bring the case to the notice of Her Majesty the Queen. If I fail, we're likely to have a mutiny of the Army, right here in Hong Kong. By your unselfish work for them, you've endeared yourself to the soldiers more than any other woman I've ever known.'

When Gideon Pyke brought *Black Swan* into the Hong Kong anchorage a few days later, the extent of the careful planning behind the move to oust Luke became known. Unable to bring his ship alongside the stone quay of Gemmell Company because McCulloch's ships filled every berth, Gideon Pyke stormed angrily up the hill to McCulloch's house and demanded to know what was happening.

He was shown the deed of purchase, which made Charles Moller the rightful owner of the land. He was also shown a letter from Moller, giving McCulloch the sole right to the use of the jetty for his ships.

Moller had made out the document with a meticulousness typical of his race. It was dated many months before Killian had announced the sale of Crown land on the island. From this, it would appear that James Killian was part of the conspiracy against Luke.

Whether Killian stood to gain monetarily from such intrigue was doubtful. It was more likely his way of repaying Luke for the stand he had taken against the Superintendent of Trade on past occasions. It might even have been the settlement of a debt James Killian felt he owed to Ezra McCulloch and Charles Moller for their support in the troubles against the Chinese.

Either way, the Honourable James Killian was not destined to remain in the colony long enough to enjoy his victory over Luke and his trading company.

On 10 August 1841 a steam-frigate arrived at the Hong Kong anchorage, having set a new record of sixty-seven days for the passage from the United Kingdom. On board was Sir Henry Rutherford, KCB. His credentials proclaimed him as Her Britannic Majesty's sole plenipotentiary and minister extraordinary to the Imperial Court of Peking.

Sir Henry also carried a letter of dismissal for James Killian from Lord Palmerston. Stripped of his offices and ordered back to England, Killian had been officially dismissed for his lack of a cohesive policy, coupled with a propensity for making decisions based, not upon facts, but upon his own whims and changing moods.

The dismissal was one of Palmerston's last acts in his present term of office. Quick as had been the steam-frigate's voyage from England to Hong Kong, there had been time for a change of government – and the war in China contributed in no small degree to the defeat of Palmerston and the Whigs.

Three hundred miles to the north of Hong Kong, Luke suffered the heat and humidity of a Chinese summer on board a 74-gun man-of-war. Around him, the expeditionary force prepared to launch a land and sea assault on the island fortress of Amoy.

Situated at the mouth of one of China's many rivers, Amoy was China's link with the great offshore island of Formosa. Plans for the attack had already been carefully laid when Sir Henry Rutherford arrived post-haste from Hong Kong and declared his intention of trying to arrange a truce.

Sir Henry Rutherford was a very experienced administrator and he was well aware of the shortcomings of his predecessor. He smiled at the questioning looks that passed between the assembled naval and army officers gathered in the wardroom of the warship. 'No, gentlemen, I am not a James Killian . . . but neither do I lust for the blood of our enemies. I intend sending an officer and an interpreter to parley with the Governor of the city. He'll be given twenty-four hours to sign a peace treaty with us. At the end of that time we will attack Amoy and not relax our efforts until the city has fallen. This will be made perfectly clear to him.'

To everyone's surprise, General Tudely-Hext agreed with Sir Henry's attempt to prevent bloodshed. More, he declared that he himself would be the officer to enter the city with Luke.

Sir Henry Rutherford led the opposition to this surprise move, protesting that the Chinese had not always honoured the white flag in the past; the commanding general's life was too valuable to risk. But Tudely-Hext remained adamant.

'If there is any chance at all of a peaceful settlement, it can only be arranged with the Governor of Amoy. We all know of the strict protocol followed by the Chinese. No matter how senior the officer I send, he will speak to the Governor through intermediaries, each of whom has his own prejudices. I agree with Sir Henry that peace overtures should be made, but if they meet with failure, as I feel they will, I want to be satisfied they have not failed through any misunderstanding.'

General Tudely-Hext stood up. 'Now the decision has been taken, I think it should be implemented immediately.'

Nodding to Sir Henry Rutherford, he said, 'With your permission, Sir Henry, I will leave straight away. Come, Luke.'

Luke was dubious of the reception they would be given by the Amoy officials. There had been no attempt by either side to call a truce until now. The garrison of the city had been seen busily adding to the formidable defences ringing the town. Luke's apprehension increased as the ship's boat, sporting a giant white flag, neared the shore. Hordes of Chinese militiamen swarmed towards the landing-place, shouting and gesticulating noisily at those on board.

'H'm! Not the most reassuring welcome I've ever had,' muttered Tudely-Hext matter-of-factly, as a huge Chinese coolie leaped upon a rock jutting out into the sea and began hurling obscenities at them, accompanied by crude gestures of intent that required no interpretation.

'Tell your men to hold off for a few minutes,' Luke called to the naval officer in charge of the boat. 'Here come some real soldiers . . . Tartars. Now we'll learn what the official attitude is likely to be.'

The Tartars, stockier than their Chinese counterparts, looked even broader because of their uncomfortably warm padded jackets. Forcing their way along the beach, they beat back the noisy Chinese militiamen. Soon the giant coolie was the only Chinese standing between the Tartars and the sea. The Tartar officer ordered him from the rock, but was ignored. The officer called out a curt order and half a dozen Tartar soldiers raised their weapons. Before the Chinese militiaman could change his mind, there was a volley of shots and the Chinese coolie crumpled and slipped off the rock into the sea.

'Good God!' ejaculated Tudely-Hext. 'That officer takes his duties seriously.'

'He's a Tartar,' replied Luke, as though this in itself was sufficient explanation. 'But it means that our flag of truce will be honoured . . . providing nobody on our ships gets the wrong idea about those shots.'

General Tudely-Hext looked anxiously back towards the fleet, but the ships' captains had been keeping a keen watch through their telescopes on events ashore. They knew exactly what was happening and passed on the news to a much relieved pleni-potentiary.

As the boat grounded on the shingle, the Tartar officer stepped forward. 'Stop! We have honoured your white flag, but come no farther. What do you want?'

Luke explained that he brought the commanding officer of the British army to speak of peace with the Governor of Amoy.

The Tartar officer was impressed with the rank of Tudely-Hext, but he insisted they should remain in the boat while one of his own officers went into the city of Amoy and informed the Governor of their presence.

It was uncomfortably hot, and they had waited in silence for half an hour when the Tartar officer said suddenly, 'I liked you better when you came in the night to Shengan dressed as one of us, Luke Trewarne.'

Tudely-Hext looked at Luke sharply. He had caught Luke's name among the unfamiliar clipped Chinese words.

'You are one of Shengan's men?' Luke was surprised and not a little concerned. He had imagined Shengan would have marched his men out of sight of Canton, to return as soon as the British withdrew. He would not want Shengan caught up in the forthcoming fight, which he now thought was inevitable. 'Is Shengan near?'

'No.'

Luke's relief was so evident that the Tartar officer gave Luke a rather gloomy smile. 'You will not have to fight Shengan. He is in the Yangtze valley. I am in command of the armies here.'

'You?' Luke looked at the Tartar officer more carefully. Only very senior officers would be given command of an army of the size needed to defend Amoy. This Tartar certainly had the air of command. 'What rank are you?'

'The Fan Qui equivalent is, I think, a brigadier.'

'Then you must be Brigadier Yih-wei!' Luke was impressed at discovering the identity of the Tartar officer. Shengan had mentioned his second-in-command on a number of occasions, as had Morna. Always in the forefront of any battle, Yih-wei was a brave and resourceful soldier. He was also a most unusual man to find in a high army rank. A kinsman of the Emperor, and a poet of some note, Yih-wei had thrown up all his prospects of an easy life and automatic high office to join Shengan's Tartar army. He had earned his promotion by ability alone. Luke thought Tudely-Hext should know some details of the man who stood between them and Amoy.

Tudely-Hext listened intently, scrutinizing his opposite number as he did so. When Luke ended his explanation, the British general said, 'He has an impressive pedigree.' Extending his hand to the Tartar brigadier, he said to Luke, 'Tell him I'm pleased to extend my hand to him in friendship. I trust it will never point in his direction during battle.'

Brigadier Yih-wei was delighted with General Tudely-Hext. 'I, too, hope we will never face each other in battle. If we do, it is better to die at the hands of one who but for war might have been a friend. Perhaps you and the General would care to wait in my quarters. They are outside the city, but comfortable enough.'

Tudely-Hext was eager to accept the invitation from the Tartar brigadier. On the way he showed such a great interest in the elaborate defences about the city that Luke felt he should distract Yih-wei, lest he take offence.

'Surely it's unusual for such a distinguished soldier to have his camp outside the walls of a city?'

Yih-wei nodded soberly. 'These are unusual times. My orders are simple. Amoy must be held. It will not fall while I live. I and my men pitch our tents outside the walls because it is here we will live and die. We fight — or we die. That is our sacred duty.'

Luke repeated the conversation to Tudely-Hext, and the British general inclined his head. 'That's what I thought as soon as I saw their defences. They've thrown everything into them.' He wore a pained expression as he looked to where Yih-wei listened to a message, brought to him from the town by a Tartar soldier. 'He seems to be a damned fine fellow, Luke. I'd rather probe his mind than the defences I've seen here so far.'

But there was to be no truce. After a couple of hours, a mandarin came to Yih-wei's camp, despatched by the Governor. There would be no talks with the Fan Qui. He advised them to go away and leave China in peace. If they did not, they would be defeated by the Emperor's army, their bones left to rot in unmarked graves, far from those of their ancestors.

It was a meaningless piece of bravado. General Tudely-Hext told the mandarin that the Governor had until dawn the next day to change his mind. If there was no white flag fluttering above the main gate of Amoy at that time, the attack on the city would commence. It would continue until Amoy had been taken.

Tudely-Hext bid Brigadier Yih-wei a cordial farewell. As they were about to step into the boat that had brought them ashore, the British general hesitated for a moment, then unbuckled his sword-belt and handed the weapon to Luke.

'Give this to Yih-wei. Tell him I will be very happy if he hands it to me in person at the end of the battle – as a symbol of honourable surrender.'

Brigadier Yih-wei bowed his gratitude, then passed his own sword to Luke in return. 'Your general will have his sword again when the battle is done. I give this to him . . . but with a different request. If I survive this battle, I wish him to use my own sword to execute me. I know – as Shengan would know – that I cannot win. I also know I cannot live, with honour.'

As Luke turned to pass the sword and Yih-wei's tragic message to Tudely-Hext, the Tartar brigadier called, 'Wait, Luke Trewarne. A horseman arrived from Shengan a short while ago.'

'He is coming?'

Shengan and the remainder of his army could probably turn the course of the forthcoming battle, as both men knew.

'No, but he has bad news. He told me to send him as many soldiers as could be spared, to search for Ping Chuan. Your country's pirate ally has seized the woman you brought to Shengan's camp. She has saved many Tartar lives, but I fear she will not be able to save her own.'

Luke went cold at the thought of Morna in Ping Chuan's hands. On the way back to the warship he tried to share his fears with Tudely-Hext, but the army commander had other things on his mind. The lives of more than three thousand men depended upon the decisions he had to make in the next few hours. One girl was unimportant to him at the moment.

Ten

LUKE was on deck as dawn broke, hoping to see the white flag of surrender flying above Amoy's main gate. There *was* a flag, and at first Luke's spirits soared. Then as it grew lighter it became apparent that it was no more than a gesture of defiance. The flag bore the golden dragon emblem of Imperial China.

The bombardment commenced immediately, led by the guns of the fleet's two battleships. A few of the smaller vessels were firing into the city, but the main bombardment was directed against the Tartar defences, between the shoreline and the city wall. For three hours the heavy and well-aimed barrage pounded the island of Amoy. During all this time, Sir Henry Rutherford and the army headquarters staff watched the fall of shot through telescopes, commenting excitedly on the destruction of the Tartar defences, cheering wildly when the occasional shot exploded a magazine.

Luke could not share their enthusiasm. His thoughts were with Brigadier Yih-wei and his men, clinging desperately to their lives under the punishing bombardment, in the certain knowledge that they would lose them on British bayonets when the cannonade stopped. The regiments of the Royal Irish and Princess Charlotte's Welsh were to spearhead the attack. Nervously eager for the forthcoming battle, they were already on their way ashore, their barges towed through a choppy sea by the armed steamers accompanying the fleet.

The deafening barrage ceased as the first troops leaped from their boats and splashed ashore. On the men-of-war the sudden silence hurt the eardrums. It was broken by the distant cheers of the soldiers on shore and the flat report of their muskets as they stormed the first defensive positions.

Incredibly, a great many Tartar soldiers had survived the cruel bombardment and a fierce battle raged all that day. The increasingly rough sea between ships and shore was criss-crossed by boats landing stores, more ammunition and artillery. Those returning to the ships carried the wounded.

Sir Henry Rutherford was anxious to go ashore and witness

the fighting at first hand, but his staff dissuaded him from such foolhardiness. The battle was by no means over. A third of Tudely-Hext's forces, the Westmorland Regiment, had been prevented by rough seas from landing farther along the coast in support of the other regiments. If Yih-wei were able to call upon any reserves, he might still turn the tide of the battle.

Luke was heartily sick of the din of battle and the excitement among the military and naval men on deck. He went below to his cabin and lay on his back in the narrow bunk, staring up at the ceiling, wondering about the future of Gemmell Company and wishing he was with Kuei in Hong Kong.

Both came a little closer to him the following morning. The weather had improved, and the Westmorland Regiment was at last able to land in support of their comrades. General Tudely-Hext went with them, leaving Sir Henry Rutherford to pace the deck of the man-of-war and fume at his enforced inactivity.

When Luke went on deck to join the plenipotentiary, he was astounded to see *Black Swan* anchored not more than a cable's length from the warship. A boat was already halfway between the two vessels. As it drew closer, Gideon Pyke waved a greeting.

Luke was at the top of the gangway, delighted to see the American captain, but his happiness faded when he looked at Gideon Pyke's serious face. This was no friendly passing visit. Something was wrong — and Luke's first thought was of Kuei.

'She's all right, Luke. Kuei is well,' Gideon Pyke replied to Luke's anxious question. 'But she's having some bother. I think you should return home. . . . Is there somewhere we can talk in private?'

Curious seamen were crowding about them, wanting to know if Gideon Pyke carried mail or despatches from England. Luke led his captain below decks to the cabin, and here Gideon Pyke told him about Moller's purchase of Luke's land and of McCulloch's part in it.

Luke was at first stunned, then explosively angry. 'This must have been carefully planned between Moller, McCulloch and Killian. Not a word of the land auction leaked out before I left. This settles it! You can take me back to Hong Kong — now. I built that house. Neither McCulloch nor his thieving man of God is going to take it from me. As for putting Kuei out of her home . . . ! Come on, Gideon, I'm sick of the smell of war. It's time I went home.'

As he spoke, Luke was stuffing clothes angrily inside a battered leather chest that had once belonged to Dan Gemmell. His hasty packing more or less completed, Luke hoisted the trunk before him and crashed out through the doorway. He almost knocked over a young captain of Sir Henry Rutherford's administrative staff.

'Mr Trewarne . . . where are you going? Sir Henry Rutherford wants you to go ashore with him. The battle is over. Our troops are in Amoy. They've found it empty. . . . The Chinese have fled. . . .'

'Sir Henry will have to find someone else to hold his hand. I'm going home. Out of my way.'

Luke pushed past the astonished officer and, with difficulty, heaved the heavy trunk up the steep ladder to the deck. Staggering with it to the gangway at the side of the ship, he dumped it heavily to the deck and straightened up to find himself face to face with the startled plenipotentiary.

'What on earth are you doing, Trewarne? I sent Captain Stott to fetch you. Amoy is ours. We're going ashore.'

'*You're* going ashore, Sir Henry. *I'm* going home. My wife needs me more than you need an interpreter. I spent half of yesterday listening to you and your friends sitting up here on deck, applauding as though you were watching a theatrical show. For you it's no more than a . . . a . . . pheasant shoot, instead of a war in which good men on both sides are dying and maiming each other. I'm sick of your war, Sir Henry. It has never been mine; and, while I've been here wasting my time with you, my house and land have been stolen from me.'

Sir Henry Rutherford was hopelessly perplexed at Luke's outburst. He looked from Luke to Gideon Pyke in bewilderment. 'I have no idea what this is all about. I think you should come down to my cabin and tell me. I must have an interpreter and I want *you*, Trewarne.'

He turned to Gideon Pyke. 'You've apparently brought bad news with you. What is it?'

On the way to Sir Henry Rutherford's cabin, Gideon Pyke condensed his news of the happenings in Hong Kong. Once inside the cabin, Sir Henry said to Luke, 'Am I right in assuming that this regrettable incident is your main reason for wanting to return to Hong Kong? Oh, I know you don't care for this damned war. Neither do I, Trewarne. I don't care for any war — and I have known a great many in my lifetime. I can even understand your conflicting loyalties, young man. I was brought up in France; my mother was French. At the age of twelve I was packed off to sea and when still in my teens I found myself fighting the friends I had shared my toys with. I'm sorry; I had no intention of boring you with my own life-story. We are talking about Hong Kong. I'll appoint a committee to investigate all claims and appeals in respect of land. Stott . . . !'

Sir Henry called his young aide. 'Stott, I want you to draft a notice setting up a land appeal committee for Hong Kong. You had better head the committee yourself.'

To Luke, Sir Henry said, 'Put your complaint in writing, and I'll have it investigated as soon as we return. Does that satisfy you?'

'It helps. Thank you. But it could be months before we return to Hong Kong. Where will my wife live until then?'

'She can move in with my wife . . . in the Governor's residence. They haven't completed it yet, but I doubt if they ever will. It seems to grow and grow. It's ridiculously large for just the two of us. Almost as big as your house, Luke. Yes, I've seen it – and McCulloch's. They were both courageous ventures, if I may say so. We need men like you, Trewarne – and like McCulloch, too. He's a hard trader and a selfish man, but without such men Britain would not be the great nation she is today.'

Sir Henry Rutherford had made a generous gesture, but Luke remembered the attitude of the British women marooned on the ships in the anchorage towards Kuei. Taking a deep breath, he said, 'I think you should know, Sir Henry. . . . My wife is Chinese.'

Sir Henry Rutherford looked faintly amused. 'My dear fellow, I am quite aware of that. One of my very first duties after my arrival at Hong Kong – and a very pleasant one, too – was presenting a scroll to your wife. The officers and men of the expeditionary force wished to express their gratitude for her work in nursing so many of them back to health. You're a lucky man to have such an attractive wife. Lady Rutherford was very taken with her. I know she'll be delighted to have her in the house. Now, you've given me some extra work to do. I'll need to write a couple more blasted letters – but I still intend going ashore to see Amoy, and I want you with me.'

Luke nodded. He would have preferred to return to Hong Kong to solve his own problems and be with Kuei, but it would be churlish to refuse Sir Henry Rutherford now. Besides, Hong Kong was no longer a remote island where strong men made their own rules. McCulloch had learned this lesson from Surgeon Pelham Barclay. Luke would need to do the same.

Sir Henry Rutherford was greatly relieved. 'Thank you, Luke. You won't regret your decision. We need to put our trade with the Chinese on a realistic basis, but I am anxious to do this with a minimum of force. I am quite certain you are the best man to help me.'

On the way back up to the deck, Gideon Pyke said grudgingly to Luke, 'I think your government has done something sensible for a change, Luke. They've actually sent out the right man for the job he has to do.'

Luke was less easily convinced. 'I'll give you my views on that when this war is over. But if by staying with Sir Henry I get some news of Morna it will be worth while. In the meantime, I'd like you to stay in Hong Kong. Take care of Kuei and the business for me until I return.'

Later that same morning, the true tragedy of the war moved a step nearer to Luke. He was in a boat, heading shorewards with Sir Henry Rutherford and an escort of marines, when he saw two figures heading for deep water off rocks to the side of the landing-area. They were Tartar soldiers, and one appeared to be wounded, being helped along by the other.

Luke watched them with only a passing interest at first; the beach was littered with dead and wounded men of both sides. Then, as the men neared the water, his interest quickened. Snatching a telescope from the hands of the boat's coxswain, he trained it upon the shore. Impatiently, he worked to focus the instrument . . . and then he saw the figures more clearly.

'Quick! Head that way. Towards those two men.' Luke's order was so authoritative that the coxswain obeyed him without question.

'What are you up to?' The question came from the captain of the marines.

'One of those soldiers is Brigadier Yih-wei, commander of the Tartar forces defending Amoy.'

Startled, Sir Henry Rutherford took the telescope from Luke and trained it on the Tartar soldiers for a full minute. Lowering the telescope slowly, he looked sceptically at Luke. 'Are you quite certain? They both look like ordinary Chinese soldiers to me.'

'I'm certain. . . . Can't you go any faster?' Luke threw the question at the boat's coxswain, who looked balefully at Luke.

'This is a 'eavy boat, sir – and I had to cut down on oarsmen because we'm taking so many personages ashore.'

The coxswain bellowed at the sailors pulling on the oars and had them stretching forward and heaving with all their might. It was still not fast enough. As the two Tartars reached the water's edge, the wounded man handed something to his companion. Then, limping painfully, he walked out into the sea.

The occupants of the boat watched in fascinated horror as the water rose up the Tartar's chest . . . to his chin . . . and then over his head. Suddenly, he was gone.

'Good God!' Sir Henry's Rutherford's gasp broke the stunned silence. 'What in heaven's name did he think he was doing?'

'Brigadier Yih-wei was ordered to prevent us from taking Amoy, whatever the cost. He failed. There was no honour left in living.'

'The other one is still alive.'

A marine sergeant made the observation and raised a musket to his shoulder. Sir Henry Rutherford closed his hand about the barrel and pulled it down gently. 'There's been enough killing for one day, Sergeant.'

Luke shouted at the Tartar soldier from the boat, and the dejected figure waited for them to land. Luke jumped from the boat and splashed to meet him. The Tartar soldier held out both his arms in front of him. In his hands was General Sir Piers Tudely-Hext's sword.

The Tartar was an officer who had more than once escorted Luke from the factories to Shengan's house in Canton. He bowed as Luke approached.

'Brigadier Yih-wei left this for your general. He said it would be a waste for such a weapon to lie rusting in the sea.'

'Thank you. General Tudely-Hext will be honoured that Brigadier Yih-wei should think of him at such a time.'

The officer bowed again and would have walked away, but Luke called to him. 'Wait. . . . What will you do now?'

'Go to find Shengan. To tell him what happened here, and give him a message from Brigadier Yih-wei.'

'What is the message? May I know?'

'Yes, Luke Trewarne. Tell it to your general. Yih-wei's message is for Shengan to take his army to the hills and not come down to fight the Fan Qui until our men have muskets as efficient as yours – and ships with guns capable of bringing a city crashing about a man's ears.'

'General Shengan will not heed such words. He can't.'

The Tartar officer inclined his head. 'Then you and he will meet again . . . but not as friends. Goodbye, Luke Trewarne.'

Eleven

GENERAL TUDELY-HEXT fought his way northwards along the coast, and Luke and Sir Henry Rutherford went with him. Ting-hai and the whole of the unhealthy island of Chusan were recaptured and held with reinforcements newly arrived from India. Tudely-Hext fought a fierce battle for the town of Chin-hai, then he swung inland and moved his troops to within striking distance of the city of Ning-po.

Here, Luke was able to persuade the city officials to surrender without a fight. It was Luke's first major success since setting out with the expeditionary force many months before. He was heartily sick of the din of battle, the acrid smell of gunpowder, and the bloody and futile loss of life that was so much a part of the China campaign.

Luke had been unable to glean any information about Morna, and General Tudely-Hext had received no reports from the officers accompanying Ping Chuan. Rumour put the rebel leader somewhere in the Yangtze valley — but the river flowed for 3500 miles from its source in Tibet to the broad estuary in the China Sea.

The huge cities on the banks of the Yangtze — Shang-hai, Chin-kiang and Nanking — were to be the targets for Tudely-Hext's army, but not until the spring of 1842, still four months away. Meanwhile, his troops would remain in Ning-po for the winter.

Luke breathed a sigh of relief when Sir Henry Rutherford announced he was returning to Hong Kong and suggested to General Tudely-Hext that Luke accompany him. Luke's whole being ached to be with Kuei again.

He was on deck when the man-of-war in which he and Sir Henry were taking passage reached the Hong Kong anchorage. It was shortly before dusk on a cool November evening, and Luke could hardly believe that this was the same place from which he had sailed only months before.

Two- and three-storey stone buildings rose on the waterfront. Behind them, permanent houses extended up the lower slopes of the high peak, with a made-up road linking them with the businesses along the shore. There was even a naval dockyard in course of construction. Around the outskirts of the rapidly developing colony were the huts of the Chinese who had doubled the population of the island in a scant three months.

Rising above all the other buildings was the Governor's residence. Although Sir Henry Rutherford had been modest when comparing its proportions with Luke's own house, the residency dwarfed all other buildings on the island, with the exception of the partly constructed army barracks. But there were no carriages on the island yet. Rather than ride in Chinese sedan chairs, Luke and Sir Henry walked to the Governor's house, surrounded by an escort of Cameronians, the island's garrison troops.

Lady Rutherford greeted her husband with affection . . . and relief. Relief because he was an elderly man who refused to acknowledge his age and stubbornly pursued the vigorous life to which he had always been accustomed. When Sir Henry introduced Luke to her, tears sprang to her eyes, and she kissed him as though he were a long-lost son.

'I guessed you would return with Sir Henry. I sent someone to fetch Kuei as soon as I was told he had arrived. She will be so happy to see you, Luke. She's a dear girl. I will miss her terribly when you take her from me. . . . But this is a happy day – for all of us. It must not be marred by even one unhappy thought.'

Luke was shown to the beautiful suite of rooms where Kuei was living. He hardly had time to remove his coat before the door was flung open and Kuei burst into the room.

She clung to him, laughing and crying at one time. 'Oh, my Luke, it has been such a long time. I was sure you must have found a beautiful Manchu girl and forgotten your water-gipsy. . . .'

'Never, Kuei. . . . Never,' Luke said fiercely.

Later that evening, when lights were springing to life in the houses about the Governor's residence and the air was noticeably cooler, Kuei got up from the bed to close the windows. Luke stretched luxuriantly, the tensions of the past months thrown off with his clothes.

The windows closed, Kuei drew the curtains. From the darkness she said, 'You did not find Morna?'

A cloud crossed the clear sky of Luke's happiness. 'No, Ping

Chuan is somewhere in the Yangtze valley. But I don't even know if she's still with him – or if she is alive.'

'Would you have come home sooner had you not been searching for her?'

'No. My duties were with Sir Henry and General Tudely-Hext. . . .'

Luke suddenly propped himself up on one elbow. 'Kuei . . . I believe you're jealous.'

'No. . . . Yes! I am sorry, husband. Yes, I have been very jealous.' She came to him again. 'I thought you would save her from Ping Chuan and she would be so grateful. It would be – what do you say? – "romantic"? Yes, it would have been romantic. Like you and me on the Pearl River. Now I am sorry you did not find Morna. Perhaps I wished too hard. . . .'

Luke reached for Kuei in the darkness. She was a whole tangle of feminine emotions, and he loved every one of them. He told her so, and she whispered in reply, 'I love you so much, Luke. It makes me afraid. I think that one day you will look at a Fan Qui girl and say, "That girl is very beautiful. White skin . . . hair with no colour. . . . She is better than an ignorant Hoklo girl. . . ." '

Luke kissed Kuei. 'You're just fishing for compliments. You know very well you're the loveliest girl in Hong Kong. The whole of the island adores you. The Governor . . . Lady Rutherford . . . Surgeon Barclay . . . Gideon Pyke, not to mention every single soldier you've ever nursed.'

'Nobody matters to me but you, Luke. I want only you to love me.'

Pulling her to him, Luke whispered, 'Your wish is my command, Princess Kuei. Love me again and I promise never to look at another girl, Fan Qui, Chinese, Hoklo or Manchu.'

The subject of Morna McCulloch came up the next morning, when Luke and Kuei were at breakfast with Sir Henry and Lady Rutherford.

'Do you believe the McCulloch girl is still alive?' asked Lady Rutherford of Luke. 'I've heard some ghastly tales about this Ping Chuan. Why we ever had anything to do with him, I don't know.'

'Expediency, my dear,' muttered Sir Henry through his toast. 'It was necessary to draw the Tartar troops away from our objectives. We'd never have taken Amoy had the whole of General Shengan's army been there to oppose us. It was a damned close thing as it was. But I do agree with you. I've heard some hair-raising stories about Ping Chuan.'

'Whatever you heard is less than the truth,' said Luke grimly. 'I've had dealings with the man – and so has Kuei, right here on this island. He's insane. But, to answer your question, Lady Rutherford. Yes, I do think she is probably still alive – if your British officers were around at the time she was captured. Ping Chuan is counting on British support. Before long he'll be needing arms, money . . . and opium. He'll be coming to General Tudely-Hext to get them. For as long as he's likely to want our aid, Morna will be safe . . . but not for one minute longer.'

Lady Rutherford toyed with her food, occasionally looking up at Luke with a thoughtful expression. She wanted to ask him to do something, but was not certain how he would take the request. She did not want to upset him, she was far too fond of Kuei, and yet. . . .

'Luke, I wonder if you will do something for me?'

'Of course, if it's at all possible.'

'I would like you to repeat what you have just told me . . . to Ezra McCulloch.'

'No!' The cry of indignation came from Kuei. 'Luke will not speak to that man.'

'What makes you think Ezra will want to know about Morna? I took her to meet him, in Canton. It proved to be a great mistake. He struck Morna and publicly disowned her. I doubt if he will have had a sudden change of heart.'

'I'm quite sure he never meant a word he said to her,' declared Lady Rutherford. 'Ezra McCulloch is a lonely and confused man. I find it terribly sad, especially as I had so been looking forward to meeting him. He has become something of a legend in Britain. A swashbuckling adventurer. The same breed of man as Drake and Raleigh. With typical Scots aggression and ability he has built up his trading empire from nothing. Unfortunately, things are changing very quickly here in the Far East, and Ezra McCulloch is too old to move with them. He is seeking solace in drink, and I fear he is destroying himself.'

'Good!' Kuei spoke with feeling. 'McCulloch killed my father with his opium, my best friend with a gun, and now he tries to take my husband's house and business. You think Luke should be kind to him? I say, No! No! No! Let McCulloch destroy himself as he has always destroyed others. He and Ping Chuan are all the same man.'

When Kuei was excited, her English deteriorated – and she was very angry now. She stalked from the table as fast as her tight-fitting silk dress would allow, her chin thrown high.

'I'm terribly sorry, Luke.' Lady Rutherford was deeply distressed. 'I should have had more sense than to mention Ezra McCulloch in front of Kuei. But I never knew about her father . . . and her friend.'

Luke folded his napkin on the table at the side of his plate before standing to go after Kuei. 'There are a great many things you don't know about Ezra McCulloch, Lady Rutherford. I'll go and see him, because he's Morna's father . . . but don't expect any miracles. Now, if you'll excuse me, I must go to Kuei.'

When the door had closed behind Luke, Sir Henry said, 'I like that young man. He will make a useful diplomat. He's honest and loyal. Perhaps a shade too much conscience, but that's becoming fashionable in these times. Yes, I think Great Britain may make good use of Luke Trewarne one day.'

Luke found Kuei in their room, staring morosely out of the window. When he came up behind her and put his arms about her, she turned in to him fiercely and Luke held her for a long time without speaking.

'Are you very angry with me, my husband?' Her voice was muffled as she spoke with her face pressed against his shirt.

Luke smiled and kissed the thick dark hair on top of her head. 'And why should I be angry with you? Because you told the truth about Ezra McCulloch? You could have said much more.'

Kuei pushed herself just far enough from him to look up into his face. 'But I was rude to the wife of your governor.'

Luke shrugged. 'She understands . . . and so do I. After what Ezra has done to us *I* should feel the same way about him; but we'll have the house and land back soon. Ezra McCulloch will have lost, once again. To the rest of the world he might appear to be a successful man – a legend. I can't help thinking of him as no more than a lonely old man. I feel genuinely sorry for him.'

'Ezra McCulloch may be old man. He is still very dangerous man. See him, if you must, my Luke. But I will tremble for you until your return.'

On the way to see Ezra McCulloch, Luke called in at his own house. It looked sadly neglected. The walls were in need of a coat of whitewash and the gardens tangled and overgrown. The faded notice signed by Killian was still attached to the front door. Luke had intended going inside, but he found the door had been secured with two heavy iron staples and a stout padlock, put there by Surgeon Pelham Barclay to prevent looting.

Luke did not approach the quay, crowded with McCulloch's ships. He feared the sight would anger him so much he might break his promise to Lady Rutherford.

Ezra McCulloch's house looked every bit as neglected as Luke's, and his servants were sullen and suspicious. After a lengthy wait, Luke was shown into the lounge that Lo Asan had once graced so beautifully. It was now an untidy mess, the air heavy with the stale smell of alcohol and tobacco.

Heavy-eyed, Ezra McCulloch sprawled in one of the large armchairs. As Luke approached him, he reached out a hand for a half-filled brandy-glass standing on the table beside him. The hand shook as though McCulloch had palsy. Luke had little cause to like the trader, yet it gave him no pleasure to see him in such a state. Ezra McCulloch was a mere shadow of the man he had been. The deterioration had worsened in recent months, but downing his drink he looked up at Luke with a touch of his former arrogance.

'If you've come about the sale of your land, you're wasting your time, Trewarne.'

'I'll get my land back, Ezra. In my own time, and my own way. But that isn't why I'm here. I've come to talk about Morna.'

Ezra McCulloch twice opened his mouth as though to say something; then he dropped his gaze to the empty glass he held in his lap. After a full three minutes' silence, Luke became concerned about the older trader. He had not moved a muscle for all that time.

'Ezra . . . you *have* heard what's happened to Morna?'

McCulloch's head jerked up, and Luke glimpsed the anguish that was in the man.

Ezra McCulloch struggled from the chair and made his way to the sideboard. Refilling his glass from a crystal-cut ship's decanter, he said to Luke, 'D'you want a drink?'

Luke shook his head, and Ezra McCulloch returned to his chair. 'You remember what I told you in Canton? I have no daughter.'

'You didn't mean it then, and you don't now. I know it, and so does Morna.'

'You believe that . . . ?'

The brief moment of eagerness faded quickly, and Ezra McCulloch shrugged his shoulders hopelessly. 'Why are we talking like this — as though she's still alive? She was taken by Ping Chuan. You know him almost as well as I do. . . . But it wasn't *your* idea that he should fight for us. If I hadn't done that. . . .'

Luke ignored the other man's drunken self-recriminations. 'I'm convinced she's still alive, Ezra.' He repeated his theory, but it seemed only to send McCulloch into a deeper melancholic state. Before Luke had stopped talking, Ezra McCulloch was shaking his head emphatically. Suddenly he stood up, spilling some of the brandy from his glass, and began pacing the room.

'You don't understand, Luke. I've heard from Ping Chuan. He sent one of his men to give me a message.'

Luke stared at McCulloch. 'What did he want? A ransom?'

'He gave me an ultimatum. Either I give my blessing to a marriage between Morna and Ping Chuan — with a suitable dowry, of course — or I could buy her back with opium.'

'Have you told anyone else about this?'

Ezra McCulloch shook his head.

'What reply did you give to Ping Chuan's man?'

Ezra McCulloch stopped his pacing. 'I had him strangled and his body dumped in the harbour. I'll not be dictated to by pirates.'

Luke felt a sudden chill go through him. Ping Chuan's man would not have travelled alone. His companions would tell Ping Chuan what had happened.

'You must have been mad, Ezra. We'll try to get an answer to Ping Chuan — and quickly. Offer him opium — promise him *anything* — but get Morna back.'

'It's too late. What we're talking about happened months ago. Morna won't be alive now. If she is, she'll be hoping for death to come. . . .'

'She's your daughter, not Lo Asan. I believe Ping Chuan will have kept her alive rather than risk trouble with his British army advisers. He's got a lot at stake.'

'More than you know,' agreed Ezra McCulloch. 'Ping Chuan is fighting for the throne of China. Not that the thought of that will save Morna, if he wants her. Ping Chuan is mad. He makes a madman's decisions.'

Luke gasped as he tried to grasp the magnitude of Ping Chuan's ambition. Then he looked at Ezra McCulloch with a new understanding. 'You seriously believe Ping Chuan can succeed.' It was not a question, but a statement. 'You think that Ping Chuan can lead a successful rebellion against the Emperor. If he does, you stand to make a fortune . . . right? Because of this mad idea, you persuaded the British to back Ping Chuan and turn him loose against the Chinese people?'

Luke was nauseated by Ezra McCulloch's greed. There *was* a remote chance that Ping Chuan might succeed in seizing the throne of China. The Manchus had never been popular rulers and their power had declined enormously in recent years. But the price that would be paid in lives and human misery was unthinkable. A madman on the throne of a country the size of China could threaten the peace of the whole world!

'I can understand Charles Moller backing such a plan, Ezra. He's as mad as Ping Chuan. But you . . . ? We've never got along, and it's no secret that I despise your trading methods, but I've always respected you as a man of some intelligence. This . . . it's just unbelievable!'

Suddenly, Luke could take no more of Ezra McCulloch's company. Turning on his heel, he left the house and made his way up the hill behind the houses. Finding a quiet spot, Luke sat for a couple of hours looking out over the anchorage to the hills of mainland China. It was a rare luxury to be alone and able to think clearly.

Later that morning, Luke made his way to Sir Henry Rutherford's office and told him all he knew about Morna, Ping Chuan and Ezra McCulloch.

Sir Henry was shocked by what Luke had to say, but he confessed there was little he could do.

'We don't know where Ping Chuan is,' he admitted. 'Even if I did get word to him, I fear it would be too late in view of what you have just told me. I agree with you; it is disgraceful that we should have had anything to do with such a man. I don't believe Ping Chuan will ever succeed in his bid for the throne. He has destroyed all sympathy for his cause by his actions, and those of his men – but he has served an important purpose, I assure you. Had we not divided the Chinese forces, this war would have taken a very different course.'

Sir Henry made a gesture of hopelessness. 'What more can I say? If you think it will help, I will give you a letter to take to General Sir Piers Tudely-Hext. He might be persuaded to move off to the Yangtze River earlier than he intended. He might be able to put a stop to Ping Chuan's depredations — but I doubt if he will save McCulloch's girl.'

As Sir Henry said, the situation seemed hopeless. But Luke sent Gideon Pyke to Ning-po with the Governor's letter to Tudely-Hext and sent one himself, giving the General every scrap of information he had on Ping Chuan.

Luke spent the remainder of that winter re-establishing his trade in Canton and Hong Kong. At the beginning of 1842, Sir Henry's committee on land purchase met to hear Luke's complaint. It ruled that the land, house and godown should be immediately returned to him and a new deed made out in his name.

Luke and Kuei moved back to their own home, but not until Lady Rutherford had thrown a farewell ball for them at the Governor's residence. The first social occasion of its kind in the new colony, it was attended by every one of the two hundred and fifty British residents, and most of the officers from the garrison.

It was a splendid evening. The more conservative residents of the colony were shocked that such a soirée should have been held to honour a trader and his Chinese wife, but they did not voice their opinions in the hearing of the colony's first lady.

Luke was aware of their disapproval, but he gave no hint of it as he danced with a radiantly happy Kuei. He was too wrapped up in his own thoughts to care. This had been a very mixed day for him. Sir Henry Rutherford had asked Luke to join General Tudely-Hext at Ning-po, in preparation for the spring offensive along the Yangtze Kiang — and Kuei had told him that she was carrying a child.

Twelve

DURING the winter months, the Chinese militia had been active outside the walls of Ning-po. They picked up any British soldier foolish enough to venture abroad on his own or tempted outside by the lurid promise of a painted Chinese prostitute. Forty men were taken in this manner and their heads exhibited on stakes within sight of the city wall.

Luke arrived at the city the day before the Chinese launched an attack there. They intended it as a surprise, but, thanks to a programme of surreptitious bribery, Tudely-Hext learned details of the Chinese plan days before it took place. With the help of a regiment of Indian troops, moved in from Chusan, the attack was repulsed, and great loss of life suffered by the Chinese.

The attack was pressed home with great determination. It was an indication of the mood of the Chinese and Tartar commanders, desperate for a morale-boosting victory against the barbarian invaders.

Luke carried a letter for General Tudely-Hext from Sir Henry Rutherford. It gave the General a free hand in the summer campaign against the Chinese.

Aware of the Chinese need for a victory — real or imagined — General Tudely-Hext was in no great hurry to move off. He delayed evacuating Ning-po until it was impossible for the Chinese to claim he had left because of their abortive attack. The delay irked Luke. He was eager to find Ping Chuan, and have the whole campaign brought to a close. Kuei was expecting a child, and he wanted to be with her when it was born.

Eventually, Tudely-Hext made his move. Embarking his forces on the troop-transports, he sailed for the mouth of the Yangtze River.

On both sides of the Yangtze Kiang estuary, the army took villages and towns in battles so one-sided that Luke was sickened by what he considered to be entirely unnecessary bloodshed. Only in the larger, walled cities was there any real resistance, and here Luke was frequently successful in arranging a truce before fighting began.

Woo-sung, the stronghold guarding the Yangtze tributary leading to Shang-hai, was one of his failures. Luke did not even get ashore to talk about a truce. His boat, prominently displaying a white flag, was bombarded by shore batteries. Although no shots hit the craft, the message was clear. The Chinese would not enter into negotiations with the Fan Qui.

Tudely-Hext lined his ships up opposite the stronghold and began a devastating cannonade. But the defenders of the city were seasoned Chinese troops, with a strong contingent of Tartars to provide them with additional backbone. They had also learned something from earlier engagements. When the bombardment began, the Chinese soldiers lay low in deep trenches, prepared well in advance in front of the city wall. They stayed in them until Tudely-Hext's troops landed. Then they emerged and fought with a ferocity never before experienced by the British expeditionary force. For many hours the outcome of this battle was in the balance. Not until a strong detachment of marines landed farther along the coast and fought their way behind the combined Chinese and Tartar force did the defence begin to crumble.

Even now, there were strong pockets of resistance. In a strongly built stone temple, close to the city gate, three hundred Tartar soldiers made a desperate stand. They inflicted heavy casualties on the British and Indian troops and fought on until their ammunition was exhausted and every man in the temple was wounded.

Much to the surprise of the colonel in charge of the attacking force, the Tartars did not continue the battle with knife and bayonet. They surrendered.

The British troops, smarting under the heavy punishment they had suffered at the hands of the Tartar troops, were in no mood to accept their surrender. As the Tartars poured from the shattered building, the British troops began bayoneting the unarmed men. Their colonel was unable – or unwilling – to do anything to prevent the massacre. The slaughter ended only when Tudely-Hext himself ordered the British soldiers to pull back, threatening to use his marines to shoot them down if they did not obey immediately. The British troops fell back from the temple, but by now only sixty Tartars were left alive.

Fuming at the barbarity of the British soldiers involved, Tudely-Hext ordered them back to the troop-transports.

'What will you do with the Tartars now?' Tight-lipped, Luke

asked the question as he looked to where the small group of Tartars huddled in a dejected group, some having their wounds bound by their comrades.

'Tell them they will be supplied with food, then are free to leave,' replied Tudely-Hext. 'It's the least I can do for them. I wish they were for me, instead of against my troops. I've met no comparable fighting men since I did battle with the Gurkhas in Nepal.'

Luke walked to where the Tartars sat and looked for an officer. He could not see one. However, there was a small tight knot of soldiers standing at the rear of the group, and he moved in that direction. Immediately, other Tartars moved to block his way. Luke became uneasy. Something was wrong here.

Then a familiar voice gave a sharp order in Manchu. Reluctantly, the Tartars moved away to allow Luke through, and he found himself looking down at Shengan. He looked as dirty and disreputable as the remainder of his troops and, in common with them, Shengan was wounded. He leaned back against a rock, the right side of his uniform jacket soaked with blood.

'Shengan!' Luke was distressed to find his friend in such a condition, but he kept his voice low. 'What are you doing here?'

Shengan smiled weakly. 'This is my country, Luke Trewarne, and these are my soldiers. Where else should a good general be but at the scene of a battle?'

'I ought to have realized. . . .' Luke was untying the leather laces fastening Shengan's coarse jacket as he spoke. 'The way your men fought should have told me you were with them. But where are the remainder of your troops?'

Luke winced as he uncovered Shengan's wound. The Tartar general had been standing close to a narrow window in the temple when a shrapnel shell burst outside. He needed a surgeon.

Shengan answered Luke's question quietly, carefully controlling his emotion. 'I had two thousand men defending this city. These are the survivors. There would have been more had your soldiers not slaughtered defenceless men.'

A few dispirited Tartar warriors, miraculous survivors from the carnage outside the city walls, had wandered along to join Shengan, but there were less than a hundred men about him.

'General Tudely-Hext is dealing with the soldiers who attacked you after your surrender. Men get carried away by blood-lust in battle. But where is your main army? You left Canton with more than twenty thousand men and their families.'

338

Shengan shrugged, and the movement caused him pain. 'They are spread the length of the Yangtze valley. Many will now be hurrying to defend Shang-hai – but we have found no answer to the guns of your ships-of-war.'

Luke pulled out a sliver of metal from Shengan's body, and the action caused Shengan to wince.

'I'm going to fetch a surgeon.' Luke stood up and looked down at his friend.

'What happens then, Luke Trewarne? Will you have me taken to meet your general?'

'No. General Tudely-Hext has given orders for you and your men to be given food and allowed to leave.'

Shengan's eyes searched Luke's face. 'He will not allow us to go when he learns he has the commanding general of the Tartar Army in his hands.'

'He won't be told,' retorted Luke. 'Stay here until I find a surgeon. I'll be as quick as I can.'

Shengan leaned back against the stone gratefully. 'Thank you. It is good to find a friend at such a time.'

Army Surgeon Pelham Barclay had come north with the British expeditionary force. Tudely-Hext now commanded twelve thousand men, and the senior surgeon felt there was more to be done here than in the now well-established hospital in Hong Kong.

Luke found Pelham Barclay working with a team of fellow-surgeons in a large hospital tent, pitched just above the water-line beside the beach. Most of their work called for swift and often crude amputation, and the surgeon was wearing a large wrap-around apron heavily stained with the blood of his fellow-men. Luke shuddered. A battlefield hospital had the smell of an animal slaughter-house about it.

Pelham Barclay agreed to accompany Luke. In common with other members of the expeditionary force, he had considerable respect for the Tartar warriors who fought with such ferocity. He was eager to meet them at first hand.

Luke took him first to examine Shengan, and the Tartar general startled Barclay by declaring, in English, 'It is nothing serious. I will live to fight another day.'

'Probably,' agreed the army surgeon. 'But it's a nasty wound. I'd like to examine you in the hospital tent and keep you under observation for a few days.'

Immediately, Shengan's eyes narrowed and he looked at the surgeon suspiciously.

'That's not possible,' said Luke hastily. 'General Tudely-Hext has said the Tartars are free to go. They're anxious to get away as quickly as they can.'

'Then I'll have to do the best I can here,' accepted the surgeon. 'It won't be a lot.'

In spite of his words, Pelham Barclay made a thorough examination of Shengan's wound, picking out a number of slivers of metal. Finally, he bound a dressing about Shengan's body, then turned his attention to the wounds of his soldiers.

'I am grateful to you.' Shengan spoke in Chinese when the surgeon had moved away. 'I was surprised when I first saw you with your soldiers. . . . Then I remember what I had been told. You are known as "the Peace Maker" and are still a friend of my people.'

Luke was deeply moved. In moments of depression, such as the one he was experiencing now, surrounded by dead and wounded men, Luke felt his efforts were wasted. Now Shengan was telling him they were not. By calling him 'the Peace Maker', the Chinese themselves acknowledged the usefulness of his work. They were brutally honest in the names they used to describe a man's activities.

'It's a pity more of your mandarins won't listen to me, Shengan. Look about you. How many of your men have died — and how many of ours? For what? Woo-sung is ours for the taking and both our countries have many more widows.'

'You speak the truth. Yet while a barbarian army tramples the sacred soil of my land I must remember I am a soldier and obey the orders of my Emperor. He has decreed that I must fight while a single Tartar soldier remains alive.'

Luke bit back a reply about the mindless arrogance of the Emperor. Shengan would not accept such criticism, even from a friend.

Rising carefully to his feet, Shengan patted the dressing about his body. 'We have much to learn from you about medicine. . . .' He suddenly became uncharacteristically hesitant. 'How . . . how is Morna? Is she in Hong Kong now?'

Luke looked at Shengan in astonishment. 'You must know. . . . She was taken by Ping Chuan.'

Shengan's hesitancy vanished. 'That was almost a year ago!

You knew well before winter that Ping Chuan had taken her. Was he not ordered to release her then?'

'No one knows where Ping Chuan is. We're hoping to meet up with him somewhere on the Yangtze. If Morna is still alive. . . .'

'*If?* What manner of men are your generals that they choose their allies so carelessly? I can understand that they do not care what Ping Chuan does to my people. That is the morality of war. But Morna is one of your own. If I took a Fan Qui woman and harmed her, your army would seek me out no matter where I hid. Yet a man – and I spit at the word – one such as Ping Chuan, can do what he likes because you call him an ally?'

Pelham Barclay had stopped treating the wound of one of the soldiers. In common with the Tartar warriors, he was taking an interest in Shengan's outburst of fury.

'I am as concerned as you, Shengan. Morna means a lot to me – to Kuei, too. *I* believe she is still alive. There are British officers with Ping Chuan's army. They'll protect her.' Shengan gave a derisive snort, but Luke continued quickly. 'Morna's father received a message from Ping Chuan. He asked for her in marriage . . . or a ransom of opium instead. He won't harm her while there's a chance of making a profit from her.'

Shengan had regained control of himself. 'Your faith in Ping Chuan behaving like a sane man is greater than my own. You have not entered towns and villages quitted by him and his men. You have not seen the heads of innocent men heaped like turnips in the fields, or heard the cries of the women and children, begging that they, too, might be killed as an act of mercy.'

Shengan called on the ragged remnants of his army to prepare to march away from the scene of their defeat, before speaking to Luke again.

'I, too, wished Morna to marry me . . . and she had accepted me. I make you a promise. If she is still alive now, she will stay alive. Ping Chuan will not have a moment to think of anything but fighting me. I will not give him time to unroll his blanket at night. Tell your general to advance up the Yangtze Kiang and he will meet with Ping Chuan running the other way. My Tartars will drive him down the river to you.'

Shengan gave an order, and his men began limping inland, away from Woo-sung. Before following them, Shengan gripped Luke's hand and looked into his face. 'Give me time to get far from here. Then you may tell your general that in exchange for my life I give him Shang-hai. There will have to be a final battle between us, but it will not be at Shang-hai. You and I will not meet again. I want you to know I have valued your friendship above all my possessions. Goodbye, my barbarian friend. I was right. You have never become a Fan Qui.'

Deeply moved, Luke stood watching Shengan's men on their way. Gathering up his surgical instruments, Pelham Barclay came to stand beside him.

'Was that General Shengan?'

Luke looked at the surgeon sharply. 'How did you know?'

'Call it an inspired guess. You and he obviously knew each other well, and Kuei has told me of your friendship with Shengan. I realized when I first saw him that he was a senior officer. Such a man had no need to wear a general's uniform.'

Luke looked at Pelham Barclay questioningly, and the surgeon smiled. 'I've served with the Army all my life, Luke. A good officer has no need of gold braid and the other accoutrements of rank. He wears his authority as naturally as he does his uniform. It's there for all to see. Shengan is such a man.'

He gazed after the receding figures. 'Will you tell General Tudely-Hext he has allowed Shengan to slip through his grasp?'

'I'll have to. Shengan just made him a present of Shang-hai. Tudely-Hext is entitled to know who it's from.'

General Tudely-Hext was philosophical about Shengan's escape, and Luke's part in it. He believed that generals should not be held as prisoners. But he was sceptical about Shang-hai falling without a fight. It would be the largest city his army had occupied to date, and he had anticipated a fierce battle.

Once he had accepted the surrender of Woo-sung, Tudely-Hext moved his troops the few miles up-river to Shang-hai. He found the gates flung wide for him to enter. There was not a Tartar soldier within fifty miles, and without the Tartars the Chinese had no stomach for battle.

The British troops entered the city cautiously but, except for an occasional isolated incident, they met no opposition. The residents of the city were fortunate that it was so. Shang-hai was rich with pickings. It would have taken little to persuade the British troops to set out on an orgy of looting. The Indian troops, their eyes on other Chinese treasures, were less inhibited than the British. Not until Tudely-Hext sent five of their number in front of a firing squad did the raping of Chinese women cease.

As a result of his discussion with Shengan, Luke was anxious to move on up the Yangtze River. But General Tudely-Hext would not be hurried. As well as the twelve thousand troops under his command, he had more than sixty troop-transports and their men-of-war escorts. It was a great responsibility and he was taking no risks.

The Yangtze River was a mighty waterway, the main artery to the heart of China. From Chin-kiang, a hundred and fifty miles up-river, there was a remarkable canal that ran northwards for six hundred miles to Peking. Along this waterway rice was carried to feed the millions residing in the Chinese capital. Tudely-Hext expected the river to be heavily defended for every foot of its length. Before setting out from Shang-hai, he sent two armed steamers up the Yangtze to test the Chinese defences. Then he sat back and waited.

A fortnight later, the first of the two armed steamers returned, and its captain reported to General Tudely-Hext. He had gone up-river as far as the entrance to the Peking canal. The only gun emplacement had been a few miles downstream from the canal. Deserted, it had been destroyed by a party of marines from the ship. The largest cannon in the emplacement was inscribed with the name of its Jesuit maker, 'M. Ricci'. A magnificent brass weapon, it had first been fired when Oliver Cromwell was fighting to overthrow his monarch in England. The marines rolled the cannon to the river-bank and dropped it into the sluggish brown water of the Yangtze Kiang.

The second steamer returned two days later, having steamed as far as the towering walls of Nanking city. On a stretch of river where a large deserted island narrowed the navigable passage to no more than three hundred yards, the river was guarded by two guns, sited in a splendid defensive position. When the steamer was still a quarter of a mile downstream, a single shot had been fired from each gun. Moments later, both gun crews and their guards were seen fleeing along the river-bank away from the strange British warship, the like of which had never before been seen in this part of China. The two gun emplacements suffered the same fate as the one encountered by the first steamer.

Greatly heartened at this unexpected news, General Tudely-

Hext embarked his troops and led them up the great river. By now, Sir Henry Rutherford had joined the expedition. He had been a fighting man for too many years to languish in Hong Kong, wielding nothing more deadly than a quill pen, when British soldiers and sailors were fighting almost on his doorstep.

Sir Henry arrived on board *The Two Brothers* with the ship's owner, Ezra McCulloch — and a full load of opium. If Morna were still alive, her father had the price for her release, albeit somewhat late.

Sailing up the Yangtze River, the fleet was an impressive sight. Divided into three divisions, it extended along six miles of river. Leading this great armada was the 74-gun battleship *Cornwallis*, warning off all Chinese river traffic.

The steam-powered warships had carried out their reconnaissance well. Not a gun was fired at them, though whole villages turned out to watch them sail by. Men and women watched in silence, but it was difficult to contain the excitement of the children at the sight of such a grand fleet. Some of the younger children would venture a cheery wave, only to be cuffed into aggrieved order by disapproving parents.

Thirteen

THINGS were not going at all well for Ping Chuan and his pirate army in the wide Yangtze valley. Part of the problem was that during the early months of campaigning the pickings had been too easy. The Chinese were expecting any attack to come from the direction of the sea. Regiments of militia had been raised and sent post-haste to the towns and cities along the coast. When Ping Chuan and his fifteen thousand men suddenly appeared from the hills, hundreds of miles inland, the surprise was complete.

Many pirates became so overburdened with their loot that they could not keep up with their companions. Others suddenly found themselves rich beyond all their wildest expectations. They deserted Ping Chuan and set off for homes and villages they had been pleased to leave many years before and had never expected to see again.

Ping Chuan was hardly aware of the loss of thousands of his warriors. Young men, disgruntled with their Manchu rulers, flocked to join his rebel army. To distract him further, Ping Chuan had surrounded himself with a harem of the most attractive girls in the Yangtze valley. A few of them were willing concubines, but most were captives.

For many months the pirates roamed the valley, doing just as they wished. The opposition from Shengan's army had diminished as more and more commitments were heaped upon it by a frantic and ill-advised Emperor.

Then, early in the summer of 1842, Ping Chuan and his hordes descended upon yet another sleepy riverside town. They were met by a withering crossfire that killed a hundred men in the first fusillade. The rebel army had become unused to opposition. In response to screams of fury from Ping Chuan, they launched a second attack on the town. The result was the same as before, but now the determined defenders poured from the town in hot pursuit of the rebels. Ping Chuan's men saw they were opposed by seasoned Tartar warriors who formed a disciplined line of advance, proudly brandishing the silk banners

345

of Shengan's regiment. The rebels broke and ran – straight into two companies of mounted Tartars who rode among them, hacking them to the ground and trampling them beneath the feet of their long-haired wiry ponies.

It was the beginning of an oft-repeated nightmare for Ping Chuan. No matter where he struck, it was the same story. Every town of any size was defended by Shengan's men. Smaller villages were deserted, the departing peasants taking all their food with them.

Shengan was keeping his promise to Luke. Ping Chuan's army was being squeezed hard, and the only way he could go was with the river, away from the lands he had terrorized for so long.

There were no easy victories now. Ping Chuan was fighting for survival.

Ping Chuan blamed everyone for his sudden reversal of fortunes. He raved at his men for growing soft. He blamed the luckless Fan Qui army 'advisers' for not planning his campaign in advance.

The British officers had suffered even more than Ping Chuan's own men. Many of them had been shot down trying to rally the rebels against Shengan's Tartars. Others had died from fever. Now only two remained. They were lucky. They had contracted malaria when Morna still had quinine.

But Ping Chuan reserved his most virulent hatred for the Reverend Charles Moller.

At the beginning of their ill-matched alliance, religion had provided them with a common bond, but it was soon apparent that the two men interpreted Christianity in very different ways. Ping Chuan's professed Christianity was typically Chinese. Much of the unpalatable ritual was ignored and the remainder was melted down and shaped to suit his needs and inclinations. He found it useful to be the representative of one all-powerful God, superior to the others. At first, the Ten Commandments had proved to be something of a stumbling-block, but Ping Chuan eventually accepted them in the same way that a Chinese abided by the laws of his land. They were issued only as a 'guide', open to argument and interpretation.

For Charles Moller, Christianity came undiluted from the Bible. As it was written, then so must it be. A man either believed, or he was damned – a heathen. Moller's sworn duty was to convert the heathen. Those who refused conversion died. They were the Devil's men – and Charles Moller was a warrior of the Lord.

As the campaign progressed, Moller lost none of his fierce eccentricity. Absolutely fearless in battle, he would stand in the vanguard of Ping Chuan's army, undaunted by spears or musket-balls, holding a bloody sword by the blade. Raised high above the heads of Ping Chuan's men, it was a symbolic crucifix to rally the flagging rebels.

Always to be found where the battle was most furious, Charles Moller bore a charmed life. On one occasion, Shengan's Tartars used an aged cannon against the rebels. The roar as it was fired at point-blank range was deafening, and the attacking rebels disappeared in a cloud of choking black smoke. When the smoke cleared, Ping Chuan's men lay dead and dying, but Moller stood uninjured in his flowing blood-spattered robe and fell upon the Tartar gun crew like an avenging angel.

It was little wonder that the legend of his immortality was accepted without question by Ping Chuan's men.

Moller also led the rebels on a successful raid against an ill-guarded supply-column. When he returned to camp, Moller conducted a thanksgiving service during which he preached a damning sermon against Ping Chuan's personal way of life. He blamed his immorality for the defeats the rebel army had suffered, declaring it was the Lord's way of expressing his disapproval. He promised that, if Ping Chuan did not dispense with his harem, God's wrath would be terrible to behold.

It was the first occasion on which Moller had openly criticized Ping Chuan, and the wily rebel leader was shaken by the roars of support that rose from his own men. That same evening, Ping Chuan had every girl in his harem executed in front of his cheering army. Charles Moller had recorded a resounding victory against Ping Chuan, but it would not be so easy to score another. The rebel leader now looked upon the mad missionary as a dangerous rival – and Ping Chuan was experienced in dealing with such men.

Morna and the two British officers were aware of the growing tension between Moller and Ping Chuan, and all three feared for their own lives. There had been no contact with British troops since leaving the Pearl River, and no arms or ammunition had reached the rebels for months. The benefits to be gained by the rebels from an alliance with General Tudely-Hext were no longer apparent, and the influence of the British officers declined accordingly. Morna's situation had become increasingly precarious. No word had been received from her father. If he sent neither dowry nor ransom, she became expendable. With Ping Chuan's harem gone, Morna was now the only woman in the camp, and the rebel leader had time to think about her.

Morna and the two officers discussed their rapidly worsening situation one evening in the bamboo and reed hut they shared. Outside, the rain beat fiercely against the hut, leaking through the roof into one corner and turning half the dirt floor into a quagmire.

'We've got to do something positive before Ping Chuan catches on to the fact that the three of us are eating more than we're earning.'

The speaker was Captain Sir Harry Darrel of the 18th Royal Irish Regiment. A young Irish baronet, Darrel had become bored with sitting outside Chinese cities while civilians haggled over terms of surrender. Knowing nothing of Ping Chuan, he had volunteered for secondment to the rebel army. Now, after more than a year's experience of irregular warfare, his aim was survival and not adventure.

'The best thing we could do would be to shoot Ping Chuan and get the hell out of here. We're not helping General Tudely-Hext by condoning the rape of China by Ping Chuan and Mad Moller. . . .'

Lieutenant Tim McKinley's contribution to the conversation ended in a bout of coughing that left him breathless and weak. Morna touched a finger to his lips to prevent him saying more and shook her head at Captain Darrel.

Lieutenant McKinley had contracted malaria a month after leaving the Pearl River. It had recurred at frequent intervals since then, and now the hot and humid atmosphere in the Yangtze valley had brought on lung disease. Unless help was obtained very soon, Lieutenant McKinley would go the way of his colleagues, whose graves were scattered along the route of Ping Chuan's long and bloody march.

Captain Darrel ignored Morna's discreet warning. 'We've got to talk about this, Morna. If we don't, we'll all die. Tim said it all when he suggested we should get the hell out of here. But where do we go? I've thought of suggesting to Ping Chuan that he's done enough campaigning in the Yangtze valley and should strike out for Nanking. Hopefully, Tudely-Hext should have taken Nanking by now.'

'What would happen to us if he hasn't?' asked Morna quietly.

Captain Darrel shrugged. 'That's a chance we'll have to take.'

'You're forgetting one very important thing.' Lieutenant McKinley spoke in a thin voice, his eyes closed. He was propped against the wall of the hut, his head lying back on part of the bamboo frame. 'Ping Chuan has raised his sights since he threw in his lot with us. He's not going to settle for being Tudely-Hext's "diversion" any more. He's convinced the whole of China will rally behind him. He might not *want* to go to Nanking.'

'He's got no choice . . . and neither have we. If we stay out here, his whole rabble army will be cut to pieces by the Tartars — and us with them.'

'There *is* another way out for us.' Mention of the Tartars had caused Morna's heart to beat faster. 'We could give ourselves up to General Shengan. He'll get you back to Hong Kong, or wherever else you want to go.'

Captain Darrel made a small gesture of irritation. This was an argument they had pursued on many occasions.

'Morna, Tim and I are helping a man who is rebelling against the Emperor. We're not even waging a regular war against the Chinese. Your precious Shengan would have our heads if we fell into his hands — and who could blame him?'

Morna was constantly frustrated and angered by the refusal of either officer to accept that Shengan possessed the chivalry and honour they believed were exclusively British traits.

'Why won't you—?'

'Shhh!'

Morna stopped in mid-sentence. She, too, had heard the scream, cut off as quickly as it had begun. There were more sounds now. Screams, shouts and the drumming of ponies' hoofs.

'Quick! Put out that light.'

Captain Darrel snatched up a percussion musket standing against the wall of the hut and removed the greased paper protecting the end of the muzzle.

As Morna snuffed out the candle that provided their only light, Lieutenant McKinley pulled a double-barrelled pistol from his belt and cocked it slowly.

Something crashed against the side of the hut and they heard the snort of a frightened pony. It made a hole in the reed wall of the hut, through which they saw the dull red of a fire gutting a nearby hut. The flames remained inside the hut, extinguished by torrential rain whenever they licked through the thatched roof. The sound of fighting was all about them now. Suddenly the door of the hut crashed open on leather hinges and a Tartar soldier leaped inside, silhouetted against the flames behind him.

One of the barrels of Lieutenant McKinley's pistol belched smoke and flame. The lead ball took the Tartar in the chest but, although he staggered, he did not fall. Captain Darrel fired his musket as the Tartar raised his sword to strike. The shot spun the Tartar warrior about and he crashed to the ground in four inches of mud and water.

Morna was choking and gagging from the gunpowder smoke, and Captain Darrel punched a hole through the reed wall to allow clean air to pass through the hut.

The pandemonium outside ceased as quickly as it had begun. The increasing tempo of the rain soon blotted out the cries of wounded men and the hissing of steam as burning huts were gradually extinguished by the downpour.

Sword in hand, Captain Darrel went out into the night, after warning Morna and Lieutenant McKinley to remain inside the hut, out of sight. He was gone for three hours.

When he returned, Captain Darrel seemed well pleased with himself. 'Well, everything's settled,' he said, coaxing another reluctant candle into life. 'We leave here in the morning.'

'Leave for where?' asked Morna.

'For Nanking. I've told Ping Chuan that's where we'll find General Tudely-Hext, and that the sooner we get there and obtain fresh supplies and ammunition the sooner he'll be able to realize his ambition and win the throne of China.'

'He agreed? Without argument?' Lieutenant McKinley was sceptical.

'Not at first. Then Mad Moller joined in the argument — against me. That settled it! Ping Chuan agreed immediately. The upshot of it all is that we're setting out at first light. No following the river, or going from village to village to steal food. We're going in a straight line to Nanking. With any luck well be there in four or five days.'

'What happens if we get to Nanking and there's no General Tudely-Hext?'

'Ah! That's where the Good Lord seems to be on our side, for a change. Word has got through to Ping Chuan that General

Tudely-Hext *is* on the Yangtze. He's taken Shang-hai and is moving up-river. Because of this, we've probably seen the last of Shengan and his Tartars. He's been ordered to Chin-kiang by the Emperor himself, to make a last stand there. There's a possibility that Nanking will be unguarded, looking for trouble to come from down-river, not from us. Ping Chuan can still muster almost ten thousand men. If he can get himself organized between here and Nanking, he'll be able to take the city and throw the garrison at Chin-kiang into utter confusion.'

'Not to mention giving Ping Chuan's men more loot and women than they'll be able to handle,' replied Lieutenant McKinley. 'Put them inside a city of that size and Ping Chuan will have no army left. They will have one aim – to get rich quickly, and then get as far away from Ping Chuan as they can.'

'And who in his right mind would argue with that?' Captain Darrel grinned like a schoolboy. 'Sure now, General Tudely-Hext ought to give us a medal for disbanding the whole sorry bunch. Keep Ping Chuan and his bandits together as an "army" and they'll prove more trouble to us than to the Chinese, in the long run.'

Morna was concerned less with the long-term dangers of Ping Chuan's army than with the details of the last stand Shengan was supposed to be taking at Chin-kiang.

'Where did Ping Chuan get all this information? If Shengan's men have all been called to Chin-kiang, who attacked us this evening?'

Captain Darrel was reluctant to say more. Details of the do-or-die stand to be taken at Chin-kiang had been brought to Ping Chuan by the survivors of the party he had sent to find Ezra McCulloch in Hong Kong. They, in turn, had tortured the information from a messenger of the regional Viceroy.

The long-absent pirates had brought less palatable news of Ezra McCulloch's reply to Ping Chuan's ultimatum. Morna's life now hung on a very slender thread indeed. Only an early link-up with the British expeditionary force would save her life.

'The raid last night was nothing,' explained Captain Darrel. 'No more than a few Tartar horsemen, on their way to Chin-kiang. They stumbled on us here and took advantage of the lax guard Ping Chuan's men were keeping.'

Captain Darrel's assumption was only partly correct. The

Tartars *had* been on their way to Chin-kiang — but it was more than a few horsemen. The raid had been carried out by Shengan himself, with an escort of a hundred mounted men.

They had located the rebels encamped in and about the village. Although heavily outnumbered, they had made a quick surprise attack before riding on.

Shengan's plans would have been very different had he known that this was Ping Chuan's own camp — and that Morna was in the village.

It was kinder, too, that Morna would never know how close she had been to the man she was to have married. It was Shengan's pony that stumbled against the reed and bamboo hut in the darkness; Shengan's pony that smashed the fragile wall as it stumbled and almost threw its rider into her arms.

fourteen

WHEN Shengan left Woo-sung, he led the Tartar survivors of the bloody battle only as far as Shang-hai. Here he had a stormy meeting with the high-ranking Governor of the city. Shengan was determined to withdraw his garrison from Shang-hai. He knew the army of the Fan Qui could not be beaten while they fought within range of their formidable ships-of-war.

The Governor complained bitterly that Shengan was forsaking his sacred duty to the Emperor by leaving one of Imperial China's great cities to the mercy of the barbarians. But Shengan had made his decision. He told the Governor to send a peace delegation to meet the barbarians. They should ask for Luke Trewarne and sue for an honourable truce.

Shengan's refusal to allow his warriors to be annihilated by the British expeditionary force proved no more acceptable to the inhabitants of Shang-hai. They had lined the streets and cheered when he had brought his army into the city to defend them against the foreign invaders. Now they watched silently from behind closed shutters and barred doors as General Shengan rode away at the head of his troops.

It was Shengan's intention to bide his time and keep back his Tartar warriors until he judged the time right to throw them into battle. He believed that, if the army of General Tudely-Hext scored enough easy victories, the Fan Qui general might be lured away from the sea and the great rivers. Given a battleground of his own choosing, Shengan was convinced he could defeat the invading army – albeit at a great cost to his own men.

Shengan was hoping to teach General Tudely-Hext the bitter lesson learned by many aggressors during China's long history. The 'Heavenly Kingdom' was so vast that it could be conquered only from within. Many fine armies had fought their way inland, only to be swallowed up by the country, defeated by the twin military problems of supply and communication. The Fan Qui army would be no different.

When the opportunity arose, Shengan knew he would need all the Tartar soldiers he could muster. He would waste no more men defending the indefensible. But first the badly shaken Tartar warriors needed to be reminded of the sweet taste of victory. He would lead them against Ping Chuan and clear the rebel army from the fertile valley of the middle Yangtze.

On his long march through the lush green heartland of the Yangtze valley, Shengan withdrew garrison after garrison of troops from towns and villages along the way. Soon he had a mighty army once more.

Shengan kept his men together until they located Ping Chuan's rebels, then he split his army into units of a hundred men. Each company formed a vital link in a long loose human chain that extended across the valley from river-bank to mountain slope. No company was more than an hour's hard ride from the next. When contact was made with Ping Chuan's men, the companies on either side were brought in — more, if the strength of the rebels made it necessary.

Shengan also brought in some of his Tartar reserves, sending them to towns and villages between Ping Chuan and the sea to throw up hasty defences — and wait.

The Tartars began to drive Ping Chuan and his pirate army before them, their momentum increasing in a bid to clear the valley before the rainy season began in real earnest.

Shengan's policy was not to take prisoners, but whenever a rebel fell into his hands he was always questioned before execution. One question was standard: 'Where was Morna McCulloch?'

Sometimes a doomed rebel was able to tell his captors where Morna *had* been. Always, when Shengan arrived at the place, Ping Chuan and his captive had moved on. But, heartened by the knowledge that Morna was alive and unharmed, Shengan never gave up hope of finding her. When he began to hear disquieting news of the dissension between Ping Chuan and Charles Moller, Shengan recognized the danger it posed for Morna and the rebels were pushed even harder.

Then the weather broke. In the face of the heaviest rain in living memory, contact between Tartars and rebels became spasmodic and confused, as both armies battled with the common enemies — mud and water.

In the midst of this discomfort and confusion, Shengan received a long and angry letter from Emperor Tao Kuang. From his palace in Peking, the Emperor expressed deep disappointment at Shengan's lack of success against the Fan Qui

354

army. Admonishing Shengan for his failure to defend Shang-hai, the Emperor ordered him to atone for his defeats. He was ordered to take his Tartar army to Chin-kiang. Here he would make a stand and prevent the Fan Qui army from moving up-river to Nanking.

The letter was couched in the strongest terms. It disregarded Shengan's carefully thought-out plan of campaign and reverted to the traditional view that a Tartar soldier must win every battle – or die at his post. The aggrieved Governor of Shang-hai had used his considerable influence at the Peking Court well.

Shengan immediately sat down and wrote a despatch to his Emperor, pleading with him to change his mind. He cared nothing for his own life, he said, offering to end it by his own hand if the Emperor doubted his courage. Shengan's only concern was for the future of China, and for the Emperor himself. It would be foolhardy to throw away the best troops in the land.

Shengan had no illusions about what would happen if his Tartars made a determined stand at the riverside city of Chin-kiang. Shengan's intelligence-gatherers put the number of Fan Qui warships at sixteen, with dozens of armed troop-carriers. Their largest ship alone carried enough guns to demolish a small town in a matter of a few hours. The combined naval force could blast the Tartar army out of existence without landing a single Fan Qui soldier.

Although he sent off such an impassioned appeal, Shengan never doubted what the reply would be. One week later, it was delivered to him by the Emperor's special messenger. Succinct to the point of rudeness, the fourteen-word message said simply: 'If Chin-kiang falls, it will be because I no longer have a Tartar army.'

Rerolling the letter carefully, Shengan handed it to his recorder for safe-keeping. He bowed three times in the general direction of the Emperor's palace, as befitted a servant who had just received a command written in the Emperor's own hand. Then he sent for his senior officers.

Splashing their way across country, Ping Chuan's army encountered no opposition from Shengan's Tartars. When the rain ceased and a scorching sun beat down on the countryside, Ping Chuan took it as a portent of better things to come. It did not depress him when floodwater rolled down the Yangtze Kiang from the hills and the river burst its banks, turning the countryside into an anonymous waist-deep lake. It would serve to prevent Shengan from stumbling upon their tracks.

The rebel army was now only a night's march from Nanking. By dawn, Ping Chuan would have his men poised outside the gates of the city. A few bold men would then scale the walls with the aid of ropes and grappling hooks, and overpower the sleepy guards. Nanking would awake to find the pirate army pouring in through its gates.

Ping Chuan was in a jovial mood when he spoke to Morna and the two British officers at dusk. They would travel at the rear of the army. Ping Chuan wanted no future historian suggesting that Fan Qui officers had masterminded the taking of the city where the Chinese had surrendered their country to Manchu overlords, two hundred years before.

Ping Chuan suffered a rude awakening. His troops crept silently to the great walls of Nanking in the darkest hour before dawn. The grappling irons were flung up to the buttresses — and then the deep boom of a giant gong echoed from wall to wall of the great city. It was the signal for the lighting of thousands of blazing torches. Hurled from the walls into prepared bonfires, they ringed the city with flames, turning night into fiery day.

Hundreds of soldiers of Ping Chuan's ragged army fell in the first volley from the muskets of the militiamen lining the city walls. A second volley put them to flight. Chaos ensued as the fleeing rebels collided with others who had not felt the musketballs of Nanking's defenders and still advanced.

Ping Chuan was in the vanguard of the retreat. Splashing through flooded fields, he did not stop until he reached the safety of high ground, a mile from the walls of Nanking.

It was futile for Charles Moller to stand before the gates of the city, fuming impotently and calling upon the fleeing rebels to return and die fighting for the Lord. They did not share his wholehearted conviction that the key to the Kingdom of God came in the shape of an Imperial musket-ball. They preferred to run, in the hope of enjoying more mundane pleasures another day.

The failure to scale the walls of Nanking was a humiliating disaster for Ping Chuan. Morna and her companions knew he would look for scapegoats. The idea of striking across country to Nanking had come from Captain Darrel. Ping Chuan might even believe he had sent the pirate army into a deliberate trap.

356

Morna and the others had seen the sudden illumination of the walls of Nanking, but it was some minutes before the shock-wave of defeat rolled back through the rebel column and reached them.

Captain Darrel made a rapid decision. It was time they parted company with Ping Chuan. As the rebel army floundered about in the darkness, Morna and her two companions made their escape. They did not care which way they went, intent only on putting as much distance between themselves and Ping Chuan as was possible before sunrise.

By the time it was light enough to make out objects about them, the sound of Ping Chuan's huge rebel army was no more than a distant excited murmur. As the light continued to improve they discovered they were dangerously close to the city of Nanking, with no trees or clumps of bamboo in which to hide. Fortunately, before the Chinese peasants ventured from their houses to inspect the flooded fields, they stumbled upon a Chinese burial-ground. Set on a hillside close to the city, the grass was high, the graveyard neglected since the beginning of the heavy monsoon rains. It was hardly likely there would be any tidying here today, with a rebel army camped on the city's doorstep.

The tombs were, for the most part, shallow caves scooped from the hillside. Faced with stone, they resembled a European fireplace. But where the fire would have been there was a small square opening, sealed with soft mortar. Sufficient to keep out wild animals, it could be easily knocked out to allow a jar containing the bones of another close relative to be placed inside.

Selecting one of the largest tombs, Captain Darrel kicked out the mortar. After removing a number of large jars containing the remains of the Yeh family, late of Nanking, the three Europeans crawled inside.

The refuge proved to be a fortunate choice. Although damp and musty, it commanded an excellent view over the Yangtze River, with its fishing villages and hamlets. By nightfall they had selected the site from which they would steal a fishing sampan and head down-river in a desperate bid to find General Tudely-Hext's army.

When night came, they crawled stiffly from their refuge – and immediately encountered their first problem. They had been without food and water all day, and now the unwell

Lieutenant McKinley complained of agonizing stomach pains. They had gone no more than a few hundred yards from the tomb-refuge when he collapsed, crying that his legs would not support him. Captain Darrel bullied him along for another quarter of a mile, then the young lieutenant fell to the ground, sobbing that he could go no farther.

With his arms about their shoulders, Morna and Captain Darrel dragged their companion through the mud to the river. Unfortunately, because of this unexpected distraction, Captain Darrel made a mistake in the darkness and they missed the unattended sampans for which they had been heading. When they reached the river they found nothing.

Captain Darrel was in a quandary. He knew there was a village nearby and he did not want to stumble upon it for fear they would have a militia guard posted. He would have liked time to reconnoitre, but McKinley was by now in a state of delirium. It was doubtful whether Morna could have kept him silent if she were left alone with him. Captain Darrel decided to move up-river.

They had not gone far when they came upon a number of sampans moored at the river-bank. Delighted, Captain Darrel whispered that it was better to be born lucky than rich. Not until he and Morna dragged Lieutenant McKinley into the nearest sampan and fell over a loudly complaining Chinese did he learn his mistake. The sampan was occupied by a family of Hoklos!

The owner of the boat rose to his feet, demanding to know what was happening. He was promptly thrown in the river by Captain Darrel. His cries awoke a woman. She promptly followed her husband over the side.

Fortunately for the escaping trio, there were no more occupants on board the sampan, but the shouts of the man and his wife had roused the occupants of the other boats. One of them jumped on board, and Morna saw the glint of metal in his hands. She shouted a warning to Captain Darrel, but he was desperately trying to untie the rope securing the sampan to the river-bank.

There was a loud report as Morna drew Lieutenant McKinley's pistol from his belt and fired off one barrel at the would-be attacker. The Chinese uttered a single grunt and collapsed in the bottom of the sampan, the sword that had been raised above his head falling beside him.

Seizing the sword, Captain Darrel hacked through the rope. The next moment, the sampan was drifting lazily out from the bank on the river current.

The dead Chinese was dumped overboard about a mile downstream. By then, Captain Darrel had an oar over the stern and was sending the sampan along as fast as his strength would allow.

Captain Darrel's initial error turned out to be fortuitous. There was Chinese clothing on board and they had need of it when daylight came and they found they shared the river with many other sampans. There was food, water and bedding, too, and Morna was able to make Lieutenant McKinley comfortable, providing him with his first meal for thirty-six hours.

Late that same afternoon, they rounded a bend in the river and were met by a sight that set Morna and Captain Darrel shouting and cheering in near-hysterical joy.

Puffing up the river towards them, its paddles churning the muddy river into a creamy froth, was the Honourable East India Company's armed steamer *Phlegethon*. Their escape attempt had succeeded. The long and gruelling ordeal with Ping Chuan and his rebels was over.

The Reverend Charles Moller was less fortunate than his fellow-Europeans. The failure of the pre-dawn attack sent Ping Chuan into a maniacal rage. When his army stopped running, he put them into camp on a hill a mile to the south of the city. Then he ordered the immediate execution of the Fan Qui officers. When they could not be found, Ping Chuan had the camp searched time and time again, convinced that Darrel and his companions were in hiding, frightened of his anger. Not until the camp had been thoroughly searched for the third time did it dawn upon Ping Chuan that the two soldiers had fled, taking Morna with them.

His fury frightened even the closest of his lieutenants. They cowered from him as he raved incoherently at their incompetence, striking about him with a sword, inflicting dreadful wounds on those of his followers unfortunate enough to be within range.

Not until sheer exhaustion forced him to stop was there a lull in Ping Chuan's senseless ranting. By this time his followers had retreated to a respectful distance from his flailing sword.

Many of them had gaping wounds, others were spattered with blood, and three of their number lay still upon the ground.

As Ping Chuan leaned on his sword, wild-eyed and panting, Charles Moller came upon the scene. Looking from the men on the ground to their leader, he said, 'Have you taken to fighting each other because you can only win battles with cowards? If no more than fifty of you had called on the Lord's name and scaled the walls of Nanking, it would have been a Christian city by now.'

'Seize him! Seize him!' Ping Chuan screamed the words and pointed to Charles Moller, his face contorted with insane rage. When none of his men made a move to obey him, Ping Chuan advanced upon them, sword upraised.

Two of Ping Chuan's lieutenants stepped forward hesitantly and took hold of Charles Moller.

The missionary shook off their hands contemptuously. 'You dare to lay your hands on me? God! Strike down these men who molest your beloved servant.'

Ping Chuan's men stepped back hastily, fear written on their faces. Such was the strength of the legend of Moller's close communion with the one true God.

Ping Chuan knew he needed to take immediate action. Another few moments and his army would be Moller's for the taking.

Striding to where Charles Moller stood, Ping Chuan drew back his sword and stabbed the missionary in his left side. Moller's exhortations ended in a sharp cry of pain. As the gasp of apprehension died in the throats of the onlookers, a scarlet stain spread down the side of Moller's long robe.

The spell Moller had cast on the pirates was broken. While his lieutenants held the struggling missionary, Ping Chuan ripped the long white robe from his body and plunged his hand into the blood that flowed from the exposed wound.

Ping Chuan held a bloody hand up to his army. 'You see? This is blood . . . human blood. The Fan Qui Moller's blood.' His voice carried to every man in his army. 'Moller is *not* immortal. He bleeds, just as you and I bleed. He claimed to be chosen by the Lord. *He lied!* It is his lying that has angered God. This is why the Lord has deserted us in battle. Has he ever failed us before? Did *I* ever fail you before the Fan Qui came to us?'

The mighty denial that rose from the throats of Ping Chuan's followers startled the swallows nesting beneath the eaves of the great wall surrounding Nanking.

'Fools!' shrieked Moller. 'You are all *fools*! Would you believe a man whose every action profanes the Christian religion? It is Ping Chuan who has offended the Lord. He is a profligate . . . a son of Satan. I am your saviour. . . . Listen to me. . . .'

'Tear out his tongue, before his blasphemy brings the wrath of God down upon us all again.'

Ping Chuan's men jumped to do his bidding. Moments later, Charles Moller's screamed curses ended in a spinechilling gurgle as he choked in his own blood.

'Now we will give him a truly Christian death,' grinned Ping Chuan, aware that he had won the leadership battle that might so easily have gone Moller's way. 'Build a wooden cross.'

Two pieces of timber were produced from somewhere and a rough crucifix manufactured. When it was completed, Charles Moller was tied to the symbol of his belief, and Ping Chuan nodded to the men who stood behind the mad missionary.

The Reverend Charles Moller died of strangulation as swiftly as any Chinese criminal. The crude operation, carried out before execution on the orders of the rebel leader, ensured that the missionary made no dying prophecy for lesser men to seize upon should success continue to elude Ping Chuan.

The rebel leader had exploded the myth of Charles Moller's immortality, but he took no chances. He and his army kept a vigil around the lifeless body of the missionary for three days and three nights, prepared to offer an abject apology should he rise again from the dead.

Fifteen

SHENGAN and his Tartar troops arrived at Chin-kiang with little time to spare. The Fan Qui army was only a few miles down-river, their transports being towed slowly against the floodwaters of the Yangtze by their invaluable steamers.

If ever a campaign proved the value of the steamer to a doubting British Admiralty, it was this one. Unaffected by adverse winds or currents, they carried the fight to the enemy along narrow creeks and inlets where no ship dependent upon sails would dare venture.

Shengan called his officers together and planned as effective a defence as was possible in the short time left to him. In the face of bitter complaints, he ordered every able-bodied man and woman in the city to help dig defensive walls and ditches between the river and the city wall. Then he ordered all those soldiers with families inside the city to be sent outside to man the partially constructed defences. Shengan reasoned they would fight harder knowing the safety of their wives and children depended upon their ability to keep the enemy at bay.

The remainder of his army Shengan put high on the city walls. They were not to leave their posts until he himself gave the order.

His preparations made, Shengan went alone to the tower above the main city gate. As he waited for the British fleet to come up-river and take up their bombardment positions, he looked about him at the green of the countryside and the paler green of the willows at the water's edge. He listened to the twittering of the swallows as they weaved flight patterns in the sky above the city, in pursuit of flies for open-beaked families. It was a day to remember all that was beautiful and enduring in China. A day when a man felt glad to be alive — or ready to die for the things in which he believed.

On board the three-decked battleship *Cornwallis*, Luke stood alone in the bows, looking towards Chin-kiang. The flagship of the British fleet had dropped anchor with her guns pointing towards the great city gates. They stood open, the city in no immediate danger from the Fan Qui army. Luke watched the women and men digging the defences and saw the sun reflected on weapons carried by soldiers high on the city walls. He knew instinctively that Shengan was here and would fight a fierce and bitter battle.

'Cheer up, Luke. The Chinese might not feel like fighting when they see the guns of the whole fleet ranged against them.' Sir Henry Rutherford had come up on deck, seeking a few minutes' peace before preparations for the forthcoming battle got under way in earnest.

Seeing Luke leaning over the side, looking gloomily towards Chin-kiang, Sir Henry thought he knew what was wrong with him. There was a strong body of opinion in England who looked upon this as an immoral war. But none of those who raised their voices, in or out of Parliament, was as personally involved as Luke – and few took their failures as seriously as he.

Luke turned to Sir Henry and shook his head. 'They'll fight. Look at them. . . .' He pointed to where thousands of Chinese worked at full speed, all the while keeping a nervous watch on the manoeuvring men-of-war. 'Shengan is making his stand here.'

Sir Henry looked critically towards the shore. The ground between the river and the city walls was flat and even, present- ing no military problems to an attacking army. 'I would have thought a general of Shengan's calibre would have chosen his battlefield more carefully. With naval support, the advantage lies overwhelmingly with us.'

'I doubt if Shengan had a choice. His army has suffered too many defeats at our hands. He's probably been told by the Emperor he *must* win here.'

Sir Henry looked at the busy scene ashore with a new inter- est. 'Then we're in for a hard battle; but it could prove to be the last we will need to fight.'

'It *will* be Shengan's last battle.' Luke was bitter. 'He's tried to avert war for years. He saw it coming before anyone else . . . and he knew China couldn't win. Now he'll succeed in buying peace with his own life and the lives of the men who meant so much to him. Ironic, isn't it?'

'A man of honour who gives his life for his country dies a worthwhile death, Luke. I'm quite certain your General

Shengan would agree with me. If by his death he succeeds in gaining all he fought for, he will die a happy man. . . .'

'Happy?' Luke straightened up angrily. Striding to the side of the ship farthest from the city of Chin-kiang, he pointed to where *The Two Brothers* was dropping anchor, well clear of the action that would soon take place. 'How can a man die happy when he sees vultures like Ezra McCulloch gathering to pick his country clean when he's dead? It's rubbing his nose in the dirt, Sir Henry. It's telling him, "Go ahead, hurry up and die. As soon as you're gone we can start selling opium and poisoning your people once more." *That's* what Shengan has been fighting against. That's what this whole imbecile war is about. The Emperor says he doesn't want opium coming into China. We say he's got to accept it. Had the British Government banned men like Ezra McCulloch from selling opium, there would have been no war. *No one* need have died. . . .'

Luke choked on the emotion he felt and turned away, returning to look towards Chin-kiang.

Sir Henry Rutherford shook his head sympathetically. Moving to Luke's side, he said softly, 'There's a new government in Britain, Luke. Lord Aberdeen is the new Foreign Secretary. He made many fine speeches against the opium trade when he was in opposition.'

'Speech costs a man nothing,' retorted Luke. 'It won't stop Ezra McCulloch from selling opium — or the "Honourable" East India Company from growing it.'

'Don't be too hard on Ezra, Luke. He's got opium aboard, yes . . . but it's a ransom for his daughter's life. . . .'

Luke's snort interrupted the plenipotentiary. 'I hope for Morna's sake that no one makes him a good offer for his cargo before Ping Chuan's found. Now, if I have your permission, I'd like to go ashore and see if anyone is ready to talk about a truce.'

Sir Henry nodded. 'If you succeed, no one will be more delighted than I, Luke.'

Ten minutes later, Luke set off in a cutter from *Cornwallis*, flying a large white flag. Before they were halfway to the shore the report of a cannon-shot boomed out from a gun emplacement beside the city walls and a warning shot dropped in the water, close to the cutter. The oarsmen stopped rowing, but Luke ordered them on. The cannon fired again. This time the shot fell close enough to send spray into the cutter and set it rocking wildly. Still Luke would have persisted in his attempt to land had not a volley of musket-fire rung out. The range was too great to pose a serious threat to the lives of the sailors, but two musket-balls smacked against the white flag and fell harmlessly into the bottom of the boat. Common sense prevailed, and Luke ordered the boat to return to *Cornwallis*. There would be no negotiations.

The same conclusion had been reached by those who watched from the British flagship. As the cutter backed and turned, the three tiers of the man-of-war's guns spat smoke and fire. The salvo blanketed the gun emplacement that had fired the shots but, when the smoke and dust cleared, the Chinese gun fired again defiantly.

It signalled the beginning of the most deadly bombardment by British ships Luke had ever witnessed. Ship after ship let fly with a mighty broadside, and the Chinese who had been constructing the city's defences fled inside Chin-kiang to escape the holocaust, leaving the married Tartar soldiers to face the enemy's guns.

An hour after the bombardment commenced, troops began disembarking from the troop-transports and were ferried ashore by an armada of small boats. Shouting defiance, Shengan's Tartars ran to the shore to meet them and a desperate hand-to-hand battle began. The water was thick with swirling bodies before the first British soldier set foot on the shore.

On board *Cornwallis*, Luke retired to his cabin. He had no wish to witness the slaughter on shore, but before long the din of the never-ending cannonade and the juddering of the ship that accompanied every broadside sent Luke back on deck again.

The fighting had been so bitter that even the members of Sir Henry Rutherford's staff were unusually subdued when they brought Luke up to date on the battle's progress.

The Cameronians and the 49th Infantry Regiment had landed farther along the river. Using the same tactics as had proved successful at Woo-sung, they were driving in through the suburbs outside the city wall, sandwiching the Tartars between themselves and their hard-pressed comrades landed outside the city. Meanwhile, the guns of the fleet were now throwing their shot into Chin-kiang itself.

Smoke and occasional flames rose high above the city walls, but the bombardment did not end until scaling-ladders rose like cobwebs against the city walls and the gates to the city were blown apart by a daring captain, leading a party of Madras Engineers.

In the uneasy silence that followed the cessation of the bombardment, the crackle of musket-fire and the muffled din of shouting men and screaming women and children could be heard from the direction of the city. Eventually, this, too, died away and there was only an occasional sporadic rattle of gunfire. At this juncture, a boat came from the shore to *Cornwallis*, with a request for Luke to join General Tudely-Hext, inside Chin-kiang.

Luke found the walk from the river to the gate of the city indescribable. The carnage was appalling. Everywhere he looked there were bodies, some lying half-buried beneath the ruins of Shengan's defences, others sprawled above them. The vast majority wore the drab uniform of Shengan's Tartars, but there were also a great many red-uniformed British soldiers sharing the fate of their enemies.

Inside Chin-kiang, the situation was hardly any better. Here, the devastation of houses and buildings added to the horror. Many fires still burned, and the stench from one in particular was nauseating. The burning building had been a slaughter-house, and the smell was of burning pig, but Luke's imagination was by this time running riot. He gagged noisily as his escort led him through the pungent smoke to the Tartar quarter of the city. It was plain to see that Shengan's troops had fought fiercely every inch of the way as they were forced back upon their own barracks.

Here, in the Tartar quarter, the final horror of the battle for Chin-kiang had taken place. The Tartars had fought until powder and shot were almost exhausted — then they turned on their own, killing wives and children before committing suicide themselves. Those who miscalculated, and had no more powder left, strangled their luckless families with bare hands, rather than leave them to the mercy of the Fan Qui soldiers.

It was a scene of slaughter of such proportions that even the hardened veterans of Tudely-Hext's army were shocked into stunned silence.

The last desperate stand of the Tartars had been made by a small group of officers in their headquarters building. Reduced to ten men, they had all committed suicide at the moment when the building was being stormed by the Cameronians.

'I sent for you to see if Shengan is among this lot,' explained General Tudely-Hext to Luke, tight-lipped at the scene of slaughter about him. 'These Tartar officers seem to wear no badges of rank and I can see no one who fits my idea of a great general.'

For a moment, Luke's hopes rose . . . but only for a moment. In the room where the Tartar officers had committed suicide, he looked about him at the bodies, then slowly walked to where a broad-shouldered Tartar lay face downwards on the floor.

Luke dropped to his knees and gently turned the body over. It was still warm. Laying it gently on its back, Luke looked down into the glassy-eyed stare of Shengan. Reaching out with thumb and forefinger, he drew the lids down over Shengan's seeing eyes, doing his best not to look at the ghastly gash across Shengan's throat.

'Is this General Shengan?' a major asked the question eagerly.

Luke nodded and rose wearily to his feet.

'Doesn't look anything special, does he?' burbled the major happily. 'I mean, he's not the sort of man one would frighten one's children with.'

Luke looked at the major contemptuously. 'General Shengan never went in for frightening children, Major. As for being special. . . . He was a great soldier who loved his country above all else. He was also the finest man I've ever met in my life '

Luke hurried from the room before he broke down and made a fool of himself in front of General Tudely-Hext and his staff.

How long he wandered about the charnel-house that was the Tartar quarter of Chin-kiang, Luke never knew. He was not quite alone there. A few aged Tartar women roamed dazedly along the narrow streets. Widows of long-dead soldiers, there had been no one to care enough to put their honour beyond the reach of the Fan Qui soldiers.

There were others, too. Furtive looters, who robbed bodies; collecting mementoes that would one day be given as gifts to the proud families of British and Indian soldiers.

Walking aimlessly along one of the streets, Luke picked his way around whole families of dead Tartars. Suddenly, as he stepped across the body of a baby boy, he stopped. Crouching down, he removed something from the child's neck. It was a locket — and it looked familiar. Luke frowned as he struggled to remember. Then it came to him. This locket had once belonged to Morna. He had watched her put it around the neck of a new-born baby. Her 'first Tartar baby', she had called it. Luke remembered the pride in the eyes of the Tartar mother and her soldier husband as they walked away with their first-born son. Now he lay dead beside his mother. Somewhere outside the city walls was his father's body.

Luke slipped the locket about the baby's neck again, tucking it inside his cotton jacket in the hope that no scavenger would think of searching the body of a baby for loot.

Blinking back tears that stung his eyes, Luke turned his back on the city of death and made his way to the beach. Here he waited for a boat to take him back to *Cornwallis*, weeping inwardly for the Tartar baby, for Shengan, for China . . . and for the tarnished honour of his own country.

That night, a company of Tartars who had reached Chinkiang too late to join in the battle carried out an act of revenge against the anchored fleet. Few guards were posted by the ships on this night of victory, and none at all on *The Two Brothers*.

Chinese fireships were floated down the river and ignited when they were attached to the anchor cable of the merchantman. The ensuing blaze lit up the river from bank to bank. Ezra McCulloch and most of his crew escaped without serious injury, but when the blaze reached *The Two Brothers*' gunpowder store the ship was ripped apart and the pieces scattered on the muddy bed of the Yangtze Kiang.

Sixteen

THE night after the battle of Chin-kiang there was a total eclipse of the moon. Coming, as it did, in the same month as an eclipse of the sun, it was a clear portent to Emperor Tao Kuang, awaiting news of the battle. China was faced with unprecedented disaster. The Emperor acted with unusual promptness.

Two days before a horseman galloped into the Imperial city with news of Shengan's death and the loss of his great Tartar army, Emperor Tao Kuang sent his Commissioners to Nanking. Their mandate was simple. They must make peace with the Fan Qui. The terms were in their hands. The Emperor made only one stipulation. The Commissioners should agree to nothing that would make trading in opium legal.

The Emperor knew that he and his navy would never be able to prevent opium from entering the country, but he swore the Chinese administration would not accept revenue obtained from the misery and corruption of his people.

Tao Kuang's belated wish for peace made Luke's task easy. When he reached Nanking under a flag of truce, ahead of the main fleet, he was received by the Emperor's Commissioners as a welcome friend. He was 'the Peace Maker', a good friend of China – or so the Commissioners told him. To Luke would go the honour of telling Sir Henry Rutherford that the Emperor himself wanted an end to this war.

Luke was given a great many gifts before returning to the fleet in triumph, an impressive escort of bannermen keeping pace with his boat on both sides of the river.

Sir Henry Rutherford was inclined to be sceptical about the Chinese and their plea for peace. 'What do you think is the real motive behind this move?' he asked Luke for the third time.

'I'm absolutely convinced that the Chinese want a quick end to the war,' Luke repeated patiently. 'They've lost their army, and they have no navy. They know we can blockade their ports and take their cities at will – Peking itself, if we wished. The Emperor has to bring this war to a close, especially now Shengan is dead. If serious revolt were to break out in the

369

provinces, he wouldn't be able to raise enough experienced troops to put it down. He needs peace in order to rebuild his country. China is on her knees to you, Sir Henry.'

Her Britannic Majesty's plenipotentiary listened thoughtfully as Luke spoke. To Luke's relief, he finally nodded his agreement. 'You've convinced me, Luke. All right. . . . Peace it shall be.'

They were in the Admiral's cabin in *Cornwallis*. All the senior army and naval officers were present. Sir Henry turned and raised his glass. 'Gentlemen, I propose a toast. To victory.'

When the answering shout had died away, Sir Henry said, 'I have a great many matters to discuss, Luke . . . but it's all military talk. Get yourself up on deck and enjoy some fresh air before you turn in. You've done a splendid job.'

Luke was glad to escape from the cabin. He made his way to the quarterdeck, the stern section of the upper deck, reserved for ship's officers. It was dark up here, the anchored fleet showing no lights.

There was a welcome breeze, but the night was still uncomfortably hot. Luke leaned against the guard-rail and ran a handkerchief around the neck-band of his shirt, wiping away the perspiration. He thought of Kuei and the baby she was expecting. Its birth would not be far off now. He hoped he and Kuei could offer it more of a future than that given to the Tartar baby – strangled by its own father when barely a year old. What would Morna have felt, had she known of its fate?

'Luke? It is you, isn't it?'

The voice startled him. It was as though his thoughts had conjured Morna up from nowhere. She could not be real. . . . But she was. When Morna was close enough to be certain it was Luke in the darkness, she flung herself at him. Her body in his arms was much thinner than he remembered, but she was no apparition.

Phlegethon and the boat taking Luke to Nanking had passed on the river, each taking a different channel past one of the many large islands in the centre of the Yangtze. Sir Henry Rutherford had known Morna was on board *Cornwallis*, but had kept the news from Luke, allowing the surprise to come from Morna herself.

'When did you get here? How did you escape from Ping Chuan?'

'I'll tell you all that later.' Morna's hands fell away from him. 'Luke . . . tell me it isn't true, what they told me. Shengan isn't dead? No one saw him . . . die? It's just rumour, isn't it?'

Luke took Morna's arm. Leading her to a low locker at the side of the quarterdeck, he sat her down.

'I wish I could tell you they lied, Morna. That there had never been a battle for Chin-kiang. But they asked me to go . . . to identify him. He's dead. So, too, is every Tartar officer in his army, together with most of his men and their families. It was . . . madness, Morna. Just bloody madness. . . .' Luke was glad Morna could not see his face in the darkness.

For a long time Morna said nothing. Captain Darrel had told her that Shengan had been ordered to make a last stand at Chin-kiang, but none of this made sense if the Emperor was now suing for peace. 'Why, Luke? Why? What happened?'

Luke reached for her. Morna's grief went far deeper than even his own. 'He had a personal letter from the Emperor. His orders were to hold Chin-kiang . . . or die. One of the Commissioners at Nanking knew I was a friend of Shengan. He thought I would like to know that Shengan died a hero. He's to be given a hero's funeral in Peking. . . .'

It was scant consolation, and Luke knew it. But he could not bear the unhappy silence between them.

Along the line of warships, bells rang out to tell the fleet it was seven o'clock. Moments later, Morna said in a near-whisper, 'We were to be married in Nanking.'

'I know. Shengan told me.'

Morna's head came up quickly, and he saw the white blur of her face. 'But . . . it was only decided on the day I was captured. You saw him after that?'

'Yes, after the battle for Woo-sung. Shengan was wounded. I had him treated by an army surgeon.'

'Poor Shengan. . . . My poor, poor Shengan.'

There were tears inside her, Luke knew, but none showed on her face. He held her close.

'The Emperor's Commissioners in Nanking asked after you. I didn't know where you were then . . . or even if you were still alive. They told me the Emperor wishes to honour you for your work among the Tartars. He would like you to return to Canton and reopen your hospital for the new Tartar garrison. It would be known as the Shengan Hospital.'

Morna said nothing, and Luke prompted, 'Will you take up the offer?'

She looked up at him. 'I'll need to think about it, Luke. At the moment it would be too painful to return to Canton . . . but time might change that. Anyway, I couldn't go just yet. I have to look after Father.'

'Ezra? What's wrong with him? He was all right when he was rescued from *The Two Brothers*. I saw him before I left for Nanking.'

'The excitement must have been too much for him. He had a heart attack soon afterwards. He's paralyzed down one side, and can't speak. I warned him long ago that if he didn't cut down his drinking this might happen. He's been drinking very heavily for a great many years. He'll need nursing for the rest of his life. I know he and I haven't got on too well in the past, but we're all the family either of us has.'

She stood back and held both of Luke's hands in hers. 'Thank you for being so kind to me, Luke. I could have told no one else about Shengan. They wouldn't have understood. What will you do now — interpret for Sir Henry Rutherford in Nanking?'

Luke shook his head. 'He has his own staff to take care of all the details of a treaty. I came here to interpret for General Tudely-Hext. As far as I'm concerned, that work is done. I'll leave on the next boat. Kuei needs me more than the British Army — she's expecting a child.'

'I'm pleased for you both, Luke. You deserve your happiness.'

Morna suddenly turned and hurried away. Luke heard her shoes clatter on the brass-edged ladder leading to the cabins. He remained on the quarterdeck for another hour. Then Sir Henry Rutherford and most of his staff came on deck for a breath of fresh air before retiring for the night. They were in jovial mood, and Luke could have done without their company tonight. But General Tudely-Hext had just won a war. He was in an expansive mood. Slapping Luke on the back, he boomed, 'You've done me proud, Luke. I made the right decision when I asked you to come with me as my interpreter. Mind you, there were times when I thought you were doing *too* damned well! I was afraid you'd talk the mandarins of every city into giving up without a fight before my army had a chance to show what it was made of.'

General Tudely-Hext's laugh was taken up by his brigade commanders, standing nearby. One of them, Major-General Bentley, of the 49th Regiment, said, 'Fortunately, we *were* able to get ashore. They won't forget the lesson we taught them at Chin-kiang in a hurry, eh, Sir Piers? Leave us here and we'll complete the job. Conquer the whole heathen country.'

'China has digested a great many lessons in her three-thousand-year history,' said Luke quietly. 'She's also swallowed up a great many so-called "conquering armies". All you've done is to touch here and there along the Chinese coast. Inland, there are four million square miles of unconquered country.'

Luke remembered what Shengan had once said, when they were discussing the changes that war with Britain might bring to China. The Tartar general had shrugged the question away, as being of no importance. 'Armies will come to China with their new ideas, Luke Trewarne. Then they will go, leaving their ideas behind them. But when the sun rises the next morning it will shine on the China we have always known.'

'Luke is quite right.' General Tudely-Hext stepped into the uncomfortable silence that followed Luke's words. 'We mustn't get carried away by our own cleverness. We've won a war, but we haven't conquered China. In this modern world we soldiers merely carry out the fighting. We have to leave the conquering to the politicians and the diplomats.' He clapped Sir Henry Rutherford on the shoulder, and the awkward moment was over. The laughter of the celebrating men followed Luke all the way to his cabin door.

Luke was given a passage to Hong Kong in the armed steamer *Medusa*. Also in the ship were Morna, the paralyzed Ezra McCulloch, and the captain and crew of *The Two Brothers*. It was a strained and unhappy voyage in the cramped quarters. Luke and Morna's thoughts on opium smuggling were well known and, with their ship gone and Ezra McCulloch patently unfit to run his trading company, Captain Obadiah Innes and his crew were concerned for their future.

Shortly before they arrived at Hong Kong, Luke asked Morna what she planned to do with the McCulloch trading company, but he was unprepared for the answer she gave him.

'My father has worked hard to build up McCulloch & Company,' she said. 'I'm not going to be the one to destroy it. My father can't speak – he can barely move – but he knows what is being said to him and his mind is still working. If he knew his company was failing, and wasn't able to do anything to save it, the frustration would kill him. Will you help me run it, Luke?'

'Help you to run McCulloch & Company? How?'

The idea of assisting a rival company was unusual, to say the least, but Morna had given the matter a great deal of thought.

'I'd like to merge our two companies. You would have a majority holding, of course—say, fifty-one per cent to my forty-nine—and you would have a free hand as far as running the new company was concerned.'

The idea was staggering. With all Ezra McCulloch's ships and Luke's own two, the combined fleet would rival that of Lancelot Fox—and come close to Jardine Matheson's total tonnage. The new company would also own a large portion of Hong Kong's waterfront.

'Gideon Pyke has a small share in Gemmell Company. Would you be willing for him to hold the same percentage in the new company?'

Morna nodded. 'Yes, and the company will need a change of name. I thought of Trewarne, McCulloch & Company.'

The name sounded good to Luke, but there were other, more serious details to be settled. The principal one was McCulloch & Company's dependence upon opium.

'I want nothing to do with opium,' declared Morna firmly. 'But can we operate such a large company at a profit without it?'

'I've always said it could be done,' replied Luke. 'This is my chance to prove it . . . or eat my words.'

'Good. Then we'll shake hands on the merger now and have the legalities sorted out when we reach Hong Kong.'

Later that day, Luke spoke to Captain Obadiah Innes about the proposed merger. Innes heard him out in silence before asking curtly, 'Where does all this leave me?'

'That's very much up to you,' replied Luke. 'Archie Wheeler is my captain in *China Wind*. He's not a young man and he's already told me he would like to retire by this year's end. *China Wind* is yours, if you want her . . . but you'll be running regular cargoes. There'll be no opium carried in any of my ships.'

Obadiah Innes looked at Luke speculatively, then he grinned ruefully. 'I little thought when I brought you from Calcutta that within a few years I'd be touching my cap to you, and calling you "Sir". No doubt it will mean putting my old Trafalgar hat into retirement, but it's not before time. I'm getting too old to run opium and fight off war-junks. All right, Mr Trewarne . . . "Sir", I'm your man.'

Seventeen

WHEN Luke arrived home, Kuei was eight months pregnant. She had been having a very difficult time. The baby lay awkwardly and Kuei was in constant pain. She had also been greatly worried about Luke. Lurid and much embellished versions of his part in the battles for Woo-sung and Chin-kiang had been received in Hong Kong.

Kuei was overjoyed to have him with her again and, in answer to his anxious questions, promised that all would be well with her now. But later that night, as they lay in bed, he heard her gasping in pain. As he held her to him, he tried to take her mind off the pain by reminding her of the first night they had lain together, in the bedroom of Dan Gemmell's factory at Canton.

'Much has happened since then, my husband.' Kuei snuggled her awkward bulk as close to him as she could. 'You are now a great man. When your people are in trouble they say, "Send for Luke Trewarne. He is the only man who can help us." My people show you much respect, too. They call you "the Peace Maker".'

Kuei wriggled happily. Luke would never know how much she had missed him during his months away – especially during the night.

'If we met for the first time now, you would say, "Who is this dirty little Hoklo girl? I no want to know her. I can get *any* girl I want. I find very rich Manchu girl, maybe. Or pretty Fan Qui girl . . . big like this all the time." '

She placed his hand on one of her milk-swollen breasts.

Grinning in the darkness, Luke heaved himself up on one elbow and looked down at her. 'Kuei, you've been spending too many hours talking Chinese to the servants while I've been away. Your English is a disgrace. As for another girl. . . . Who else would undress for me on an island in the Pearl River, on a moonlit night?'

Kuei giggled in delight. 'That was very wicked of me, my husband. Were you very shocked?'

'Very.' He bent down and kissed her where his hand was resting. 'And I wanted you very much.'

'I wanted you, too, my Luke. I wanted you then . . . and I have wanted you for many months. But I am not a thin and innocent Hoklo girl now.'

'Your body is the most wonderful I have ever touched, Kuei . . . especially now. I love you.'

'I love you, too, my very special-for-me husband.'

That night, her loneliness over, Kuei would have changed places with no one.

Much later, Luke woke as Kuei wriggled from his grasp.

'Are you uncomfortable? It's my fault. . . .'

Kuei turned with some difficulty and kissed him. 'No, my Luke. It is the fault of our son.'

'You're very sure it's going to be a boy!'

'I *know* it is. He kicks too much for girl. What name shall we call him?'

Luke already knew the answer to this question. He had thought about it many times as he lay awake in his bunk on board *Cornwallis*.

'He will have a long name. First, Thomas, for my father. Then Fang, for yours. . . .'

'Fang is not a good name. He will not have that. What others?'

Kuei made it clear there was no room for argument, and Luke said, 'Daniel — for Dan Gemmell, the man who gave me his trading company.'

Kuei nodded vigorous agreement. 'Thomas Daniel is a fine name.'

'He'll have one more name, Kuei . . . a Chinese name. I want my son to bear the name Shengan — after a very special friend.'

'Shengan is a Manchu name. A very good name. General Shengan would be very pleased.'

She repeated the names, enunciating them very carefully, 'Thomas . . . Daniel . . . Shengan . . . Trewarne. Oh, yes! They *very* good names. Our son will be a great man one day.'

When Luke fell asleep, Kuei was still murmuring the names to herself.

When Luke woke in the morning, Kuei was sleeping peacefully for the first time in months. She was still asleep when he left her and went outside the house to look at the godowns and the ships which would soon fly the new flag of Trewarne, McCulloch & Company.

Friday, 9 September 1842 was an eventful day for many people on Hong Kong island. It was the day when the survivors of Ping Chuan's long-haired rebel army crossed from the mainland in the early hours of the morning and fell upon sleeping inhabitants of a prosperous fishing and trading village, a few miles along the coast from the European community. After murdering half the luckless villagers, Ping Chuan and his followers made off with a number of fine junks. Ping Chuan had given up his grandiose designs on the throne of China and reverted to his original occupation – piracy.

On the same day, the Honourable East India Company's steamer *Sisostris* arrived from Nanking with details of the treaty signed between Sir Henry Rutherford and Emperor Tao Kuang's Commissioners.

It was a good treaty for the British. The first clause promised lasting peace between the two nations. The second was an agreement by China to pay the cost of Britain's expeditionary force. The sum involved was an estimated twenty-one million dollars. In addition, by the terms of the treaty, the hitherto forbidden ports of Amoy, Fuchao Fu, Ning-po and Shang-hai, together with Canton, were to be thrown open to commerce. British consular officials would be appointed to reside in each place. There would be no more Hong merchants to act as middlemen and take a huge cut of trading profits.

This last was the clause most lauded by the traders. They had suffered at the hands of the Canton Hong merchants for as long as trading had been carried on there.

The final clause of the treaty declared that, once the treaty had been ratified by Emperor Tao Kuang, the bulk of the British troops would be withdrawn, leaving only a garrison force on Hong Kong island. Such a garrison had already been anticipated. As long ago as June of that year, a troop-transport had brought a hundred and twenty women and children to the island. They were families of men of the Prince of Wales Regiment.

The third event of this momentous day was the birth of Thomas Daniel Shengan Trewarne. In fact, Kuei had gone into labour the day before, but the birth proved to be as difficult as Kuei's pregnancy. At the first sign of labour, Luke sent for

Morna, but even after her arrival Kuei would not allow Luke to leave her side.

'Please . . .' Kuei pleaded with Luke, looking at him with pain-filled eyes. 'Stay with me, my husband.'

Luke stayed, trying not to look when Morna examined Kuei in an attempt to see why the baby would not come and Kuei squirmed and gasped in his arms. It reminded Luke of the way his father had sometimes to help a calf into the world, by plunging his arm, elbow deep, inside the cow.

He held Kuei's shoulders as Morna shouted at her to strain harder – and still harder. Luke feared Kuei would burst a blood vessel as veins stood out like cords on the side of her neck. Each prolonged effort ended in the same way as the one before it and the unsuccessful attempts to bring the baby into the world went on all through the night.

When dawn coloured the curtained window, Kuei was close to exhaustion – and Morna admitted defeat. She sent a servant to the hospital for one of the army surgeons. The skill of the army medical men varied greatly, and Luke breathed a great sigh of relief when Pelham Barclay, newly roused from his bed, strode into the room.

'Well, well! What do we have here?' he said cheerfully to Kuei. 'Don't you worry about a thing, my girl. I've never yet known a child destined to make a mark on the world who wasn't the devil's own job to drag into it. You just lie back and leave us to get on with the work.'

He and Morna began talking together in a low voice. At the bedside, Luke squeezed Kuei's hand and gave a smile of reassurance.

Pelham Barclay examined Kuei thoroughly before walking slowly from the room, jerking his head almost imperceptibly for Luke to follow him. There was a moment of panic from Kuei as Luke freed his hand and rose to follow the army surgeon, but Morna moved in and assured Kuei he would not be long, as she fussed over Kuei's pillows and the bedclothes.

Outside, Pelham Barclay waited only until Luke had closed the door behind him before coming straight to the point. 'We have problems, Luke – serious problems. I'm very concerned, not only for the baby, but for Kuei as well. I could baffle you with medical jargon, but I'll spare you that. Put quite simply, the problem is that the baby is too big to come out. I'm un-decided what action is best to take at this moment. What I would like to do is send for one of my junior surgeons; he has taken a great interest in the problems of childbirth.'

'Send for whoever you wish,' said Luke desperately. 'But for God's sake be quick. Kuei's been in labour for long enough.'

Kuei looked up at Luke as he re-entered the bedroom, her eyes deep and dark in her unnaturally pale face. 'All is not well, my husband?'

Luke forced a smile. 'It's nothing that Surgeon Barclay can't cope with.'

Kuei was about to reply, when a fierce pain racked her body. She gritted her teeth until it had passed.

'You do not speak the truth, my husband. I see fear for me in your eyes.' She struggled to sit up, ignoring the protests of Luke and Morna. 'Bring Mo She to me.'

Mo She was one of the servants and, like Kuei, a Hoklo girl.

'Why . . . ?'

'Please, my husband. We have wasted much time already.'

Mo She was a kitchen servant. She entered the room in a state of near-terror at finding herself in the presence of so many Fan Qui men and women.

Kuei spoke quickly to the girl in the Hoklo language of Fu-kien, which Luke had never completely mastered. He knew only that Kuei was sending the servant-girl to fetch someone from the floating village of the Hoklo people.

Pelham asked what was happening, and Luke told him, adding, 'I'll stop the girl going if any interference is going to upset you.'

'No, let her go. I've heard rumours of an old water-gipsy who attracts more Chinese patients than all the doctors at the hospital together.'

Seeing Luke's anxious frown, Pelham Barclay added, 'Don't worry. I'll stay here to keep an eye on Kuei, but at the moment I'm prepared to accept any help.'

The old Hoklo woman arrived at the house at the same time as the second army surgeon. She was not happy at having the Fan Qui surgeons in the room with her, though she raised no objection to Morna. When Kuei explained who the surgeons were, the old lady spat her contempt on the bedroom floor. She finally agreed to their presence, after making it clear, through Kuei, that they must make no attempt to interfere. But she would not have Luke in the room. He was sent out.

For two hours, Luke paced the downstairs rooms. He paused

frequently at the foot of the stairs, listening for any significant sounds from the bedroom.

He was downing his third brandy when he heard the first thin cry. He froze, not daring to be certain. Then the sound came again and there could be no doubt this time. It was the cry of a new-born child.

Luke cleared the stairs two at a time. He reached the bedroom door as it was opened by Surgeon Pelham Barclay to allow the old woman to pass through. Seeing Luke, the surgeon stepped outside the room and closed the door behind him, preventing Luke from entering.

'Is something wrong?' Luke studied the surgeon's face in alarm. 'I heard the baby. . . . It's not Kuei?'

'You have a wife – and you have a son, thanks to that old woman.' Pelham Barclay nodded his head towards the old Hoklo woman, who was finding it difficult to descend the unfamiliar stairs, despite the assistance of Mo She. 'But it was a very difficult birth. The baby suffered considerable distress.'

'But it's alive. I heard it. . . .'

'Yes, it's alive . . . and that in itself is a miracle, the secret of which is known only to that incredible woman who has just left. But how long the baby lives is entirely in God's hands. The child has a defective heart.'

Luke tried desperately to master his distress. 'Does Kuei know?'

Pelham Barclay shook his head in genuine sorrow. 'It would have taken a much braver man than I to tell her, Luke. I am afraid the sad news must come from you . . . but choose your words carefully, for I fear it will break her heart.'

The surgeon stood back from the door and Luke went inside the bedroom.

Thomas Daniel Shengan Trewarne was buried in the Hong Kong cemetery on the day the British expeditionary force sailed from China. He had lived for fourteen weeks. The only mark he had made upon the world was to carve a niche for himself in the hearts of Luke and Kuei that would never be filled. He was the first baby to be born to the small European community on the island – but he was not the first to die. Hong Kong was proving almost as unhealthy for the British garrison troops and their families as Chusan had been. Neat rows of headstones in the military section of the cemetery provided a frightening record of the mortality among them.

The death of her son was a tragedy for Kuei. She refused to believe what Pelham Barclay had told Luke, although it became apparent to everyone else that baby Thomas waged a constant battle against death every minute of his day.

Even so, it seemed at first that Kuei would accept the death of her baby with the same stoicism she had shown at the loss of her father and Tik-wei. Luke breathed a prayer of thankfulness – but it was premature. At the funeral service on the hill, Kuei's composure cracked wide open. She collapsed sobbing at the graveside, and Luke had to carry her home.

For weeks afterwards, Kuei would wake from a recurring nightmare, screaming for her son. Then, after he succeeded in consoling her, she would lie in Luke's arms sobbing quietly until the dawn.

One day, soon afterwards, Sir Henry Rutherford sent for Luke. He offered him the post of British Consul in Shang-hai. It was a post he had earmarked for Luke many months before.

Under normal circumstances, Luke would not have considered leaving Hong Kong, with trade booming as never before, but he thought it possible that the change might do Kuei a great deal of good.

Since the expansion of Gemmell Company, Gideon Pyke had become much more involved with its affairs. After a discussion with Morna, Luke agreed to accept Sir Henry Rutherford's offer, and leave the running of Trewarne, McCulloch & Company in the hands of Gideon Pyke. It did not mean that Luke would be out of touch with the Company's affairs. The post of Consul would not occupy all his time in Shang-hai, and he intended opening a company office there and building a lucrative trade in the silks for which the city was justly famous.

There was another factor which influenced Luke's decision. As British Consul he would be in a good position to crush the opium trade which flourished in the Shang-hai area. It would be another positive step forward in the fight being waged by men like Luke to eliminate it altogether.

Eighteen

SHANG-HAI was a large and bustling city, full of new things to see and new people to meet. Great Britain had fought and won the war with China on her own, but the fruits of victory had been distributed generously. Portugal, America, France and Denmark had all been invited to send consuls to the important sea-port.

For a while, it seemed the change had achieved the desired effect for Kuei. She had periods of depression, but they rarely lasted long, and she was one of the most popular hostesses in the growing trading community.

A year came and went. Then, within weeks of the Chinese New Year, in 1844, Luke was called to the Shang-hai office of the Provincial Governor. After sipping tea and exchanging information about the health of Emperor and Queen, China and Great Britain, and members of their respective families and communities, the Governor came to the reason for Luke's summons.

'I am deeply troubled, Peacemaker' — this was the title by which Luke was still known among the mandarins and senior officials of China. 'It is well known to our people that you will not allow opium to be carried into Shang-hai, yet a ship belonging to one of your countrymen brings regular cargoes of opium to my province. The ship trades with pirates in a creek in Hang-chow Bay. This makes me very unhappy, Peacemaker.'

Luke sighed. As the Governor had said, Luke had managed to discourage opium traders from Shang-hai. But the British Government had avoided passing effective legislation to outlaw the trade. The most that had happened was that Lord Aberdeen, the British Foreign Secretary, had bowed to popular pressure. He warned traders that they could not expect official help if they were arrested for trafficking in opium. It was a hollow warning, as he well knew. The traders were quite capable of looking after themselves, and China still had no navy worthy of the name. In a later letter, written when some of the pressure at home had been taken off him, Lord Aberdeen made his position even clearer. He warned the Governor of Hong Kong that he had no powers to restrain those traders who chose to ignore his warning.

'Do you have the name of this ship?' Luke asked the Chinese Governor.

'Yes, it is the *Eileen Lelant*.'

Luke pursed his lips. *Eileen Lelant* was a fast clipper owned by Lancelot Fox, the Hong Kong trader who was now a Member of Parliament in London. Fox was in the same category as Jardine Matheson. His company made its own laws — as often as not ignoring those made by governments. It would not be easy to bring a Fox Company ship to heel. Nevertheless, he had to try, if he was to retain the goodwill and respect of the Chinese Governor.

'Leave this matter to me. *Eileen Lelant* will stop bringing opium to your province. You have my word.'

The Governor beamed and inclined his head gratefully. 'Thank you, Peacemaker. I will tell the Emperor the problem is already ended.'

Giving his word was one thing. Implementing the promise was something quite different. HMS *Calypso*, an armed steam-frigate, was anchored off the city. Luke invited the lieutenant in charge to dinner that evening, to discuss the problem.

Lieutenant John Hope immediately dismissed the idea of taking action against the *Eileen Lelant*. He had good reason for such a refusal. A few months before, at the request of the Chinese authorities, he had boarded a ship known to be carrying opium up the Yangtze River to Nanking and ordered the captain to take his ship and its illegal cargo back to Hong Kong. For this 'interference with the free trade of British merchants', Lieutenant Hope received a severe reprimand from his Admiral. He was not ready to risk another.

'What would be your reaction if, instead of asking you to take unofficial action against a British trader, I made an official request — on behalf of the Chinese Government — for help in subduing the pirates who are threatening shipping in the vicinity of Hang-chow Bay?'

'Ah!' Lieutenant Hope's interest quickened immediately. There was an Act of Parliament in being which approved an award of twenty pounds sterling per head for every pirate killed or captured — plus a worthwhile bonus for the destruction of a pirate vessel. 'If you were to put such a request in writing, it would be quite clear where my duty lay.'

'I'll bring the request to you on board *Calypso* tomorrow, together with a Chinese to guide us to the pirate hideaway.'

Hang-chow Bay was just south of the Yangtze River estuary, seventy-five miles wide, and a hundred in depth. For four days *Calypso* steamed aimlessly from one end of the bay to the other as the Chinese guide sought unsuccessfully to locate the pirates' sanctuary.

During the evening of the fourth day, Lieutenant Hope announced his intention of returning to Shang-hai if they did not find the pirates in the next twenty-four hours.

Luke had anticipated some difficulty in locating the pirates' refuge. He had seen the Chinese guide's dismay when he came on board and learned that *Calypso* was not part of a huge fleet setting off against the pirates. Taking the guide to the stern of the warship, Luke pointed to the triangular fins of the sharks that sliced a criss-cross pattern in the wake of the armed steamer. Then he passed on his own ultimatum. Unless the guide took them straight to the pirates' hideout, Luke would cast him over the side for the scavenging sharks. One of the sailors added unexpected emphasis to Luke's words. Climbing the ladder from the wardroom, he heaved a bucket of galley-slops over the stern. Immediately, the sharks converged hungrily on the slow-spreading stain of rubbish, churning the water to a frenzy in their greed.

The dramatic warning worked. At dawn the next day, the Chinese guide piloted *Calypso* along a deep channel that wound its way through a cluster of high-cliffed islands. Suddenly, the channel ended and they were in a wide and deep harbour. Luke saw instantly why the Chinese guide had been so reluctant to bring them here.

A pirate village sprawled for a quarter of a mile along the shoreline, and Luke saw twenty large pirate junks getting under way before a cannon-shot caused him to stop counting.

The battle that followed was hard-fought, frequently at point-blank range. The steam power of *Calypso* gave the warship a tremendous advantage, but Lieutenant Hope needed every pound of steam that his engineers could raise. The junks were crewed by desperate men at banks of sweep-oars. Twice, broadsides from *Calypso* exploded powder magazines on board pirate junks and blew the vessels out of existence.

Then the battle took a new turn as a large junk flying a crimson flag edged with gold bore down on them – and Luke recognized the figure of Ping Chuan standing on the high-decked stern. Snatching a loaded musket from one of *Calypso*'s marines, Luke took careful aim and fired. He saw Ping Chuan stagger, but at that moment *Calypso* fired another broadside and choking black smoke obliterated the pirate vessel. When it cleared, Luke saw the badly listing pirate junk heading towards the fishing village.

Luke clutched Lieutenant Hope's sleeve and pointed towards the pirate chief's junk. 'I'll give you and your crew an extra ten thousand dollars if you sink that junk.'

Lieutenant Hope brought his ship about in pursuit of Ping Chuan, but the opportunity was already gone. Other junks were pressing him hard, and the listing junk was beached on the sand in front of the village long before *Calypso* could close on her.

The savage battle lasted for an hour. At the end of that time, six junks had been sunk, three were burning to the waterline, and five more had been beached to prevent them from sinking. The remainder had lost their taste for battle. *Calypso* steamed back and forth along the coast, lobbing shells into the village, setting it ablaze from end to end. When the blaze reached the pirates' arsenal there was a spectacular explosion which destroyed a third of the village.

As *Calypso* steamed out of the hidden harbour, Luke saw with some satisfaction that *Eileen Lelant* had gone aground on rocks close by the winding channel. The captain of the opium clipper had tried to make his escape in the confusion of battle. Without the help of a pirate boat, propelled by oarsmen, the opium smuggler had quickly come to grief in the winding channel. *Eileen Lelant* was close enough to land for the crew to be able to scramble to safety, and *Calypso* steamed past the opium clipper without reducing speed.

It had been a most successful operation. Luke's only regret was that he had not been able to bring about the death of Ping Chuan. He had wounded the pirate chief, of that he was certain, but his instinct told him the wound had not been mortal. Ping Chuan would live to fight another day, and never again would Luke come so close to him.

'Well, how do you think we did?' Lieutenant Hope broke in upon his thoughts. 'I estimate we must have killed at least six hundred pirates.'

The statement was made somewhat tongue-in-cheek by the

naval officer. At twenty pounds a head, it represented a sizeable fortune in prize-money.

To Lieutenant Hope's delight, Luke replied, 'My own estimate is closer to a thousand. Perhaps we should split the difference. My report to the Governor of Hong Kong will give the figure as eight hundred pirates killed . . . with nine junks sunk and five more almost total wrecks.'

'Not to mention the opium clipper, aground without a shot being fired at her,' grinned the young lieutenant. 'I think this calls for a celebration . . . once we've cleared the channel.'

The success of Lieutenant Hope and *Calypso* cost the British Government almost twenty thousand pounds, which they paid somewhat ungraciously.

The Chinese Governor of Shang-hai was far less grudging with his praise for the feat of the small warship. The pirate village had been the scourge of the province for many months. The Governor personally visited the armed steamer, with all the considerable pomp commanded by his high rank. He gave gold and silver presents to the officers and crew. In addition, he added ten thousand dollars to their prize-money, to show the gratitude of the people of the province. Relations between Great Britain and the Chinese had never been so satisfactory.

But the incident had a less happy sequel for Luke. While he was away, Kuei had gone shopping in the market where she had become well known. Unfortunately, on this day a great many Tartar women were also there, camp-followers of the new Tartar garrison which had recently arrived in the city. Many of the women had lost husbands and relatives in the war with Britain. Kuei was punched and kicked as the women crowded about her, calling her a Fan Qui's whore. Cut and bleeding, she was rescued by some American seamen who were also in the market.

The Tsotang of Shang-hai was quick to call on Kuei and offer the city's apologies, but the ugly incident caused Kuei more than physical injury. It demonstrated that her recovery from the death of her child had been only temporary. She lost all her self-confidence and refused to leave the house.

For the first time in all their years together, Luke found it impossible to bring any comfort to Kuei. She had built an emotional wall about herself that even his love could not break through. There was a strangeness in her, too, that Luke found disconcerting. She wanted to return to Hong Kong to visit the grave of their dead son, insisting that his spirit was upset by her neglect.

Luke was aware that it was almost the time of 'Ching Ming', the annual Chinese ceremony to commemorate the dead. At this time, the Chinese visited their family graves, decorating them, and offering food and incense for the comfort of the spirits. Luke decided to take Kuei back to Hong Kong for a visit. By allowing her to carry out the traditional ceremonies, he hoped she might return to normal.

Kuei slept a great deal on the voyage to Hong Kong, and as he watched over her Luke compiled a long report for Lord Aberdeen on the effects of the opium trade on relations between China and Great Britain. He listed all the incidents of the past which could be directly attributed to opium smuggling. Finally, Luke pointed to the excellent results achieved in Shang-hai, where a serious attempt had been made to stamp out the illicit trade. He ended by urging the British Foreign Secretary to make a positive stand on the issue.

Luke's letter could hardly have arrived on Lord Aberdeen's desk at a worse time. Lancelot Fox was an influential party man in Parliament, and he had lodged an official complaint about the action of Her Majesty's Consul in Shang-hai resulting in the loss of Fox's clipper, *Eileen Lelant*.

In the same week, the Foreign Secretary received a clear warning from the Earl of Ellenborough, Governor-General of India. Ellenborough reminded Lord Aberdeen that, if the opponents of opium succeeded in having its sale to China banned, the economy of India would collapse. That vast country would become an intolerable burden on Great Britain. Such a calamity would bring down the strongest government – and Sir Robert Peel's Tory administration was far from secure in office.

On a personal level, Lord Aberdeen was inclined to agree with Luke on the opium issue, but the Tory peer was not a man to allow principles to interfere with his duty to country and political party. He sent a sharply worded reply to Luke, pointing out that the duties of a British Consul did not extend to dictating government policy.

Lord Aberdeen's accompanying letter to the Governor of Hong Kong went farther. Sir Henry Rutherford had recently been succeeded by Sir Francis Cunningham, and the new Governor was informed of a policy change. He was to do all in his power to *ease* restrictions on the trade in opium. With this in mind, Lord Aberdeen suggested it might be better for everyone if the British Consul in Shang-hai were replaced by a more 'flexible' representative of Her Majesty's Government.

Luke had fought hard for many years to protect the Chinese from unscrupulous opium traders. His recent successes had led him to believe he was at last winning his battle. But when he was called to the Governor's office and told he was being replaced as Consul in Shang-hai he knew he had lost the final round in his personal war against opium. He did not need to look towards the twenty-odd opium clippers, riding at anchor in the harbour, to understand that commercial pressure had proved too strong for moral argument.

Luke was not sorry to have been relieved of his consular post. Only the circumstances that had brought about his dismissal disappointed him.

Luke determined that he would now devote all his time to Kuei. Far from improving, her mental state was causing him great concern. The return to Hong Kong had merely given her tortured mind a focal point. She frequently disappeared from the house – but Luke knew where to find her.

Trudging up the hill to the cemetery, he would see her kneeling at their son's graveside, talking as any mother might to her baby. All the while, her never-still fingers plucked to shreds the flowers she had taken with her. As he led her back to the house, Kuei would chatter incessantly about the imagined behaviour of their son during that day. It broke Luke's heart to listen to her.

There were many times when Luke wished they had friends in Hong Kong with whom he could talk over Kuei's problem, but they had all gone. Morna had left the island many months before, when Luke and Kuei were in Shang-hai. Ezra McCulloch had finally died peacefully in his sleep, and Morna sold her interest in the company to Luke and returned to the country of her birth. She wrote regularly, but Kuei's problems could not be discussed in a long-range correspondence.

Surgeon Pelham Barclay had gone, too, sent to South Africa to take charge of medical services in the escalating wars against the tribes there.

Gideon Pyke was the only man left with whom Luke felt comfortable, but the American was not often in Hong Kong. Gideon Pyke spent much time travelling between Hong Kong, Canton and Shang-hai, on company business. He also made an occasional trading voyage to Manila, to satisfy the urge for the freedom of the sea that sometimes came over him.

As 1844 drew to a close, an epidemic of lung fever struck down many of Hong Kong's residents. Kuei was one of its first victims, and it hit her particularly hard. For months she had eaten no more than was absolutely essential to keep her alive and she had no resistance to the debilitating illness.

For many anxious nights, Luke sat by her bedside as she tossed and turned in fever, growing steadily weaker.

After one particularly bad night, Luke fell asleep in his chair from sheer exhaustion. He awoke to find her dark-ringed eyes studying him in concern.

When he started up, she held out her hand to him. 'Hello, my husband. I have brought you much unhappiness. . . .'

A fit of coughing cut her sentence short, but they were the first rational words he had heard her utter for many months.

'No, Kuei. You have always given me great happiness.'

Kuei smiled at him sadly. 'We have never been able to lie to one another. It is good that it has been so. You will believe me when I say I could never have loved another man as I love you. You have been a very special husband for me.'

'We've both been very happy together, Kuei . . . and we'll be even happier when you're well again.'

Kuei closed her eyes and shook her head. 'I know I will never be well again. I do not mind for me . . . but I am sorry I must leave you so alone. . . .'

'Hush, Kuei. I'll have no more of this talk. You're going to get better — soon. When you do, we'll take a long holiday. Maybe we'll go to England.'

Kuei smiled drowsily. 'Yes, I will like that. Perhaps we make another baby there, you and I. . . . Yes, I think I will like that very much.' She closed her eyes and in a few minutes she slept.

They were the last words Kuei ever spoke. That evening she opened her eyes and smiled at Luke, before drifting back into sleep. By the morning, her spirit had slipped away to join that of her baby son, Thomas Daniel Shengan Trewarne.

Beside himself with grief, Luke was given one final example of the way in which Hong Kong was changing. He went to make arrangements for Kuei's funeral with the preacher of Hong Kong's newest and most impressive church. The preacher had been on the island for only a few weeks and he and Luke had never met before.

Taking details of Kuei, his pen stopped short at mention of her name.

'She . . . your wife. She was Chinese?'

'Yes.'

'Ah. . . . I'm afraid that poses something of a problem, Mr Trewarne. We've had so many deaths on the island lately that it's been necessary to reserve the hillside cemetery for Europeans only. However, there's a very nice cemetery just outside the town. . . .'

Luke rose to his feet so abruptly he knocked over the chair on which he had been sitting. Leaning across the desk, he looked down into the startled face of the preacher.

'Mister . . . the very first body laid in your cemetery was a Chinese girl named Lo Asan. Killed by a man who has a Christian grave in the same cemetery. The second was my wife's sister — also Chinese. I dug both their graves and buried them myself. That was before you, or your church, had ever heard of Hong Kong. Since then I've buried my son and many friends there. All of them are surrounded by the graves of soldiers who were nursed by my wife when they were dying. Now you tell me my wife doesn't belong in the same cemetery. By God . . . ! I should wring your scrawny neck. My wife will be buried beside her son, Preacher — and I'll have three hundred armed men ashore from my ships to deal with any objections.'

The armed men were not necessary, but the incident proved once and for all to Luke that the island was no longer a place where he could be happy. Now that Kuei was dead he could no longer work up any enthusiasm for trading.

Not yet thirty years of age, Luke sold his majority holding in Trewarne McCulloch & Company to Gideon Pyke and sailed from Hong Kong a wealthy but disillusioned man.

Luke thought the battle to prevent opium from entering China had been totally lost. In England, he soon learned there was a strong vociferous movement in the land intent on outlawing the sale of opium anywhere in the world.

Luke threw himself wholeheartedly into this movement. With his wealth he was able to secure a seat in the House of Commons. Here he became the acknowledged leader in the fight against opium — in opposition to Lancelot Fox and his friends.

It was a battle that was not to be resolved in Luke's lifetime. Halfway through the century, so much opium was being sent into China via Hong Kong that the trade was made legal by the

Chinese upon the death of Emperor Tao Kuang. It would be another fifty years before the trade was finally outlawed, and the legacy left by the opium traders of the nineteenth century is with us still.

Luke found more success in his personal life. For five years he mourned Kuei, with whom he had shared so much – but the link with his Hoklo water-gipsy was not completely broken when he married again.

In the society column of the *West Scotland Gazette*, dated August 1849, the following was reported.

The marriage took place on Saturday, 4th August, 1849, at Strathnay Church, between Luke Trewarne, MP, and Morna Fionna McCulloch of Oban. Mr Trewarne, once British Consul in Shang-hai, is well known in Parliament for his stand against the sale of opium in China. He still retains many business connections in that country.

It is understood that his bride also has a knowledge of China.